STRUGGLE FOR EMPIRE

STRUGGLE FOR EMPIRE

THE BATTLES OF GENERAL ZUO ZONGTANG

KENNETH M. SWOPE

Naval Institute Press
Annapolis, Maryland

Naval Institute Press
291 Wood Road
Annapolis, MD 21402

Library of Congress Cataloging-in-Publication Data

Names: Swope, Kenneth, author.

Title: Struggle for empire : the battles of General Zuo Zontang / Kenneth M. Swope.

Description: Annapolis : Naval Institute Press, [2024] | Includes bibliographical
references and index.

Identifiers: LCCN 2023051079 (print) | LCCN 2023051080 (ebook) | ISBN
9781682472859 (hardback) | ISBN 9781682472866 (ebook)

Subjects: LCSH: Zuo, Zongtang, 1812-1885. | Statesmen—China—Biography.
| Generals—China—Biography. | China—History, Military—19th century. |
China—History—Xianfeng, 1850-1861—Biography. | China—History—Tong-
zhi, 1861-1875—Biography. | BISAC: HISTORY / Asia / China | HISTORY /
Modern / 19th Century

Classification: LCC DS763.63.T76 S96 2024 (print) | LCC DS763.63.T76 (ebook) |
DDC 951/.034092 B—dc23/eng/20231229

LC record available at https://lccn.loc.gov/2023051079

LC ebook record available at https://lccn.loc.gov/2023051080

32 31 30 29 28 27 26 25 24   9 8 7 6 5 4 3 2 1
First printing

All maps prepared by Glynn Seal.

CONTENTS

MAPS

PREFACE

From simple beginnings this book has taken a convoluted journey. Ironically, what I originally envisioned as the easiest of my monographs to research and write turned out to be the most difficult, not least because of complications arising from the pandemic of 2020–2022. From the time I started seriously studying Chinese history I have received casual questions from friends and acquaintances about "that General Tsao/Cao/Tso/Zuo guy," particularly if we happen to be eating in a Chinese restaurant.[1] I would often reply with something along the lines of, "Yes, he was a real person and someday I'll write a book about him to give you the full story of his life." So, for many years, as I became a full-time professor and researcher and eventually earned tenure, this was a project I knew I would eventually get to. The eventuality started crystallizing into reality in the fall of 2015, when I was a visiting member of the Institute for Advanced Study at Princeton. At the time, I was finishing the research and starting to write my monograph *On the Trail of the Yellow Tiger*. One day I was eating lunch in a Middle Eastern restaurant near the Princeton University campus. There were several graduate students sitting at the table next to me, and I overheard one of them ask an Asian student, presumably Chinese, if "that General Cao" was a real person. He responded, "I don't think so, man. I think they just use that name to make the dish sound cool." I leaned over and corrected him, but only got a shrug and a "Good to know" from my unwilling audience.

Around the same time, one of my colleagues mentioned the film *The Search for General Tso*, directed by Ian Cheney, which was then streaming on Netflix.[2] Watching this film led me to track down the book *The Fortune Cookie Chronicles* by Jennifer Lee, which is a broader examination of Chinese food, such as General Zuo's Chicken, and how it has been integrated into the American culinary scene.[3] Both these mediums offered interesting and quirky takes on how the famed General Zuo Zongtang (1812–1885) came to be associated with the spicy-sweet chicken dish that is ubiquitous in American Chinese restaurants but virtually unknown in China itself. Indeed, as Jennifer Lee notes, most chefs in China have never heard of the dish.[4] In a nutshell, a transplanted (from Hunan to Taiwan to New York) Chinese chef created the dish in the 1970s and decided to name it after one of his home province's most famous citizens, perhaps second only to Mao Zedong himself.[5] (For the record, General Zuo's own favorite dish was apparently roast dog.)

Even though Cheney and Lee did go to Zuo's home village of Xiangyin, Hunan, however, neither the film nor the book provides much information on Zuo himself or his tremendous significance for Chinese history. In fact, alongside his contemporaries Zeng Guofan (1811–1872) and Li Hongzhang (1923–1911), Zuo was one of the foremost Chinese officials of the nineteenth century.[6] He helped crush the Taiping Rebellion (1850–1866), which is widely regarded as the bloodiest civil war in recorded history, resulting in perhaps 30 million dead, and helped set up China's first modern naval yard at Fuzhou in southeast China. He was crucial in stamping out the pesky Nian rebels who ravaged north and central China from 1851 to 1868. After this, he put down a loosely connected series of Muslim revolts in northwest China and reconquered Central Asia, which had fallen into the hands of a Muslim adventurer from Khokand known as Yakub Beg. Zuo's rapid and surprising success in the latter venture resulted in the successful resolution of the so-called Yili Crisis and the return of much Chinese territory that had been occupied by the Russian empire in 1871. These lands subsequently were incorporated into the regular administrative structure of the empire as the province of Xinjiang. Not coincidentally, there are currently tensions with the Muslim Uighur population there. After these accomplishments Zuo returned to China proper, where he presided over numerous irrigation projects and tax reforms before ending his long career helping defend the empire and its interests in the Sino-French War of 1884–1885. So, while they are unfamiliar with the popular American dish named for him, most Chinese are quite familiar with Zuo himself.[7] Moreover, in 2000 when *Newsweek* magazine listed its Forty Smartest People of the Last Millennium, Zuo was one of just three Chinese on the list, along with Chairman Mao and Chinggis Khan, who was, of course, technically Mongolian.[8]

Yet, despite his many achievements, the only full-length biography of Zuo in English was published in the 1930s, though a few more recent studies focus on his efforts in Xinjiang and the northwest.[9] In China, on the other hand, there has been a boom in interest in Zuo and his accomplishments, especially as China continues to assert itself on the world stage against the backdrop of nineteenth-century Western imperialism and Westerners' criticisms, concerns, and fears about China's policies and intentions.

Thus when I decided to write a military biography of Zuo Zongtang for Western audiences, I figured he would be a fairly easy subject to research and that the book, with its connection to Western imperialism, would have a built-in audience. When I was presenting my work on Zhang Xianzhong at the Annual Meeting of the Society for Military History in 2016, Glenn Griffith of the Naval Institute Press attended the panel and approached me afterward to see if I was looking for a publisher for the project. I told Glenn that project was already under contract, but I gave him a quick outline of what I had in mind for a biography of Zuo Zongtang. Not long after that Glenn invited me to submit a full proposal, which I did; a contract followed soon thereafter. Now that I had a publisher, I went about gathering sources. To my delight, surprise, and dismay, Zuo's collected works had recently been republished in fifteen volumes, each running around five hundred pages in length. So much for my quick and easy biography! I soon discovered that many of the other primary sources were equally long and detailed. While I never intended my research to be exhaustive, I knew I had to consult the most important primary sources in order to tell the story properly. As a result, the research dragged on far longer than originally planned, further hindered by the restrictions imposed by the pandemic. To his great credit, Glenn has been supportive throughout the process, and I'm thrilled to finally be here, having learned the valuable lesson not to underestimate the extent of the surviving primary sources from the nineteenth century in China.

On the positive side, my research not only confirmed Zuo's seminal importance in nineteenth-century China but also revealed how his life and career can serve as a microcosm for China's experience in modern power politics spanning the period from 1800 to the present. Zuo's experiences also shed light on practical military matters ranging from the development and implementation of counterinsurgency strategy to social and institutional reforms, to analyses of the impact of modernization on traditional societies.

Tracing how Zuo has been appraised in China from his own time to the present provides a barometer of the ever-changing vagaries of nationalist politics and China's self-perception of its place in the world. Zuo has gone from hero to traitor-collaborator with the Manchu conquerors, to suppressor of the revolutionary peasant masses, and back to a nationalist hero whose concern for the people and for maintaining the territorial integrity of China has made him a shining example for contemporary Chinese and a popular subject for biographies that can be found in bookstores and airports all over China. And as I discovered firsthand on my last research trip to China in the summer of 2019, Zuo's impact is still evident in museums and monuments across the country. Trees he ordered planted in the wake of his northwestern campaigns still line the modern highways in some of these areas. Schools he founded still stand. And more tragically, unrest still exists among certain segments of the large Muslim population of Xinjiang. From all this and more I hope my readers will come to realize that General Zuo's legacy is much more than just a chicken dish. Read on and find out for yourselves!

ACKNOWLEDGMENTS

For various reasons this was the most difficult book of my career to research and write. It was also the one for which I received the least outside aid and funding. Nevertheless, I am extremely grateful to all those who helped and supported me along the way. First and foremost, I want to thank Glenn Griffith and everyone else at the Naval Institute Press. Glenn was an enthusiastic supporter of the project from our first preliminary conversation at the 2016 Annual Meeting of the Society for Military History. He remained unbothered three years later when I met with him when I was serving as the Leo A. Shiffrin Chair in Naval and Military History at the U.S. Naval Academy and informed him that delivery was going to be a bit slower than initially projected owing to the amount and detail of the primary sources. Little did we know at the time that a global pandemic, accompanied by my wife's bout with a life-threatening illness, would delay things still further. With every communication Glenn was supportive and understanding, and I sincerely hope he feels that the wait was worth it.

As anyone who has done research in China knows, it can often be difficult to find places and sources, and one often has to rely on friends and local contacts. Ying Zhang procured articles for me from Chinese databases. Gang Zhao helped me acquire copies of primary sources through friends of his in China. Tonio Andrade likewise put me in touch with graduate students in China who emailed scanned copies of source materials. My friend Su Yang purchased Zuo's collected works for me and shipped them to the United States. Kate Hammond at Brill secured me gratis access to the electronic database of the *North China Herald* held by Leiden University for a full month in the summer of 2020. Martin Heijdra at the East Asian Library and the Gest Collection at Princeton worked with Nadine Phillips of the interlibrary loan office at the University of Southern Mississippi to help me borrow rare primary sources during the pandemic. The Dale Center for the Study of War and Society at Southern Miss provided funds for conference travel and to assist with paying for the maps and the index.

Professionally I enjoyed talking about the project in its earlier stages when I was at the USNA in Annapolis, particularly with Ernest Tucker, Rick Ruth, and Wayne Hsieh during our informal lunch gatherings in the Sampson Hall break room. Ernest still owes me a Naqshbandi lunch. Or maybe I owe him one. In terms of other specialists on the late Qing, Hannah Theaker and Eric Schluessel graciously provided me copies of works in progress. Yingcong Dai answered various questions about Qing documents and compilation practices, particularly with respect to the *fanglue*. I also want to thank the organizers of the various panels, conferences, and invited lectures where I presented earlier stages of this research, most notably the amazing Nineteenth-Century Counter-Insurgency Conference organized by Mark Lawrence at the University of Kent in October 2018. My findings were also presented at meetings of the Chinese Military History Society, a public lecture at the College of Wooster in 2022, and the Society for Global Nineteenth-Century Studies World Congress in Singapore in 2023. I benefited significantly from the feedback provided at these venues.

Special thanks as well to Eric Setzekorn and Peter Lorge, who reviewed the manuscript for the press. They helped greatly with clarification and organization. Glynn Seal created the maps. Heidi Blough prepared the index. Jim Bonk and Stephen Platt helped me locate images from the period for inclusion in the book. Most significantly I want to thank my wife, Jin Yun (Lucy Jin), and our son, Princeton Jin (PJ). We traveled all over China in the summer of 2019 visiting sites related to Zuo's life. PJ was just two years old, but he was a real trooper. As I was researching and taking notes, PJ would often climb on my lap to watch episodes of *Peppa Pig* on his tablet just to hang out where I was working. I would be remiss if I did not also thank my mother, Diane D'Angelo, for coming to help with Yun and PJ when Yun got ill in the summer of 2020 and staying through her surgery the following spring. During those dark months, immersing myself in Zuo's life and travails was a welcome distraction. If I have forgotten anyone, you have my apologies and my thanks.

STYLISTIC CONVENTIONS

All Chinese personal and place names are rendered in the pinyin system of romanization without tone marks. For the sake of consistency this includes titles of works published in Taiwan as well as their authors' names. The only exceptions are books published in English by Chinese authors who used variant forms of romanization. Japanese names and terms are rendered in the standard Hepburn system. For Mongolian and Manchu names and places, I use the system employed in *The Cambridge History of China* volumes, though in a few cases I follow the transliteration provided in *Eminent Chinese of the Qing Period*. Central Asian personal and place names are more problematic, as there are many competing forms. I tried to use the form most commonly found in English writings (e.g., Yakub Beg rather than Yaqub Beg), while also providing competing common alternatives the first time a person or place is introduced (e.g., Khokand/Khoqand). For translation of Chinese official titles into English, I follow Charles Hucker, *A Dictionary of Official Titles in Imperial China*. For converting lunar dates into their Western equivalents, I follow *A Sino-Western Calendar for Two Thousand Years, 1–2000 A.D.* by Bi Zhongsan and Ouyang Yi. Specific dates are generally rendered into their Western equivalents, but when a reference is made to a month—say, the fourth month—this refers to the lunar month.

With respect to citing specific works, in general I cite them by the page numbers in the modern published edition if possible. Otherwise, citations are given by *juan* (chapter) and fascicle number within the *juan*. Because the works in question were usually printed on woodblocks, each page had two sides, hence the first side or face of page 12 of *juan* 15 of a work would be rendered 15:12a. In the case of the *North China Herald*, which I accessed online, later issues included only dates, not the issue numbers. Page numbers were not always indicated either, so I cited stories simply by date. Multivolume works include the short form title, followed by the volume and page number.

QING REIGN TITLES AND DATES

TEMPLE NAME	REIGN TITLE	DATES
Taizu	Tianming	1616–1626
Taizong	Tiancong	1627–1636
Taizong	Chongde	1636–1643
Shizu	Shunzhi	1644–1661
Shengzu	Kangxi	1662–1722
Shizong	Yongzheng	1723–1735
Gaozong	Qianlong	1736–1795
Renzong	Jiaqing	1796–1820
Xuanzong	Daoguang	1821–1850
Wenzong	Xianfeng	1851–1861
Muzong	Tongzhi	1862–1874
Dezong	Guangxu	1875–1907
	Xuantong	1908–1911

CHINESE WEIGHTS AND MEASURES

CHINESE UNIT	U.S. EQUIVALENT	METRIC EQUIVALENT
1 *fen*	0.141 inch	0.358 centimeter
1 *cun*	1.41 inches	3.581 centimeters
1 *chi* (linear)	14.1 inches	35.814 centimeters
1 *chi* (itinerary)	12.1 inches	30.734 centimeters
1 *zhang*	141 inches	3.581 meters
1 *bu*	60.5 inches	1.536 meters
1 *li*	1,821.15 feet	0.555 kilometer
1 *mu*	0.16 acre	0.064 hectare
1 *qing*	16.16 acres	6.539 hectares
1 *liang* (tael)	1.327 ounces	37.62 grams
1 *qian* (cash)	0.1327 ounce	3.762 grams
1 *jin* (catty)	1.33 pounds	603.277 grams
1 *dan* (picul)	133.33 pounds	60.477 kilograms
1 *shi* (stone)	160 pounds	72.574 kilograms
1 *sheng*	1.87 pints	1.031 liters
1 *dou*	2.34 gallons	10.31 liters

DRAMATIS PERSONAE

Bai Yanhu	Muslim rebel leader active in the 1860s–1870s; escaped to Russia
Bao Chao	Qing military commander active in fighting Taipings
Cao Kezhong	Military commander involved in defeating Dungans
Cen Yuying	Yunnan official involved in crushing Panthay Revolt and participating in Sino-French War
Chen Yucheng	Taiping military leader
Chenglu	Manchu commander in the northwest frequently accused of corruption
Chonghou	Manchu diplomat who bungled talks with Russia concerning Yili
Ci'an	Senior consort to Xianfeng emperor; later dowager empress who served as regent
Cixi	Dowager empress, mother of Emperor Tongzhi, and de facto ruler of China from 1862 to 1908; her given name was Yehonala
A. P. Courbet	French admiral who sank the Chinese fleet at Fuzhou during the Sino-French War
Paul D'Aiguebelle	French ally of Zuo who helped direct the Fuzhou Navy Yard
Daoguang	Emperor of China (r. 1821–1850)
Ding Richang	Modernizing official who assumed control of the Fuzhou Navy Yard in the 1870s
Duolonga	Manchu military commander active in the northwest
Duxinga	Manchu military commander who fought the Taipings and Nian
Enlin	Manchu official who failed to contain the Dungan rebels
Feng Yunshan	Cousin of Hong Xiuquan and architect of the God Worshippers Society

*Gao Liansheng	Military commander who served under Zuo against the Taipings and Nian
Prosper Giquel	French adventurer who helped Zuo establish the Fuzhou Navy Yard
C. G. Gordon	British military officer who inherited command of the Ever Victorious Army
Guangxu	Emperor of China (r. 1875–1908)
Guo Baochang	Military officer who served Zuo battling the Nian and the Dungans
*Guo Songtao	Qing statesman who served as the first Qing envoy in Britain
*He Changling	Statecraft scholar and bibliophile; brother of Xiling
*He Xiling	Master of the Chengnan Academy in Hunan; brother of Changling
Hong Ren'gan	Taiping prime minister and cousin of Hong Xiuquan
Hong Xiuquan	Founder of the Taiping Heavenly Kingdom; believed he was the younger brother of Jesus Christ destined to saved China from the Manchu demons
*Hu Linyi	Qing military commander and statesman; early patron of Zuo
Huang Shaochun	Military official who fought the Taipings under Zuo
Jahangir	Khokandi ruler who raided Kashgaria in the 1820s
*Jiang Zhongyuan	Official involved in organizing the Hunan Braves against the Taipings
Jiaqing	Emperor of China (r. 1796–1820)
Jinglian	Manchu official and logistics coordinator in Xinjiang
Jinshun	Manchu commander in the northwest
Kang Guoqi	Military official who served under Zuo in the south
Lai Wenguang	Nian leader and sometime Taiping commander
Lei Zhengwan	Military commander active against the Dungans

Li Hanzhang	Younger brother of Hongzhang; impeached by Zuo
Li Hongzhang	Statesman and diplomat; longtime rival of Zuo Zongtang
Li Shixian	Taiping military commander who battled Zuo in Zhejiang
*Li Xingyuan	Qing official involved in the Opium War and in fighting Muslims in southwest China
Li Xiucheng	Chief Taiping military commander
*Li Xubin	Student of Luo Zenan and leader of the Hunan Army
*Li Xuyi	Early commander of the Xiang Army
Liang Afa	Christian convert and author of *Good Words to Exhort the Age*
Lin Fengxiang	Taiping commander; one of the leaders of the Northern Expedition
Lin Zexu	Qing official and patriot who instigated the First Opium War
*Liu Changyou	Qing official who battled the Taipings and Nian and governed several provinces
*Liu Dian	Military commander who joined Zuo's *mufu* early and served with him for decades
*Liu Jintang	Military commander and nephew of Liu Songshan; first governor of Xinjiang province
Liu Mingchuan	Qing official who battled the Nian and served in the Sino-French War
*Liu Rong	Qing official and grand coordinator in the northwest
*Liu Songshan	Military commander killed battling Dungan rebels at Fort Jinji
Liu Yongfu	Military adventurer and commander of the Black Flag armies in Vietnam
Luo Bingzhang	Censor who later served as governor of Hunan and supported Zeng Guofan and Zuo Zongtang
*Luo Zenan	Qing official associated with the creation of the Xiang militia
Ma Duosan	Muslim rebel leader at Xining

Ma Hualong/ Ma Chaoqing	Muslim rebel leader in northwest China based at Fort Jinji
Ma Wenlu	Muslim rebel who seized Suzhou
Ma Zhan'ao	Muslim leader at Hezhou who submitted to the Qing and helped them suppress the Dungan Rebellion
Ma Zhenghe	Muslim rebel; ally of Ma Hualong
Miao Peilin	Adventurer and military commander with a penchant for changing allegiances
Mutushan	Manchu civil and military commander who served in northwest and central China
*Peng Yulin	Qing riverine and naval commander
Qishan	Manchu official involved in the negotiations during the Opium War
Saishanga	Manchu prince tasked with defeating the Taipings early in their existence
Senggelinqin	Mongol noble and military commander slain by the Nian rebels
Shen Baozhen	Qing official who battled Taipings and worked with Zuo to establish the Fuzhou Navy Yard
Shengbao	Manchu military commander infamous for his military blunders
Shi Dakai	Taiping military commander noted for skills in mobile warfare
Song Qing	General who fought Taipings, Nian, the rebels in Central Asia, and the Japanese
Suo Huanzhang	Muslim rebel allied with Tuo Ming in Urumqi
Tan Tiyuan	Last Taiping King; he killed Wang Haiyang but was defeated by Zuo's forces
Tang Jingsong	Qing military commander involved in the Sino-French War
Tang Jiong	Qing military commander involved in the Sino-French War

Tao Maolin	Qing military commander active in the suppression of the Dungans
*Tao Zhu	Scholar, official, and patron of Zuo Zongtang
Taqibu	Manchu military commander who gained fame fighting the Taipings
Tongzhi	Emperor of China (r. 1862–1874)
Tuo Ming	Muslim rebel who instigated uprising in Urumqi
Thomas Wade	British diplomat and adviser to the Qing court
Wali Khan	Khoja leader who raided western Xinjiang in the 1840s–1850s
Wang Depang	Qing military commander who served under Zuo in the southeast
Wang Haiyang	Taiping leader defeated by Zuo in the southeast
Wang Tao	Journalist, translator, and proponent of modernization
F. T. Ward	American adventurer and commander of the Ever Victorious Army
*Wei Yuan	Late Qing statecraft scholar and historian
Wenxiang	Manchu grand councilor who favored more engagement with Westerners
Xiang Rong	Qing general who fought the Taipings in the early 1850s
Xiao Chaogui	Early Taiping commander killed at Changsha
Xu Xuegong	Adventurer and guerrilla commander; helped the Qing fight rebels in Central Asia
Xu Zhanbiao	Military commander who a played major role in the Xinjiang campaign
Yakub Beg	Tajik adventurer who proclaimed himself overlord of Xinjiang
Yang Xiuqing	Taiping military commander; purged in 1856
*Yang Yuebin	Qing naval commander

Ye Mingchen	Qing official involved in the Taiping Rebellion and the *Arrow* War
Yixin	Prince Gong; generally viewed as a moderating influence in the late Qing court
Yuan Baoheng	Logistics officer for Zuo in the northwest
Yuan Jiasan	Civil official who battled the Nian; father of Yuan Baoheng
*Zeng Guofan	Qing statesman and general who organized the first Hunan Army
*Zeng Guoquan	Qing general and conqueror of the Taipings; younger brother of Guofan
*Zeng Jize	Qing diplomat; son of Zeng Guofan; helped resolve the Yili Crisis
Zhang Dejian	Adviser to Zeng Guofan
Zhang Lexing/ Luoxing	Nian leader
*Zhang Liangji	Civil official and patron of Zuo Zongtang
Zhang Peilun	Qing official associated with the "purist" faction
Zhang Yao	Military commander active against the Nian and Muslims
Zhang Zhidong	Late Qing official and reformer associated with the "purist" faction
Zhang Zongyu	Nian rebel leader
*Zhou Yiduan	Zuo Zongtang's wife
*Zuo Xiaowei	Zongtang's eldest son; married He Xiling's daughter
*Zuo Zongtang	Late Qing civil and military official; self-strengthener and proponent of Han culture; our hero

*Denotes native of Hunan province

TIMELINE

1812	Zuo Zongtang is born in Xiangyin, Hunan
1816	The Zuo family moves to Changsha
1820	Birth of Yakub Beg; Jahangir starts raiding into Kashgaria
1821	Official start of the reign of the Daoguang emperor
1827	Zuo's mother dies; Jahangir is captured by the Qing
1830	Zuo's father dies; Zuo meets He Changling
1831	Zuo enters Chengnan Academy, which is run by He Xiling, Changling's brother
1832	Zuo marries Zhou Yiduan; Zuo and his elder brother, Zongzhi, attain *juren* status
1833	Zuo fails the *jinshi* examination for the first time
1835	Zuo fails the *jinshi* examination for the second time
1837	Zuo starts teaching at the Lujiang Academy, where he meets Tao Zhu
1838	Zuo fails the *jinshi* examination for the third time
1839	Tao Zhu dies and Zuo is made tutor to his son; Lin Zexu arrives in Guangzhou and the First Opium War begins
1840	Zuo moves into the Tao household
1841	First Opium War ends; Lin Zexu is exiled to the frontier
1842	Treaty of Nanjing formally ends the First Opium War; Zuo becomes close to Hu Linyi, son-in-law of Tao Zhu
1843–1848	Zuo buys a farm in Xiangyin, moves his family there, and experiments with agriculture
1845–1847	Hong Xiuquan and relatives organize God Worshippers Society
1847	Wali Khan begins incursions into Kashgaria that will continue for the next ten years
1849	Zuo meets with Lin Zexu in Changsha

1850	Start of the Taiping Rebellion; death of the Daoguang emperor; Lin Zexu dies en route to his new post where he was to combat the Taiping rebels
1851	Outbreak of the Nian Rebellion; ascension of the Xianfeng emperor
1852	As Taipings push into Hunan, Zuo joins the staff of Zhang Liangji and coordinates the successful defense of Changsha
1853	Taipings capture Nanjing; Zuo briefly retires to Xiangyin; Zeng Guofan organizes the Hunan (Xiang) Army
1854	Zuo becomes military adviser to Luo Bingzhang; the Taipings are defeated in a naval engagement at Xiangtan
1856	Outbreak of the Panthay Rebellion in Yunnan; the *Arrow* incident in Guangzhou provokes the Second Opium War, also known as the *Arrow* War
1858	Treaties of Tianjin signed by the Qing
1859	Zuo is charged with insubordination but is saved by the intercession of Hu Linyi and Zeng Guofan; Senggelinqin defeats the Anglo-French force at Dagu Fort
1860	While en route to Beijing to take the *jinshi* exam Zuo is diverted by a letter from Hu Linyi urging him to join the *mufu* of Zeng Guofan; Zuo does and soon creates his Chu Army; Anglo-French forces take Tianjin and burn the Summer Palace at Beijing; resulting negotiations confirm the Treaty of Tianjin and extend Western trading and missionary rights; F. T. Ward begins creation of Ever Victorious Army
1861	Zuo's Chu Army helps turn the tide against the Taipings; death of Emperor Daoguang
1862	Zuo is made governor of Zhejiang; Li Hongzhang organizes the Huai Army; Dungan Rebellion begins in northwest; Tongzhi emperor ascends the throne with the backing of Cixi; France creates Cochin China by annexing part of southern Vietnam
1863	Zuo is appointed governor-general of Zhejiang and Fujian; Zuo recaptures most of Zhejiang and advances toward Hangzhou

1864	Zuo recovers Hangzhou; Taiping forces are defeated at Nanjing and Hong Xiuquan dies; Tuo Ming revolts in Urumqi
1865	Burzurg Khan and Yakub Beg attack Kashgar as Muslim unrest spreads across Xinjiang; Zuo is sent in pursuit of Taiping remnants; Senggelinqin is killed by the Nian
1866	Zuo's forces defeat the Taiping remnants in Fujian and Guangdong; Zuo begins construction of the Fuzhou Navy Yard; Zuo is appointed governor-general of Shaan-Gan to quell the Dungan Rebellion
1867	Zuo moves to Wuhan and sets up a supply base; Zuo moves to Shaanxi but is redirected to battle the Nian rebels
1868	Zuo and Li Hongzhang defeat the Nian
1869	Zuo moves into Shaanxi, and Qing forces clear most of the province of Dungan (Muslim) rebels, pressing in on their base at Fort Jinji
1870	Liu Songshan is killed in the assault on Fort Jinji and replaced by his nephew, Liu Jintang; Zuo's wife, Zhou Yiduan, dies; Tianjin massacre
1871	Qing forces capture Fort Jinji and execute Ma Hualong, ringleader of the Dungans, though his associate, Bai Yanhu, escapes west
1872	Zuo's forces recapture Hezhou and Xining and gain the allegiance of Muslim leader Ma Zhan'ao; Zuo moves headquarters to Lanzhou; Zeng Guofan and Zuo's elder brother, Zongzhi, die; Yakub Beg signs a commercial treaty with Russia
1873	Zuo recovers Suzhou in Gansu, ending the Dungan Rebellion in China proper; Panthay Rebellion quelled; British mission travels to meet with Yakub Beg; Yakub's envoy meets with the Ottoman sultan; Bai Yanhu flees to Xinjiang to aid Yakub Beg; Liu Yongfu defeats the French near Hanoi
1874	British sign a trade agreement with Yakub Beg; Japanese send naval expedition to Taiwan; the Tongzhi emperor dies; France moves to make Vietnam a protectorate
1875	Great Policy debate; Zuo is made supreme commander of Qing forces tasked with recovering Xinjiang from Yakub Beg; Emperor Guangxu ascends the throne

1876	Zuo moves his headquarters to Suzhou; Qing Northern Expedition led by Liu Jintang and Zhang Yao sweeps through northern Xinjiang
1877	Qing forces sweep across southern Xinjiang; Yakub Beg dies
1878	Qing complete mop-up operations in Xinjiang; Bai Yanhu flees to Russia
1880–1881	Yili Crisis
1881	Zuo is recalled to Beijing and given oversight of empire's military affairs
1882	Zuo is appointed governor of Liang-Jiang and oversees many infrastructure and military modernization projects
1883	Tensions with France increase as Liu Yongfu expands operations; Zuo retires on sick leave but is recalled to combat sectarians in Shandong
1884	Sino-French War begins; Zuo is named governor of Fujian to coordinate coastal and naval defenses; Xinjiang becomes a province
1885	Sino-French War ends; Zuo dies in September in Fuzhou

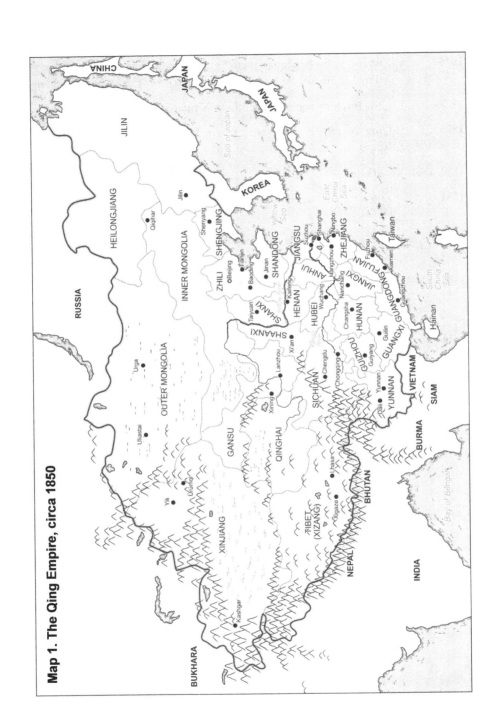

Map 1. The Qing Empire, circa 1850

1

THE NEXUS OF THE CRISES

ZUO'S EARLY YEARS

The voices sound deadly; sometimes I hear echoes of empire spread throughout the skies.
—Blue Öyster Cult, "Wings Wetted Down"

All free time should be spent in study for it nourishes the spirit.
—Zuo Zongtang

On the seventh day of the tenth month of the seventeenth year (November 10, 1812) of the reign of the Jiaqing emperor (r. 1796–1820) of the Qing dynasty, an eighty-year-old matron of the Zuo family in Xiangyin, Hunan province, dreamed that a heavenly spirit visited her family. Shortly thereafter, her daughter-in-law gave birth to a son.[1] The child would grow to be one of nineteenth-century China's most famous officials, statesmen, and military commanders—known to history as Zuo Zongtang, styled Jigao, later canonized as Zuo Wenxiang gong, the Duke of Literary Accomplishments.[2] The Zuo clan had lived near the south shores of Lake Dongting since the Song dynasty, and one member had been a district magistrate who had resisted the Manchu conquerors.[3] Zongtang had two elder brothers and three younger brothers. By the time he was born, his mother was already thirty-eight and short on milk, so the crying baby Zongtang had to get by on rice soup. He was rather sickly and weak as a small child, with a paunchy, distended stomach and a protruding belly button, though he would grow into a robust adult.[4]

Zuo lived with his grandfather Zuo Renjin (1738–1817) as a young boy and was noted for being smart, courteous, and talented but never covetous or selfish. It was obvious to all around him that he was destined for great things. He started reading at an early age, being taught alongside his elder brothers by his father, Zuo Guanglan (1778–1830), and grandfather, both of whom were of *xiucai* (flowering talent) status, the lowest rank of Qing officialdom, and engaged in teaching others to become officials.[5] His grandfather had been a student at the Guozijian, the National Confucian Academy in Beijing.[6] Like most literati children, Zuo began by learning the *Three Character Classic*, followed by *The Hundred Surnames* and then *The Thousand Character Classic*. By the tender age of four, Zuo could recite classical poems from memory. Zuo was a confident young man, full of spirit and more than a little cocky, often likening himself to the great strategist and commander of the Three Kingdoms era Zhuge Liang (181–234).[7] He was said to be rather arrogant, boastful, conceited, and intolerant of others and was not well liked at school. But his few friends were good ones, and to them he expressed his feelings openly and fully.[8]

The family moved to Changsha, the provincial capital, in 1816 when Zuo's father got a new teaching job. Changsha was the home of the famous Yuelu Academy, "a central node in a coalesced Hunan nexus of lineage ties, Neo-Confucian study, and literati relationships."[9] His brothers subsequently advanced to petty posts as instructors, and at the age of fourteen Zuo Zongtang entered the Yuelu Academy and was granted *shengyuan* (government student) status. He finished second in the county-level exams, a noteworthy achievement for one so young, as the pass rate for this lowest level of the exams was around one in two hundred applicants.[10]

The family had several dozen *mu* of land and took in about forty *shi* (piculs) of rice annually, but this was not a lot of wealth for a family with so many members, and they sometimes suffered from food shortages. Zuo later said they sometimes had to make rice buns from chaff.[11] Nonetheless, his family regularly gave famine relief to local peasants and participated in local public works efforts to improve the lot of the common folk, instilling in Zuo a sense of responsibility that he never abandoned.[12] This was despite the fact that Zuo's mother was often sick and they lacked money to pay for medicine. She died in the tenth month of 1827. When Zuo's father died in 1830, most of the family's meager savings went toward their burials. The family survived by growing their own food and raising chickens. This hardscrabble existence would have a profound impact on Zuo and his policies in later years. Zuo also learned the Confucian virtues of filiality by attending to his sick grandfather for many years, accompanying his father to the nearby river to help wash his grandparents' laundry and performing regular sacrifices at the family shrine.[13]

Like any aspiring literatus, Zuo was steeped in the Confucian classics from an early age, studying the *Four Books* (*The Analects* of Confucius, the book of Mencius, *The Doctrine of the Mean,* and *The Great Learning*) as well as later commentaries on these classics by Confucian scholars, especially those from the Han (202 BC–220 AD) and Song (907–1279) dynasties. He also studied Chinese history, literature, and poetry. Perhaps even more significantly, Zuo developed an early interest in strategic geography, military history and strategy, agriculture and irrigation works, and the great works of the "statecraft" tradition.[14] The material available to him dated all the way back to China's Warring States (430–220 BC) era and also included works produced throughout the imperial period—massive compilations of government documents and policy memorials such as the massive *Zizhi tongjian* (Mirror of governance) compiled by the Song historian and official Sima Guang (1019–1086). Zuo adopted a critical eclectic approach to reading these texts and valued practical applicability over flowery rhetoric, though his own writings offer ample evidence of his broad erudition.

Additionally, he was fascinated by scholars of the Ming–Qing transition— many of whom were officials endeavoring to put their philosophies into practice to save their failing dynasty—not least because one of his ancestors had been such an official. Zuo was born into an era of turmoil and change in China but also one of great opportunity. Indeed, throughout Chinese history constellations of like-minded officials have tended to appear in times of dynastic crisis and decline.[15] Drawing further inspiration from the scholarship of the high Qing, Zuo read the newly published collection of statecraft memorials, *Huangchao jingshi wenbian*, compiled by Wei Yuan (1794–1856) in 1826. Wei's proposals for shipyards, translation bureaus, and an arsenal were ahead of his time and exerted tremendous influence on Zuo's thinking.[16]

Zuo took these early lessons to heart and eventually "paid it forward" by setting up schools and printing presses and distributing works of both a

Confucian and a more practical nature to people in the far-flung reaches of the empire.[17] In this sense Zuo came to embody the ideal of the socially conscious Confucian scholar-activist putting principles into practice for the betterment of society. Significantly Zuo also embraced many of the new Western ideas and practices that entered China during the nineteenth century for the expressed purpose of making China strong again and resisting Western imperialism, in the process spawning a nationalism animated by a specifically Han Chinese outlook that defies easy categorization but was instrumental in laying the groundwork for the notion of the modern Chinese nation.

THE STATE OF THE QING IN THE EARLY NINETEENTH CENTURY

Many historians over the last two hundred years have contrasted the supposed vibrant dynamism of the expanding West at the dawn of the Industrial Revolution with the xenophobic and hidebound traditionalism of the tottering Qing empire. For example, the editors of the inaugural issue of the *North China Herald*, published in August 1850, referred to the Chinese as "the most positively stagnant people on the face of the earth."[18] While this description reflected the imperialist context of its time, the lingering presence of such sentiments illustrates the tenacity of such beliefs. *The Cambridge History of China*, volume 10: *Late Ch'ing,* part 1, a classic reference work published in 1978, poses a clear dichotomy between the "expanding Western civilization of international trade and warfare and the persistent Chinese civilization of agriculture and bureaucracy."[19] Studying modern Chinese history from the perspective of missionaries and traders, the first generation of Western scholars of China created the "Impact-Response" model of Chinese history, which casts China as a country that allowed change only within tradition, in contrast to the dynamic and all-embracing West.[20] In the view of these scholars, many of whom were missionaries or the children of missionaries, China's nineteenth-century experience was a "certainly enormous decline and fall almost without equal in history."[21] Even a recent survey of Chinese military history by Maochun Yu directed at a broader audience observes, "Rarely in the course of human history do we see a mighty empire decline so precipitously and helplessly as the Qing dynasty (1644–1912) of China."[22]

And while China doyen John King Fairbank admits that the reality of Qing decline was far more complex than this overview suggests, he repeats platitudes about how Chinese culture in general and Confucianism in particular disesteemed individual prowess and aggressiveness, including the use of violence.[23] John Rawlinson's study of China's nineteenth-century naval development blames the "Confucian system" for the Qing's supposed inability to adjust to the myriad challenges China faced.[24] Sadly, some forty-plus years later, textbooks and popular accounts continue to spew such canards. As James Bonk notes, "Depictions of a military lacking in discipline, leadership, and technology have remained entrenched in and indeed fundamental to many narratives of China's nineteenth century history."[25] Accounts championing the exportation of European military institutions and technology lambast Confucianism's supposed deprecation of military exploits.[26] "In the last decade," Emily Mokros notes, "scholars have revised our understanding of the nineteenth century, replacing stagnation, corruption, and dynastic decline with revitalized agendas and pioneering institutions."[27]

In essence, the Qing was a victim of its own unprecedented success. Population explosion accompanied the restoration of peace and order after the tumultuous wars of the seventeenth century. Military triumphs over traditional enemies such as the Zunghar Mongols bred a sense of complacency, and corruption crept into every element of the civil and military bureaucracies.[28] Eager to embrace Confucian principles of light government, the Qing rulers eschewed expansion of the bureaucracy and froze land taxes, with deleterious effects that multiplied as demographic and environmental crises mounted in the early nineteenth century. These practices and mindsets created glass ceilings for aspiring officials. Among the common folk, these same stresses and pressures led to the proliferation of secret societies, banditry, and the steady militarization of society in a fashion not dissimilar to what happened in the last decades of the preceding Ming dynasty.[29] Widespread competition for land sparked feuds between rival clans, brotherhoods, or religious groups. The secret societies, native place associations, and brotherhoods of various kinds that permeated China in this period offered social intercourse, financial support, and military protection, but they also, as we shall see, had the potential to foment unrest.[30]

THE TURN TOWARD PRACTICAL STATECRAFT

The White Lotus Rebellion (1796–1804), ably chronicled by Yingcong Dai, was a wake-up call for the Qing and led to efforts to reform the military decades before the First Opium War.[31] Two major trends emerged in the aftermath of the White Lotus Rebellion. The first was a relative loosening of state control over the military apparatus; the second was a military that attempted to apply the "lessons learned" from the war.[32] There was also a growing interest in military matters, perhaps reflecting the increasing prominence of Han Chinese in military campaigns vis-à-vis the Manchus and Mongols. A cohort of Han Chinese officers rose through the ranks together and contributed to an expanded discourse on military topics that included writing autobiographies and publishing their own reflections on military affairs.[33]

This insight is significant in that it connects to the growing interest in practical statecraft among the literati of this era. These two groups—military and literati—forged extensive ties and patronage networks that blurred the lines between civil and military matters. In fact, the real architects of the Qing victories of the middle and late nineteenth century were the civil officials, like Zuo Zongtang, who most effectively embraced the statecraft philosophies and established extensive networks with military officials including Han Chinese, Manchus, and Mongols.[34] Indeed, some of the works that so influenced Zuo as a young scholar, such as Wei Yuan's *Shengwu ji*, an account of Qing military actions from the inception of the dynasty written after the Opium War in part to help explain the Qing defeat, included detailed exploits of heroes of the White Lotus War.[35]

THE ASPIRING OFFICIAL

In 1830 Zuo, already recognized as a prodigy, came to the attention of He Xiling (1788–1846), who ran the Chengnan Academy in Shanhua, an old and prestigious school with ties to the legendary Song Neo-Confucian scholar Zhu Xi (1130–1200). Xiling's brother, He Changling (1785–1848), had previously served in a number of important financial posts in eastern China and would later become governor of Guizhou province.[36] He Changling had a vast library in his house, and Zuo often went to the He family compound to borrow books that he could not afford to buy.[37] Thus began a career fostered by personal ties, what the Chinese call *guanxi*, most significantly with other natives of Hunan province. Zuo's daughters would marry the children of his close friends, and the friends frequently recommended each other for government positions. The luminous alumni of the aforementioned Yuelu Academy would include Wei Yuan, Tao Zhu, Guo Songtao, Hu Linyi, and Zeng Guofan. These men also shared ideas and programs. Tao Zhu's revitalization of the salt monopoly in his jurisdiction served as a model for Zuo's later reforms along these lines.[38]

By the end of the nineteenth century it could veritably be said that a "Hunan mafia" of sorts practically ran the country.[39] Philip Kuhn notes that "Hunan in the nineteenth century partook of the self-reliant and martial character of the south China mountains with their unceasing ethnic conflict and the resulting high degree of militarization as well as of the cosmopolitan character and rich culture of the central Yangzi area."[40] The Hunan connection is also significant with respect to stereotypes about its people in modern China. Hunan's most famous native son is undoubtedly Mao Zedong (1893–1976), and in many ways he and Zuo Zongtang embody popular perceptions of the Hunanese. They are said to be rude, unreasonable, reckless, and hard to repress. The Hunanese don't care about monetary gain and are not very interested in official ranks but are willing to sacrifice their lives in pursuit of their aims. Zuo himself was referred to as a "stubborn old mule from Hunan" by contemporaries.[41] He tended to trust old friends and frequently clashed with those he considered arrogant, including Zeng Guofan and Zeng's protégé, Li Hongzhang. But Zuo could put such differences aside and work with rivals—even those he personally disliked—when he recognized talent, a quality sorely missing in today's politicians.[42]

In 1832 Zongtang and his brother Zongzhi earned the *juren* (recommended man) degree in the provincial exams held in Changsha. Zuo Zongtang had purchased the right to sit for the exam, a practice that was becoming more common in the cash-strapped dynasty. He was technically ineligible for the exams because they were held within the officially prescribed mourning period for his parents.[43] Nonetheless, he was eminently qualified to take them, placing eighteenth out of the forty-two men who passed.[44] His essay topics included discussions of waterworks and irrigation, reflecting his inclination toward statecraft.[45] He also wrote an essay on military preparedness and the historical role of emperors in setting up military institutions, particularly in the capital region.[46]

Having achieved this significant career milestone, Zuo married Zhou Yiduan and started his own family in Xiangtan, where his eldest daughter was born in 1835.[47] The Zhou family was fairly well off, and Zuo moved into their home, where he remained until 1843. Although he seemed poised for success, he failed the highest level *jinshi* (presented scholar) exams three times in the next five years and indeed never did pass the highest exam, making his career all the more remarkable.[48] One reviewer wanted to pass Zuo when he took the exam the second time, but others charged that Zuo's writing "lacked grace," and he just missed the cut.[49] Indeed, although he was well versed in both the classics and more eclectic subjects, Zuo was not particularly adept in writing in the formulaic "eight-legged" style that dominated the scene in the Qing.[50] Upon returning to his hometown, Zuo put his principles into practice, devoting time to experiments with agriculture and starting mutual aid programs for growing and saving grain, worthwhile activities in this time of frequent strife, drought, and famine. Zuo's frequent discussions with He Xiling centered on the need for officials to study the past and put their knowledge into practice for the betterment of society. As Zuo later summed up this period in his life, "I didn't even have half a *mu* to my name. But my mind worried about all under heaven. Reading myriad crumbling texts, my spirit touched the ancients."[51]

After one of Zuo's failed examination efforts he composed the following poem presaging his later efforts in the northwest:

> For countless years troops guarded the western territories
> Those were the days when our dynastic founders were devoted to opening the frontiers
> Teams of camels carried grain for ten thousand *li*
> Deserts of one thousand years remain stony fields
> Making it a province awaits planning
> Money was spent on colonies

Generals were not the only ones worried in their sleep
The livelihood of people in the Central Plain deserves sympathy.[52]

In 1837 Zuo started teaching at the Lujiang Academy in Liling, Hunan, where he met Tao Zhu (1779–1839), then the viceroy of Liang-Jiang.[53] Tao was highly impressed by the twenty-five-year-old Zuo, praising him as "an unusual talent."[54] In 1838 Zuo failed the *jinshi* exam for the third and final time. Undeterred by his official failure, Zuo decided to pursue the path of statecraft, intensifying his studies of geography and military matters while also immersing himself in local and regional histories through reading local gazetteers. Zuo was not alone in these interests. The broadening government crises of the early nineteenth century stimulated sociopolitical concerns in many scholars and officials and set the stage for a desire to "reorder traditional political and social norms."[55]

Zuo began writing on a variety of subjects, including agriculture, although these works were not published during his lifetime. Significantly and true to his character, Zuo did not rely solely on book knowledge in his writing but also drew on his practical experience and conversations with local farmers.[56] It was during this period of Zuo's personal disappointment and reassessment that the Opium War (1839–1841) between China and Britain erupted. Although by the standards of the era the conflict was relatively limited, it is impossible to overstate its psychological and cultural importance for modern Chinese. The details of the war itself and the resulting seismic shift in Qing foreign relations practices have been amply chronicled by others from both the Western and Chinese perspectives, so we will not dwell on them here.[57] Suffice it to say that the war served as a call to action for statecraft scholars. It is also noteworthy that the Chinese themselves considered this a trade war at the time. It was not called the Opium War (*yapian zhanzheng*) until after the fall of the Qing in 1911, when it became an indelible part of the evolving narrative of national humiliation.

BIRTH OF A STATESMAN

The war heightened Zuo's interest in the affairs of the empire and in the current plight of the Qing. He also developed a lifelong distrust and dislike of the British during this time, though he was not, as some critics charge, xenophobic.

At the same time, having studied military affairs, Zuo appreciated the implications of superior Western technology. He agreed with Wei Yuan's assessment of the situation: China may have lost this war, but the ship of state could still be righted. For the time being, Zuo withdrew further into the countryside, immersing himself in village and family life. Despite his best efforts to avoid them, however, within a few years he would be dragged into national events.

Ironically, Lin Zexu (1785–1850), who probably deserves much of the blame for starting the Opium War, emerged from it a national hero.[58] After a few years' exile in Yili, he returned home a respected senior statesman and was granted further official posts. Even today, Chinese view Lin as a paragon of virtue. Movies depicting him in a positive light abound in China, and New York City's Chinatown features a statue of Lin that dwarfs the one of Confucius not far away. Not all his contemporaries regarded Lin in this light, however. Wei Yuan attributed China's defeat to Lin's inflexibility regarding military modernization and accountability.[59]

FOLLOWING A STRATEGY OF PLOWING AND READING

In the aftermath of the war, Zuo Zongtang wrote a letter to He Xiling in which he expressed his rage over China's defeat, the terms of the peace treaty, and the fact that opium was apparently not going to be prohibited.[60] The Qing's time-honored strategy of "overawing the enemy" had not worked, and more concrete, practical measures were required if the dynasty was to survive.[61] Already demonstrating his awareness of the significance of embracing new technologies, Zuo called for a new, integrated system of defenses that combined building modern ships and cannon with training and equipping soldiers, while also relying on older technologies such as fireboats. Most significant, Zuo recognized that the superiority of Westerners lay in their firearms, and that was where the Qing should focus.[62]

At least in the short term, Zuo's career aspirations had changed. He was now living a life of "plowing and reading" (*gengdu*). Indeed, he romanticized his role as a gentleman farmer, calling himself "the Farmer of Xiang River" (*xiangshang nongren*) when he finally established his own household, separate from his in-laws, in 1843.[63] Disenchanted scholars have taken a similar route throughout Chinese history, including the early Qing scholar Gu Yanwu (1613–1682), whom Zuo greatly admired as a paragon of dynastic loyalty (to the Ming) and a scholar of practical learning.[64] His life in the country also afforded Zuo the opportunity to put his principles into practice by regularly consulting with local farmers concerning his techniques and agricultural innovations. As one modern biographer notes, Zuo was unusual among his contemporaries in recognizing that the strength and livelihood of the common people were as vital to the survival of the state as raw military power.[65] In a letter to He Xiling written in 1837, Zuo expressed concern for the starvation among the peasants caused by banditry and criticized how higher level officials handled such matters, with their maladministration often creating further trouble.[66]

Drawing on texts but eager for practical experience, Zuo raised mulberry trees, tea, and bamboo, trying different strains and methods of cultivation. These early experiments exerted a profound impact on Zuo as he realized the potential of new crops and crop strains to avert famine and provide alternatives to the production of opium. He would later draw on these experiences when he was posted to China's northwest frontier, where he introduced sweet potatoes and new rice strains in addition to promoting mulberry cultivation.[67]

Of course, Zuo also had a family to feed. In 1838 he had become head instructor at Lujiang Academy, where he instituted a curriculum modeled after that of Zhu Xi.[68] Two more daughters were born within the next year, and after Zuo failed the *jinshi* exam for the third time he returned to tutoring as an additional source of income. He also participated in scholarly activities such as producing local gazetteers.[69] He remained keenly interested in broader current affairs, meeting with officials who came through the area and discussing the topics of the day with them. He also became increasingly interested in frontier and geography studies and their relationship to military affairs and found much wisdom that might be applied to China's current problems.[70]

In fact, Zuo had written letters to powerful friends during the war itself requesting that his ideas be presented to the emperor.[71] In a letter to He Xiling written in 1840, Zuo emphasized the need for the Qing to modernize and mechanize their army, essentially arguing that the key to survival in this new imperialist age was wealth and an awesome military, anticipating the mindset of Japanese reformers more than two decades later.[72] Proper supplies at the provincial level were essential. Training needed to be improved and additional fortresses established for both land and sea defense. "In order to strengthen our defenses, we must be able to fight," he insisted. "In the end this will help the whole empire."[73]

In another letter to He, Zuo criticized decisions that had been made as far back as the Kangxi reign (1662–1722) that had compromised Qing coastal defenses and led to the current crisis with Britain.[74] Zuo's solution was to create layered defenses along the coasts and rivers, augmented by constant patrols and joint land-sea operations, made viable by improved training methods and the adoption of new technology. In subsequent letters to friends Zuo blamed traitorous officials who prevented the monarch from knowing the real situation and dragged their feet when it came to concrete reform measures.[75] In 1844 Zuo wrote to He Xiling that he feared that the awesomeness (*wei*) of the dynasty had dissipated; if such reverses accumulated, the nation's decline would be difficult to stop. The West was like a river overflowing its banks threatening to inundate the whole realm.[76]

Zuo continued to entertain powerful friends such as Hu Linyi (1812–1861) while writing his agricultural books and raising his family. Hu Linyi had served in the prestigious Hanlin Academy in the Forbidden City and had been an imperial censor noted for his memorandums to the throne on foreign and domestic problems. He would later become the governor of Hunan province.[77] Zuo's first son, Xiaowei, was born in 1846, and his second son, Xiaokuan, was born the next year. His eldest daughter was betrothed to a member of the Tao clan, cementing the relationship between the families. Zuo Xiaowei later married the daughter of He Xiling. In addition to forging ties among the elites, Zuo integrated himself into local society, assuming the roles expected of Confucian literati. Whenever flood and catastrophe struck, Zuo took the lead in collecting and distributing relief, saying it was the responsibility of the Zuo clan to protect the locals.[78] He also kept up his reading, remarking to He Xiling how useful he found Wei Yuan's *Shengwuji* and how rewarding he found his simple life of private study interspersed with manual labor alongside family and friends.[79]

Nevertheless, the affairs of China and the wider world drew Zuo into public life. The pace of social disorder, particularly in Guangdong and Guangxi provinces, accelerated in the wake of the Qing defeat in the Opium War. In 1841–1849 alone there were some 110 peasant uprisings, a tenfold increase since the 1820s.[80] Zuo referenced the unrest in letters to He Xiling in 1844 and 1846, discussing unrest in Yunnan alongside accounts of his farming efforts in the mountains.[81] Guangdong and Guangxi were steadily militarized as locals adopted survival strategies ranging from building stockades, to joining bandit gangs or secret societies such as the Elder Brother Society (Gelaohui), to raising private militias or some combination of all of these measures.[82]

Throughout the 1840s the beleaguered emperor and his officials attempted to right the Qing ship the only ways they knew how. There were appointments and dismissals. Minor skirmishes were fought with foreign ships and Chinese pirates along the coast. Famine relief was distributed. Artillery batteries were updated and repaired. Quietly and gradually, many of the disgraced officials who had been exiled to the frontier were restored to prominent posts and rotated back to the interior, several after helping restore order in Xinjiang.[83] Yet even as these efforts to restore order proceeded apace, trouble was emerging elsewhere, including Muslim uprisings in the southwestern province of Yunnan. Lin Zexu was eventually dispatched to handle matters there, which he did in comparatively efficient fashion, earning a number of honors and recognitions for his successful efforts.[84] Qishan followed on Lin's heels, assigned to tamp down unrest in neighboring Sichuan province before assuming oversight of Shaanxi and Gansu provinces in 1849.

While declining invitations from Hu Linyi to join his secretariat in Yunnan, Zuo remained a local leader in public works projects and relief efforts. When famine struck in Hunan in 1848–1849, he donated some 90,000 pounds of grain from local stores to the starving peasants and set up a local pharmacy to treat those who became ill.[85] He also continued with his agricultural experiments, consultations with locals, and lively correspondence with his official friends. He does not appear to have joined any secret societies, despite some suggestions that he was a member of the aforementioned Elder Brother Society. Indeed, Zuo's later strenuous efforts to remove the Elder

Brother Society from the ranks of the military serving under him attests to his disdain for such organizations.[86]

There is an old Chinese saying: "In a small calamity, flee to the city. In a big one, go to the village. But when things really get bad, you hide in the mountains."[87] Local disturbances in the late 1830s had forced Zuo's family to temporarily relocate, but they had returned to Xiangyin. In 1843 Zuo bought seventy *mu* of land near Xiangyin and dubbed the place "Willow Manor" (Liuzhang) in the style of the literati.[88] When famine and flood hit Xiangyin in 1848, Zuo's family hid in the mountains east of Xiangyin, where Zuo, like many at that time, built a defensive edifice as protection against roaming bandits and desperadoes.[89] Many in the household became ill and the family was in dire straits, so in 1849 Zuo returned to Changsha and greatly expanded his circle of contacts.

In the winter of 1849–1850 Zuo met with Lin Zexu, who was then en route to Fujian from his tenure as the provincial governor of Yun-Gui (Yunnan and Guizhou). Lin had been recalled to service in 1844, had distinguished himself in multiple posts, and was now hoping to retire. Zuo had long been an admirer of Lin's and had corresponded with Lin's eldest son, Lin Ruzhou.[90] Zuo met his idol on a boat in the Xiang River beneath Yuelu Mountain in Changsha on the twenty-first day of the eleventh month of 1849 (January 3, 1850). The two scholars discussed border events, minority affairs (Lin had recently managed minority revolts in Yun-Gui), and the situation in Yili, Xinjiang, with regard to both the ongoing Muslim unrest and the threat posed by Russia.[91] Lin had presided over extensive irrigation projects in Xinjiang in the 1840s, and he saw colonization of this region as key to unlocking the region's resources. In essence, Lin viewed Xinjiang as the answer to the problem of land scarcity that was causing many of China's current ills. This conversation had a profound effect on Zuo's subsequent career because it reified much of his own thinking about these subjects. As it turned out, Lin Zexu was not allowed to retire. He was recalled to service to battle the Taipings and other rebels in Guangxi, but he died en route to his assignment.

Zuo understood that Lin's hands had been somewhat tied during the Opium War owing to the inferiority of Qing naval technology. This realization later prompted Zuo to initiate the construction of the Fuzhou Navy Yard,

China's first such modern facility. It was no coincidence that when Zuo was forced to abandon oversight of the shipyard to assume another military post in the northwest, the man who replaced him was Shen Baozhen (1829–1879), the son-in-law of Lin Zexu.[92] There would be more connections between the two men as Zuo's career advanced. As noted above, Zuo's close friends were relatively few, but he had a keen eye for talent and was loyal to those who served him well.

Zuo and his family faced further hardships in 1850 as the floods worsened and the Taiping Rebellion picked up steam. Again Zuo fled into the mountains, this time with his friend Guo Songtao (1818–1891), another Xiangyin native, who would later be the first Chinese minister stationed in a Western country (Britain).[93] The Tiandihui (Triads) were active in Guangxi, and Li Xingyuan (1797–1851), yet another native of Xiangyin, had recently replaced the deceased Lin Zexu and wanted Zuo to come work with him.[94] But Li himself died just after he started his appointment, so Zuo returned to being a country recluse, albeit for just a short time.

Zuo had kept up his correspondence with old friends in the field, most notably Hu Linyi, then serving as prefect in Liping, Guizhou, offering military advice such as the classic "clear the fields, strengthen the walls" (*qingye jianbi*) strategy of local defense.[95] They also discussed methods for recruiting and creating local defense organizations and militia.[96] When Hu Linyi became the provincial governor he wanted Zuo to come and serve as his military adviser, but Zuo was reluctant to abandon his family ensconced in the mountains.

Like the Opium War, the story of Hong Xiuquan (1813–1864) and the "Heavenly Kingdom of Great Peace" (Taiping Tianguo) is amply chronicled in both Chinese and English sources.[97] Ironically Hong's attempt to establish his Heavenly Kingdom resulted in the bloodiest civil war in recorded history and an estimated 30 million deaths. Although the Taiping Rebellion threatened the very existence of the Qing dynasty, it also inspired a coterie of visionary and capable officials to initiate reforms that not only preserved the Qing for another half century but also paved the way for the rise of modern China in the twentieth century. Hong's upbringing was not much different from Zuo Zongtang's, and he had similar training and aspirations, which makes their subsequent life trajectories so fascinating to compare.

THE QING RESPOND TO THE TAIPING CHALLENGE

As evidenced by the appointment of Lin Zexu, after allowing the movement to fester for several years the Qing were now taking the threat of the Taipings more seriously. But in addition to Lin's death a number of factors hindered their response. First the bureaucracy was hamstrung by overlapping responsibilities, factionalism, favoritism, and corruption. Over time military powers had accrued to civil officials, not all of whom possessed the inclination or ability to handle such matters. Deficiencies remained in equipment and training. There were no modern military academies in the Qing at this point. And diversity in the military forces' unit size and composition, among the Green Standard armies in particular, made it difficult for units from multiple regions to integrate and cooperate. Since it was standard Qing operating procedure to overawe domestic foes by bringing in units from across the empire, this issue proved particularly troublesome.[98] Further complications arose when these units had to cooperate with the multitude of quasi-official militia and village defense organizations that had mushroomed in response to the militarization of the countryside.[99]

Lack of leadership at the very highest level exacerbated the situation. The Daoguang emperor had died in February 1850 and was succeeded by his nineteen-year-old son Yizhu, the Xianfeng emperor (r. 1851–1861).[100] The new monarch was confronted with an empire in disintegration, beset with social unrest, ravaged by natural disasters, crippled by scheming factions, and faced with anti-Manchu sentiments from increasingly larger segments of the populace, Han and non-Han alike. "The government had lost vitality," notes S. Y. Teng; "officials lacked dedication, initiative and the ability to cooperate; the treasury was depleted."[101] To his credit, the young emperor did not shy away from responsibility. He eagerly sought advice from many quarters. He issued imperial commands for investigations into local conditions in order to improve official services and ameliorate the hardships of the common people.[102] A note published in the *North China Herald* urged the emperor to investigate military reforms because "village braves" and "untrained militia" had proven ineffective, as demonstrated by recent events in Hunan and Shandong. The writer railed at the "useless and undisciplined . . . troops everywhere," urging the restoration of order and discipline among officers and the military as a necessary first step to barring foreigners from China's coastal cities.[103]

Among Xianfeng's significant appointments was to name the Mongol prince Saishanga, a member of the Grand Council who had been in charge of Qing defenses at Tianjin during the Opium War, to the post of imperial commissioner to suppress the Taipings.[104] And not unlike modern politics, character impeachments tended to fly around faster than concrete solutions. In reference to the expanding Taiping influence, Xianfeng echoed the *Herald* writer cited above, remarking, "It seems to me that they [the Taipings] ought to be intercepted, surrounded, and annihilated, but the troops have no discipline, the soldiers are insolent, and the officers are lazy."[105] The bandits' ranks continued to swell, and the Qing received reports that the rebels were cutting off their mandated queues and refusing to shave their foreheads in a pointed rejection of Qing authority.[106] News of these "long-haired bandits" was quickly picked up by the foreign press.[107]

Saishanga engaged the rebels at Guilin and prevented the city's capture, and then reported several more victories. But the Qing forces were inconsistent at best in the field, and it was unclear how significant the "victories" Saishanga reported actually were, given that the rebel movement was still expanding.[108] The Manchu commander Shengbao (d. 1863), who would later be embroiled in multiple controversies for command incompetence and gaining office only through favoritism, complained about the pettiness of the officials hampering field operations.[109] Dispatches from one Qing field commander reprinted in the *North China Herald* contained the usual accounts of imperial bravery, harsh discipline, and rebel perfidy even as they acknowledged the need for reinforcements.[110] By late April 1851 the emperor had authorized the disbursement of another 2 million taels toward suppressing the rebellion.[111]

When Saishanga proved ineffective, Xianfeng started appointing Han Chinese such as Xiang Rong (d. 1856) to positions of authority, setting an important precedent for how the Qing would henceforth handle sensitive military problems.[112] While Manchus had constituted the majority of governors-general appointed by the Qing over the course of the dynasty to this point, from 1850 to 1860 nineteen Han Chinese governors-general were appointed versus fifteen Manchus; from 1861 to 1890, there were thirty-four Chinese and only ten Manchus in such posts.[113] The numbers of regular provincial governors were similarly skewed. Throughout the history of their dynasty the Manchu conquerors had prided themselves on their military prowess and sought to protect and nurture it via the so-called Banner system, which divided the army into components identified by banners of a particular color.[114] The Manchus lived in separate districts in the major cities, and Manchuria itself was theoretically off limits to settlement by non-Manchus. Qing emperors received martial training in archery and horsemanship and encouraged their Manchu subjects to practice regularly. The Banner armies were the elite forces called up in national emergencies or for extending the reach of the empire, as in the eighteenth-century campaigns that wiped out the Zunghar Mongols and led to the annexation of Xinjiang. Even during the recent Opium War the Manchu forces had earned a measure of grudging respect from some European observers for their spirited resistance, so the appointment of Chinese reflects the changing sociopolitical environment of the Qing more broadly.

There were still prominent Manchu and Mongol commanders, of course, such as Duolonga (1817–1864).[115] But the move toward a policy of using the best man for the job, regardless of ethnic background, was an important new direction in Qing governance. Even more striking was the increasing number of military officials appointed to high offices in the late Qing without the highest degrees that had long been considered a virtual prerequisite for such posts. Rather than a sign of weakness, as some historians have charged, these measures showed the flexibility of the late Qing administration.

The rebellion in Guangxi raised some red flags at court and brought limited attention from Western observers, but information remained sketchy. The Taiping rebels rampaged through Guangxi in 1851 and finally captured the city of Yongan in September 1851—the first walled city they had taken. It was here that Hong Xiuquan bestowed titles of royalty on the other Taiping leaders, naming them the kings of the four directions, along with an assistant king, Shi Dakai.[116] Some accounts claim there was a Taiping co-sovereign named Hong Daquan residing at Yongan whom the Qing captured and later executed. Hong was supposedly related to the Ming rulers, which accounts for the fact that some Western reports initially reported the uprising as being a Ming restoration effort.[117] The Western press had previously reported concerns over heterodoxy running rampant in the empire, echoing the feelings of some Qing officials.[118] And since the Triads were connected to Ming restorationist goals, some versions of the story ascribe Triad membership to Hong Daquan, further muddying the waters.[119]

Qing forces besieged Yongan from the winter of 1851 until April 1852,[120] using troops from multiple provinces bolstered by local militia units. Despite the serious issues of command and coordination that entailed, the Qing hoped this campaign would nip the rebellion in the bud. Abandoning Yongan under heavy pressure from government forces, the Taipings advanced toward Guilin. Repulsed there, they moved east toward Hunan but were defeated again near the entry to that province when Feng Yunshan fell in battle with the Qing in June 1852.[121] The defeat prompted the Taipings to split their forces and move north into Hunan. They continued to attract followers, swelling to more than 50,000 and capturing many cities and towns as they approached the provincial capital of Changsha late in the seventh month of 1852.[122]

The subsequent battle for Changsha marked the turning point in Zuo Zongtang's life and career. Though he had avoided accepting appointments in distant provinces owing in part to his many family responsibilities, this threat was in his own backyard. And despite his failures at the highest level of the Qing examination system, Zuo had created a network of friends and supporters over the previous fifteen years in Hunan who respected him for both his deep knowledge of history and statecraft and his integrity. Moreover, in the changed political and military climate, Zuo's lack of the highest degree was not nearly as important as his inborn talent. The government desperately needed men of action who could back up their lofty words. Zuo's supreme self-confidence had already made him a polarizing figure; it was now time for him to justify his arrogance. He proved to be more than up to the challenge.

Map 2. The Taiping Rebellion

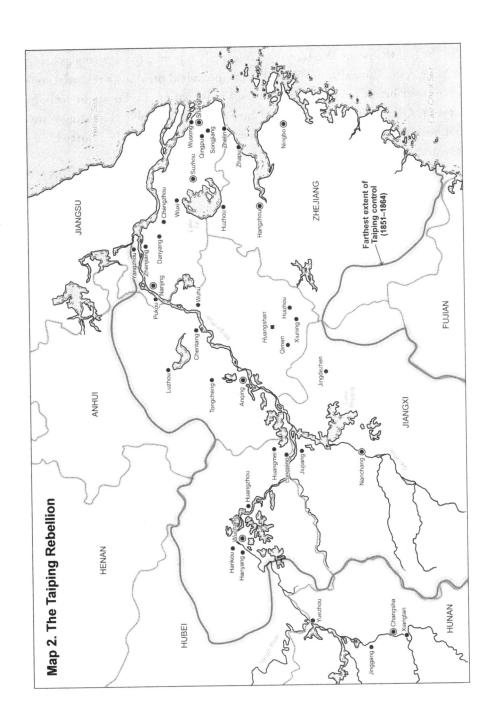

2

A KINGDOM NEITHER HEAVENLY NOR PEACEFUL

The spectacle of a great nation convulsed in its centre in the struggle for empire not only challenges our earnest attention as a grand political problem . . . but also behooves us to look into the future.
—*North China Herald*

By the time the Taipings were pushing into Hunan, Zhang Liangji (1807–1871) had been appointed governor of the province and was urging Zuo to serve on his secretarial staff. Zhang belonged to Zuo's circle of close friends in Xiangyin and was well aware of Zuo's strategic acumen. As Zuo and his family were still holed up in the mountains east of Xiangyin, Zhang dispatched a courier to retrieve him. Zuo was at first reluctant, but other officials, most notably Hu Linyi, urged him to go. Hu praised Zuo as an expert in geography, military arts, planning, and strategy and as a man who did not spout empty words or covet rewards. He also said that Zuo "had the spirit of Lin Zexu."[1] Guo Songtao and Zuo's elder brother Zongzhi also pressed him to join Zhang, using the argument that he could put his high-flown principles into practice and make a difference.[2]

High Qing officials at this time generally had private secretariats, known as *mufu*, that combined clerical functions with the responsibilities of a general staff in the Western sense. The *mufu* was a clever solution to a vexing problem because it allowed officials to circumvent the cumbersome and factionalized bureaucratic appointment process and hire men of specific talents to serve specific needs. In essence the *mufu* institution was a response to conditions such as insufficient subordinate personnel, more burdens of office, and fewer career opportunities for talented men such as Zuo Zongtang. Thus it came to straddle the boundary between public and private service and became an end in itself for men who failed or were marginalized in the examinations. The institution could be abused, of course, but in the right hands it was an efficient means of tapping talent to solve tough problems.[3] Indeed, Zuo himself would make great use of his informal networks to staff his administration with such marginalized individuals, and the generally positive results he obtained speak to the viability of the practice.

THE SIEGE OF CHANGSHA

As the Taipings rolled through Hunan, the Qing court grew increasingly angry and alarmed. The rebels reached Changsha on September 11 and found the local Qing defenders panicked and unprepared. The Taiping units fanned out and captured weapons, livestock, and artillery.[4] Eager for a scapegoat, the court dismissed the commander, Xiang Rong, for cowardice and faking illness and sentenced him to a labor camp in Xinjiang. He was almost immediately recalled, however, and was assigned to support Saishanga.[5] The assignment proved to be brief because Saishanga himself was subsequently replaced for his poor performance in the siege of Changsha. Beset by troubles on all fronts, the Qing leaders needed results and fast.

The rebels dug trenches around Changsha in efforts to sap the walls and mounted five assaults on the city, all of which failed. Zuo, meanwhile, finally agreed to join Zhang Liangji. He arrived in Changsha on the nineteenth day of the eighth month of 1852 (October 2) with his seal of authority in hand, going, in the words of a critical modern Chinese communist author, "from local landlord to counterrevolutionary military commander."[6] The Taiping forces had been besieging the city for about three weeks by this point, but Zuo and Zhang managed to sneak into the city, and Zhang gave Zuo full control over the military situation.[7] Zuo immediately recognized one key problem: too many Qing commanders with too many overlapping responsibilities were involved. The Qing had perhaps 50,000–60,000 troops in the area, more than enough to drive off the attackers, but they failed to coordinate their activities.

And the rebels had clearly picked up valuable experience and confidence over the course of their advance from Guangxi.[8] Zuo went about clarifying responsibilities and, with Zhang, organized relief measures to bolster the morale of the city's defenders. They brought in militia and mercenary bands to augment the regular troops and burned peasant homes outside the city proper to implement the *qingye jianbi* strategy (clear the fields, strengthen the walls).[9] As the Taipings retreated following one attack, Zuo pushed for cutting off their escape route and pinning them against the Xiang River.

Some sources suggest that Zuo personally met with Hong Xiuquan and Shi Dakai on a boat on the Xiang River and was offered—or even sought—a position with the Taipings, but most scholars think this story is a fabrication.[10] In the wake of the Changsha campaign Zuo started creating smaller militia units and created a new office for awarding military ranks and titles, the *zhongyi tang*, or Hall of Righteousness and Loyalty, following Zeng Guofan's practice of creating new offices to promote loyalty to the state.[11] Or, to use the colorful language of the early People's Republic, Zuo "assumed an increasingly greater counterrevolutionary role." He then hooked up with another counterrevolutionary landlord, Zeng Guofan, and they formed the Xiang Army to suppress the Taipings.[12]

This early clash presaged many of the later engagements between the rebels and the Qing. It featured siege warfare, riverine operations that included cooperative land-water tactics, the use of floating bridges to transport men and supplies, and extensive augmentation of regular forces with locally raised militia. The Qing managed to claim the final victory by planting gunpowder charges over a wide area and detonating them simultaneously to drive the Taipings away. Official reports claimed the Qing killed one thousand rebels and captured two hundred more, but many others escaped, so the court urged pursuit of the enemy.[13] When Zhang Liangji was praised for his efforts, he complained that if the court had followed the advice of Zuo and Jiang Zhongyuan earlier, matters would not have gotten this bad and the Qing would have claimed an even greater victory.[14]

Following the victory at Changsha, Zuo helped Zhang devise a new plan for local defense, integrating different levels of administration, rebuilding walls, protecting rivers and key points, and making use of cannons and small firearms.[15] He also believed in using harsh public justice, executing hundreds of bandits at the same time to set an example for the rest of the populace. Though such measures might seem cruel to modern readers, they were in accordance with standard practices, which mixed the paternalism of Confucianism with the firmness of Legalism.[16] In the wake of this success Zhang Liangji remarked, "There are only three people I can rely on, and Zuo Zongtang is the one who brings them all together."[17]

These early engagements with the Taipings crystallized many of Zuo's ideas about the importance of local gentry in saving the dynasty. In a letter to his son-in-law, Tao Guang, Zuo emphasized the leading role the local gentry should play in raising militia, especially if the local officials had been lax. He advocated sterner measures of local government, restraining the wicked, and employing *qingye jianbi* to deny the rebels' resources. Zuo also expressed his dissatisfaction with the general official response to the Taiping threat.[18] In another letter to Tao, Zuo talked about the useful strategies found in the *Huangchao jingshi wenbian*, again showing his own statecraft studies. Zuo admonished his son-in-law that one should not neglect such works for even one day and recommended that "all free time should be spent in study for it nourishes the spirit."[19]

Zuo saw the potential to nip the rebellion in the bud if the Qing could kill the Eastern King (Yang Xiuqing) and the Yi King (Shi Dakai) right away. Without their leadership the movement could be crushed. Given that these two men went on to become the most distinguished and successful of the Taiping field commanders, Zuo's assessment was prescient indeed. Zuo added that in his estimation the true believers were relatively few and many of those following the rebel banners were opportunistic bandits. Cutting out the heart would kill the beast. To do this, Zuo offered two suggestions. First, the Qing should double down on their advantage in heavy artillery. All city walls should have cannon emplacements, and additional towers with cannons should be erected along the rivers. Second, knowing that the rebels would retreat from stout defenses, the Qing should survey the terrain to ascertain where the enemy might go and establish killing grounds there.[20] Unfortunately for the Qing, they were unable to implement Zuo's strategy at this juncture.

Zuo's early experiences at Changsha proved seminal because he met others serving in Zhang's *mufu* with whom he would enjoy long and productive associations. These men spent their evenings discussing the minutiae of campaigning and logistics, as well as the means of raising additional funds and equipping and training soldiers. In effect, service in such an environment offered the same kind of education a Western military officer might receive in a state-run military academy. If anything, it was more valuable and practical because the men were forced to think on their feet and devise concrete solutions for immediate, pressing problems. They also had to serve as intermediaries between the high court-appointed officials, the soldiers, and the common folk. It was their job not only to win the hearts and minds of the people but also to ensure they stayed on the side of the Qing.

As for the Taipings, after the defeat at Changsha they advanced toward Yiyang, on the north shore of Lake Dongting. The rebellion was still picking up steam, but the rebels' ultimate goal was still unclear, especially as they had lost one of their primary military commanders, Xiao Chaogui, at the siege of Changsha. The Qing monitored the movements of the Taipings and bandits while calculating their own mobility and ability to pursue and contain them. The locally raised militia were generally confined to their own areas, and it was hard to maintain steady pressure on mobile rebel bands that crossed jurisdictional lines.[21] A few victory reports rolled in, but these largely chronicled the number of bandits slain or captured. The victories themselves had little impact on the overall situation.[22] Unfortunately, this "body bag" mentality was a feature of late imperial Chinese warfare; bureaucrats wanted concrete measures of "success" and tended to reward soldiers based on the number of enemy heads taken.[23]

THE REBELS ADVANCE TO NANJING

The Taipings seized Yuezhou, acquiring artillery, ammunition, and some five thousand boats along with a Qing naval commander. In December 1852 they captured Hanyang and Hankou. Wuchang, the last of the Wuhan tri-cities, was taken in January 1853.[24] A slaughter followed, with allegedly 90 percent of the defenders and more than 100,000 commoners killed. The rebels also captured more than 1.6 million taels of silver and conscripted people to fight for their army and serve as porters.[25] The emperor complained that many officials had abandoned their posts on the pretext of "guarding strategic points," thereby leaving actual strategic points open to capture by the rebels.[26] The Taipings continued down the Yangzi River toward the wealthy cities of the river valley as the Qing scrambled to bring in units from multiple provinces to counter them and tried to raise more militia auxiliaries.[27] The emperor issued another diatribe complaining that the *Capital Gazette* (*jingbao*), a quasi-official news source for officials, was giving the rebels valuable intelligence on government countermeasures.[28]

Demonstrating their understanding of the significance of riverine warfare, the Qing bolstered riverine defenses with more gunboats and troops to thwart the Taiping advance.[29] Xiang Rong had advocated a strategy of burning bridges around Wuhan and using gunboats to deny river crossings back in 1852.[30] The Qing interest in building and improving a riverine force to combat the Taipings was inspired by the rebels themselves, who had realized early on that one key to defeating the Qing and establishing the Heavenly Kingdom of Great Peace was mobility—the ability to seize key objectives without being tied down defending strongpoints. Using the extensive river system of south-central China was the most expeditious way of doing this. Additionally, the very nature of the Taiping movement necessitated the use of boats for transportation because the families of the soldiers traveled east with the armies. In fact, the initial Taiping "fleet" was really an ad hoc affair consisting of seized vessels—mostly passenger and freight ships—that were used for movement, supply, storage, refuge, and as floating fortresses.[31]

The aforementioned factors impelled the rebels to use combined operations from the inception of the Taiping Heavenly Kingdom. In the early years of the rebellion the Taipings lacked large cannons, and in any event the small vessels they had appropriated could not stand the recoil of heavy artillery. There was often insufficient space to maneuver a large fleet on the rivers, so the riverine forces worked in tandem with land units to effect passage toward the rebels' ultimate goal, Nanjing. Their prioritization of mobility proved vital in allowing the Taipings to seize Nanjing in 1853.

At this juncture the court authorized Zeng Guofan to organize his Hunan Army, a force essentially based on earlier traditions of militia (*tuanlian*) organization dating back to the White Lotus Rebellion. The Qing court publicly announced (again) that Manchu troops were being brought in, hoping to use their (admittedly tarnished) mystique to overawe the enemy. Despite the strengthened river defenses and continual shuffling of officials aimed at preventing the Taiping from pushing too far east, the rebels continued to advance. Even the death of the Western King Xiao Chaogui at Changsha was not sufficient to stem the tide of their advance.[32] The Qing retook Wuchang, but the well-supplied Taipings again slipped east, heading downriver. In February 1853 they moved into Anhui and captured the provincial capital of Anqing, a strategically vital location that would become the lynchpin of the war in later years.

As conflicting reports about the rebellion trickled into the treaty ports, Westerners' main concern was that a Taiping victory would seriously disrupt trade. They had already seen a diversion of trade from the rivers to the coast and were strident in their criticism of the lax and effete Qing government. Again bending with the wind, the editors of the *North China Herald*, recognizing the rebels' growing strength, advised Britain not to make enemies of them. On the day the rebels seized Nanjing, the *Herald*'s editors wrote that the Taipings' final success was "next to certain."[33] Westerners were advised to remain neutral, bolster the defenses of Shanghai (where most foreigners lived), and wait to see what transpired.

Nanjing fell on March 19, 1853, and Yangzhou followed on April 1. The magistrate in command of Nanjing committed suicide as more than 30,000 Bannermen and their families were slaughtered in the Inner City.[34] This was a vital moment in the Taiping movement's history. Nanjing was a wealthy and important city. It had been a capital under previous dynasties, including in the early Ming, and was a hub for trade and commerce. But the Qing, still reeling from the rebels' rapid advance, did nothing to stop them. Some of the Taiping military leaders advocated a quick strike toward Beijing, believing they could topple the Qing and establish themselves there. Others argued that Nanjing, being more centrally located, would be a better "Heavenly Capital" (*tianjing*).[35] One adviser to Hong Xiuquan argued that the Yellow River in Henan was too shallow for the Taiping navy and that the Taiping forces might be slowed and isolated. It made more sense to hold Nanjing and keep the river route along the Yangzi open, allowing supplies to flow into the capital for use in longer campaigns later.[36]

Although the decision was made to fortify Nanjing as the Heavenly Kingdom's capital, a smaller northern expedition of 75,000 troops was launched in May 1853. By mid-June the Taipings had captured the city of Guide. They got to within twelve miles of Tianjin, the gateway to Beijing, in October 1853 but were overstretched and were forced by Qing counterattacks to fall back to Shandong province in the following months.[37] The Taipings remained entrenched near Tianjin until the end of 1853, but they had missed their real chance to seize Beijing.[38] As will be seen below, they never adequately relieved the Qing forces' pressure on Nanjing, so they could never bring enough force into the field to both take and hold far-flung locations. They also failed to take Shanghai. Had they done so early on, they might have gained valuable revenues and persuaded the Western powers to swing to their side, an issue we will take up below.[39]

Once established in Nanjing, the Taipings requisitioned supplies and manpower from the surrounding areas, with varying degrees of success. There were already signs of Taiping shortcomings that would later prove fatal. They lacked modern firearms and powder, although unscrupulous Western sailors had already created a black market in arms and powder.[40] Further, Xiang Rong had arrived outside Nanjing some ten days after the Taipings took the city and immediately laid siege to it. The Qing were unable to retake the city, but the pressure they exerted throughout the Taipings' existence drained the rebels' resources and prevented them from using their full strength for offensive operations. Even in the early fighting in 1853 in Henan and other places to the north the Taipings struggled to hold territory.

In late 1853 Shengbao and the much more competent Mongol prince Senggelinqin (d. 1865) were given command authority in Henan and the north to both battle the Nian and to keep the Taipings away from Beijing.[41] They drove the rebels east into Shandong, where Shengbao's cavalry then (allegedly) routed them in the spring of 1854.[42] The Qing commanders, especially Senggelinqin, proved resourceful, diverting rivers and canals to flood rebel camps and curtail their movements until they could be isolated and annihilated. By the first month of 1855 this was largely accomplished. Senggelinqin later gained fame by killing the Taiping commander Li Kaifang, again using flooding as a weapon.[43]

THE EMERGENCE OF THE HUNAN ARMY

Amid the chaos of the Taipings' initial onslaught, only Hunan province had shown much determination to resist. Jiang Zhongyuan (1812–1854) defeated the rebels at the Battle of Suoyi Ferry and then helped to lift the siege of Changsha.[44] Jiang had previously organized a detachment of Hunanese volunteers known as the Chu Braves (Chu yong) who fought the Taipings in Guangxi province on multiple occasions. In fact, Jiang's stout defense of the rivers had been partly responsible for the Taipings' decision to take land routes into Hunan. Zuo Zongtang wrote to Jiang advising him to "be clear in orders and aims and properly mobilize good people to aid the troops in contesting the bandits." He also told Jiang to carefully investigate local conditions to have a sense of what concerned the common people and to take care in military operations "lest stone and jade both be lost in the fire."[45]

Zeng Guofan, recalled from mourning by the emperor to help manage the crisis, organized the Xiangjun, or Hunan Army, one of the new-model armies that would prove crucial in the Qing defeat of the Taipings.[46] Inspired by the late Ming commander Qi Jiguang (1528–1588), who had raised forces to battle Japanese pirates in the southeast and Mongols along the frontiers, armies like the Xiangjun were an innovative response to the military decline of the Qing.[47] Troops were recruited and trained locally and bound to specific commanders and officers, unlike regular forces, which were regularly rotated to prevent mutinies. Specific training methods modeled after Qi Jiguang's manuals instilled a sense of camaraderie and loyalty in the soldiers.[48] Funding came from the newly established transit (*lijin*) taxes. As the war dragged on, funding sources diversified and changed according to conditions.[49]

The Hunan Army was organized as follows. The lowest unit, the team/ platoon (*dui*), led by a corporal, comprised ten to twelve soldiers and one cook. Two teams equipped with long guns plus six regular teams made up a company (*shao*). Each company had one commander, one vice-commander, five guards, and one cook. Four companies plus six teams of battalion guards (*yingguan qinbing*) constituted a battalion (*ying*), which had one commander. Battalions had 360–500 men on average.[50] The generals were chosen personally by Zeng Guofan, again circumventing standard bureaucratic procedures, and the various commanders chose their own subordinate officers.

Zeng had four criteria for selecting his commanders: (1) they must be able to govern people; (2) they must be fearless; (3) they were not to seek personal fame or glory; and (4) they had to be able to cope with hardship.[51] Discipline and training were strict, but pay rates were higher than the norm. Infantry soldiers made around fifty-one silver taels per year and battalion commanders around five hundred. By comparison, the typical farmer earned around five taels a year.[52] Training and equipment standards were also higher than the norm, and Zeng sought to create uniform standards of appearance and behavior to cultivate esprit de corps.[53] Naval battalions had 10 companies, each with an armed ship and sampan, for a total of 21 ships manned by 447 officers and sailors. Each battalion had an admiral, and Zeng himself rode in the flagship.

Not wanting to overburden the local populace, Zeng stipulated that local markets should be established to facilitate trading with merchants and country folk. The soldiers were forbidden to smoke opium or gamble. There were to be no women in camp, and local women were off limits. Camps were expected to be quiet and orderly. There was to be no gossip and no discussion of the supernatural. The reference to the supernatural is explained by a passage in Zhang Dejian's *Zeiqing huizuan* noting that "the colorful uniforms and pennants contributed to Taiping military success by confounding the eyes and ears of the militia soldiers to the extent that some believed the Taipings had supernatural powers."[54] They were to wear standard uniforms; "bright or strange-colored" clothes were forbidden. Finally, soldiers were strictly prohibited from joining secret societies or brotherhoods or following heterodox faiths.[55]

The Hunan Army was broadly split into two departments: military affairs and supplies. The supply department had eight offices: (1) secretariat, (2) interior cashier, (3) exterior cashier, (4) arsenal for native implements, (5) arsenal for firearms, (6) intelligence bureau, (7) military court, and (8) editorial office. There was also an office for selling official ranks to raise funds.[56] It is amusing to note that there were separate offices for firearms and "native implements," considering the Chinese themselves had invented firearms. But clearly this reflects the realization that the new Western guns were essential to winning the conflict.

Both Zeng and Zuo were sensitive to the need to win the people's hearts and minds. Qing propagandists derided Taiping strategies as coming from popular novels such as *The Water Margin* (*Shuihu zhuan*) and *Romance of the Three Kingdoms* (*Sanguo yanyi*). The Taipings were also criticized for foul eating habits and were labeled "destroyers of culture" who allegedly used classic texts as toilet paper.[57] Conversely Qing loyalists cast themselves as paragons of virtue. Righteous martyrs allegedly emanated luminous vapors after death, and there were even accounts of "righteous bones" dripping blood.[58] Loyalists valued "morally charged things, including books, antiques, and human remains," which were said to "illuminate a bright line dividing the righteous from the wicked, the loyal from the rebellious, the civilized from the savage, even as theatrically-inspired regalia differentiated the imitative regime from a dynastic state."[59]

THE VIEW ON THE GROUND

The surviving reports of Qing officials such as Zhang Liangji give an excellent sense of what was going on in the field. In early 1853 Zhang admitted that controlling the rebels was difficult and he had been thrown on the defensive while trying to reassemble scattered militia and government troops. As he tried to coordinate activities with Zeng Guofan he continued to report scattered victories involving hundreds of deaths but admitted that it was not necessarily clear if those slain were Taiping rebels or merely unaffiliated local bandits. He was also beset by issues pertaining to staffing due to alleged illnesses and the slowness of appointees to take up new posts in war-torn regions.

Lawlessness was spreading.[60] The scarcity of wood hampered his ability to construct defensive structures on which to mount cannons, and a shortage of boats forced his troops to rely on crude rafts for transportation.[61] Zhang urged the repair of defenses damaged the previous year, such as the walls of Changsha and Wuhan, and pushed for more significant riverine defenses. Strong river defenses with cannon would hinder the rebels' movements and deny them the resources available in riverine communities.

There were also still issues within the command and coordination structures of the Qing, some of them stemming from the diverse nature of the forces. Apparently, some Green Standard troops had accidentally killed Hunan Army forces during the siege of Changsha. The Hunan Army forces were mercenaries explicitly linked to specific officers and commanders, whereas the Green Standards were national troops who lacked strong ties or chains of command because they were transferred from place to place, often under different officers.[62]

These problems persisted over the following months. Victory reports were followed by accounts of defeat. Many official posts remained unfilled. There were not enough troops on hand to properly garrison locations once they had been seized. On top of this, the Taipings were destroying or stealing government grain stores, hurting both the military and civilian populations while aiding and abetting local bandits.[63] Qing countermeasures remained compromised by a lack of officials and mid-ranking military officers, shortages in supplies and equipment and inability to distribute them, and arrears in salaries. The army was unable to respond to rebel moves lest they run out of supplies in the field.[64]

ZUO ENTERS THE FIELD

Zuo was promoted to magistrate when Zhang Liangji was sent to attack Wuchang. When Zhang was transferred north to battle the Taipings in Shandong, Zuo declined the minor post he was offered there, opting to remain close to his family in Hunan. He seems to have briefly retired, as Luo Bingzhang repeatedly sent him letters trying to coax him back into service.[65] In a letter to Zeng Guofan, the self-confident Zuo argued that a prefectural post, normally given to officials shortly after they passed the civil service exams, was beneath him.[66] Zuo would not have to wait long for a post befitting his talents. On April 1, 1854, with the Taipings still rampaging through the Yangzi Valley, Zuo was named chief military adviser to Luo Bingzhang (1793–1867), governor of Hunan.[67] Luo had previously worked with Zuo in defending Changsha and had supported Zeng Guofan against impeachment charges after his first riverine flotilla had been defeated by the Taipings, and he had been among Zuo's circle of correspondents when he was still hiding out near Xiangyin.[68]

Zuo was soon at odds with Zeng, however, over a report Zeng sent to the court concerning the military activities of Zuo's friend Wang Xin.[69] Zuo and Zeng and their respective friends and protégés would butt heads repeatedly over the next two decades, but they generally managed to work together, and there was respect, if not friendship, between these two luminaries of the late Qing. Indeed, Zeng's praise of Zuo earned him honors and imperial rewards as early as 1856, when Zuo was still serving under Luo Bingzhang.[70] Zeng himself was subject to criticism as well, as jealous rivals repeatedly smeared his name and belittled his accomplishments throughout the 1850s. Ironically, Zeng's strongest supporters tended to be the Manchu and Mongol grand councilors.

BATTLING ALONG THE YANGZI RIVER

The war between the Qing and the rebels seesawed back and forth through the 1850s, particularly in the strategically vital Yangzi River Valley. The Taipings were keen to keep their supply lines to their capital in Nanjing open and disrupt communications between the Qing forces to the north and south. In effect, the Taipings became plunderers with little in the way of long-term strategic goals. Repeated triumphs and reverses were punctuated by battles that often proved less decisive than it first appeared. When the Taiping captured Wuchang (again) in June 1854, Zeng Guofan tried (again) unsuccessfully to commit suicide. Some of Zuo Zongtang's biographers portray Zeng as an utterly mediocre field commander despite his organizational innovations. He was supposedly inadept in unorthodox warfare and sluggish in field maneuvers, often failing to adapt to changing battlefield conditions.[71]

While various smaller Taiping expeditions penetrated into such distant places as Shandong, Shaanxi, and even Qinghai, the main struggle continued in Hunan and along the Yangzi. In the first month of 1854 the Taipings took Huangzhou and besieged Wuchang again. The next month they took Yuezhou and Zuo's hometown of Xiangyin. With his family apparently safe in hiding, Zuo stayed at Baishuidong sending out letters calling for assistance. Zeng Guofan and Luo Bingzhang subsequently moved to counter the Taiping forces, and there were clashes across the region, with both sides winning at some points. Still, at this juncture the Taipings generally scattered and fled before the disciplined Qing forces as Zeng advanced by land and water from Hengzhou. Wang Xin subsequently recovered Yuezhou, and Hu Linyi scored a victory with braves from Guangxi at Tongcheng. Nonetheless, renewed Taiping attacks in the following months resulted in the Qing loss of Yuezhou once more, and Zuo was forced to relocate his family deeper into the mountains.[72]

Both sides of the conflict made good use of the waterways crisscrossing Hunan. Luo Bingzhang was tasked with coordinating the defense of Hunan and containing incursions into neighboring provinces, and he used riverine forces and flotillas to a significant degree. Hu Linyi likewise recognized the value of superior firepower on the rivers and purchased some 1,700 pieces of foreign ordnance to improve his boats' firepower.[73] The Qing used joint land-water amphibious operations to recover Wuchang and Hanyang in late summer of 1854. So far as the government was concerned, Hunan was vital to screening off Triad elements in the south who might potentially ally themselves with the Taipings. This in fact proved to be the case a couple of years later when Shi Dakai absorbed Triad elements to bolster his forces after a bloody purge tore through the upper echelons of the Taiping leadership.[74]

THE SIGNIFICANCE OF RIVERINE WARFARE

After lifting the siege of Changsha, Zuo's first major assignment was heading a gun-manufacturing bureau that was essentially China's first modern arsenal.[75] Recognizing the importance of riverine warfare for the campaign against the Taipings, Zuo invented (or repurposed) the *dishanpao*, or "mountain-splitting cannon," and placed them on sampans.[76] Zuo was fascinated with steamers and naval vessels in general and recognized their utility in riverine warfare, drawing on his discussions with other officials, including Lin Zexu, concerning the effectiveness of the British navy in the recent Opium War. China, too, must acquire and deploy such technology. He made increasing use of steamers in his subsequent campaigns against the Taipings, even though the Qing's early efforts to manufacture steamers from scratch were less than satisfactory.[77] But even at this early stage the Qing were regaining initiative from the Taipings, at least with respect to riverine campaigns. In the assessment of one modern scholar, the Taipings' defeat at Xiangtan in late April 1854 "marked the turning point of the rebellion,"[78] because it allowed the Qing to clear the Xiang River Valley from Changsha to Hengzhou and subsequently use this region as a base for recruiting troops and extracting supplies.

While Zeng Guofan traditionally gets credit for organizing the river fleet, the idea actually came from Guo Songtao, who in turn allegedly got the idea from questioning a Taiping soldier captured during the siege of Nanchang during the summer of 1853. Guo suggested the idea to Jiang Zhongyuan, who approached Xianfeng with the idea on September 14, 1853.[79] In fact, the practice of interrogating former Taiping soldiers and followers was crucial to Qing success, as evidenced by the *Zeiqing huizuan*, a work written early in the war by a local official named Zhang Dejian for Zeng Guofan's Hunan Army that was based primarily on captured Taiping documents and rebel testimony. This work "applied recent intellectual trends to the crisis at hand by spotlighting the utility of new ideas about governance and the role of men working across or beyond formal bureaucratic boundaries."[80] In other words, it encapsulated the mentality that animated the innovative late Qing statecraft reformers discussed in chapter 1.

The *Zeiqing huizuan* has a short chapter devoted to the importance of boats and riverine warfare. In it Zhang notes that the emphasis on the use of boats for military and supply purposes had been a hallmark of the rebels' operations since they first moved into Jiangxi and Hubei, and they had already amassed a fleet of more than 1,300 vessels.[81] Zhang discusses how riverine transport had been central for both the rebel and the Qing forces and how the Taipings had concentrated on building up their riverine capabilities over the previous couple of years (ca. 1851–1853). And while Zhang expresses confidence that the Qing will ultimately prevail, he also recommends that they burn as many rebel boats as possible to deny supplies to the rebel capital at Nanjing.[82] In a later chapter Zhang references the efficacy of Qing gunboats in curtailing rebel movements and repulsing Taiping attacks on vulnerable riverside communities.[83]

In the late summer of 1853 Zhang Liangji sent up a memorandum that called for the Qing to build four hundred boats to patrol the rivers and aid in the siege of Nanjing—one hundred boats of the first and second classes, and two hundred smaller third-class vessels—providing suggested dimensions for each. These would be equipped with cannon of sizes and calibers appropriate to the size of the boat. Large boats required 52 crewmen; mid sized ones, 33; and the small boats just 5—a total manpower allotment of 9,500 for 400 boats. He further estimated that 4,700 workers, preferably experienced shipwrights, would be needed to build these ships. A company would consist of one first-class, one second-class, and two third-class boats, and twenty companies would constitute a squadron. Fifty companies would be under the purview of an admiral. All would have dedicated instructors, and gentry would be tasked with helping select trainers. He envisioned his fleet being divided into five squadrons.[84] Due to an apparent dearth of capable sailors in Hunan and Hubei, Zhang suggested bringing in more from Guangdong.

The original riverine fleet assembled by the Qing was destroyed at the First Battle of Tianjiazhen, between Hankou and Anqing, in early 1853, as the Taipings were advancing toward Nanjing. Jiang Zhongyuan urged Zeng to rebuild the fleet and established a dockyard at Hengzhou in December 1853. Another yard was opened at Xiangtan. Officers and crews were brought in from Guangdong and Guangxi, again demonstrating Zeng's willingness to tap all the resources at his disposal and the creative approaches the late Qing commanders took to resolving the challenges they faced.[85] By the second month of 1854, Zeng's riverine force was reportedly 17,000 strong.[86] It was this fleet that helped carry the day at the Battle of Xiangtan in late

April 1854 by combining a land ambush with riverine support that was ably commanded by the redoubtable Taqibu (d. 1855). In this engagement rebel bullets, fire arrows, and incendiary rafts were bested by superior government firepower and tactics, as Taqibu feigned retreat and lured the enemy into an ambush. Over the course of several days, hundreds of Taiping boats were destroyed, and the flames of the battle illuminated the night sky for a hundred *li*.[87] The strategy for this battle had been proposed by Zuo Zongtang.[88] Unfortunately, around the same time, Zeng Guofan was defeated in a naval engagement at Jinggang when strong winds blew his fleet into an artillery barrage. He despaired and even asked to be dismissed, but the court retained him.[89]

The triumph at Xiangtan and other victories helped the Qing recover a bit from the reverses of the previous months. Taqibu on land and Peng Yulin (1816–1890) on the water proved a formidable combination, killing thousands; capturing weapons, boats, and rebel banners; and severing Taiping communication lines and driving them south.[90] The Qing were also aided by the receipt of one hundred foreign-made cannon brought up from Guangdong and reinforcements transferred in from other provinces.[91] Through the year the officials in the field worked on plans to contain the Taipings using gunboats and combining militia forces with regular units. Firepower was also stressed. As Luo Bingzhang noted, "Not only does victory in naval warfare lie in boats; it also resides in cannon."[92]

When Zeng Guofan recaptured Wuchang in late 1854, he placed Zuo Zongtang in charge of coordinating all supplies and armies in Hunan. Zuo initiated a boat construction program at Changsha and it was in conjunction with his oversight of arms manufacture that he helped develop the "mountain splitter" (*pishanpao*). Its shot weighed around half a catty, and it had a range of four to five *li*.[93] As the manufacturing and placement of cannon for both city and riverine defenses proceeded, Zuo sent a steady stream of letters to Zeng with strategic advice, not all of which Zeng heeded.[94]

As part of his duties Zuo centralized the salt monopoly and other local revenues pertaining to commerce and transit taxes to ensure a steady flow of revenue without imposing undue burdens on the already sorely pressed local populace. Indeed, probably as a result of his own rather impoverished background, Zuo was always acutely sensitive to preserving the livelihood of the people under his purview. Zuo's plans for combating the Taipings combined social revitalization with military innovation. He advocated integrating different levels of administration, rebuilding walls, protecting river routes, and making extensive use of Qing superiority in firepower on both land and water.[95] Zuo and Guo Songtao were also keen on keeping trade flowing between localities to ensure the livelihood of the people and deter them from joining the rebels. Additionally, Zuo was a firm believer in holding territory once it was captured rather than engaging in an endless series of mobile encounters that might bring rewards and recognition to the commander but do little for the people. In this sense Zuo, not unlike Chairman Mao a century later, believed that the army should serve the people.[96] To this end Zuo's troops built and repaired buildings, canals, streets, and farms.

The Qing also benefited from their position as an established government with a fully formed, albeit often corrupt and factionalized, bureaucratic apparatus. The Taipings were initially forced to capture most of their vessels, and their "navy" consisted primarily of trading ships fitted with small cannons. Qing ships, on the other hand, generally carried at least three cannons, ranging in weight from two hundred to three thousand *jin*. Moreover, as the war dragged on, an increasing number of the Qing cannons were foreign made (at least eight hundred of two thousand by 1857). The newer cannons had greater ranges and could sustain firing for longer times. According to Guan Wen's report of the Battle of Jinkou in January 1856, the Taiping fleet could fire only four rounds against the imperial fleet's six rounds, allowing the latter to advance fifty yards per firing.[97] Additionally, the Qing were now casting steel cannon as opposed to wrought iron, with more than six hundred being cast between 1852 and 1855 alone.[98]

Furthermore, unlike the Taipings' ragtag navy, the Qing had purpose-built specialty ships. The *tuogu* was a floating fortress with large-caliber guns. The *kuaixie* (fast crab), *changlong* (long dragon), and *sanban* (sampans) were designed for maneuverability and shallow-water operations. Opium smugglers favored the fast crabs for precisely these capabilities, and the Qing took the lesson to heart. The Qing also had dedicated supply ships. This early Qing fleet was much like a modern brown-water navy, except that most of the riverine vessels were made of wood and powered by sails or oars—though this, too, would change over the course of the war. Zuo Zongtang added cannons to boats he captured in his campaigns in early 1854, and the navy adapted in other ways throughout the campaign.[99]

The Taipings were less able to acquire foreign arms and, being largely cut off from Western contacts, especially after 1860, had less ability to acquire ammunition and replace arms that were destroyed or lost in battle. They also lacked the technicians and ready access to foreign trainers that the Qing increasingly enjoyed. Nevertheless, between 1854 and 1856 the Taipings established their own shipbuilding facilities in Jiangxi, Hubei, and Anhui and continued to contest the Qing for riverine supremacy, recognizing its vital importance for maintaining their Heavenly Capital at Nanjing. And despite their shortcomings, the Taiping fleets dominated parts of the Yangzi through the 1850s. They achieved their successes largely with tactics that took advantage of their technological inferiority, such as using smaller vessels to attack larger, less maneuverable ships in tight quarters as shore batteries covered them. It was difficult for the larger Qing ships to depress their guns enough to fire down on the small boats.

THE STRUGGLE FOR HUNAN

Even though the Hunan Army had largely driven the Taiping rebels out of the province over the second half of 1854, there were still problems there. Shi Dakai was refining his knowledge of training and naval operations and was becoming a more formidable commander. Wuchang fell to the Taipings yet again in the second month of 1855, prompting Zeng Guofan to send more naval units south at the request of Luo Bingzhang as Luo obtained assistance from Luo Zenan (1808–1856), who had been instrumental in organizing the Hunan Army and was another friend of Guo Songtao and Zuo Zongtang.[100] Although he was an able commander, Luo Zenan fell ill and did not wish to assume full command of the armies. Peng Yulin, who had assumed control of the naval forces, was a solid strategist, but he lacked battlefield acumen.

Moreover, operations against the Taiping were still hampered by incursions of large bandit gangs from Guangdong and Guangxi that forced the Qing to divert forces south to combat them.[101]

The government's successes multiplied across southern Hunan and into Guangxi and Guizhou in the second half of 1855 as Qing forces secured multiple routes in and out of the province and started tightening the screws on Wuhan.[102] But the presence of unaffiliated bandits kept the situation unstable. If the Taipings managed to break through into the southeast, not only would they have potential domestic bandit and pirate allies, but they would also have readier access to Westerners and their trade and technology. Additionally, the opportunity of fleeing by sea would be there. This threat was curtailed in the early autumn of 1855, right around the time Luo Zenan was driving the Taipings back in Hubei.[103] After a victory in the eleventh month of 1855 Luo Zenan and Hu Linyi requested more foreign cannons from the court. The request was approved, and six hundred cannons were purchased and sent by river from Hubei to Hunan.[104] Qing reports through the end of 1855 continued to emphasize successes, with the lion's share of the credit accorded to the gentry-led militias.[105]

Zuo himself trumpeted the superiority of the gentry-led militia model. It was useless to rely on soldiers who "fear death and covet merit," he said; troops with the proper spirit and sense of duty were necessary. Zuo also criticized some central appointments, noting that one such naval commander "not only didn't understand soldiering, but was also unimaginative in battle."[106] And Zuo reiterated that putting down the rebellion was going to be a long process due to the great numbers of rebels still at large. "Defeating the rebels is like cutting down a great tree," he wrote to one colleague. "You must first peel off the bark and leaves, then you cut up the trunk. This is the proper plan."[107]

Throughout this year Zuo's experience in Luo's *mufu* proved invaluable as he accumulated practical experience in logistics, planning, coordination, and rehabilitation operations. These experiences shaped the way he would later approach large-scale military and recovery efforts in the northwest. He also learned much about the vagaries of the Qing bureaucracy. One needed to cultivate contacts and friendships and not be afraid to bestow and call in favors. Most important, his experiences with Luo's *mufu* reified his own views on hiring the best people for the job, regardless of their official degree status or political connections. In a letter to Zeng Guofan, Zuo criticized the selfishness of the current generation, saying no one cared for study or principles, which should be paramount in selecting officials.[108] Zuo himself benefited greatly from personal relationships, but that does not mean he didn't earn his positions. And he expected the same from those he appointed. In another letter Zuo blasted the residents of Jiangxi, complaining that there "was not a single worthwhile soldier" in the entire province, in stark contrast to his Hunanese troops.[109]

A TAIPING RESURGENCE

The early months of 1856 marked a revival of Taiping fortunes. The rebels seized much of western Jiangxi province, distributing ranks, bestowing posts, and attracting many followers.[110] By the second month a fearful Zeng Guofan was holed up in Nanchang. The Taipings' strategic position strengthened as they retained control over much of Hubei and the city of Wuchang. Taiping armies raided everywhere, sometimes bolstered by reinforcements from Nanjing.

In a letter to the Xiang Army commander Li Xuyi (1824–1863) Zuo lamented the dearth of men of talent to arrest the situation. Even worse was the lack of people who knew how to properly make use of men of talent. In another letter addressing the broader situation in early 1856 Zuo frankly stated,

[The army] on the north bank [of the Yangzi in] Hubei consumes 120,000 taels per month and the commander has stayed at Xingou for a long time without advancing, sending forth victory reports though not even one is reliable. His troops and militia number 20,000–30,000 yet at this time they tremble in fear in the ranks. Not only do the cavalry always look for opportunities to save their lives, they are terrified of drowning in rivers swollen by spring rains and the horses and troops alike are equally useless. As those in charge of the troops continually take bribes to use the regiments for their own ends, how can we discern what lies at the bottom of their hearts?[111]

Zuo went on to note that the Nian rebels in the north now numbered more than 100,000 strong, and it was no longer possible to manage them. "The siege of Zhenjiang has not yet been resolved and the strategic situation of the bandits has not worsened, yet every month the victory reports roll in, none of which can be believed. That things have come to this really freezes my heart!"[112] Recognizing the need to maintain morale in the countryside, Zuo again targeted corrupt local officials, reasoning, "If we can rein in the wicked, we can embolden the hearts of the good subjects."[113]

In order to counter the threat posed to the Qing if the Taiping forces should push farther into the southeast, Zuo recommended a three-pronged rescue mission into Jiangxi, spearheaded by his own Chu Army.[114] Over the course of 1856, these forces, augmented by those of Zeng Guoquan, helped contain the Taipings. But a general stalemate continued: the Qing could not stamp out the Taipings; the latter could not relieve the pressure on Nanjing; and local bandits continued to take advantage of the chaos, killing Qing and Taiping appointees alike. In some places disaffected minority groups like the Miao joined with local rebels.[115] The Miao were embroiled in their own ongoing rebellion against the Qing in Guizhou, which had erupted in 1854.[116] To retain loyalty and improve performance Zuo suggested a general pay increase for mercenaries. He also encouraged officials to be accurate in their representation of the number of troops under their charge, because inflating numbers to secure extra supplies or pay led to serious problems in the field concerning expectations and deployment.[117]

At the end of 1856, the Qing armies swept through Hubei, securing the region for the first time in more than five years.[118] In a letter to Xiang Army commander Yang Yuebin, Zuo said that the Qing must improve their river defenses in order to retain control of Wuhan. He suggested making use of captured ordnance and recently purchased foreign cannons for land defense while getting more gunboats on the river. Zuo admitted that it was currently difficult to procure guns from the British, presumably owing to the *Arrow* War (see below), but ships should be purpose-built as soon as possible for the Qing to retain their strategic advantage. The Qing could then mimic the success of the foreigners on the rivers in the previous war.[119]

Nonetheless, the situation remained precarious. There remained a short-age of quality officials to fill vacant posts. Supplies were inconsistent. As Zuo related in a letter to Hu Linyi, "In Hunan we still have rice, but are short on salt. In Hubei they still have salt but are lacking rice. So now I'm requesting salt be sent by river from Sichuan."[120] Zuo eventually set up a rice-for-salt exchange program in Hunan, prefiguring similar efforts elsewhere later in his career. Local bandits and heterodox associations continued to inflame the masses as they crossed provincial lines to cause havoc. By early 1857 Zuo was finally able to move away from primary defensive and rescue operations to more offensive tactics and dispatched small strike forces to engage the enemy. Following his own advice, Zuo stepped up his training programs and weapons manufacturing.[121]

The Taipings were on their heels through much of 1857 as Shi Dakai, now the rebels' primary field commander, sought to reorganize the armies and regain the initiative.[122] In the late summer and fall the Qing won a dozen battles over the Taipings in Jiangxi, reportedly killing more than 45,000 rebels. Finally seeing positive results, the Xianfeng emperor invested more authority in Zeng Guofan, Luo Bingzhang, and Zuo Zongtang, encouraging them to step up their efforts to coordinate militia and regular forces.[123] Zuo praised the militia forces in particular, calling them better trained and more disci-plined than regulars, and suggested that they should serve as the model for the others.[124] The Qing also gained sweeping victories over the rebels in Hubei and Guizhou. Zuo moved his family to Changsha that year and celebrated the birth of his fourth son.[125]

In 1858 Shi Dakai pushed into Zhejiang province, prompting Zuo and Hu Linyi to intervene there.[126] Shi moved briefly into Fujian when harassed by Zeng Guofan's riverine forces but then returned to Jiangxi. Meanwhile Hu Linyi recovered Jiujiang in May 1858, aided by Bao Chao (1828–1866) and the Manchu commanders Duolonga and Duxinga.[127] Shi Dakai kept up his raiding throughout the year, sometimes aided by local bandits, but did little to improve the grand strategic picture for the rebels, though he pushed back into Hunan in early 1859. Luo and Zuo rushed 40,000 troops to southern Hunan to set up defenses against him. In a letter to Guo Songtao in late 1858

Zuo admitted, "Managing supplies is difficult, managing generals is difficult, and managing the braves is not easy either."[128]

As these seesaw struggles raged across south-central China, more men who would become vital cogs in Zuo's operation emerged on the scene. One such individual was Liu Changyou (1818–1887), another Hunanese, who had been a friend of Jiang Zhongyuan.[129] Liu played a major role in driving Shi Dakai from Hunan into Guangxi. After Jiang died in 1854 at Luzhou, Liu worked with Luo Bingzhang to defeat the Taipings at Dong'an and Xinning.[130] On suffering a defeat in late 1857 he tried to kill himself but eventually regrouped and rallied his forces, gaining several notable victories the following year.[131] Liu would later serve as a provincial governor in multiple provinces and be involved in battling the Nian rebels. The summer of 1859 saw another clash at Baoqing as Shi Dakai again tried to move into Sichuan. But once more the Xiang Army carried the day, finally triumphing in August after a three-month siege.[132] Shi retreated to Qingyuan in Guangxi with some 300,000 troops, but by winter many were deserting due to lack of food. He led troops from Guilin to Guiyang in Guizhou as he probed for routes into Sichuan in late 1859.[133]

In the spring of 1861 Liu Changyou, now the governor of Guangxi, started pressuring Shi again. Shi slipped into Sichuan with a much-diminished force in the autumn of 1861, right around the time Luo Bingzhang was transferred there to become governor-general. During his tenure there Liu had cleaned up local administration, organized militia, and created a riverine defense force.[134] Helped by this infrastructure, Luo would drive Shi out of Sichuan after a series of battles in late 1862 and 1863. Continually harassed by the Qing, Shi was bottled up trying to cross the Dadu River and surrendered to Tang Yugang on June 13, 1863. He was executed in Chengdu less than two weeks later.[135]

Returning to the main theater of operations, by mid-1858 the Hunan Army had seized most of the central Yangzi region, with the capture of Jiujiang on May 19, 1858, marking the culmination of a four-year campaign.[136] Nonetheless, the Taipings still controlled much territory on the north bank of the Yangzi and had even killed Zeng's Guofan's brother, Guohua (1822–1858), in a battle at Sanhe, Anhui, where they slaughtered the nearby garrison force.[137] This victory temporarily relieved some of the Qing pressure on Nanjing. But matters turned against the rebels the following spring when many of their erstwhile Nian allies defected to the Qing side. The Qing steadily increased their control over Jiangxi through 1858, planning to secure Jiangxi and then push into Zhejiang and use Zhejiang as the springboard to recover Nanjing. They also moved more troops into Anhui, as the recovery of Anqing was also vital to their plans.[138] Qing victories continued through much of 1859, especially in the western campaigns. By the late summer it appeared that the Qing would be the aggressors, though as we will see, the Taipings were not quite out of steam. Guangxi was largely pacified by the end of the year after a series of bloody campaigns.[139] Guizhou was likewise more or less under control, and Hubei had been cleared to a significant degree.

IMPEACHMENT AND EXONERATION

Meanwhile, though he had formerly foresworn taking the exams, Zuo considered going for the *jinshi* degree one final time in 1860, and even set out for Beijing.[140] But Zeng Guofan, considering the strategic situation too dicey, asked Zuo to raise another five thousand troops to help defend Anhui. Thus was born Zuo's own Chu Army. Initially conceived as a branch of the Hunan (Xiang) Army, Zuo's force was also modeled after the forces of Qi Jiguang.[141] The Chu Army had 4 divisions of 1,400 men each, totaling 5,600. These divisions were split into brigades (*ying*) and companies (*shao*) of 500 and 320 men, respectively.[142] Again following Qi, Zuo took to heart the adage that an army travels on its stomach. Food and supplies, not to mention adequate pay, were paramount. Every 500 men had a brigade commander and a pay officer, and the group was allocated 2,500 taels per month. Travel rations were 2,800 taels per month. In individual terms this worked out to 4 taels, 2 cash per month per soldier, with extra funds allocated for squad leaders and firearms. In total, Zuo's new force cost 70,000 taels per month as approved by Luo Bingzhang.[143]

Liu Songshan (d. 1870), who would eventually become one of Zuo's most trusted commanders, led the Hunan Army into Guangdong, killing some eight thousand more rebels, including several dozen officers and commanders.[144]

The Chu Army also racked up victories in Guizhou, a sign that the court had relaxed its restrictions on these quasi-private forces being confined to their native areas. Not unlike the situation that evolved under Qi Jiguang in the late Ming, the court decided that efficacy trumped all other concerns. The best armies would be sent to battle the biggest threats, pure and simple.

Zuo and Luo Bingzhang had managed to stockpile 1,300,000 taels of supplies over the past several years, which they estimated could support an army of 40,000 for 6 months.[145] But recognizing that his troops had little practical battle experience, Zuo emphasized that he viewed them as primarily serving a defensive role. When he first set up the new force Zuo himself oversaw the drilling exercises in Changsha. Despite his own background as a scholar, Zuo was not particularly impressed with intellectual commanders. He wanted experienced fighting men as his generals. And he was reluctant to put his troops into unfavorable situations. When Hu Linyi initially requested Zuo to come to his aid in Sichuan, Zuo refused, saying, "My charge is to pacify Hunan, not enter Sichuan."[146] Some argued that sending Zuo's small force to Hunan would be pointless because a larger force was needed there. Proving his supporters right, however, Zuo's small force was immediately successful, winning its first three battles in Hunan. He soon took Wuyuan, Anhui, relieving the pressure on the Qing forces besieging Anqing, which the rebels still held. As a result of these successes, Zuo was promoted to grade 3 (of nine) in the official hierarchy.[147]

It was about this time that Zuo was impeached on bogus corruption charges stemming primarily from his refusal to grovel before a superior official. Hu Linyi and Guo Songtao intervened, and Zuo was pardoned.[148] Hu Linyi praised Zuo's planning acumen, even though he was only a "lowly fourth grade official in the Ministry of War."[149] Luo Bingzhang also came to Zuo's defense, noting that his advice had been invaluable in securing the defense of Jiangxi, Hubei, Guangxi, and Guizhou from rebel depredations. "The empire could not survive a single day without Hunan," Luo said, "and Hunan could not survive a single day without Zuo Zongtang."[150] Zeng Guofan also pushed for Zuo's reinstatement. Despite this support, Zuo was a bit shaken, and he briefly curtailed his activities and contemplated retirement.

Fortunately for the Qing this did not happen, and Zuo was soon back to criticizing his fellow officials. In a letter to Hu Linyi, Zuo maintained that many were greedy and covetous, fearing death but craving wealth. And it was not just in Hunan; all the southern provinces were afflicted with these craven incompetents. In one place with a listed strength of 1,200 soldiers there were just 300, and many of those were carpenters and support staff, not actual soldiers. How could such groups be relied on to contain the rebels? Once again Zuo stressed accountability in the form of higher standards for lower-grade officials and penalties such as flogging for those who failed to assume their posts in a timely fashion.[151] Zuo tried to set an example by investigating crimes committed by his own commanders, most notably charges of killing innocent civilians.[152]

Zuo and Zeng Guofan maintained a regular correspondence discussing the tactical and strategic situations. Zuo continued to emphasize the importance of smaller groups of highly trained militia/mercenaries. He favored training a small group initially, then having those men train others. Zeng was concerned by the fact that his own force was reduced and the Taipings were closing in, but Zuo reassured him that help was forthcoming, though he also complained that his small force of 5,000 was costing 60,000–70,000 taels per month.[153]

RAISING FUNDS FOR THE ARMY

This brings us to the ongoing problem of funding. The Qing used a variety of measures to finance their military, including soliciting funds from local gentry, selling official decrees and student status, and devising new taxes. The most successful of the last was the *lijin*, or transit tax,[154] which emerged in direct response to issues stemming from the ongoing warfare and social dislocation. In 1849, 77.2 percent of the Qing government's annual revenue came from traditional land taxes. By 1884 this figure had dropped to 38.8 percent.[155] Qing officials had been aware of the revenue loss for some time, and many had been pushing to implement new commercial and other taxes since the early 1840s. But tax increases were hard to implement during this time of general unrest and hard to justify in light of the ongoing hardships experienced by the people. The Qing instead instructed officials in the provinces to devise new policies and modify existing practices to meet the projected shortfalls.[156] In many cases, for example, it was simpler to centralize collection and eliminate middlemen and overlapping exactions. Zuo did this to great effect when he centralized the salt monopoly in areas under his jurisdiction.[157] The idea for *lijin* apparently came from Lei Yixian (*jinshi* 1823), who first implemented it at Yangzhou in 1853, though he credited Lin Zexu with the idea.[158]

There were two major methods of collecting *lijin*. It could be collected at designated points as a transit tax or solicited from resident merchants. By the late 1860s more than 5 million taels per year were coming in via *lijin* revenues. And while figures are still unclear, some scholars estimate that one-third of the base military expenses for suppressing the Taiping Rebellion derived from *lijin* taxes.[159] This would amount to around 100 million taels in total. But irregularities in collection and the propensity of officials to create surcharges detracted from the tax's efficacy.

For his part, Zuo, not unlike modern tax reformers, thought that simplification was the answer. He advocated decreasing some taxes and diverting tribute rice destined for the court in Beijing to feed the troops. And he thought that by simplifying assessment and collection and cutting out intermediaries who added "customary fees" (like Ticketmaster) he could bring in more than 200,000 extra taels annually while passing along savings of more than 1 million taels to the people. In this fashion Zuo was not only curbing landlord abuses but also "rectifying social contradictions in the countryside," to adopt the parlance favored by modern Chinese historians.[160] Records suggest Zuo was successful in these efforts; when he served as the adviser to Luo Bingzhang, tax rates were reduced by as much as 50 percent.[161] Indeed, Zuo's son Xiaotang would later claim that his father's real revolutionary achievement was in securing supplies from disparate sources to supply his men, since Zuo generally operated in impoverished areas.[162] A *lijin* bureau was set up in Hunan in 1855, largely through the efforts of Hu Linyi, who worked closely with Zuo, Zeng, and Luo Bingzhang.[163] Salt and additional transit tax bureaus were soon established throughout the province.[164]

While the Qing state continued to have trouble collecting taxes from foreign trade, it was doing a better job of tapping the domestic market and in ways that somewhat shielded the poorest people, who were not usually merchants and did not travel far (thereby avoiding *lijin* stations) unless dislocated by war. Stephen Halsey further argues that *lijin*, being domestically implemented and controlled, helped to preserve Qing authority, concluding that "the transit fee administration incorporated a number of earlier institutional practices, but it served the new purpose of protecting China's sovereignty within a predatory international environment."[165] This observation draws well-deserved attention to one of the underappreciated aspects of the Taiping Rebellion: it spurred the Qing to adopt new methods of preserving and extending sovereignty that had significant repercussions not only for the dynasty's continued existence but for the development of modern China in the twentieth century as well. Zuo was intimately involved in this as in so many other reform practices.

In addition to *lijin*, the government took in revenue from the sale of official posts. For his part, Zuo Zongtang was opposed on principle to such measures. It threw a wrench into the established hierarchies, and there was no way to distinguish between those who had purchased ranks and those who had earned them.[166] In 1866 Zuo had asked the government to curtail the sale of military offices on the grounds that officials with purchased degrees were less competent than those who earned rank through service.[167] But as in other areas, Zuo's position on this issue would evolve as he recognized the need for revenue from as many quarters as possible. Zuo himself knew how lucrative the sale of offices could be. In Hunan as much as 30 percent of the annual revenue in the era of the Taiping Rebellion came via selling offices.[168] When Zuo was later in charge of military efforts to battle the Dungan rebels in Gansu province, he too sought to fund his campaign by selling offices, including the right of opening bureaus to sell offices in other provinces.[169]

The latter practice was an expedient way to get money from provinces that had pledged funds for campaigns elsewhere but not yet contributed them. Indeed there was a constant struggle between the Ministry of Revenue, the throne, and the provinces when it came to allocating funds. Moreover, many of the poorer provinces, such as those in the northwest, had been the recipients of aid from other provinces for most of the dynasty. These new military campaigns just increased the amount of revenue they consumed. Interprovincial finance expanded and diversified to meet new war aims even as the central government maintained considerable authority in directing allocations. This included the creation of temporary assistance programs such as Zuo's own *Xizhong jingfei*, created in 1867 in Xi'an to raise funds for his western campaigns.[170] By 1870 it had branch bureaus in Shanxi, Henan, Hubei, Sichuan, Jiangsu, Gansu, and Zhejiang provinces.[171] In the end, more than 70 percent of Zuo's funds for crushing the rebellions in Shaanxi and Gansu came from such interprovincial programs, though he would use other measures to raise revenue for the reconquest of Xinjiang.[172]

THE DEBATE OVER WESTERN INVOLVEMENT

Given their at least nominally Christian background, the Taipings sought to enlist Western aid for their crusade against the Qing. But from the start their efforts were contradictory and marred by distrust and misunderstandings. As the Taiping forces neared Shanghai in 1855, for example, their ships exchanged gunfire with Westerners' ships.[173] In another instance the Taipings fired on the British ship *Hermes*, thinking it a Qing vessel.[174] Although they emphasized their supposed Christian brotherhood with the Western powers as a selling point, meetings with both the British and French produced no formal alliance. There were, of course, private individuals who sold arms and supplies to the Taipings, creating friction between the Qing government and the European representatives. Unlicensed ammunition trading was outlawed in Hong Kong in 1854.[175]

There were vigorous debates in the British press over which side to back, and opinions shifted with the changing fortunes of the war. Within just a few months of the rebels' seizure of Nanjing the Qing reportedly were trying to get Western naval units to help defend Shanghai, but the British were largely inclined to believe that the Son of Heaven should settle his own quarrels with his subjects.[176] Others in Britain saw an opportunity to press for revision (or stronger enforcement) of the Treaty of Nanjing in exchange for British support of the Qing.[177]

The Qing faced a dilemma. From the beginning they appreciated the importance of Western gunboats, steamers, and artillery and were eager to purchase them and hire Western trainers, but at the same time they were reluctant to involve their erstwhile enemies too deeply in this domestic conflict.[178] The Westerners themselves remained ambivalent, intrigued by the Taipings but preferring to remain neutral and see how things developed. Staff writers and editorialists for the *North China Herald*, for example, initially assessed the Taipings as merely another group of Ming restorationists who would easily be dispatched by the government forces. Although they had no high opinion of the government forces, the *Herald* writers predicted "that should the rebels venture to any considerable distance from the southern mountain range where the nature of the country affords them every advantage, the government forces, ill-led and ill-disciplined as they are, and suffering the privations entailed by defective arrangements, and a corrupt commissarial administration will not, in the open country, fail to crush them."[179]

The Treaty of Tianjin, signed on June 27, 1858, had already tilted things against the Taipings because it granted the British expanded rights of navigation on the Yangzi.[180] The Qing court had been discussing expanded river navigation rights for the Western powers since 1854, in part as a result of strategic concerns related to the war, but majority opinion had opposed such measures up until this point.[181] In the interim they had considered various plans to create a more cohesive defensive strategy while also appointing various officials to coordinate riverine defenses against the Taipings.[182] In the wake of the new treaty, the Englishman Lord Elgin traveled up the Yangzi from November 1858 to January 1859 as a show of power. When the Taipings fired on the British ship *Lee* as it approached Nanjing, the British responded in kind, destroying the Taiping batteries and setting the Heavenly Capital aflame.[183] This having helped set the stage, as soon as the Qing and British concluded their peace talks in 1860 after the sacking of the Yuanmingyuan, Qing courtiers approached the British about formally cooperating with them to crush the Taipings.

As these matters simmered, Zuo and Luo Bingzhang recognized that the court's marked inability to select the right people for important posts and to win back the people's support and trust were responsible for many of the ongoing difficulties. Both men favored a more active defense against foreign encroachment, building on China's strengths by using loyal subjects, fighting under circumstances of their own choosing, and properly rewarding loyal and competent officials. But Zuo contended that the court "was not of a mind to fight and went out of its way to be pliable [*quyi qurong*]."[184] Such frank assessments helped cement Zuo's reputation and earned him celebrity and support in certain circles at court, though it also earned him an undeserved reputation for xenophobia among certain Westerners. Guo Songtao sang Zuo's praises in a personal meeting with the emperor, adding to Zuo's reputation and paving the way for his subsequent promotions.[185]

But despite the enthusiasm of at least some of the court officials in Beijing for wider cooperation with the West against the Taiping, field commanders such as Zeng Guofan and Zuo Zongtang remained rightfully suspicious of Western motives and were loath to allow foreigners too much influence in key locales, not least because they themselves had been fighting for nearly a decade and did not want to be denied the final credit for crushing the rebels. Zuo in particular still bore a grudge against the British for the First Opium War.[186] For the rest of his career, when he worked with foreigners he preferred working with the French, Germans, and Russians rather than the British, whom he never trusted. The Qing's improving relations with the West was transpiring just at the wrong time for the Taipings, who had resolved to push for Shanghai in the summer of 1860 after they had captured Suzhou. The Foreign Rifle Corps (*yangqiangdui*) under the command of the American Frederick Townsend Ward had formed on June 2, 1860, and the British formally adopted a policy of defending Shanghai on July 25 of the same year.[187]

THE *ARROW* WAR AND ITS IMPLICATIONS

The British policy of nonintervention in the civil war had been predicated on multiple factors, including the rise of Napoleon III in Europe and concerns elsewhere in Britain's growing empire.[188] The British also put some faith in the existing treaty port system and had begun asserting their rights and angling for more, as evidenced by an article published in the *North China Herald* in 1851.[189]

Opium remained a key sticking point, although some British argued that its trade should be open and legal because it was more benign than alcohol.[190] A letter to the editors of the *North China Herald* in 1850 had grumbled that China complaining about the evils of opium was like England complaining to the French and the Dutch about brandy and gin.[191]

The pot finally boiled over in October 1856 when a dispute arose in connection with the *Arrow,* a ship registered in Hong Kong that had a British captain but a Chinese crew. The *Arrow* attempted to dock in Guangzhou with an expired registration and was searched by the Chinese authorities, who claimed to find a wanted pirate hiding on board. The British protested this infringement on their rights and responded by bombarding the forts outside Guangzhou. The Chinese official in charge closed the customs house and halted trade in Guangzhou. Two months later, foreign trading factories were burned. After vigorous debate in Parliament the British government decided to send a force to Guangzhou in the spring of 1857, but it was diverted to India to suppress the Sepoy Mutiny. At the end of the year, however, the British bombarded Guangzhou, captured the governor-general, and then proceeded to govern the city (with a Qing-appointed Mongol official) for the next three years.

Zuo Zongtang was predictably angered by this turn of events, writing to a colleague that the "Guangdong barbarians [i.e., the British] get worse by the day, aided by Han traitors." And now the English and domestic bandits were obstructing the rivers, hindering Qing efforts to combat the Taipings.[192] In a letter he wrote to Hu Linyi toward the end of 1857 Zuo lamented the British occupation of Guangzhou, saying that once more the awesomeness of the dynasty had been tarnished, and not merely by the British.[193]

The British and other powers used a show of force near Tianjin in 1858 to force new treaties on the Qing.[194] Most significantly, the British gained the right to station a permanent resident minister in Beijing. The treaties also levied additional indemnities, nearly tripled the number of treaty ports, allowed foreigners to participate in China's coastal and riverine trade and travel in the interior, opened the Yangzi all the way to Hankou, provided for new tariff and transit tax duties, and legalized the opium trade.[195] Although certain elements at the Qing court remained opposed to full and equal trade and treaty relations with the West, others advocated favorable relations in order to gain Western help against the Taipings. The potential for this had already been demonstrated when Western gunboats traveled up the Yangzi to inspect potential future trading sites and intimidated the Taipings with their firepower.

But the treaties unraveled in June 1859 when a foreign mission traveling to Beijing was stopped and destroyed by Senggelinqin at the Dagu Fort.[196] This victory emboldened the Qing, and in August 1859 they abrogated the Tianjin treaties of the previous year. The British and French responded with reprisals that included attacks on Tianjin and Beijing and the sacking of the Yuanmingyuan, the imperial retreat just outside of Beijing (also known as the Summer Palace), which burned as the hapless Xianfeng emperor went "on holiday" to the imperial summer retreat at Rehe in the northeast in August–September 1860.[197]

Prince of the Blood Yixin, better known as Prince Gong (1833–1898), stepped in at this point and negotiated a settlement that did in fact signal a sea change in relations with the British.[198] Prince Gong had been raised alongside Emperor Xianfeng, and the two were close. He was also much more open-minded than many of the Manchu courtiers and more willing to deal with the Westerners on an equal footing. His moderating influence, though often challenged or even eclipsed, would be an asset to the Qing court over the remainder of his life. Within a month a new agreement was signed, the Westerners pulled back to Tianjin, and the disgraced Senggelinqin was given a chance to redeem himself by battling the Nian.[199] In the twelfth month of the year, Prince Gong was named the first leader of the newly created Ministry of Foreign Affairs (Zongli Yamen), and other Manchu nobles were placed in charge of trade with foreigners.[200] These appointments were even more significant steps in the unraveling of the old tributary system than the Treaty of Nanjing because they involved a literal reordering of the Qing administrative apparatus at its highest levels. Over the next three decades the British would work much more closely with the Qing and often assist them, largely in an effort to preserve the rights that had finally been gained by virtue of two decades of gunboat diplomacy.[201]

THE TAIPINGS TRY TO REGROUP

Though the purge of 1856 had severely compromised the Taiping military leadership and resulted in Hong Xiuquan himself retreating into the pleasures of his palace, a revival of sorts was engineered by his cousin Hong Ren'gan, who had arrived in Nanjing in April 1859 and was appointed Shield King and prime minister. Ren'gan had lived in Hong Kong and Shanghai and thus had far more contact and experience with Westerners than many of the Taiping leaders.[202] Hong Ren'gan helped create a plan for lifting the siege of Nanjing by feigning an attack on Hangzhou and Huzhou to draw Qing forces away. The attackers succeeded in capturing the outer city of Hangzhou, though Manchu troops retained control of the inner city. This opening also allowed the Taipings to pick off many of the Qing units surrounding Nanjing, resulting in the death of the commander, Hechun, as some 100,000 Taiping troops overran the Qing siege lines.[203]

Hong Ren'gan then recommended taking Shanghai and recapturing Hubei in order to strengthen the rebels' defensive position and possibly curry Western support. Initial operations proved successful as the rebels seized Danyang and Changzhou in May 1860 and Suzhou on June 2, aided by fifth columnists. Some historians argue that many of those who joined the Taipings in these later operations were mere opportunists who in the long run undermined Taiping morale and effectiveness.[204] There was also the old problem of holding places once they were captured, never a Taiping strength.

Hong Ren'gan, being fairly well informed of Qing activities, had advocated striking at Beijing when the court fled to Rehe, but Li Xiucheng had favored gathering troops at Anqing first, thinking he could drive the Qing away once and for all.[205] Anqing now became the lynchpin of the struggle.[206] As the Taiping armies advanced within sixty *li* of Zeng Guofan's armies, Zuo held his lines to the southwest at Jingdezhen while also battling Taiping forces between Anhui and Jiangxi.[207] Yang Yuebin and Peng Yulin kept up the pressure from the rivers with Peng's new fleet built on Lake Tai.[208]

The Manchu commander Shengbao was also dispatched to help, though modern scholars question his contributions. Shengbao gained notoriety after being promoted to the Grand Secretariat, where he proffered advice on quelling the Taipings. The court told him to put his money where his mouth was and sent him to Henan.[209] Liao Zhenghua describes Shengbao as "utterly lacking in ability, with few accomplishments and many failures." Privately the leaders of the Xiang Army referred to him as Baibao (secure defeat), but the court protected him because he was a well-connected Manchu Bannerman.[210] Shengbao had a habit of sending in fulsome victory reports that were often exaggerated to cover up greater failures, so he was shuffled from post to post.[211]

The short-term gains for the Taipings led the court to reinvest Zeng Guofan as governor-general. During the period of mourning for his father from March 1857 to July 1858 Zeng had planned how he might restructure his forces and mount the final assault on Nanjing.[212] Zuo had criticized Zeng for going into mourning, writing to him that abandoning his military responsibilities at such a time was "neither loyal nor righteous and did nothing to honor the memory of his father."[213] Within the Neo-Confucian context, however, such mourning gestures were deemed very important, and officials who obtained permission from the emperor to curtail mourning, which normally lasted twenty-seven months in the case of deceased parents, often came under heavy fire from their peers. Throughout Zeng's mourning period, Zuo and Luo Bingzhang sent letters to the court asking that Zeng be reinstated. When he was finally recalled to service, Zeng met with Zuo and Luo Bingzhang on July 22, 1858, to discuss their long-term strategy for defeating the Taipings.[214] Over the next several years Luo, Hu Linyi, Li Hongzhang, and Zuo Zongtang devised a winning strategy. According to the *Qing shigao* it was Hu Linyi who devised the original plan (in late July 1857) of attacking Nanjing from multiple directions by taking Jiujiang first, then Anqing, and then converging on the Taiping capital from all four directions.[215]

TURNING THE TIDE

The campaign did not proceed smoothly. At one point Zeng Guofan's forces were nearly encircled and received no provisions for thirty days. Zuo sent forces to the rescue, but they were repulsed. Bao Chao and Zuo then moved to engage the Taiping forces near Yangtang and Hukou, southwest of Anqing upriver on the Yangzi, but heavy rains delayed Bao's army on its approach to the rendezvous. Perceiving an advantage, the Taiping forces closed in. Zuo had his men erect banners on a hill with Bao's name on them, tricking the rebels into thinking Bao had in fact arrived, and they retreated. Bao arrived the next day and joined the battle. Zuo directed from the rear until Bao sent him a message asking him to advance. Bao's forces had taken low ground rather than a strategically better high position, and that should have been disastrous, but because of Bao's fearsome reputation the Taipings were afraid to engage him, and they were smashed by Bao in successive battles and forced to retreat toward Anqing.[216] Zuo rushed to Wuyuan in northern Anhui, cutting bridges to prevent the rebel forces from crossing rivers.[217]

A battle for control of Leping to the south broke out, with Li's force of 100,000 attacking the city for two weeks. Zuo ordered his men to dig ditches and build counter-siegeworks to flood the area around the city and hamper the Taiping cavalry. The government forces then sallied forth for a three-pronged assault against the Taiping.[218] At the moment the armies clashed, a thunderstorm erupted. The Taipings were routed, losing more than four thousand men in a battle near Jingdezhen that avenged an earlier defeat Zuo had suffered there.[219] In a letter written to his son Xiaowei, Zuo described how the rebels trembled before the awesome might of the Qing during the final assault.[220] In a subsequent letter he wrote that the locals had not seen such a demonstration of Qing awesomeness in more than a decade and that the Qing were finally winning the battle for hearts and minds.[221]

The Taiping commander Li Shixian lost more than ten thousand soldiers over the course of the campaign and headed back east into Zhejiang. All told, Zuo fought more than twenty battles in this campaign and won most of them. In the wake of these triumphs Guo Songtao praised Zuo to the emperor, calling him "an upright, talented and true hero, with a firm grasp of all matters."[222]

Crucial in these battles were the exploits of Liu Dian, yet another native of Hunan, who had risen through the military ranks quickly due to his innate skills and joined Zuo Zongtang's *mufu*.[223] Liu was a master of night attacks, and his exploits helped Zuo and Zeng keep their supply lines open as he repeatedly stymied attacks by Li Shixian and Li Xiucheng. It was Liu Dian who recaptured Leping for the Qing and later mobilized the people in southern Anhui to keep Qing lines open as the government force closed in on Hangzhou. It was said that he was so respected that the people "regarded Liu's army like a timely rain shower."[224] Liu played a major role in mopping up Taiping remnants in Fujian and Guangdong and later accompanied Zuo on his campaigns in the northwest, again serving with great distinction.

Zuo's efforts to mop up Taiping remnants were hampered by disease running through his troops.[225] As Zuo's forces continued to chip away at Taiping positions around Anhui and the Zhejiang border, the Taipings under Li Xiuqing decided to attempt one more hammer blow to dislodge the Qing besiegers, then under the command of Zeng Guoquan (1824–1890), Guofan's younger brother.[226] But Zuo's savvy use of combined operations and firepower proved lethal to the Taipings, whom he defeated at Songshuling. This prompted further honors from the throne, including Zuo receiving the position of Minister of the Court of Imperial Sacrifices.[227] In early 1862 Zuo told his son that most of Zhejiang was back under Qing control.[228]

The siege of Anqing dragged on through the hot summer months as starvation and desertion plagued the defenders. The government siege tightened as outlying forts were taken. The Taiping commander Chen Yucheng tried to save his compatriots but was repulsed by Bao Chao and Duolonga, prompting more rebels to surrender.[229] The Qing forces finally recovered Anqing in September 1861.[230] The Taipings managed to seize the port city of Ningbo in December 1861, but a mixed force of Western mercenaries and Chinese fighting alongside the regular forces of Zeng Guofan, Li Hongzhang, and Zuo Zongtang were gaining victories by land and water.[231] A Taiping assault on Shanghai was repulsed in the spring of 1862.[232] Even as the Taiping commander Li Xiucheng (d. 1864) mustered his troops for a renewed offensive, he was recalled to save the crumbling defenses of Nanjing.[233]

The British tried to advance their own interests and leverage their influence with the Qing field commanders but to little avail. Qing officials were willing to use Western troops and weaponry but seldom deferred to foreigners on matters of strategy or planning. Zuo, for example, wanted to ensure that there was clear Chinese control over Westerners in the armies associated with him. This included oversight of everything from command decisions to appearance and decorum. Zuo disliked bushy Western beards and wanted his troops cleanshaven, which also helped distinguish them from the Taipings, who were often called the "long hairs" (*changmao*) because they refused to shave their foreheads in the Manchu style as required by law.[234] As of the spring of 1862, however, the Qing did permit the British and French to patrol the Yangzi with their gunboats, freeing up some Qing forces for other duties, and approved the training of select Qing officers on Western gunboats.[235]

A NEW BOY MONARCH

Emperor Xianfeng died in the seventh month of 1861 at the "mobile palace" in Rehe. He was succeeded by his son Zaichun, who would reign as Emperor Tongzhi (r. 1862–1874).[236] His original reign title was supposed to be Qixiang, meaning "auspicious" but was changed to Tongzhi, meaning "restoration of order," on the day of his enthronement.[237] Tongzhi's ascension to the throne was momentous for the Qing in that his birth mother, a concubine named Yehonala (1835–1908), was named one of his regents. The Empress Dowager Cixi, as she is best known, dominated the court and its affairs until her death. While she is today remembered as the embodiment of shortsighted conservatism, manipulation, and corruption in late Qing politics, she was also a savvy ruler, and her repeated support of Zuo Zongtang over the next two decades gave him the opportunities he needed to implement his policies and successfully defend the empire against numerous threats.[238] She was said to have been particularly impressed by Zuo's tenacity and ability to bounce back from defeat, traits she also embodied.[239] Zuo praised the new emperor as a "truly sagacious Son of Heaven" in a letter to one of the Xiang Army commanders.[240]

The subsequent "Tongzhi Restoration" era has been evaluated in varying ways. At the time and shortly thereafter, despite the creation of important new institutions such as the Zongli Yamen (Ministry of Foreign Affairs) and the defeat of the Taiping and Nian Rebellions, the reign was portrayed as a largely propagandistic series of half-hearted reforms that paled in comparison to the dramatic successes of Meiji (1868–1912) Japan. The bankruptcy of the reforms was revealed in the Qing's defeat by Japan in the war of 1894–1895. The Qing loyalists who edited the *Draft History of the Qing Dynasty* (*Qing shigao*), published in 1927, were more laudatory, crediting Luo Bingzhang and Hu Linyi in particular with assembling the military talents involved in reviving Qing power. "Concerning the Restoration can anyone be considered greater than these two in that enterprise?" they asked.[241] Writing in the 1950s, Mary Wright cast the Tongzhi era as marking "the last stand of Chinese conservatism," comparing it to the similarly failed measures of Chiang Kaishek's Guomindang in the 1920s–1930s.[242] More recent evaluations have been more positive in pointing out how innovations pioneered in the late Qing paved the way for China's comparatively successful modernization in the twentieth century.[243]

ZUO BECOMES A NATIONAL FIGURE

Returning to our hero, Zuo had been given an honorific post in the Court of Imperial Sacrifices back in 1860 and was increasingly a public figure. Given purview of military affairs in Jiangnan, he led the eight thousand troops of his Chu Army into Zhejiang. But he had more than seven hundred *li* of front to protect and his army was stretched thin. When Hangzhou fell to the Taipings on December 29, 1861, the court put Zeng in supreme command of all military affairs in Jiangsu, Anhui, Jiangxi, and Zhejiang. At the recommendation of Zeng Guofan, Zuo was delegated to command the military in Zhejiang.

Wary of having his own supply lines cut, Zuo suggesting spreading his forces out and holding key points so as to avoid a static defense that would cede the initiative to the enemy.[244] In the second month of 1861 he took Suilan. Repeatedly luring rebel armies into engagements that favored his forces, Zuo and his commanders took several more cities, and by early 1862 most of eastern Zhejiang was pacified.[245] True to their vision, Zeng and Zuo resisted meddling directives from the court as they implemented their plan. Zuo also called in various favors to obtain sufficient supplies for his army.[246]

Meanwhile, returning to the river campaigns, the British admiral James Hope toured the Yangzi in February 1861, and it was formally opened to British trade the following month.[247]

In 1862 Zuo was promoted to provincial governor, a remarkable climb for a man who had been impeached just a couple of years earlier for disrespecting senior officials.[248] At this point the provincial capital had been held by the rebels for twenty days, and numerous other important cities and prefectures were in their hands. Just a few places were holding out before the Taiping onslaught. The new appointment gave Zuo the clout to request more troops and supplies from neighboring provinces.[249] Zuo envisioned a gradual, but lasting, recovery of Zhejiang, moving city by city while tapping resources from his neighbors. He also needed more troops to continue his joint land-river operations.[250] Having observed that the troops of Zhejiang suffered heavy losses owing to their lack of discipline, he prioritized training and officer selection.[251] Confident of his success as always, Zuo was poised to enter the national political and military arena. As significantly, Zuo's accumulated experiences now provided him with the opportunity to fully implement his statecraft principles to make his mark on China, an opportunity he would not squander.

3

EMBRACING
SELF-STRENGTHENING

SUPREME COMMANDER IN THE SOUTHEAST

We need machines that make other machines.
—Zuo Zongtang

I t had taken Zuo fifty years to rise to the apex of the Qing bureaucracy. He had advanced via channels that were considered unusual but would become increasingly common as the dynasty adopted new measures to suit the rapidly changing times. Early in his life Zuo had sought wisdom from the classics and read all the traditional histories and philosophical texts. But he also recognized the value of gaining wisdom from other sources and people from all walks of life. He was not content to lecture peasants on how to farm. He wanted their input so that he could apply it to his academic studies and produce manuals that would be of value to all. Thus, despite his general antipathy toward the British, it should not be surprising that Zuo also appreciated the significance of Western science and technology and sought ways to harness it to serve the needs of China. In this sense Zuo was one of the first proponents of "Self-Strengthening" (*ziqiang*), also sometimes called the "Western Affairs Movement." Traditionally, this movement began at the conclusion of the *Arrow* War and the ascension of Emperor Tongzhi and concluded with the Qing's disastrous defeat at the hands of Meiji Japan in 1895. It is also often portrayed in a negative light. One source, for instance, observes that "Self-Strengthening became less a rallying cry for genuine efforts at innovation than a shibboleth that served to justify expenditures and vested bureaucratic interests" and notes that it consisted essentially of halfway measures that never produced significant institutional changes.[1]

But as we will see in the following chapters, the reality is quite a bit more complicated. The progress made by the Qing in Self-Strengthening was integral to its struggle to retain its administrative and territorial integrity and had far-reaching implications for the subsequent history of China. Zuo would be at the forefront of these activities for the next two decades, the most active and fruitful period of his life.

MOVING INTO ZHEJIANG

The autumn of 1861 had been a momentous one for Zuo. His old patron, Hu Linyi, passed away in September. Hu had long been Zuo's greatest supporter, calling him a "modern day Zhuge Liang," a compliment Zuo enjoyed so much that he sometimes signed his letters "Liao Liang."[2] Zuo was whipping his new armies into shape, increasingly taking on the Taipings in mobile engagements and moving away from the siege warfare that had characterized much of the civil war to this point.[3] The Taiping force entrenched in Nanjing began to resemble an octopus with tentacles stretching outward. Although they continued to attack Qing forces, the rebels had no real plans for reversing the course of the war. They were simply lashing out in response to Qing probing missions. The Qing were keen to recover the strategically and culturally significant city of Hangzhou, which had fallen to the Taipings on the twenty-eighth day of the eleventh month of 1861, prompting the Qing commander there to commit suicide.[4] The loss had hastened the appointment of Zuo as provincial governor of Zhejiang and prompted the court to send additional troops to that theater. Zuo immediately adopted a strategy of "defending Wuyuan so as to aid Huizhou" (which was the gate into Zhejiang), and the last month of 1861 featured sharp engagements along the border between Zhejiang and Anhui.[5]

Qing commanders greedy for the spoils of victory started squabbling over who would be the first to take various important sites, including Hangzhou. Zuo, however, was cautious, not wanting to assail Hangzhou until outlying areas had been taken, both to preserve Qing resources and to help starve out the enemy.[6] He also wanted to establish secure supply lines and create a stable base of operations grounded in local support.[7] In encouraging local gentry to use militia to keep order, Zuo said, "One kills bandits in order to protect the people, and it follows that in order to protect the people one is allowed to kill bandits. This is certainly the principle. So we must widely promulgate the directive to drill and train militia and the gentry must keep love of the people foremost in their minds."[8]

Zuo's prescriptions also included establishing multiple supply routes so that the effectiveness of his army would not be compromised if one was severed.[9] This was to be combined with more training for soldiers and careful selection of their commanders. Deserters had to be rounded up and set to rights, and plans carefully laid to effect a gradual and complete recovery. With these points in mind, Zuo continued to amass supplies as he chose his commanders.[10] Zuo had around 39,000 troops under his direct command and had arranged for 130,000 taels per month in extra funds beyond taxes and *lijin* revenues.[11]

While he had previously enjoyed success with his Chu Army, that force was far too small to confront the forces now arrayed against him. He needed more troops to carry out the kind of offensive and defensive operations he had in mind. Troops started coming in, but Zuo, as was his style, pressed for more. "We will begin with a strong defense," Zuo noted, and "then we will be able to tie up the bandits [*zigu zhiji keyi zhi zei*]."[12] Reiterating his previous points concerning the intimate links between the provinces, Zuo said that securing the borders with Anhui and Jiangxi would serve as a springboard for his operations in Zhejiang, starting with Kaihua, the literal and figurative entry to the province.[13] It was obvious to him that many of his predecessors knew little of basic soldiering, let alone the finer points of training, distributing rewards, and selecting competent commanders.[14]

Several engagements at the end of 1861 resulted in many Taiping deaths, the freeing of prisoners, and the capture of significant numbers of horses and equipment.[15] Around this time Zuo and Liu Dian led twelve brigades into western Zhejiang. They won a series of engagements, killing more than one thousand rebels and capturing supplies and livestock in seizing their objective of Kaihua on the fifteenth day of the first month of 1862.[16] Zuo next moved to Quzhou and distributed relief to the people, appointing local officials and detailing 2,500 men for the city's defense, repulsing a Taiping counterattack on Kaihua as he did so.[17]

Simultaneously, other commanders assailed various Taiping positions in Zhejiang, killing tens of thousands and capturing still more weapons and supplies.[18] Supply depots were established to facilitate the Qing advance. Advancing to take Sui'an, the Qing supposedly killed ten thousand more rebels, rescued more than one thousand POWs, and recovered many false seals of office.[19] By the middle of the second month of 1862, Zuo's forces were camped around Changshan. But Zuo was still concerned about the number of combat-effective troops at his disposal and wary about maintaining his supply lines. Zuo's force dislodged Li Shixian's forces in Changshan and drove him to Jiangshan, but the rebels recaptured Ningguo in southern Anhui.[20] In the fourth month of 1862, Zuo was promoted to governor-general of Zhejiang and Anhui, and Liu Dian was ordered to set up camps in the south of the latter province.[21] It is worth noting that by 1863, five of the eight governors-general in the empire were natives of Hunan.[22]

Over the next two months the Qing advance continued, with Li Shixian repeatedly ceding territory to Liu Dian and Huang Shaochun.[23] From a military standpoint, these battles were noteworthy for how the Qing used a diverse repertoire of weapons and tactics ranging from deft cavalry maneuvers, to blasting their way through entrenched positions with heavy artillery, to riverine operations. In the summer of 1862, Zeng Guofan appointed a superintendent of Yangzi River operations after consulting with the court.[24] The Qing government was finally bringing its innate superiority in resources and technology to bear. In conjunction with the employment of brave and experienced commanders such as Bao Chao, the government forces had finally recovered the "awesomeness" that Zuo and others had accused them of losing.[25] Zuo went about punishing officials deemed culpable for losing cities to the rebels, thereby fulfilling his promise to clean up and instill discipline and accountability in the lower ranks. In some cases, known Taiping collaborators were publicly executed and their bodies left to rot in the streets as an example.[26]

Early in the fifth month Li Shixian tried to rally his units to brake Zuo's advances. But the Qing again defeated them on multiple fronts, with Wang Depang, who would enjoy a long and distinguished career under Zuo, playing a major role. In addition to killing many rebels, thousands of captives were rescued, military equipment was recovered, and the Qing further restored their legitimacy by recovering Taiping seals of office.[27] As the court continued discussing the creation of a new riverine flotilla to aid in the final campaigns against the rebels, Li Shixian's forces were put on the run again, and he lost more than a thousand of the ten thousand troops under his direct command. He retreated to Jinhua and bolstered the walls and moats to resist the Qing while Zuo deployed his forces in the surrounding areas to keep Li hemmed in.[28]

Throughout that summer and into the fall, Zuo and his forces chipped away at the Taipings' defenses. Zuo oversaw the siege of Longyoucheng himself, a tough task because the rebels were well dug in there, with deep moats and additional stockades erected outside the main city walls.[29] The rebels also had a fair number of cannons there and put up a spirited defense when the Qing tried to force their way in. The Taiping forces at Longyoucheng and Jinhua were keen to defend the south bank of the Yangzi as the strategic gateway to their rapidly dwindling realm. Zuo thus relocated his tent to Tanshiwang, some fifteen *li* away, to plan and coordinate the Qing efforts.[30] The two sides battled intermittently, with the Qing intercepting relief columns and Li Shixian sending out probes. Zuo attacked a couple of other sites in hopes of weakening the resistance at Longyoucheng, killing around one thousand rebels and capturing one hundred more, including several officers.[31] Seeing mixed results from this strategy, he decided to attack the two cities by river but did not yet have enough ships. The delay ended up serving the besiegers, who got word that the defenders of Longyoucheng were now starving to death. Li Shixian hunkered down and refused to come forth.[32]

The situation intensified when an estimated 50,000–60,000 Taiping forces advanced over multiple routes to try and lift the sieges. The fighting was intense, but again the Qing had the better of it, killing more than a thousand rebel soldiers and capturing more guns and officers. Li Shixian himself was seriously wounded but managed to escape, pursued by Liu Dian.[33] Battles raged through the fall of 1862 with heavy casualties on both sides.[34] Steady skirmishing lasted through the end of the year and into 1863 as combined land and water offensives tightened the screws on Taiping defenses and the rebels scrambled to reinforce Hangzhou.[35] Zuo pushed doggedly onward, swatting away local bandit forces that tried to hinder him. Amid these struggles, Zuo also received the happy news that his eldest son had earned the *juren* degree.[36]

In the first month of 1863, Gao Liansheng, Wang Depang, and others recovered Jinhua in addition to Shaoxing, putting eastern Zhejiang once again fully under Qing control. Zuo was confident that he would soon hold all of Anhui along the Yangzi as well.[37] With Hangzhou thereby imperiled, the Taipings bolstered their defenses at Fuyang. The Qing killed some ten thousand rebels in an ambush after feigning a retreat and then seized Jinhua, slaughtering nearly all within.[38] From Jinhua the Qing advanced to Yanzhou, killing more than ten thousand rebels and destroying some two hundred of their boats in a surprise night attack that featured bloody street fighting.[39] Zuo ordered Liu Dian to take eight thousand troops to join with the Manchu commander Wenrui to defend Huizhou and sent Pei Yuan and Wang Depang to Chun'an and Kaihua, while the Manchu commander Yili assailed Fuyang, just eighty *li* southwest of Hangzhou, forcing Liu Xiucheng to reorganize his defenses there.[40] As the Qing encircled the city, the defenders sent raiding missions into the surrounding countryside to replenish their supplies. Zuo reported that the population of Fuyang was reduced by two-thirds as a result of the Qing encirclement.[41] The court sent Zuo more supplies and officers and remitted taxes in the Fuyang area to alleviate the stress on the local people and encourage their loyalty.[42]

A number of local officials and military officers were impeached or dismissed for dereliction of duty during this time, while others were promoted for positive achievements, demonstrating Zuo's commitment to improving local government. Zuo warned court officials to verify incoming reports. He wrote to a colleague, "How can we know what's true or not? Army commanders repeatedly speak of victories, but never talk of defeat. Small victories are then reported as major victories and even if you deeply investigate reports and question what you've heard, it still may not be enough" to discern the truth. As Emily Mokros in *The Peking Gazette in Late Imperial China* observes, "In their attempts to circumvent the penalties that would follow the revelation of malfeasance or defeat, the empire's officials were complicit in undermining the military capacity of the state."[43]

The Qing were not only killing rebels by the hundreds and thousands; they were also capturing large quantities of supplies, including boats. They burned boats they could not use and kept the gunboats as they cut their way down the rivers. At Fuyang, the Qing fought a fierce naval artillery battle with the Taipings that lasted for days until the attackers gained the riverbank and torched the Taiping fleet.[44] Indeed, destruction of Taiping naval capabilities proved critical in ending the war.[45] The river battles could be quite large, with some involving hundreds of boats and lots of artillery. Qing gunboats would strafe targets adjacent to the rivers and keep up a steady barrage. Thousands of rebels were slain in these battles in the first few months of 1863 as the Qing adroitly combined regulars, provincial armies, and militia; traditional and modern arms; and land and river fighting.[46]

Local militias were a necessity in Zhejiang, which lacked preexisting defense systems.[47] What is striking here is how effectively Zuo and the other commanders melded these disparate forces together. In fact, the Qing had a long history of using specialist troops, including artillery, musketry, and naval specialists, and of tailoring units to terrain—using muskets in central China and bows on the steppe, for example.[48] Metal specialists helped turn weapons into tools for reconstruction work. Boat carpenters assisted in bridge building. Pay rates for such specialists varied but were generally higher than those of ordinary laborers.[49]

Zuo praised the contributions of irregular units. The local militia, he wrote, "serve as guards for the army and augment our awesomeness; furthermore, they help procure supplies and aid in the troops' advance."[50] Militia units were also deployed to defend river crossings to allow regulars to engage in pursuit-and-destroy operations. The Qing reaped a grim harvest. In some places rivers and streams were said to be clogged with corpses.[51] In a letter to his son, Zuo estimated that his troops had killed some 50,000–60,000 rebels in the first few months of 1863 alone. He also complained that the local officials in Zhejiang were "useless and untrustworthy" and were obfuscating his plans. "It's always people who make things difficult," he lamented.[52] Some of his concerns about shortages of supplies and men were alleviated when medicine and troops from Fujian arrived. Westerners had joined the forces as well. The

Frenchman Paul D'Aiguebelle and his foreign gun division, connected to the Ever Triumphant Army organized by Prosper Giquel (1833–1886), assisted in the attack on Fuyang.[53] After their initial meeting Giquel described Zuo as "a man from Hunan, fifty years old with a black mustache. He appears intelligent and energetic but talks too much."[54]

Zuo's forces got bogged down in Fuyang by food shortages and a malaria outbreak.[55] Drought had retarded crop growth in Zhejiang, an issue Zuo hoped would be resolved by the spring rains.[56] Once southern Anhui was secured, Zuo could focus on Yanzhou, which he considered the crucial point for capturing Hangzhou.[57] Working in tandem with China's French allies, the Qing forces recovered Shaoxing in the second month of 1863.[58] Though he had initially expressed concerns about working with the French, Zuo noted the effectiveness of foreign artillery in reducing Shaoxing's walls and the value of foreign training in firearms in his report to the throne.[59] He also advocated buying more foreign ships and guns for China's own forces.[60] With Shaoxing recovered, the avenues to Hangzhou opened and the Qing could once more open ports and tap their customs and tax revenues.

Even as they pursued these offensives, Zuo was bringing in rice from other provinces for his troops and the starving locals. He also donated significant funds from his own coffers.[61] He worked hard to end bribery and corruption among the officials by setting up local markets and taking measures to curb inflation and price gouging. As in other places, Zuo reorganized the salt gabelle and established *lijin* stations.[62] Zuo overcame his earlier scruples about selling offices and established bureaus for the sale of official degrees. He recommended using salt revenues to fund land troops and customs receipts for naval troops. He also proposed a tea tax.[63]

The Qing continued pressing toward Hangzhou by land and water, torching Taiping flotillas and executing spies along the way.[64] Through the summer Qing forces killed or captured many more rebels, recovering more seals of office as well as livestock and other resources as they pounded their way toward Hangzhou.[65] The terrified residents of the city hunkered down behind a protective network of walls and bastions extending outward some forty *li*.

Zuo divided his forces, including the foreign units under D'Aiguebelle, to attack from multiple directions. The Taipings tried to attack the allied forces, but they were rescued by Gao Liansheng.[66] With the capture of Xinqiao by Gao Liansheng and Liu Qingliang, by early autumn 1863 the Qing were within five miles of the outer defenses of Hangzhou.[67] Shortages of supplies and food continued to worry Zuo, who repeatedly requested more of both from Zeng Guofan.[68] Kang Guoqi kept pressure on the east side of the city, allowing Gao Liansheng to steadily reduce the outer defenses as other commanders hit the west and north walls. Li Hongzhang's capture of Suzhou also helped cut off another escape route, and Li advanced toward Hangzhou.

The Qing also moved to secure the sea-lanes, both to prevent the Taipings from escaping and to make sure they did not receive supplies or aid from outside sources. They destroyed pirate fleets trying to sell supplies to the rebels and executed the ships' captains. Troops were sent from Fujian to Taiwan as well, apparently as a deterrent to both the Westerners and the rebels.[69] Although Li Hongzhang would later claim that Zuo had no understanding of the strategic significance of coastal defense, these actions make it clear that Zuo was acutely aware of its ramifications.

True to his personal beliefs, from the start of his tenure as the governor of Zhejiang, Zuo enacted policies to ameliorate the suffering of the masses. He offered tax remissions and tried to bring new settlers into the province by offering start-up funds for enterprises as well as agricultural equipment and free seeds.[70] Zuo also distributed food, medicine, and clothing to refugees. Killing two birds with one stone, Zuo hired local women to pick tea, which they could exchange for rice. Zuo then exchanged the tea for military provisions.[71] He tried to restore a sense of normalcy by encouraging locals to dig wells and return to animal husbandry and other activities.[72] Formerly cultivated lands were overrun with weeds, and fierce animals such as wolves and tigers roamed freely.[73] Some districts had reportedly lost 95 percent of their populace. Such horrific accounts are typical in times of endemic warfare and strife in China and can be considered part of what I dub the "rhetoric of catastrophe," whereby civilization, as imparted by a stable government run by Confucian-trained officials, is contrasted with a lawless world inundated by natural and man-made disasters and overrun by savagery.[74]

Zuo slowed his operations for a couple of months in the summer of 1863 as he rebuilt supply reserves and French instructors drilled his troops in firearms use. When he resumed operations, the results were immediate. D'Aiguebelle in particular earned distinction for assisting the Qing troops, whose infantry and gunboat firepower proved decisive in multiple engagements.[75] The Qing court wanted faster action, but the Manchu field commander had to be recalled due to illness. Gao Liansheng and Wang Yueliang picked up the slack as the cordon closed around Hangzhou. The Qing used captured resources to fuel their advance, refitting captured supply and transport vessels with cannon for riverine warfare.[76]

As the Qing readied for a multipronged land and water offensive on Hangzhou, the cornered Taiping commanders split their defenses and erected stockades, ditches, and other counter-siegeworks. Fighting was especially fierce southeast of the city. The Qing gunboats moved down the Qiantang River toward Hangzhou, their steady fire keeping the Taipings on the defensive, occupying Shilicheng and other towns along the way. Early in the ninth month rebel relief troops came down from the mountains, but they were repulsed. The Qing sent out commando raids that killed hundreds of relief forces and intercepted shipments of grain bound for the rebels.[77] Previewing the style of warfare Zuo would use to master northwestern China later in his career, his troops used carts to shield their artillery as they dislodged some eight to nine thousand rebels from a fortified position.[78]

In at least one case the Qing used fire arrows to drive the Taipings out of a fortified post. They also built artillery platforms from which they could fire down into the city. Concerned that the city was still not fully encircled and the rebels might break out or be rescued, the court issued the order to advance and take Hangzhou in the tenth month of 1863.[79] Liu Dian was promoted, and more low-level officers were appointed to facilitate the operation. Zuo reassured the court that the Qing campaigns across Zhejiang were progressing steadily and Hangzhou was increasingly isolated.[80]

With a thousand troops as his personal guard, Zuo stayed at Yanzhou to hold the bridges and rivers and cut off relief units from aiding the rebels. In the eleventh month of 1863 he moved his base to Fuyang and was focusing on attacking the outer gates of Hangzhou as Qing forces pushed toward Shimen Bridge. Hangzhou was defended by Chen Bingwen, described in one Chinese source as a "notorious homosexual" whose inner circle had been infiltrated by the Qing, although the much more competent Wang Haiyang was also present.[81] Another Taiping sally was cast back, and the struggle intensified. The next month Zuo sent Gao Liansheng and the allied French forces in a joint land-water assault on Fengshan Gate.[82] The rebels fell back, and the Qing blew through the first line of defenses, killing more than two thousand rebel troops as they attacked from multiple directions to divide enemy strength.[83]

Qing artillery bombardments steadily reduced the outlying defenses. As the Qing pushed forward, corpses filled the Qiantang River, obstructing its flow.[84] The Taiping defenders grew increasingly desperate. Wang Haiyang, the fiercest of the Taiping commanders, tried unsuccessfully to divert the flow of the river to flood out the Qing.[85] Early in 1864 D'Aiguebelle and Gao Liansheng killed one thousand rebels at Wangjiang Gate and pushed closer to the city proper amid a hail of cannon fire.[86] In the middle of the second month Kang Guoqi killed a thousand more as the Qing tightened their siege. Zuo called for a complete bombardment from all sides using both cannon and arrow fire. Casualties mounted as the Qing stepped up the pressure. Zuo planted spies within the city to sow dissent as rumors circulated that relief was coming from Nanjing.[87]

Zuo detailed D'Aiguebelle to supervise the artillery bombardment, concentrating it near Fengshan Gate. A final rescue effort was repelled, and the allied government and foreign troops began breaching the defenses. Gao Liansheng temporarily pulled back under heavy fire, but the city's defenses crumbled section by section as Taiping defenders readied to flee.[88] Gao Liansheng entered via the Qiantang Gate and D'Aiguebelle came in through the Fengshan Gate. At this point yet another relief column tried to save the city but was driven off. Under cover of darkness the Qing sent assassins into the city to kill random defenders and undermine morale. When the Qing entered in force the next day amid a driving rain, they killed several thousand more, captured around a thousand, and freed many prisoners. Hangzhou was recovered on the night of March 31–April 1, 1864.[89] When it was finally taken, the city allegedly contained just 10 percent of its previous population.[90]

Prosper Giquel described the scene: "White walls rise up mournfully to the sky, demanding back their lost roofing."[91] At least some of the troops looted after they entered the city, against Zuo's expressed orders. In general, though, Zuo's soldiers refrained from looting and slaughter, unlike those of Zeng Guofan and Li Hongzhang. Authors sympathetic to Zuo claim that the looters were connected to the Ever Victorious Army and were not under Zuo's direct command.[92]

Wang Haiyang managed to escape the slaughter, and over the next couple of years he and Li Shixian would create considerable havoc in the region. Zuo immediately ordered pursuit of the rebels as mop-up operations commenced. Thousands of rebels were killed at Wukang and more supplies were recovered, though Wang and Li still eluded capture.[93] Zuo received a number of awards, honors, and promotions for his efforts, including being named Junior Guardian of the Heir Apparent as well as Earl of Kejing and receiving the Yellow Jacket from the emperor.[94]

MOPPING UP IN ZHEJIANG

After Hangzhou fell, Zuo went about the business of pacifying the countryside. He was suspicious of the motives of surrendered rebels and leery of pockets of resistance. But he also was concerned about reports that innocents were being killed after submitting to the Qing. He stipulated that former rebels were to hand over all weapons and seals of office and shave their heads to demonstrate their sincerity.[95] His officers made steady progress securing Zhejiang through the summer of 1864.[96] But natural disasters such as famine and epidemics continued to plague the region, necessitating tax remissions and the distribution of relief, which hampered recovery efforts.[97] In a letter to his son, Zuo lamented the widespread famine and disease and the ruined countryside left by the warfare, which had created a huge refugee crisis. He estimated it would take twenty to thirty years for the province to recover.[98] An official told Prosper Giquel that wolves and tigers prowled the roads and the population of Zhejiang was reduced by 40 percent; but this was only half as bad as the situation in neighboring Anhui.[99] Zuo was concerned about rations and supplies for his troops and hoped that he could be supplemented by revenues from maritime customs. He also complained about graft and tried to implement measures to curtail it.[100]

With the enemy "scattering like ants" before them, Qing forces continued to cut a swath through western Zhejiang. The desperate Taipings tried to mount river defenses with cannons and boats seized from locals, but the Qing repeatedly overwhelmed the defenders, seized their boats, and killed thousands in pursuit as they fled inland.[101] Forest ambushes and other desperate gambits availed them not. By this point it was readily apparent that the Qing side enjoyed superior leadership and much better coordination of forces. While many of the Taiping generals were experienced, they were too often unwilling or unable to support one another. On the other hand, even though Qing commanders like Zuo Zongtang and Li Hongzhang were far from being friends, in their respective theaters they effectively discharged their responsibilities and cooperated enough to steadily limit the rebels' strategic options.

The Taipings were driven back to the defenses around Huzhou, where their camps were arrayed twenty to thirty *li* deep. The Taiping commander Huang Jin had reportedly received nearly 60,000 reinforcements in recent months. Zuo sent river units under Cai Yuanji, Gao Liansheng, and Wang Yueliang from Deqing in the southwest and Liu Shuyuan and others from the southeast. Gao Liansheng assumed control of the boats, allowing the others to push forward. Over the next two months the Qing sustained attacks from the front and rear as they pushed on against stout Taiping defenses. A relief column of ten thousand was pushed back. Cao Yuanji used a division of two hundred foreign gunners to lay an ambush that killed several hundred rebels.[102] The overall Qing strategy was to press forward on land while simultaneously bottling up the rivers. In this fashion they steadily reduced the rebels' defenses and eroded their naval capabilities while making judicious use of foreign auxiliaries. Those who professed a desire to submit to the Qing but remained entrenched when government forces arrived were simply exterminated as an incentive to encourage others to desert.[103] Corpses piled up through the summer. By the end of the sixth month the Taiping commanders in Huzhou started submitting.[104]

Toward the end of the seventh month fires erupted in Huzhou as the Qing fire arrows, in tandem with artillery, finally achieved their aims. A rainstorm that night dampened the flames but also hindered rebels trying to flee. Some seven to eight thousand were captured and many others killed. The Qing rode in on the tide of victory, killing rebel troops and recovering discarded weapons and animals. The corpses of slain rebels littered the roads stretching more than twenty *li* outside the city. Thousands more died or submitted in neighboring areas, the Qing recovering more seals of office. This scene would be replayed across the province over the next few months. The last rebels were chased from Zhejiang by early autumn of 1864.[105] Zuo set about punishing and replacing officials who had fled their posts or defected to the Taiping side. He also solicited funds from court to restore Ningbo and other devastated cities.[106]

Another battle for Fuqiao was being waged at the same time. This conflict was notable in that the foreign forces, directed by D'Aiguebelle, were using exploding shells against the Taipings in addition to steamboats.[107] Zuo was impressed by both and would adopt them in his later campaigns in the northwest. The Xiang Army also maintained a strong naval presence, plying the rivers to good effect as the broader campaign to take Nanjing unfolded. The havoc created by the exploding shells allowed the Qing to take control of the rivers leading toward the Taiping bastions.[108]

WORKING WITH THE FOREIGN DEVILS

The Qing court and provincial officials had been vigorously debating the possibility of using foreign support to crush the rebels since at least 1854. The Americans even sent a representative to open talks, but they were scuttled by Xianfeng.[109] The resolution of the *Arrow* War and resulting treaties (see chapter 2), along with the creation of the Zongli Yamen, had finally opened the legal doors for such cooperation.[110] In fact, contrary to popular belief, such relationships were well within the framework of traditional Chinese practices. As Richard Smith notes, "Behind the basic rhetoric of the Chinese world order throughout the imperial era lay realistic, sophisticated, and generally effective policies ... which were neither inherently 'unmodern' nor uniquely Chinese."[111] But questions remained as to exactly what forms such cooperation would take. Qing officials were leery of any large Western expeditionary force operating on Chinese soil. They were also loath to put themselves or their troops under Western commanders.[112] Zeng Guofan was a strong critic of working with the foreigners initially, as was Zuo, who warned the Zongli Yamen about the machinations of the French.[113]

The strategy adopted was essentially a compromise. The United Defense Bureau was established in Shanghai to provide payment, uniforms, and munitions for up to ten thousand foreign soldiers. Chinese officials in Shanghai referred to this as "borrowing British and French troops." Elites interceded with Xue Huan, then governor of Jiangsu, to solicit foreign help, but it took considerable lobbying. The court finally acceded in February 1862 but noted that the measure was temporary and should be handled locally, not through the Zongli Yamen.[114] Western mercenary captains, along with a few officers in the employment of their respective governments, would create hybrid armies led by a few foreign officers who trained and led troops mostly comprising natives. These captains would generally be under the control of Chinese officials, however, as most would be given ranks in the Qing armies.[115] In addition the Qing would greatly expand their purchase and deployment of the latest military technology in accordance with their new mantra centering on Self-Strengthening.

The most famous of these forces was the Ever Victorious Army (*changsheng jun*), originally organized in Shanghai in 1860 as the Shanghai Foreign Arms Corps by the American Frederick Townsend Ward (1831–1862) with the cooperation of Frenchman Henry Andrea Burgevine (1836–1865), British admiral James Hope (1808–1881), and French admiral August Leopold Protet (1808–1862).[116] Ward, a dropout of the American Literary, Scientific, and Military Academy (now Norwich University) in Vermont, was a colorful adventurer in the mold of many nineteenth-century soldiers of fortune; he is even reputed to have met Garibaldi in his wanderings in Latin America in 1850–1851.[117] The original Ever Victorious Army consisted of just a couple hundred troops, mostly European mercenaries of various backgrounds, and it never exceeded five thousand. The army generally operated within fifty miles of Shanghai, belying the long-standing perception that it and similar foreign-led forces were primarily responsible for crushing the Taiping Rebellion. A modern biographer of Ward goes so far as to assert that "more than any other person or organization, Ward and his Ever Victorious Army had pointed the way toward a different kind of China, one in which Manchu chauvinism would have given way to a reasoned Chinese acceptance of outside assistance."[118]

While the foreign forces did help to broaden Chinese knowledge of modern drilling tactics and military organization, they merely accelerated processes already underway. Carr contends that Ward's army "was a synthesis of the warlike arts of China and the West and without it the Chinese empire might not have survived,"[119] when in fact virtually every "innovation" credited to Ward and other foreign officers was already present somewhere in Qing forces by the early 1860s.[120] Visionary Chinese officials had been reorganizing their forces for decades before Ward arrived in China, and officials such as Zuo were well aware of the superiority of Western technologies and were already integrating it into their units. Moreover, the lion's share of the fighting was carried out by Qing troops far removed from Shanghai. But because that city was the center of the Western presence, events there were amplified by Western observers and have been unduly stressed ever since in Western scholarship. Further, the Western officers were not necessarily well educated or trained; many lacked the practical field experience of their Chinese counterparts. They were also accused of being "soft" by their Chinese counterparts. For example, Li Hongzhang said of the Ever Victorious Army that while their weapons and techniques were good, the soldiers themselves were overly cautious, not brave, and would not pitch or sleep in tents.[121]

Zuo was none too pleased about working alongside the foreign mercenaries and initially rejected French offers to join his forces. But he also recognized the advantage the foreign gunboats offered his troops in combined operations, and this apparently convinced him to soften his stance.[122] Still, Zuo would later stick to his principles and thwart an effort by French officers under his command to increase the size of their force.[123] Zuo's fears were realized when H. N. Lay, slated to be the point man for the proposed British flotilla that was to aid the Qing, produced a series of outrageous demands, including provisions for greater shares of customs revenue flowing into British (specifically Lay's) hands and independent command authority for British commanders operating alongside Chinese provincial authorities.[124] When the Chinese authorities refused the demands and subsequent compromises failed, the ships were returned to England and sold.[125]

Nonetheless, multiple forces were created, often with names recalling other forces in Chinese history such as the Green Turbans and the Patterned Turban Braves (*huatouyong*).[126] The recapture of Ningbo in the fifth month of 1862 was an early success for Sino-Western cooperation.[127] Significantly, in this battle the French commanders held Chinese ranks and served under Chinese officers while also helping train Chinese troops in modern tactics.[128] Victories such as this spurred commanders in other regions to request small contingents of foreign gunners or naval commanders. In fact, mercenary gunners were being recruited in groups of one to three thousand to augment Qing provincial armies in the summer of 1862.[129] Qing sources indicate that foreign mercenaries were serving on the Taiping side as well, and one account of a battle near Shaoxing reported that the Taipings had the services of fifty to sixty "black barbarians" (*heiyi*), though it gave no other specifics.[130]

THE DEFENSE OF SHANGHAI

The Western powers' most significant contribution to the Qing cause was in the defense of Shanghai and its environs. Shanghai was the main treaty port for Western commerce and housed most of the foreign community in China at the time. It also housed the Imperial Maritime Customs Service, founded in 1854 to assist the Qing state in collecting revenues from overseas trade. The service's scope of operations steadily expanded to include domestic customs administration, postal administration, harbor and waterway management, and antismuggling activities. These developments served to tie the Western community of Shanghai together and draw its interests closer to those of the Qing state.

Taiping commander Li Xiucheng had launched a probing attack at Shanghai in August 1860 but, still hoping to gain Western support, instructed his troops to avoid firing at foreigners.[131] The government forces' recovery of

Ningbo with British help in May 1862, greatly strengthening the strategic position of Shanghai, helped build at least a local groundswell of support for the creation of allied Western forces. Prosper Giquel, who had also participated in the *Arrow* War and would later advise Zuo Zongtang on the construction of the Fuzhou Navy Yard, formed his own force, initially called the Franco-Chinese Force but also dubbed the Ever Triumphant Army (*changjiejun*), which helped retake Hangzhou. Giquel had served in the customs house in Ningbo in addition to his prior military experience.[132]

The Taipings were driven back from Shanghai by the end of May 1862 but returned in September with a force of 80,000 to assail the city again, now defended by Li Hongzhang's Huai Army. The Taipings were repulsed once more but soon returned and surrounded a Qing force nearby. Ward was killed by a Taiping musket ball in a follow-up engagement at Cixi and was succeeded (against his prior wishes) by Henry Burgevine.[133] That appointment proved an abject disaster. Burgevine was unable to lead or discipline the men, got embroiled in a pay dispute, stole 40,000 taels from Yang Fang, and defected to the Taiping side before finally being replaced by C. G. Gordon in March 1863.[134] Nonetheless Li Hongzhang and Cheng Xueqi, assisted by the Ever Victorious Army, managed to rally the Qing forces and drove the Taipings back with heavy casualties by the end of September.

THE FINAL PUSH FOR THE HEAVENLY CAPITAL

As for Nanjing, Zuo did not believe that taking the Taiping capital in and of itself would end the war. He wanted to take the outlying fortresses and cities first to end the long siege of Nanjing once and for all. He knew that the rebels still commanded well over 100,000 troops who could wreak havoc if they broke through the Qing siege lines and escaped into neighboring provinces.[135] It appeared that Zuo's strategy of stretching out the Taiping forces in order to weaken their defense of Nanjing was bearing fruit. But Zeng now waffled a bit in his support of Zuo because he wanted his brother, Zeng Guoquan, to be credited with capturing the ultimate prize. There is also evidence that Zeng Guofan was a bit jealous of Li Hongzhang and Zuo Zongtang, even though he had once been a patron of both men.

There was some discord among the Qing commanders with respect to strategy. Li did not want to release his river corps before he took Suzhou, a canal-rich city sometimes likened to Venice. Li also complained that his own men were on half rations because they had to pay so much to their Western allies.[136] But with Shanghai now secured, another front was opened for the advance to the Taiping Heavenly Capital.[137] There was discord among the Taiping leadership as well, and these rifts aided the Qing. Hong Ren'gan, arguably the most visionary of the remaining Taiping leaders, lacked military forces of his own and could do little to stem the Qing tide. The Taipings also exhausted themselves in capturing isolated sites of limited value.[138] Zeng's final assault plan called for three routes of attack: Li Hongzhang was to advance from Jiangsu, Zuo Zongtang from Zhejiang, and Zeng Guoquan from Anqing. Zeng Guoquan reached the outskirts of Nanjing by the end of May 1862, but the ensuing siege would last more than two years.[139]

Suzhou fell to Li Hongzhang in the tenth month of 1863. The Taiping commanders of Suzhou surrendered to Li believing that they and their men would be spared if they murdered Tan Shaoguang, the general Li Xiucheng had left in command of the city. When the Taiping captains met Li's subordinate, Cheng Xueqi (d. 1864), they requested that they be left in command of half the city and receive Qing military ranks. Cheng pretended to accede to their request but urged Li Hongzhang to kill them in order to control their troops.[140] After initially refusing Cheng's request, Li massacred the rebels at their surrender banquet, claiming that their surrender was insincere and they were planning treachery because they had not yet shaved their heads in the Qing style to demonstrate submission. Li also killed some 20,000 surrendered troops.[141] The massacre earned the ire of General Gordon, then in command of the Ever Victorious Army, who threatened to attack Li.[142]

The Taiping navy was decimated on Lake Tai in the summer of 1864 as its defenses crumbled before the Qing onslaught.[143] Gunboats, both Chinese and Western, swept away resistance on the rivers. Zuo estimated that "not less than 100,000 rebels," including many leaders, were killed in these operations. Jiangsu was secured as rebel remnants fled southeast toward Guangdong.[144] Zuo himself defeated the rebel leader Huang Wenjin at

Bainiuqiao. Over the next several weeks, tens of thousands more rebels were slain, more than 200,000 people were liberated, and 6,000–7,000 mounts, several hundred false seals of office, and more than 1,000 foreign guns were captured. Zuo estimated that no more than a few thousand rebels remained in Zhejiang.[145]

Nanjing fell on July 19, 1864. The Qing army burned and looted the city in retaliation for what the Taipings had done when they captured it a dozen years before. Zeng Guoquan's men committed such abuses that he was impeached.[146] Hong Xiuquan's body was found in a sewer under the palace on July 30. The cause of his death has been variously reported as due to suicide by hanging, food poisoning, suicide by poison, or a poisonous centipede bite.[147] Hong's son, the heir apparent, escaped to Jiangxi with the aid of Li Xiucheng, although Zeng Guofan initially reported that he was dead. When Zuo later informed that court that Zeng's report on the status of the heir was incorrect, Zeng was furious, and the two sniped at each other in letters to the emperor.[148] Li Xiucheng was captured by the Qing on July 22, having been separated from the Taiping royal party in the chaos after the fall of Nanjing. He was turned over to Zeng Guofan and penned a lengthy confession that remains one of the key "insider" primary sources on the Taiping Rebellion.[149]

Other Taiping forces fled south, pursued by Liu Dian. In the sixth month of 1864, Zeng Guoquan retook Jiangning. The tough fighting continued through the summer, with Cai Yuanji's forces reduced to eating leather—and reputedly each other—at one point. The countryside was littered with corpses, but the inexorable Qing advance brought all of Jiangxi and Zhejiang under control by late summer.[150] Lamenting the scenes of destruction and the skeletons and rotting corpses littering the landscape, Zuo instructed local officials to dig mass graves and erect stone markers for the dead.[151] Recently promoted to the rank of the Earl of Kejing, Zuo continued his efforts to restore trade, improve water routes, and revive the economy even as he detailed troops to quell local bandits and sent others in pursuit of Li Shixian and the Taiping remnants, still over 200,000 strong.[152] As he had done previously in Hunan, Zuo set up a new salt gabelle and brought in rice from other provinces.[153] But he also complained that his forces were badly depleted and weakened by sickness. Liu Dian's three thousand new mercenaries had already battled across a thousand *li* without rest.[154]

CRUSHING THE TAIPING REMNANTS

Li Shixian sent his agents out to take Zhangpu as he fled south, then skirmished back and forth with the Qing forces in Fujian. The government forces killed the Taiping leader Ma Tangdong and some six thousand of his followers, but Li remained at large. Li hoped to get back into Zhejiang and flee west, but he was finding it increasingly difficult to feed his estimated 140,000 troops. The Qing had their own supply woes, though Zuo had already arranged for 140,000 taels of supplies to be shipped monthly from Zhejiang. Moreover, the mountainous terrain of western Fujian was ill-suited to agriculture, and Zuo was concerned that without proper guidance and leadership the people "would turn their hearts to banditry" again.[155] These concerns were heightened by the presence of Wang Haiyang, another Taiping leader with long experience battling Zuo, who was trying to link up with Li Shixian. Zuo considered Wang the fiercest of the remaining Taiping commanders.[156] Zuo estimated the total number of Taiping forces to be close to 300,000, and he asked the court to appoint many of his old cronies to important command posts to fight them, establishing a pattern he would follow for the rest of his career.[157]

Zuo's initial force of around 20,000 entered Fujian along 3 routes.[158] Zuo then dispatched Gao Liansheng and Liu Dian, two of his best commanders, to besiege the Taipings at Zhangzhou, where Li Shixian had hunkered down with an estimated 200,000 troops after killing the local military superintendent.[159] Gao's men headed south from Ningbo on steamers.[160] Zuo set up his own camp at Yanping and immediately commenced wrangling with other officials, notably those in the northwest, over allocation of funds and supplies, an ironic situation given where Zuo would next be posted.[161] He eventually secured some of these funds from Zhejiang, in part because his previous efforts there had helped restore productivity.[162] Zuo arrayed his force, by now numbering some 29,000, across hundreds of *li*, making it hard to prosecute a tight siege despite his troops' superior weapons and discipline. Zuo had more officers, supplies, and troops brought in as sharp engagements erupted along the lines.[163]

The impatient court pressured Zuo to step up the pressure. He reported that he did but was hampered by a lack of boats to ensure a full blockade, allowing the rebels to obtain weapons and supplies from foreigners. Zuo asked Li Hongzhang to send patrols to guard the coast, prevent supplies from reaching the rebels, and deter Taiping remnants from escaping by sea.[164] Zuo also asked the court to issue a prohibition against anyone, foreign or domestic, having private relations with the rebels.[165] Zuo's fears were realized when some officers under Huang Shaochun joined the Taiping side, briefly putting Huang on the defensive.[166]

Meanwhile, Li Hongzhang had dispatched Huai Army forces that reached Xiamen by the middle of the third month of 1865; within a month they joined the battle for Fuzhou.[167] Fujian was relatively secure by late summer, and the Taiping remnants were streaming into Guangdong.[168] Gao Liansheng continued to focus on harassing Li Shixian, even though he had been ordered to move north to assist in quelling the Nian rebels.[169] Zuo detailed troops to guard strategic river routes leading out of the southeast into Hunan, using it as an opportunity to experiment with using his gunboats in patrol operations.[170] Zuo reported that they had taken Zhangzhou early in the fifth lunar month of 1865, plowing through the Taiping defenses as flames and smoke filled the air. The attackers moved to funnel escapees inland.[171]

After complaining about corruption and incompetence at the lower levels of government in Guangdong, Zuo was given greater administrative oversight and the resources he needed to finish the job.[172] Huang Shaochun and Kang Guoqi, two more experienced commanders, were brought in to assist Gao Liansheng. But an epidemic struck Kang's troops, forcing the government to send in doctors and medicine.

An effort by Li Shixian to sally forth from Zhangzhou was stymied, with the Qing killing four thousand and capturing ten thousand. But Liu Dian was in turn beaten back by Li Shixian, and Zuo pulled back to Longyan, marshaling strength from various quarters.[173] Zuo's forces attacked in the first month of 1865, cutting Li Shixian's supply lines and wiping out half of Wang Haiyang's crack troops at Liancheng. Li Shixian tried to cut the Qing supply lines but failed, so he contented himself with augmenting the defenses around Zhangzhou. Li mounted another sortie in the third month of 1865 but was again thrown back by Gao Liansheng and Huang Shaochun. In yet another attempted Taiping breakout, foreign gunners strafed the Qing and Huang Shaochun's mount was shot out from under him. Undeterred, he got to his feet, brandished a great spear, and led the Qing troops to victory, reporting two thousand rebels killed against just one hundred losses of his own.[174]

Li Shixian rallied his forces once more, using exploding shells to fight off the attackers. The Qing countered with a heavy artillery barrage and launched an amphibious assault. Liu Dian moved his force to within sixty *li* south of the Taipings, testing Wang Haiyang's defenses. Rescue efforts over the next couple of weeks claimed three thousand more rebel lives.[175] Zuo cautioned his commanders to be wary of Li Shixian escaping by sea and then coming back to ravage Guangdong. Coastal patrols were increased, and 13,000 troops were detailed to patrol the rivers, with others sent north to prevent help from arriving from Jiangxi. As rebel losses mounted, Li Shixian tried to solicit aid from local bandits. Zuo repositioned his commanders, cutting off more escape routes and killing thousands more rebels. When Zuo's forces were within ten *li* of the inner bastion, more outlying forts started falling as fire arrows, aided by heavy winds, burned through the Taiping defenses. Li Shixian led his men in a bloody street fight and managed to escape westward. Thousands of rebels were slain the following morning before they could flee.[176]

Liu Dian subsequently retook Nanjing, where Wang Haiyang was entrenched, and Wang's force fled as well, heading for Jiangxi.[177] When Liu Dian's army defeated Wang Haiyang near the Jiangxi border, the rebels were forced back to the southeast.[178] Wang tried to flee south to Guangdong but was stymied by the Qing army when his force of 70,000 was ambushed at Lion-Dragon Peak. The next day they were bested again by Kang Guoqi's force of just eight thousand, demonstrating the efficacy of Qing firearms in these later engagements.[179] Throughout the Qing reports we see rebel losses generally twenty times greater than those of the government forces.[180] Wang fled into

Guangdong again.[181] By mid-July he was in Zhenping, planning to reunite with Li Shixian.[182] Zhenping had tall mountains and deep valleys to protect it, but it could also be bottled up, and the rebels lacked the supplies to survive a long siege. Li had been skirmishing with Qing forces for months, unable to fully escape but nevertheless eluding capture. As Zuo battled Li Shixian through the summer of 1865, he explored a number of avenues for supplies and funding, including using the newly secured sea-lanes for delivery.[183] The Qing dislodged the Taiping remnants from Zhenping early in the eighth month of 1865 and chased them into Longnan County.[184] The rebels moved toward the safety of the mountains once again, hoping to flee west into Jiangxi, as Zuo redeployed his men to cut off their escape routes.

Zuo split his forces and advanced by land and sea, taking care to ensure that the Taiping commanders could not join other troops in the region. Zuo advanced inland from the coast: Liu Dian from the north, with Jiangxi troops coming in from the west and Guangdong troops arrayed to the south.[185] Zuo worked with the military superintendent of Fujian to make sure the Taiping forces were denied escape routes by sea.[186] Li Hongzhang was involved in securing Xiamen, where the discovery of foreign arms and medicine on board a ship indicated that rogue foreign elements were still clandestinely aiding the rebels. The Qing also captured guns and gunners en route to the Taipings from Macao.[187] Zuo set up more coastal patrols, inspected seaports, and discharged "worthless soldiers and opium smokers" serving in coastal defense capacities.[188] The Qing also captured and destroyed the boats of coastal raiders, capturing ten great cannons in the process.[189]

On August 19, 1865, Li Shixian arrived in Zhenping, where he was apprehended by Wang Haiyang's aides and killed.[190] Wang apparently hoped he might be able to save his own life by turning over Li Shixian's corpse, though Zuo referenced an old grievance between Li and Wang as being at the root of the assassination.[191] At this point, the Taipings were essentially in survival mode. The Qing bombarded Zhenping with artillery, and Wang decided to attempt a breakout.[192] The rebels burst out from their encircled position at Zhenping and rushed about pell-mell from place to place, unable to take fixed positions or turn the tables on the Qing, though Wang did lure Gao Liansheng into an ambush and killed thousands of his troops in October 1865.[193] Thousands of Wang's own partisans were sacrificed in his escape, and more than four thousand surrendered.[194] Wang hoped to flee into Jiangxi and possibly join the Nian, but he was forced back into Guangdong, where the rugged terrain helped him elude his pursuers.[195]

Zuo chased Wang for more than two months, dislodging him from stockades and skirmishing in the wilderness. The government took one redoubt in a daring night fire attack. Though thousands of rebels escaped into the mountains,[196] the Qing claimed 16,000 killed and 10,000 "good people" liberated. Another 60,000 soon tossed down their weapons as the calendar turned to 1866. Gao Liansheng was promoted to provincial military commander of Zhejiang as mop-up operations proceeded there. He also assisted Zuo in reestablishing schools and proper Confucian leadership in the countryside.[197]

Zuo was critical of the caliber and dedication of the officials and troops in the southeast as he continued his pursuit of Wang Haiyang. He complained that "their authority lies in books, not in their offices, which they can barely discharge, being unable to even determine correct taxes." He wanted these bookworms to be replaced by activist and engaged officials.[198] Zuo also criticized the military commanders, saying, "Not even one Guangdong general was useful, but all craved merit and wealth."[199]

Yet another problem for the Qing was the alleged presence of Gelaohui (Elder Brother Society) elements within the army who stirred up trouble, incited mutinies, and encouraged desertion.[200] The late Qing military was supposedly plagued by the Gelaohui, and Zuo would target its members in his subsequent campaigns in the northwest. Modern studies suggest that the Gelaohui were widespread, particularly in Sichuan province, and some sources even argue that it was infiltration by the Gelaohui that eventually led to the dissolution of the Hunan Army.[201]

Next the Qing set about torching the rebel lairs near the coast. There were several reinforced stockades near Yunxiao that required heavy artillery to destroy. The Qing fired rockets into the stockades and then charged in through the smoke, with their doughty commander, Guo Songlin, at the head of his troops. They captured and decapitated the Taiping leader Zhu

Qiyan.[202] But Zuo informed the court that there was still widespread local banditry, looting, and disruption of farming and requested more coastal patrols to augment his efforts. Local bandits were taking advantage of the chaos to harass the populace, and Zuo dispatched Guo Songlin and Wang Depang to arrest and kill the ringleaders. Zuo also stressed the need to restore local order so he could stop the tax remissions then in place and get revenue flowing again.[203] He proposed new taxes such as new commercial levies to rejuvenate the local economy.

The remainder of 1865 saw running skirmishes through the mountainous regions of Fujian and Guangdong. Gao Liansheng was at the forefront of these battles and made adroit use of his foreign gunnery units.[204] After fleeing Zhenping, Wang Haiyang split his forces at rivers and in forests, trying desperately to elude capture. After being pursued across Fujian for several months, Wang Haiyang fled to Jiayingzhen in Guangdong and holed up in the vicinity from November 1865 to February 1866.[205] This would be the last county seat the Taipings ever occupied. Zuo reported that disease had hampered his pursuit over the previous months, but he was in the process of encircling Wang's position. Bao Chao, Kang Guoqi, and Zuo Zongtang arrayed their forces around the city, driving back rebel forces that tried to rescue Wang. The Qing steadily destroyed the outlying defenses with heavy fire. The court accepted Zuo's report but ordered an inquiry into the officials who had allowed Jiaying to fall to the rebels.[206]

By this point Zuo had brought his best commanders into the fray, including Liu Dian, Huang Shaochun, Gao Liansheng, Kang Guoqi, Wang Depang, and Liu Qingliang, with Bao Chao detailed to lead 12,000 troops to guard Wuping in the event of a breakout by Wang Haiyang.[207] The Qing built gunboats and advanced along the water routes as well. Calling Wang Haiyang "the greatest traitor under Heaven," Zuo carefully deployed his forces and waited for Bao Chao to get into position.[208] He criticized some of the local officials for laxity in delivering supplies and on charges of embezzlement and made new appointments in both Guangdong and for Taiwan, as there was still pirate activity off the coast. He also traded with Westerners to bring in more supplies for his army.[209]

One source reports that some of Wang's advisers urged him to flee and find a more defensible position, but Wang now had a family and war spoils, and he chose to spend his time in carnal pleasures.[210] Wang finally sallied forth in late January and won a skirmish. The rebels then tried to brake the Qing advance with a combination of cavalry and Western guns. As the fighting intensified, Gao Liansheng sent in his own gunnery units. Some Qing officers were forced to dismount and fight on foot when their horses were shot. An eight-hour battle resulted in a Qing victory, and the rebels withdrew. Subsequent attempts by the rebels to break out or flank the Qing were foiled. Wang himself took the field at the head of his men, but his efforts to break out of the north section of the siege also failed and the action shifted to the other fronts. The Qing broke through the outer defenses and advanced to within thirty *li* of the central redoubt of Jiaying. Zuo was still concerned about supplies, however, and his forces had to contend with local bandits who aided the rebels. Some of these bands were wiped out by one of Zuo's subordinates nearby.[211]

The court continued to push Zuo to intensify his assault, but he contended that supplies were low and casualties had depleted his forces so much that some of his battalions had just six hundred to seven hundred of their paper strength of one thousand. Yet even as he made these excuses Zuo was mounting his final offensive. Wang Haiyang was a fighting general, not a master strategist, and he was outplayed by Zuo the strategist, who finally lured him out. The first day of heavy fighting saw two to three thousand rebels killed. Wang tried the desperate maneuver of smashing right into the center of the Qing lines. Feigning collapse, the Qing forces retreated, drawing Wang into their siegeworks, and opened fire from all sides. Rebel corpses and blood covered the battlefield as Gao Liansheng waded through the gore to cut off the rear. He met the retreating rebels in three columns and pinned them against a mountain, killing hundreds more and capturing twenty-nine. Another Qing assault captured the fort of Huangzhuyang. A report arrived that Wang was wounded and had retreated to the city proper, but Zuo was skeptical and pressed on.[212]

Wang was killed on February 7, 1866, by his subordinate Tan Tiyuan, who then crowned himself the last Taiping king. Even as this was transpiring the Qing killed 10,000 of his troops in another clash.[213] Another 50,000 surrendered to the Qing as Zuo coordinated the final assault.[214] The Qing spent a week building up their siegeworks and pressing in. The rebels burst out in three columns, but after a four-hour battle in which they lost hundreds, they pulled back into their innermost defenses. Bao Chao then sent probing attacks to test their strength, and another 4,000 rebels were killed as they withdrew.[215] In yet another battle 3,000 more were killed, 20 leaders executed, and 1,000 were captured. Many drowned in the nearby river, and thousands of captives were freed. Still more surrendered as corpses littered the roads.[216] Within a week another 30,000–40,000 had submitted to Wang Depang.[217] Bao Chao killed another 8,000 in mop-up operations, and Kang Guoqi reported slaying another 6,000 and capturing more.[218] Zuo's estimate was that the Qing had killed 17,000 of the 100,000 in the city proper, taken 1,000 captives, freed 50,000 commoners, and recovered 1,600 horses, though these figures do not appear to include those slain in mop-up operations around Jiaying.[219]

Tan Tiyuan fought until the bitter end, finally falling off a cliff, only to be captured and executed. He had joined the Taipings at the age of fifteen and had served under Shi Dakai, Chen Yucheng, and Li Shixian over the course of his career. This latter connection may have prompted his decision to kill Wang Haiyang.[220] Some Taiping remnants hid in the surrounding mountains, some surrendered, and others simply starved to death. The rebellion in the south was ended, though some Taiping units melded into the Nian forces in the north. Zuo and Bao Chao, in fact, received immediate orders to head north themselves to augment the forces of Zeng Guofan and battle the Nian.[221]

Thus ended the bloodiest civil war in the history of humanity. In this final campaign alone, Zuo's forces killed more than 20,000 Taiping rebels and captured more than 50,000.[222] Zuo kept some forces in the area, establishing regular patrols on land and sea and even refurbishing an English gunboat for Qing service.[223] He was rewarded with the Imperial Peacock Feather, and his eldest son received a hereditary post.

While the Qing were understandably overjoyed at the final victory over the Taipings, their erstwhile Western allies remained critical of the Qing, including its technological and institutional advances. An editorial in the *North China Herald* criticized the British for selling out "fellow Christians" in favor of the Manchus, who had already returned to "their old practices of indolence and fraud."[224] Statements such as this are the origin of the "stagnation versus change" debate that has characterized so much scholarship about late Qing China. This supposed hidebound commitment to "tradition" on the part of Qing officials in the face of obviously superior Western technology arose from the expansionist discourse of such "China hands" who lobbied for expanded rights against Qing officials determined to preserve the dynasty and its sovereignty. As Anne Reinhardt notes, many of the officials accused of such myopic viewpoints were in fact the same ones involved in the creation of the Zongli Yamen and the implementation and deployment of new technologies.[225] This includes Zuo Zongtang, perhaps the epitome of the conservative nationalist reformer.

Gao Liansheng was left in charge of the military affairs of Guangdong as Zuo readied for his next assignment in the north. The Nian rebels he would face had emerged around the same time as the Taipings and had long been a thorn in the Qings' side, but they were less organized than the Taipings and had no recognized central leader, making them both less threatening and more difficult to pin down and defeat. But their diffuse "rebellion" took on a more serious tone when they forged an alliance with the Dungan (Muslim) rebels in China's northwest in the mid-1860s. In response, the court quickly ordered the transfer of troops and commanders to that theater from all over the empire.[226] Zuo did not go right away, however. He noted that it was difficult to get to Gansu by either land or water, and he needed time to prepare for what he expected to be a lengthy campaign. Plus he needed to remain in the south for a while to ensure that local bandits did not reemerge and to manage matters from Fujian so as to "discern the wicked from the good and bring order to the region."[227]

Until the local bandits were quelled, there could be no peace.[228] Zuo noted that 90 percent of the people in Fujian were suffering from sickness and starvation. And the banditry and devastation wreaked on the countryside meant that the army was also short on food.[229] Zuo worked on getting food supplies shipped in from the neighboring provinces and even from Taiwan by sea. He drew up detailed plans for famine relief, noting where and how it should be distributed and offering suggestions to quickly restore agricultural productivity based on personal experience, noting that this would also help the government more quickly restore normal taxes.[230] With respect to the troops, Zuo noted that the soldiers should never be a burden on local society. They should distribute some of the rice confiscated from bandits for famine relief. They should also help restore barter and support local industries to aid in the economic recovery.[231]

Zuo's subordinates battled bandits from Fujian to Jiangxi.[232] The composition of these bandit groups varied. Some were merely small groups of toughs; others claimed Taiping links or titles; still others spread heretical teachings and practiced sorcery.[233] Plus, the widespread starvation and deprivation made the region fertile recruiting ground for the Gelaohui.[234] So Zuo's most consistent advice centered on the need to establish a close relationship between local officials, the gentry, the army, and the common folk. All needed to support and rely on another for society to function properly. Echoing Mencius, Zuo noted that the people were the most important factor in calculating national safety and prosperity. Those writing the account of Zuo's success in Zhejiang maintained that these all stemmed from his investment in "human capital" (*min li*).[235]

BUILDING A MODERN NAVY

Zuo returned to Fuzhou after defeating the Taiping remnants. His wife and family had relocated there, so they were reunited for the first time since 1859. But there was little time for respite. The Nian and Muslim rebellions were gaining steam in north China. And Zuo was working on plans to further Self-Strengthening by building a modern navy. He revisited the writings of his old favorite Wei Yuan as he sketched out his ideas.

For its part, the court realized the vulnerability of Beijing and the need for ships—both paddleboats and steamers—for defense and to protect coastal trade. As Li Hongzhang put it, "If China . . . had heavy guns and steamers Westerners would draw in their horns [and sail away]."[236] In fact, the Qing had been waging a trade war of sorts with the foreign powers that were using steamships for internal trade, and had granted a monopoly on inland riverine trade to the domestically owned China Merchants Steam Navigation Company.[237] The creation of this enterprise has been lauded as "an effective tool for mercantilist statecraft in the late nineteenth century."[238] They also prohibited Westerners from transporting certain strategic commodities such as iron, oil, and timber.[239] Although their methods may appear heavy-handed, the Qing were using the resources available to them to defend their sovereignty. By the 1870s the Chinese were becoming more savvy about the vagaries of international law and learning how to use it to buttress their own position.

By 1865, influenced by Wei Yuan and others, Zuo had been discussing how to update the Chinese naval forces for more than a decade. He remained wary of allowing foreigners to be involved, however, especially the British. In a letter to the Zongli Yamen, Zuo described the British as "the craftiest" of the foreign powers, though he believed all of them had sinister designs. As for China's grand plan, Zuo said that they must first rectify government affairs, then train troops, and then build gunboats in order to become self-reliant in defense.[240] Having served in the southeast, Zuo recognized the supreme importance of naval power.[241]

From the beginning of these discussions Zuo favored China building its own ships rather than buying them from Westerners. In his mind this was the key to China restoring its national pride and power. The nation needed to become self-sufficient in the production of modern weapons, technology, and ammunition. He saw the value in using foreigners to help hire and train sailors, engineers, and scientists, of course, recognizing that building inferior ships was no better than having no ships.[242] But an infrastructure needed to be put into place. In addition to ships China would need factories to build machines, parts, and munitions. And every ship built would need a trained crew to operate it.[243] In fact, it appears that some Chinese had been training on Western gunboats for a few years already as a result of a program initiated by Zeng Guofan in the aftermath of the *Arrow* War in connection with a court directive that Zeng and the Manchu commander Duxinga create an Ever Victorious Navy for patrolling the Yangzi. The court purchased steamboats from Western powers to jump-start the project.[244]

It was against this backdrop that Zuo proposed setting up a shipyard in Fuzhou in Fujian province to make "machines to make machines."[245] He and Prosper Giquel got more serious in their discussions in 1865, and by 1866 Zuo was pushing for a full-scale modern naval yard in Fuzhou.[246] With Japan now embarking on its own program of naval reform, it was imperative that China do the same. Furthermore, the Qing might soon be renegotiating treaty agreements with the Westerners, and having an actual modern navy in the works could improve their hand. As Zuo colorfully put it, "If others gallop forward while we continue to ride the donkey, then what can we do?"[247] He continued, "First, we need to make a ship. Once we make a ship then we can train troops to man the ship. Then from one we can make one hundred. This can be done in five years. Once we have more, we can establish naval defenses for all the provinces. And from this we can increase our mechanization so that we can make guns, cannon, ammunition, and the like."[248]

Zuo recognized that the generally conservative gentry might not embrace such a plan, so the central government needed to provide incentives. As far as funding was concerned, Zuo envisioned using *lijin* revenues and following his usual strategy of badgering friends and colleagues from other provinces. He estimated the initial outlay being along the lines of 300,000 taels, then another 30,000–60,000 for workmen for the first year. Overall, he estimated a cost of around 600,000 taels for the first two years plus another 300,000 for building the first boats over a period of five years, with the total cost estimated at 2.4 million taels.[249] The key, for Zuo, was making seaworthy vessels from the start, not wasting time on obsolete construction.

Because China lacked technicians, foreigners would be hired to oversee the initial construction and provided with military ranks. But there were already natives in Ningbo with nautical expertise, and these men could be brought in as well. Sailors could get practical experience patrolling the coasts and battling pirates, which in turn would benefit commerce. Indeed, a modern navy would solve many of China's problems at once, facilitating internal and external trade, opening ports, stopping pirates and bandits, and improving China's international stature in the process, thereby helping China in the broadest geostrategic sense.[250]

In making his pitch, Zuo also stressed how foreign countries considered practical skills important while China emphasized philosophical principles (*daoli*) as the root of practical learning. China needed to make technical skills

important too, Zuo contended, noting that, contrary to what his more conservative contemporaries believed, such notions were not incompatible with
Chinese tradition. The Ming had purchased cannon from the foreigners to
use against the Manchus and improve national defense, and the Qing had
done the same.[251] In this Zuo was taking a more radical position than some of
his Self-Strengthening contemporaries such as Zhang Zhidong (1837–1909),
who famously proposed the idea of "Chinese Learning as Substance, Western
Learning as Function [*zhongti xiyong*]."[252] Zuo thought it was high time for
China to change its thinking and methods by aggressively taxing commerce
and recognizing the value of what we today call STEM.[253] Zuo's old friend
Guo Songtao likewise argued that "basic education was the root, technology
was the branches." Classical education needed to be revised with input from
the Western tradition to make China stronger.[254]

Zuo highlighted benefits beyond the obvious ones of coastal defense and
the preservation of territorial integrity. A modern navy could help modernize
China's transportation system, assist in the delivery of tribute rice and other
provisions to the north, and enrich the people through providing both jobs and
the means to avert calamities because food and medical supplies could be more
easily delivered to distressed regions. By making these points Zuo attempted
to justify the high initial outlay costs to the budget-conscious officials at court,
noting that the broader applications of new technology such as turbines would
have a ripple effect on the modernization of China as a whole.[255] As Yang
Dongliang frames it, Zuo envisioned creating a modern shipping industry
for China as a means of raising the economic prosperity of the people in order
to strengthen the nation. This is the very essence of what the Meiji Japanese
slogan "rich nation, strong army" later came to embody.[256]

Zuo distinguished between domestic and foreign threats in his proposal,
identifying naval power with defending against the depredations of foreigners.
Even though England and France had helped the Qing defeat the Taipings,
China should be wary lest they turn on her next. If the foreigners were to aid
bandits, for example, what recourse would China have? Zuo repeated his perception that the English were duplicitous, meaning that China should work
with the French. Zuo described the different types of cannons his shipyard

would build and their applications, and the broader uses of machines to build other things without military uses, also noting that China needed to identify and cultivate talent as a means to achieving self-sufficiency.²⁵⁷

In addition to his Ming example, Zuo cited Tang and Song precedents as evidence of China getting valuable technology from foreigners. He also referenced his own experience in using steamers on West Lake in Hangzhou and in subsequent military operations.²⁵⁸ And he pointed out the obvious fact that European influence was predicated on sea power. The French and British coveted trade and used their gunboats to get what they wanted. Why could China not do the same? Zuo was neither overly conservative nor xenophobic in his pitch. He was fully aware of Western strengths and Qing shortcomings, and every bit as much as his Japanese contemporaries he realized that the only way to beat the Westerners at their own game was to join them. Unfortunately for the Qing, China was far more diverse than Britain or France and was beset by problems, not the least of which were squabbling factions among both the Manchus and the Han that undermined efforts to create a unity of purpose.²⁵⁹

Zuo's argument was persuasive, and the court gave the order to establish the Fuzhou Navy Yard on the third day of the sixth month of 1866.²⁶⁰ The yard itself would be established at Maweizhen, twenty *li* from Fuzhou and about sixty *li* from the seacoast. The site was surrounded by high mountains and had a deep natural harbor that could accommodate 6,000–7,000-ton vessels. More than three hundred *mu* of land was set aside for the structures. Giquel and D'Aiguebelle were advisers from the start. The first keel was laid on January 18, 1868. Zuo himself would oversee the project for barely a year before he was called north to deal with the Dungan rebels. Fearing what might become of his project, he used his influence to secure the appointment of Shen Baozhen, the former governor of Jiangxi and son-in-law of Lin Zexu, to assume oversight of the naval yard.²⁶¹ Zuo urged the Qing to give Shen the same level of authority he would have enjoyed. He helped select many of the mid-ranking officers before he left Fuzhou on December 18, 1866, and also left detailed reports and recommendations for his successors, stressing good appointments and diligent training. As he put it, "without training it is impossible to earn military merit and [the province] cannot be defended for a single day."²⁶² He remained keen on not giving too much influence to foreigners in the yard's management and reiterated the qualities needed in good commanders such as trust and selflessness.

Once the facilities were set up, Zuo estimated that China could build eleven large ships and five small ones within five years. Large ships were defined as having 150 horsepower and displacing 1 million catties; small vessels had 80 horsepower and displaced 30,000–40,000 catties. Zuo estimated ship costs at 3 million taels and troop upkeep at 40,000 taels per month. Another 2 million taels would be needed for the factories. It appears that costs had risen from his preliminary estimates, perhaps after discussions with his French advisers, in whom he expressed much confidence, also noting that the French were currently helping the Japanese build steamers.[263] He continued to jockey for funding for his project, emphasizing the paramount importance of ships to Self-Strengthening. In addition to customs revenues Zuo attempted to tap land taxes and tariffs in places such as Fujian to cover shortfalls that were already emerging even as he started raising funds for his upcoming expedition to Gansu.[264]

The Fuzhou Navy Yard contained furnaces, stamp/pattern yards, leather works, sailmakers, wheelwrights, ironworks, casting foundries, smelting facilities, and classrooms for training, among other things. A translation bureau was established to translate Western works into Chinese.[265] Zuo had previously favored giving incentives to officers and soldiers to train in modern tactics as he believed it improved the overall level of professionalism.[266] Institutionalizing this training was the logical next step. Schools taught basic arithmetic and other subjects pertaining to ships. Students enrolled in the school earned four taels per month, enough to buy two piculs of rice.[267]

At any given time there were around two thousand Chinese employees and fifty to seventy-five Europeans working at the shipyard. Most of the recruitment for laborers and students was done in the south. Cadets had to be under sixteen years old. Room and board were provided, along with a stipend of four to nine taels per month. The curriculum included navigation, geometry, astronomy, arithmetic, and geography. Cadets also studied English, French, and steam engine theory. By 1873 some Chinese officers were deemed qualified to command their own ships.[268] But turnover was quite high. Only 35 of the original 105 students remained in the School of Naval Construction after 5 years.[269] Some found the curriculum too difficult; others got homesick or found more traditional avenues of employment that promised faster advancement. Nonetheless, the first ship, the *Wannian Qing* (*Eternal Qing*) was completed on July 18, 1869. The warship was 238 feet long and had 6 guns that could carry 466 tons of ammunition and displaced 1,450 tons.[270] Significantly, the entire crew was Chinese.[271]

A report from the *North China Herald* from the end of 1869 was generally positive about developments to that point. The report noted that there were then 57 foreign employees at the shipyard: 52 were French and 5 were British. Overall, the shipyard employed 500 carpenters, 500 ironsmiths, 500 coolies, 500 soldiers, and 120 sailors. Classes were taught in Chinese, English, and French. The forge was producing 6,000 pieces of iron a week and the foundry was casting 13–15 tons of metal. The brick factory was also quite productive. Average expenditures were reported at around 50,000 taels per month. There were four slips for shipbuilding, and a gunboat, the *Meiyun,* had been launched after the *Wannian Qing.* The *Meiyun* was 183 feet long with one 50-pound rifled gun and two smaller ones. The *Herald* expressed admiration for the language skills of the students, particularly in French, but seemed mildly concerned that one student essay noted that "once China attained the ability to make and command gunboats they would be able to dispense with the foreigners."[272] The author was also impressed with the management skills of Giquel and Shen Baozhen, commenting that Shen "not long ago tried, convicted, and executed a coolie for stealing brass—all in the space of half an hour."[273]

Through 1874 the yard manufactured some fifteen ships totaling 15,933 tons. Over its entire history through 1907, it produced around forty ships.[274] In 1873 the yard also started building merchant ships, thereby realizing another of Zuo's goals. But the yard foundered without Zuo at the helm, and the French instructors departed in 1873. Because China's industrial base was still comparatively small, there were quality control issues that set the leaders of the naval yard at odds with the governors of Zhejiang and neighboring provinces. The ships often had low-quality iron and less-than-ideal horsepower. Discord arose between Giquel and D'Aiguebelle, attributed to the machinations of the governor of Fujian in the mid-1870s, who reportedly was prejudiced against the shipyard.[275] At one point the government wanted to turn the shipyard into a munitions plant, but Zuo's opposition carried the day.

Even during his eventful tenure as military commander in the northwest, Zuo remained connected to and interested in developments in Fuzhou. He maintained contact with Prosper Giquel, sending him letters concerning hiring teachers and training artisans and navigators.[276] With Shen Baozhen he discussed the importance of training the students in the use of advanced exploding artillery shells and the building and use of ironclad vessels.[277] He peppered the Zongli Yamen with letters concerning a variety of matters from recruitment and training to the need for employing more Westerners to keep pace with the Japanese. These latter suggestions took on special significance during the crisis over Taiwan in 1874.[278]

Zuo fired off detailed memorandums on modernizing China's naval forces by building more ships, manufacturing newer weapons, and upgrading coastal defenses. These included erecting coastal batteries, improving revenue and supply streams, better training, and plans for converting steamers to gunboats. China needed to consider its own circumstances and needs and not simply copy Western boats. The Chinese navy had to be adapted for China's coasts and waterways, and navigators and captains had to be trained with this in mind. The subsequent naval debacles against the French and Japanese proved Zuo right. Zuo also recommended the creation of a marine corps—troops that were competent in land, sea, and amphibious operations.[279]

Zuo recommended establishing three main regions for coastal defense, each with its own geographic area of responsibility, roughly corresponding to north, central, and south China, and each with its own supreme commander. The respective provincial governors from the coastal provinces should have no purview over the naval commanders. Each area should have its own shipyard with three designated areas—one for building ships, one for manufacturing guns, and one for manufacturing machinery. Zuo recognized that the existing facilities at Fuzhou, Shanghai, Tianjin, and Dagu were expensive, but he reckoned that the long-term benefits would more than outweigh the initial outlays. In essence, he retained the views first articulated when building the Fuzhou Navy Yard and urged that the Qing stay the course and even double down on naval defense.

From the perspective of the central government, costs remained a bone of contention. The Ministry of Revenue complained that repairs were too frequent. When the dockyard manager successfully defended the repair schedule, conservatives at court argued that there was widespread fraud and peculation. Zuo himself sent 20,000 taels from his post in Gansu to help with costs.[280] Defenders of the dockyard blamed Giquel for deliberately slowing production and encouraging the purchase of foreign ships and materials, from which he supposedly profited. But it was also true that production was slowed by the fact that the yard had to repair and refit older vessels in addition to building new ships. And the pace of naval advances worldwide in this era made it difficult to keep abreast of developments elsewhere, not to mention advances in ordnance, which outpaced those in shipbuilding.[281] Nevertheless, by 1882 the Chinese navy had around fifty steamships of various sizes and designs. About half were built domestically, with the rest having been purchased from various European countries.

The Fuzhou Navy Yard was also hampered by revenue shortfalls. Customs duties were overcommitted, as that seemed to be the revenue stream every provincial governor tapped when extra funds were needed. This meant that Zuo and subsequent directors were constantly wrangling with the Ministry of Revenue and the provinces over funds. Costs ended up being far higher than Zuo's initial estimations, particularly with respect to maintenance, and provinces bickered concerning paying for and having access to the ships.[282] The Fuzhou Navy Yard got a bit of a reprieve in 1874 when a crisis erupted over Taiwan and funds flowed in to aid in the bolstering of the island's defenses. By the early 1880s Fuzhou's operations were in an era of "forced parsimony." Zuo himself attempted to address this issue when he became governor of Nanjing by initiating the practice of making recipient provinces pay half the costs of ships manufactured at Fuzhou. He also remitted an annual subsidy of 40,000 taels from his funds for the yard and urged other governors to do the same since the institution served the defense of the entire empire.[283]

It must be remembered that the Fuzhou Navy Yard was constructed against the backdrop of broader debates about national defense, particularly with respect to the coast. One of the most prominent proponents of creating a dynamic new plan of coastal defense was Wang Tao (1828–ca. 1885), a reporter and essayist who was based in Hong Kong for much of his life and therefore well versed in foreign ideas.[284] In the 1860s he emphasized the importance of establishing a modern navy by acquiring modern weapons, building Western-style gunboats, and erecting shore batteries. In the 1870s he directed his focus toward devising strategies to counter the imperialist designs of Russia and Japan. In the 1880s he pushed for separating science and technology from strategy, believing that both could flourish only if separated. In a nutshell, his recommendation was, "Get close to England to resist Russia; protect Taiwan to guard against Japan."[285]

Wang's predictions would prove prescient in the subsequent decades. The Qing did divide the navy into separate fleets, but when war came there was little cooperation between them. In 1875 the court created a defense system that divided the coast broadly into northern (Beiyang) and southern (Nanyang) zones under separate commands. Ding Richang (1823–1882), another strong proponent of a rich country and strong military, recommended creating three fleets, stationed at Guangzhou, Weihaiwei, and the mouth of the Yangzi.[286] The court initially favored three fleets as well but stationed at Guangzhou, Fuzhou, and in the Bohai Gulf to protect Beijing. They later added another one at Shanghai. Although the government's strategy was to keep the naval forces divided but under central control, it instead nurtured jealousy and provincialism that severely hampered subsequent naval operations. Training irregularities aggravated these problems. Because of a lack of quality instructors and because Li Hongzhang had greater influence at court than his counterpart in Fuzhou, the best teachers and students were relocated to Tianjin on the eve of hostilities with the French, weakening the southern navy on the eve of its first major test.[287] Li's perception of the navy was far more defensive than Wang's or Zuo's, however, and he proved utterly incompetent in overseeing it.[288]

Despite these shortcomings and the inconsistent (at best) direction from the center, Halsey notes, "provincial authorities constructed a coherent system of coastal defenses in the late nineteenth and early twentieth centuries to pro-tect the empire's fiscal base in southeastern China."[289] Even when China lost wars in this era, the Qing control of the coasts and the revenue derived there-from was not compromised, although the loss of Taiwan to Japan and the removal of Korea as a strategic buffer were significant geostrategic setbacks. Progress was made, to be sure, but the Qing did not realize their goal of creat-ing a fully modern and capable seaborne defense force.

EVALUATING SELF-STRENGTHENING

Even though the Qing had made significant progress in modernizing the military and in creating new governmental institutions, many contemporary Western observers remained underwhelmed. A critic writing for the *North China Herald* observed that some modernization of weapons and systems had taken place under the leadership of Li Hongzhang and others during the Taiping Rebellion, but the improvements were made for largely personal reasons. The Chinese, he continued, "are stamped with the same arrogance, the same prejudice, and the same ignorance which prevailed in the Dark Ages. Treachery and deceit, chicanery and theft, are none the less prevalent amongst the highest officials although some few are now in a better position to raise the standard of revolt on their own account than they were a few years ago."[290] The writer went on to rail against the intractable opposition to innova-tion in China and expressed uncertainty as to whether any serious progress in advancing European ideas could be made.

Modern appraisals of Qing Self-Strengthening efforts have likewise tended to be critical, especially in comparison with Meiji Japan.[291] Some point to the Qing defeat at the hands of Meiji Japan in 1895 as being the ultimate litmus test, which the Qing failed. Others draw attention to the numerous institutional and personal issues that hampered uniform modernization.[292] But as Stephen Halsey aptly notes, the war with Japan was not really a contest between the Qing and the Meiji; it was between the Meiji empire and a politi-cally isolated Li Hongzhang, whose precious Beiyang Navy was essentially hung out to dry because he had similarly ghosted his countrymen in the south during their struggle with the French a decade before.[293]

Some critics of modernization efforts simply point out that the Qing itself fell in 1912.[294] Others ignore deeper dimensions of Qing Self-Strengthening efforts and repeat a superficial narrative grounded in only some of the facts. Gideon Ch'en, for example, asserts, "Chinese efforts to modernize the country by purchasing and imitating foreign mechanical inventions and by borrowing foreign experts, without at the same time developing a tradition of science and engineering, were not enough to produce the desired results."[295] In fact, we have seen how Zuo and others appreciated the importance of developing internal capabilities so as to attain self-sufficiency. Halsey and other more recent scholars have shown how the Qing managed not only to preserve but also to extend its sovereignty in important areas, paving the way for the development of the modern Chinese state after the Qing fell. Halsey contends that foreign pressures "inaugurated the most innovative period of state-making in China since the early seventeenth century." He further argues that a military-fiscal state emerged, and "this form of political organization combined money, bureaucracy, and guns in new ways and helped ensure the country's survival in a hostile international environment."[296]

For his part, Zuo Zongtang saw Self-Strengthening in general and naval power in particular as means to increase national resolve, pride, and self-reliance. He also recognized that Western science and technology were vital to this enterprise. He contended that China's long emphasis on fine arts rather than hard science was at the root of its weakness in the nineteenth century.[297] The Chinese put principles first and artisanal skills second, whereas the reverse was true in the West. But they could still catch up so long as they learned the techniques for themselves and did not rely solely on foreign teachers and officers. Seeing the obvious potential of superior military technology, the Qing state tended to prioritize the establishment of arsenals such as the Hanyang Iron and Steel Works and the Hubei Arsenal, though issues of quality control remained.

Another hallmark of nineteenth-century Western military culture, the dedicated military academy, would not appear in China until after the Sino-French War of 1884–1885, pioneered by the aforementioned Zhang Zhidong, who appears to have taken many of his cues from Zuo Zongtang.[298]

The education program of the Guangdong Military Academy, founded at Guangzhou in 1887, strongly mirrored that of the Fuzhou Navy Yard. The same was true of the military academy established at Tianjin in the north, and both featured foreign instructors.[299] They even sent a few students to Germany, the Royal Naval College in Greenwich, England, and the École de la construction in France for additional study.[300] The curricula were still often above the heads of the students, who were often selected based on their background in Chinese tradition and classics. These successes, however quali-fied, eventually led to the creation of formal Western-style military academies where graduates from the earliest institutions served as teachers alongside more limited numbers of foreigners.[301] While some authors have charged that the Chinese focused on military drill over practical officer education, the soldiers trained in these experimental institutions eventually came to be regarded as the most skilled in China and were transferred to trouble spots throughout the empire.[302]

I am thus inclined to agree with Halsey's assertion that "the security crises of the late nineteenth century encouraged the development of a new concep-tion of statecraft in China and this framework focused on amassing the sinews of power to protect the empire's sovereignty."[303] He also notes, "From 1860 to the present, Chinese statecraft has continued to emphasize the acquisition of wealth and power in defense of sovereignty in spite of marked differences in the ideological orientation" of successive Chinese governments. Although "the Self-Strengthening Movement could never have transformed China into a military and industrial superpower overnight," it did take the first tentative steps to narrow the power disparity between China and the West.[304] These new conceptions of statecraft significantly encompassed an emergent sense of Han Chinese nationalism that initially served Qing interests in retaining sovereign authority in the far-flung regions of the empire and among the tributary states. Finally, one must not discount the emergence of Han military commanders during the campaigns to defeat the Taipings. Qing victories in campaigns led by Chinese commanders proved that "Manchu generals were no longer the sole bearers of military prowess in China" and undermined the prestige of the Manchu overlords.[305]

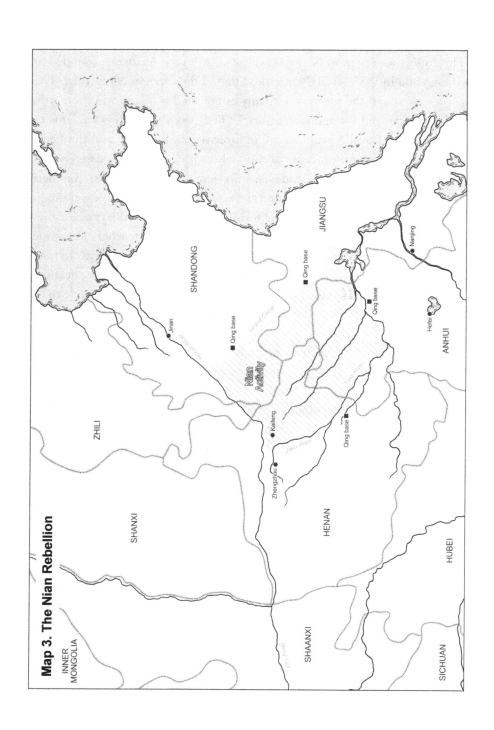

Map 3. The Nian Rebellion

4

CORRALLING THE NIAN

I cannot exterminate the Hui until I first manage to contain the Nian.
—Zuo Zongtang

Of all the rebels Zuo faced in his long career, the Nian most resemble the archetypal Chinese peasant rebel. Their tactics closely resembled those of the wandering bandits (*liu kou* or *liu zei*) of the late Ming period, and they proved just as difficult to eradicate for many of the same reasons.[1] Their main bases of operations were in the same areas as those of their Ming forebears, attesting to the region's reputation as a rugged frontier that both bred and offered sanctuary to foes of the state. It is thus not surprising that the Qing officials assigned to suppress the so-called Nian bandits drew on the precedents established in the Ming. Likewise, as we have seen elsewhere, northwest Chinese society itself underwent a progressive militarization that mirrored that of the late Ming. Zuo was well equipped to meet this new challenge, but he was a man of south China. He would need to adapt to the cultures and societies of the north and northwest, not to mention learn how to fight in environments that were drastically different from those of the south and southeast. His ability to adapt to these new circumstances and conquer challenges that had bedeviled his predecessors for years—even decades—attests to his strategic and logistical acumen.

THE ORIGINS OF THE NIAN

While the Nian Rebellion is generally considered to have lasted from 1851 to 1868, references to Nian bandits date all the way back to the White Lotus Revolt of 1796–1805 or even earlier according to some Qing accounts.[2] In her classic typology of rebels in north China, Elizabeth Perry classifies the Nian as "predatory" rather than "protective" bandits.[3] Perry argues that "predatory activities of smuggling, feuds, and banditry were . . . adaptive survival strategies" for peasants in north China. "An ongoing phenomenon, predation escalated during periods of natural calamity. Ad hoc bandit groups grew first into semipermanent gangs and then into massive bandit armies that razed the countryside in search of a living."[4] Because there was a surplus of single young males in the region owing to the prevalence of female infanticide as a "sedentary survival strategy," there were always ample recruits for the bandit gangs.[5]

The loess soil environment of north China where the Nian originated was prone to flooding and famine and was suitable for only a few sturdy dryland crops such as wheat and sorghum. It was also characterized by uneven land-holding patterns. In the hometown of the Nian leader Zhang Luoxing, for example, less than 20 percent of the families owned more than 70 percent of the land.[6] For these reasons, Perry says, in the mid-nineteenth century north China "witnessed a dramatic rise in predatory aggression, a clear reflection of worsening ecological circumstances."[7] Replicating patterns seen elsewhere in China, local communities formed local militia and built earthen fortifications for self-defense.[8] Furthermore, the lack of industry and paucity of local gentry meant that the region was only minimally integrated into the national government and economy.

The situation was further complicated by the emergence of the Taiping rebels and the strong government response required to defeat them and defend the capital. In Perry's assessment, "These external forces merged predators and protectors in a common antagonism towards the state. What began as simple predation was pushed into a rebellious posture. But bandit origins could not be entirely overcome and, for most participants, the movement continued to be a means for securing household income rather than a self-conscious effort at toppling the dynasty."[9] Qing sources substantiate this, invoking the rhetoric of catastrophe discussed in chapter 3. As one account puts it, "When the Guangxi bandit Hong Xiuquan occupied Jinling (Nanjing) he sent the false prince Chen Yucheng to take Anqing and his troops spread north and south, galloping forth. For a thousand *li* one saw no people or cooking fires; the fields were barren and the people had nothing to eat so those who followed the Nian multiplied daily."[10]

In some circles the Nian heartland was known as the "region of the three no-governs" because regional and provincial authorities denied responsibility for dealing with events and hid behind jurisdictional overlap and confusion. Northern Anhui became "a dark region where officials, yamen staff, wicked bullies and landlords oppressed the people, devising all sorts of means to extort their money."[11] The barren landscape combined with poorly maintained waterworks contributed to frequent flooding as rivers often silted up and overflowed their banks. The Yellow River burst its dikes three times in the 1840s alone and eventually shifted course entirely to empty into the sea north, rather than south, of the Shandong Peninsula, aiding Nian raids into southwestern Shandong.[12] Heavy rainfall in the 1850s caused more flooding and destroyed crops, which led to famine and even reports of cannibalism. Taiping incursions proved to be the last straw in this cycle of despair.[13]

The term Nian (捻) literally means "to twist" and probably derives from the wrapped torches the bandits carried in their nighttime raids.[14] Another homonym means "to knead or pinch" and refers to assembling bands for raiding. It is unclear if the rebels used this name themselves, and it is worth noting that referencing the Nian as a coherent "movement" is for the sake of convenience. Contemporary sources indicate that the term "Nian" at times referenced a common "brotherhood or society."[15] While there were a few prominent Nian chieftains, the Nian were inveterate opportunists and had no definitive overarching aims or strategies like the Taipings, with whom they sometimes formed alliances—as they also did with the Dungan rebels in Shaanxi. They also intermingled with various local bandit groups, drifters, and local power brokers.[16] Prior to 1853 Nian bands were reported in Henan, Zhili, Shandong, Jiangsu, and Anhui provinces.

The key to the Nian's longevity lay in their intimate links with local society. They often forged alliances with local gentry, defending certain areas in exchange for sanctuary and providing protection (for a fee, of course) from other predatory groups. They intervened in local feuds and used the influence thus gained to further insinuate themselves into local society, sometimes fighting other Nian groups in "family feuds" (*qiujiazi*). Interestingly given their later connection to the Dungan rebels, some of these feuds involved disputes between Han and Muslims.[17]

Nian leaders had varied backgrounds but all were products of their hardscrabble environs. The Nian leader Zhang Luoxing (aka Zhang Lexing, d. 1863) hailed from Zhanglaojia village. He had gotten his start as a salt smuggler working with a band of sharpshooting retainers known as "the Eighteen Gunmen."[18] Zhang was illiterate and had turned to a life of crime after his family lost their lands. Aided by a man known as Blind Gong (who could, in fact, see), Zhang cut a striking figure as he traveled through the countryside in elaborate costumes in a sedan chair with incense burned ahead of him. His cousin Zhang Zongyu, who later succeeded him as the most prominent Nian chieftain, was an illiterate opium addict with a gift for military command. It was Zhang Zongyu who would forge alliances with the Dungan rebels after the Taipings had been defeated.[19]

Nian leaders often came from the gentry, while peasants made up the rank and file. Since the latter were often too poor to steal from anyhow, they frequently shielded Nian members when government forces cracked down. Some government officials were even "sworn brothers" of Nian leaders. The Qing government found it nigh impossible to distinguish Nian adherents from other peasants, and simply killing all suspected Nian was bad for morale, so it offered rewards for those who turned in Nian leaders and spared their peasant followers.[20] When convenient, the Nian redistributed plundered wealth in the fashion of social bandits such as Robin Hood, building up more goodwill among the peasantry.[21]

THE NIAN EXPAND

Nian organization was primarily clan- and locality-based, with different groups adopting particular colors for easy identification. Bands ranging in size from as few as three to more than a thousand were geographically dispersed and operated independently of one another. Each leader designated himself a "lodge master" (*tangzhu*).[22] Like their counterparts elsewhere in the empire, the Nian initially took advantage of administrative laxity and loopholes to move freely across provinces and jurisdictions. Many magistrates or their underlings were bribed to allow the Nian free passage, or, as noted above, were related or otherwise already connected to a Nian leader.[23] Taiping successes to the south facilitated the expansion of the Nian bands and allowed the diffuse movement to assume at least some of the trappings of a full-blown rebellion. In the winter of 1852–1853 some eighteen Nian leaders proclaimed Zhang Luoxing their "head," though this confederation soon broke apart and Zhang himself enlisted in a militia unit, again emulating the example of late Ming peasant rebel leaders. In late 1853 four Nian chiefs again banded together as the Four Deva Kings (*sida tianwang*) but did little in the way of coordinating their activities. Not much planning was done along these lines until 1855, when five large Nian bands, including one commanded by Zhang Luoxing, made joint plans to invade Henan.

Building on preexisting local practices, Nian groups relied on earthen walls and stockades for defense, integrating them with natural defenses to transform the strategic landscape. They sometimes cut deals with other local strongmen and petty warlords or local militia organizations. The earth walls that defended their villages were usually about one *zhang* tall and surrounded by moats about two *zhang* wide. The walls were usually outfitted with gun ports, attesting to the overall level of militarization in late Qing society.[24] Indeed, despite their reputation as mounted guerrilla fighters, the Nian often operated from strongholds defended by heavy guns. It was only later in the movement when they had been dislodged from their bases that their weaponry became more primitive.[25] Usually three to four communities would band together, so even if Qing forces breached one wall they would have to contend with other defenses. Ironically some of these defenses had originally been built to defend against the Taipings.[26] The Muslim rebels in northwest China and Central Asia would adopt similar tactics.

Nian operations greatly expanded in 1855 as the Taipings consumed the Qing government's attention. In the first month of 1856 Zhang Luoxing was named "Lord of the Alliance" (*mengzhu*).[27] At this point the Nian divided their forces into five colored banners, each with bordered banners within them, not unlike the military system of the Qing, though the practice may have been derived from the White Lotus.[28] Zhang Luoxing's banner was yellow. Banner chiefs assumed titles as lords (*qizhu*), and the leaders of small banners were known as headmen (*niantou*). Some top leaders were named princes of the Taiping movement as well. This organization into banners provided more cohesion to the movement, but it also underscored the threat the Nian posed to the Qing, especially when Nian leaders started cooperating with the Taipings.[29]

The Qing first tried to use local militias to combat the Nian but with little success. They appointed one Mao Changxi as a coordinator for militia training. He made a bad beginning by executing many of the locals for incompetence or for colluding with the rebels. Subsequently when his subordinates arrived in local areas to recruit for the militia, people ran away. And when he did get forces into the field, they were outmaneuvered by the Nian, who rained arrows down on the government forces, encircled them, and cut their supply lines. In addition to bows and arrows the Nian were adept at using lances. The short ones were two *zhang* (about twelve feet) long and could keep foes at bay. When the Qing used guns against them, the Nian would disperse, reform their ranks, and charge before the government forces could reload. Because of these tactics it was said that the government forces "came to dread the Nian above all else."[30]

From 1856 to 1859, as the Qing war with the Taipings crested, the Nian consolidated their area of influence around "old nests" between the Huai and Sha Rivers. Their core area encompassed 45,000 square *li*, and at the height of their influence in the early 1860s they may have had nominal control of some 6 million people.[31] Qing generals such as Shengbao and others fought the Nian throughout this period, scoring many pyrrhic victories but doing little to win hearts and minds.[32] The locals alternately feared the Nian for their harsh reprisals against Qing supporters and welcomed them for distributing famine relief and aiding local grain-growing operations.[33]

Local banner chiefs retained considerable autonomy, and the clan structures prevalent in north China meant that if a clan leader was allied with the Nian, the whole community usually followed suit.[34] Nian ranks were further swelled by Qing and Taiping deserters, petty smugglers, and local bandits. Mimicking their Ming predecessors, some local bandits appropriated colorful titles for themselves such as Yu the Monk and Zhang the Bat.[35] Nian leaders might accept Taiping titles and cooperate with the Taipings for common goals, but they prized freedom of operation above all else. They relied on cavalry and mobility to stay ahead of government forces, often riding horses they had stolen from the government.[36] Their mobility exhausted their Qing pursuers and caused lapses in judgment and discipline. Indeed just such a lapse might explain how the Nian managed to kill the formidable Qing commander Senggelinqin.[37] Further, the Nian depredations enabled and inspired other local warlords such as Miao Peilin, who controlled a large swath of the Huai and alternately operated alone or took titles from the Qing in a scenario not unlike that which prevailed in this region in the 1640s. Miao changed sides multiple times through the early 1860s, serving nominally under Shengbao before rejoining the Taiping-Nian allies, only to rejoin the Qing before turning coat again. He was either assassinated by a former bodyguard of the Taiping leader Chen Yucheng in December 1863 or slain by Senggelinqin.[38]

In this middle period there were three major Qing officials tasked with combating the Nian, and each adopted a different strategy. Yuan Jiasan (1806–1863) was cautious and frequently clashed with the generals and other civil officials.[39] Shengbao, whose position was connected to his previous support for Cixi's regency, was primarily an appeaser and dealmaker.[40] Though he claimed numerous battlefield successes in the late 1850s, Shengbao pushed a dual policy of creating strong local militia and offering deals to Nian leaders and local warlords, such as the aforementioned Miao Peilin, a former militia head turned Nian chieftain. That strategy backfired for the most part, as leaders would accept titles and pledge loyalty to the Qing only to revert to their old plundering ways when the opportunity arose.[41] Shengbao was eventually transferred to the west to battle the Muslim threat and even tried to get Miao Peilin to join him there. While he was in the west, he was accused of greed and licentiousness as well as taking bribes and skimming military supplies.[42] His missteps eventually got Shengbao impeached and recalled to the capital, though his reputation was restored somewhat by his actions defending the approach to Beijing during the

Arrow War.[43] In 1861 Shengbao was sent back into the field to help Senggelin-qin battle the Nian.[44] He obtained the surrender of the Nian chief Song Jingshi and enrolled Song's troops in the Qing army, earning greater responsibilities in Henan and Anhui, though he was soon embroiled in more controversy.

Senggelinqin might be considered the most successful of the trio because he defeated and killed Zhang Luoxing in 1863.[45] He also sketched out a plan for establishing a cordon around the Nian, then damming up their water supplies and moving in after they were depleted and weakened.[46] He proved unable to fully put this plan into practice, and despite the symbolic significance of killing Zhang Luoxing, in military terms this had little impact because Zhang's nephew, Zhang Zongyu, simply took his place. Senggelinqin also seems to have suc-cumbed to the "body bag mentality" that afflicted many late Qing officials. His reports indicated that he killed more than 100,000 rebels, but he never articulated a clear plan for pacifying the Nian or reconstructing local society.[47] Senggelin-qin was hampered by petty rivalries and his lack of facility in Chinese,[48] but he nevertheless worked effectively with the Chinese commander Zhang Yao, one of the more innovative and effective field commanders battling both the Nian and the Taipings. For a time, Zhang also served as vice-censor of Henan prov-ince, but he was impeached for illiteracy by a jealous rival and his position was converted to a purely military one.[49] Some of Senggelinqin's other subordinates were corrupt and undisciplined, and he himself underestimated the Nian, which contributed to his final defeat, though he had scored numerous triumphs over the rebels from 1863 to 1865, including killing the slippery Miao Peilin.[50]

Initially Senggelinqin's strategy of denying resources to the Nian seemed to be bearing fruit. He harried them endlessly, and they could not find any-thing to loot. The Mongol prince pursued the rebels for ten days, running his horse ragged. When the Nian split their forces, Senggelinqin stopped his pursuit to consider his options. Unfortunately he failed to send out scouts to properly appraise the situation. Senggelinqin met his end when he led a small cavalry detachment into a Nian camp. Though his force killed hundreds, his horse was shot out from under him. He continued to fight on foot and sus-tained eight spear wounds before succumbing, brandishing his sword till the end. His men managed to recover his corpse when they withdrew.[51] He was posthumously showered with honors by the Qing court. Memorial shrines were erected, he was canonized as a "loyal official," and his portrait was hung in the Hall of Purple Glory (Ziguange) in the Forbidden City.[52]

Meanwhile, the Qing continued to apply the "clear the fields and strengthen the walls" (*qingye jianbi*) policy against the Nian. While the practice denied supplies to the rebels, it also forced the Qing forces to carry more of their own supplies. The rebels built earthen-walled counterforts from which to attack Qing positions. The Qing commanders were eventually forced to devise a dual strategy of seizing the nests and cutting off escape routes, steadily restricting the movement of the Nian forces. This included securing the waterways, because the Nian moved freely across rivers and the Grand Canal. Initially the Qing tried to counter the superior Nian cavalry by sending more horses against them, but the horses did not reach those who needed them. Qing commanders competed with one another for the mounts or simply commandeered them. The Qing also failed to follow the lead of Zuo and others in the south by implementing plans of rehabilitation once areas were seized from the Nian, despite suggestions they do so, including a plan that called for replanting barren lands and establishing local schools.[53] It was not until Zeng Guofan assumed oversight of anti-Nian operations in May 1865 that the Qing started making headway in winning local support.[54]

Zeng identified four major strengths of the Nian: (1) their pikemen, who were equipped with spears up to twenty feet long, (2) their cavalry, (3) their general combat skills and experience, and (4) their mobility.[55] They preferred either encircling their foes or conducting running battles of attrition. They were also adept at ambushes and using disguises, and they maintained hidden weapon caches throughout the countryside. Zeng needed to reshape local society in such a way that he could alter battlefield scenarios in favor of the Qing and force the Nian to fight *his* war. Zeng realized that Qing armies could realistically move only twenty to forty *li* per day, and they had to keep their supply lines open.

There was also the matter of overlapping jurisdictions. Officials were often content to simply chase away or wait out the bandits, hoping they would cross into someone else's area of responsibility. And those who *were* willing to take action might be wary of stepping on the toes of fellow officials in the factionalized atmosphere of the court.[56] The Nian had no such restrictions. Defenses therefore needed to start at the local level, and the court needed to appoint officials with sweeping authority and independence of action. But vigorous debates ensued over who should be appointed to various roles and how supplies and equipment would be allocated. There were even skirmishes between Qing commanders over equipment. Zeng Guofan demoted or replaced particularly contentious officials.[57]

Zeng issued proclamations promising to spare the loyal and punish the seditious and offered new titles to "Earthen-Wall Lords."[58] Commissioners were sent to local communities to ferret out the seditious and install loyal officials in their places. Invoking a classical expression, Zeng noted that it was important to discern who was loyal, "lest jade and stones both be consumed in the fire."[59] Certificates of rank and authority were issued to counter those who "outwardly proclaimed submission but secretly aided the Nian."[60]

Loyal recruits could also be enrolled in the Qing army.[61] Presaging the later actions of Zuo and Li Hongzhang, Zeng created flexible, responsive units and stationed them at key points to constrain Nian movements. He established key operational bases at Jining, Xuzhou, Zhoujiakou, and Linhuai and tried to entice the Nian into pitched battles.[62] He called his strategy *huahe quandi* (to encircle with rivers and dikes). He also ordered that local communities must have sufficient resources to withstand a siege of at least half a month, affording government forces time to relieve them and thereby allowing for the proper implementation of the *qingye jianbi* strategy.[63] Zeng moved to secure the routes leading to Beijing and tried to keep the Nian out of Shandong, albeit with mixed results. He also bolstered river defenses.[64]

The strategic situation became more complicated for the Qing in the autumn of 1866 when the two major Nian leaders, Lai Wenguang and Zhang Zongyu, elected to split their forces after their assault on Nanyang in southern Henan failed, with Lai moving east and Zhang heading northwest toward Shaanxi.[65] The Dungan Rebellion was gaining traction, and Zhang hoped to gain the Dungans' support. In fact, one reason the Qing were so keen to get gunboats on the Yellow River was to protect their supply shipments heading west to Shaanxi.

Meanwhile, the Qing armies in Henan and Anhui increased their cooperation to drive the Nian back. They won a major victory on the south bank of the Hong River and successively smashed some twenty rebel stockades. Lai Wenguang and Ren Zhu, the most prominent leaders in the east, remained thorns in the Qing side. The government hoped to sweep Shandong clean by combining infantry and cavalry forces with stoutly defended local areas, but there was simply too much ground for their available troops to cover. Liu Mingchuan had to content himself with sending out strike forces from his base at Zhoujiakou in Henan.[66] Lai's forces briefly moved into Hubei but were pushed back into Shandong.

On December 7, 1866, under pressure from jealous rivals, Zeng resigned as imperial commissioner for suppression of the Nian and, on Zeng's recommendation, was replaced by Li Hongzhang.[67] Li combined the strategies of all his predecessors and pursued them simultaneously while also stressing superior training and indoctrination of his troops.[68]

The survival of the disparate Nian groups was aided and abetted by the existence of other, more pressing threats, most notably the Taipings but also the Dungan rebels to the northwest. With the defeat of the Taipings in 1864, large numbers of Taiping adherents fled north to join the Nian and morphed into the kind of wandering bandits that had so plagued the late Ming.[69] Some of the more enterprising Nian leaders forged connections with the Muslim rebels as well. As the Muslim rebellion that had been percolating since 1862 was showing signs of being connected to other uprisings farther west, the Nian now assumed a much higher position in the hierarchy of threats. The death of the formidable Senggelinqin underscored this danger. Thus the Qing were now willing to assign their most accomplished military commanders to the task of stamping out the Nian menace.

ZUO IS APPOINTED COMMANDER TO CRUSH THE NIAN

By the time Zuo was sent north to crush the Nian he had forged an impressive network of skilled military commanders whom he trusted and respected. He naturally requested that the Qing court allow him to bring many of these men with him, including Guo Songlin and Liu Songshan, though he was concerned that most of them lacked experience fighting in the very different terrain of the region.[70] Nevertheless Zuo stressed that his close ties with these men would avail the Qing well and contribute to the speedier eradication of the Nian threat.[71] In fact Zuo's former subordinate Liu Changyou had already been appointed supreme military commander in Zhili and had killed the prominent Nian leader Zhang Xizhu back in 1864.[72] The court acceded to Zuo's suggestion and, on November 19, 1866, appointed Shen Baozhen to oversee the Fuzhou Navy Yard and Liu Dian to supervise military affairs in Shaan-Gan. Zuo's ability to persuade the court to follow his recommendation reflects his growing national stature. Zuo was summoned to Beijing for a court audience to discuss military affairs in Gansu, but ten days after he was summoned, another order instructed him to first hasten to Shaanxi and take charge of the deteriorating situation there.[73]

Zuo advanced to Wuchang and then sent a missive to the throne that read in part,

When your minister made war in the southeast advantage lay in boats. In the northwest, advantage lies in horses. The Nian and Muslims rush about the Central Plain on horseback, but if we try to fight them with government troops on foot, surely we will not have success. But when it comes to talking of strength in horses, the north is not the same as the west in terms of resources. The Nian rely on northern produce. Therefore, the Nian are more fierce than the Muslims. But right now your minister has only 6,000 troops. So now I wish to purchase fine northern horses and train cavalry units and combine them with mobile battle carts. From Xiang[yang] to Deng[zhou] we'll advance from Jinxing Pass and traverse through Shangzhou to Shaanxi. We'll establish military farms so as to facilitate long-term campaigning. Therefore, when we advance our troops to Shaanxi, we'll first clear the areas beyond the [Tong] pass of bandits; then we will advance to Gansu. Once we advance to Gansu, we'll first clear

Shaanxi of bandits. When we station troops at Lanzhou, we'll first clear the various roads [around it] of bandits. Afterward we'll be able to move armies and supplies without obstructions.[74]

Clearly, Zuo already had a broad vision for bringing peace to the northwest, and he often repeated these points when the court pressed him for faster action. Zuo added that it would take several months to make all his preparations and begged the court to indulge him. He noted that bringing troops from the southeast to the northwest was problematic, as food, climate, and customs differed. Previous efforts to send troops to the northwest had resulted in mass desertions, so Zuo had to consider morale and take steps to prevent desertion while also assessing how to operate under very different environmental conditions. He was careful to choose commanders he trusted and who had a good relationship with their troops.[75]

The situation in the northwest was dire when Zuo was appointed, for matters had been festering there for decades. Zuo's immediate predecessor, Yang Yuebin (1822–1890), incidentally another native of Hunan who had formerly worked with Peng Yulin in creating the riverine navy, had alternated policies of extermination with persuasion when dealing with the rebels, but failed to attain lasting success with either. He finally requested dismissal due to illness.[76] Things rapidly got worse in the winter of 1866–1867 as the Western Nian besieged the provincial capital of Xi'an and scattered the Qing armies in Shaanxi.[77] The court quickly reinstated Zeng Guofan, who dispatched Liu Songshan to protect the Yellow River as the Qing fanned out in seventeen brigades, crossing Tong Pass and advancing toward Xi'an in early 1867. Liu would go on to smash a Western Nian army just outside the city in the second month.[78]

True to his nature, Zuo paid careful attention to accumulating adequate supplies, ample funds, and trusted subordinates as he made his preparations. In a letter to the Manchu commander Yinghan he noted, "Managing military funds is harder than managing the troops and managing grain supplies is harder than managing funds."[79] Zuo also admitted that the situation in the north was more tangled than he had anticipated, and "it was not a simple matter to distinguish the good from the wicked, and traitors amongst the Hui are still rousing the people." Local bandits mixed freely with rebel groups, and the rugged terrain gave them ample opportunity to slip into the mountains and valleys and avoid Qing traps. The best the Qing might do initially was to station troops in key locations and alternate pacification with persuasion. The approaching winter would make operations even more difficult. Natural disasters had already cut into food reserves, making it difficult to feed the troops currently in Shaanxi, let alone new ones.[80]

Initially, owing to supply issues, Zuo brought just six thousand crack troops; half were from Fujian and under his command, and the other half were Hunanese under Liu Dian. Upon considering the vast terrain he would have to cover, he decided to raise another six thousand troops in Hunan. He also enlisted the help of his old friend Wang Boxin, who was familiar with the situation in Shaanxi.[81] Wang recommended the extensive creation of military farms (*tuntian*) to sustain the armies in the northwest, reckoning that it would take several years to restore order.[82] He also provided perceptive advice on acting tough but also showing compassion by resettling local Muslims and providing them with the means to recover their livelihoods. Zuo also got information from Liu Rong, another frontier veteran, who reiterated the need for *tuntian* and recommended using Shaanxi as the springboard to pacifying Gansu. Gao Liansheng and Wu Shiwan would join Zuo in Hankou as well.[83] Zuo was appointed governor-general of Shaanxi and Gansu on February 22, 1867.

Zuo emphasized the need to control transportation arteries because it was impossible to manage troops if one could not manage supplies. As always, he looked at the bigger picture and articulated a broad plan for success: "Now I have been called to service on the western frontier, but I cannot exterminate the Hui [Muslims] until I first manage to contain the Nian. We cannot manage the supply situation in Gansu until we first manage supplies in Shaanxi."[84] Along these lines he was eager to get supplies into Gansu from neighboring Sichuan and brought in private salt merchants to facilitate things. But he also recognized the need for positive action, writing to Gao Liansheng that "the best defense is a good offense [*yichao weifang*]."[85]

In a letter to his son Xiaowei written in 1867, Zuo outlined his broad plan for corralling the Nian, which revolved around extensive use of firearms and the deployment of war wagons to curtail the rebels' mobility.[86] He thought the wagons could break cavalry formations and entice the rebels into battles where firearms could decimate their ranks and his own cavalry could then sweep in to finish them off.[87] Superficially, at least, the plan resembled the strategy employed by the great Ming general Qi Jiguang when he was assigned to defend the northern frontier against the Mongols in the 1570s.[88] And in fact, Zuo referenced the late Ming firearms expert Zhao Shizhen (1553–1611), author of the text *Shenqi pu*, for demonstrating the efficacy of battle carts equipped with small cannon against mobile opponents because they could help break cavalry charges.[89] In each squad of ten, six men had guns while the other four used spears. Each cart was managed by four men and one officer who were responsible for maneuvering the cart, readying gunpowder, igniting the fuses, and other support activities. All told, Zuo planned to deploy fifteen cart battalions with thirty-eight carts per battalion. Zuo claimed that these formations were very effective against large groups of cavalry, but Zeng Guofan found them less useful, and evidence suggests that the cart formations were not widely used after some of the early engagements against the Nian exposed their limitations.[90]

Zuo also thought that bolstering river defenses would help bottle up the Nian so that they could be redirected into killing grounds. Land and river defenses, augmented by militia, could be used to deny the rebels both resources and sanctuaries. In a letter to Liu Songshan, Zuo suggested funneling the Nian into areas lacking inhabitants. For example, an area near the Wei River in which nine out of ten houses stood empty was a perfect place to isolate and destroy the enemy.[91] In effect, Zuo was advocating the type of amphibious warfare that had worked so well against the Taipings.[92]

In another letter to Xiaowei, Zuo expressed consternation over the general level of militarization in local society, which had trapped the realm in an endless cycle of violence. He thought the government needed to prohibit wandering braves and implement martial law among the troops. As long as the people felt insecure and unprotected by the government, they would continue to establish local militia and take matters into their own hands.[93] Zuo also noted that the Qing's ongoing logistical difficulties were made worse by the propensity of local bandits to cast their lot with the Nian and the frequency with which local militia broke in the face of rebel attacks.[94] Zuo argued for more trainers and more time to prepare his forces.[95]

Zuo felt that he would be seriously hampered by the lack of cavalry at his disposal. Because most of his units were drawn from the south, where infantry and riverine war prevailed, he began with fewer than five hundred cavalry troops.[96] The Eastern Nian, on the other hand, reportedly had more than 100,000 troops, half of which were mounted, and the Western Nian had 30,000 troops, a third of which were cavalry.[97] Zuo complained that there were only three thousand troops currently engaging the Nian, and most of them were infantry. He needed more guns and horses.[98] In comparing the Nian to the Muslim rebels, Zuo deemed the Nian stronger but perhaps easier to manage due to their lack of coherent goals and leadership. And it is worth noting that although he had yet to fight the Nian, Zuo was already sketching out plans for defeating the Hui Muslims he would face next and recovering all of Gansu.[99] The Nian had to be quelled first, however, in order to secure the rear, because the campaign against the Muslims would involve long supply lines.[100]

While he remained in Hankou to assemble provisions, Zuo sent some of his subordinates north, first to train militia to assist in fighting the Nian and then to engage the rebels themselves. Zuo's family joined him in Hankou, marking the last time they would all be together. Zuo stocked up on artillery, procuring Krupp guns and hiring foreigners to help train his men to operate them.[101] Every brigade had thirty-eight "short mountain splitting cannon [*duanpi shanpao*]" on carts and was bolstered by the latest Western firearms, including arms purchased in Shanghai and guns procured from German sources. He also had more gunpowder brought in from Zhejiang.[102] Some two thousand guns were ordered from Hong Kong, though Zuo continued to stress the importance of China achieving self-sufficiency in firearms production.[103] Indeed, these shortages were what eventually convinced Zuo to establish his own arsenals in Xi'an and Lanzhou for the campaigns against the Muslim rebels. Likewise, uniforms were originally sent from Hankou, but Zuo later built uniform factories in Lanzhou, Suzhou, and Qinzhou.[104]

As the court pushed him to act faster, Zuo argued that it would be foolish to rush into battle unprepared.[105] He submitted urgent requests for more funds, saying he needed 40,000 taels per month just to get mobilized, but most of the customs revenues had already been allocated to build the Fuzhou shipyard. Funds earmarked for Zuo's western operations had been diverted to the southeast, but he hoped to raise additional money from Guangdong and Zhejiang. Zuo asked the court to investigate each province's revenues to ascertain their ability to subsidize the western campaign and to determine realistic timetables for the delivery of funds and supplies. The court responded by issuing directives to Zeng Guofan and other officials to contribute more funds, also giving quotas for the various provinces.[106] Localities were expected to provide some food for troop upkeep, but Zuo endeavored to prevent abuses by having troops donate surplus grain to local stores and encouraging peasants to return to agriculture once rebels had been cleared out of an area.[107] Zuo also investigated reports of grain speculation by soldiers selling their rations for profit.[108]

In a memorandum to court Zuo stressed that he had done extensive research on the region in the course of his prior studies.[109] Ever the keen student of military history, he referenced the disastrous defeat of the Ming commander Sun Chuanting at the hands of peasant rebels in this region in 1643.[110] Zuo observed that many people had fled when the fighting started and there were few left tilling the fields and paying taxes. He promised to rehabilitate local society and clean up the military there, weeding out old and weak soldiers and instilling proper discipline. He also sought to open new fields for cultivation and set up grain stores for commoners to purchase grain in times of dearth.[111]

To beef up his cavalry Zuo hired Manchu Bannermen to help train recruits in horsemanship. He also tried to bring in cavalry from Jilin and Chahar, but many of them deserted or never arrived. Although he had purchased some three thousand war horses from Jilin, only a third that number were present when he reached Shaanxi; the rest had reportedly died from sickness.[112] Zuo was able to wangle more funds to buy additional mounts but still had only four of his projected ten cavalry battalions when he started his campaign. In any case, Zuo felt that employing a smaller, better trained and equipped force was superior to relying on sheer numbers. It would literally provide more bang for the buck. In a letter to Li Hanzhang, Hongzhang's brother, he was free with his criticism of some of his predecessors and their armies, charging that they were guilty of only reacting rather than actively engaging the rebels.[113]

Zuo created a strategy for a three-pronged advance that would be under the overall command of Liu Songshan. His forces mobilized in waves following the establishment of supply depots. He recommended that supply depots be set up every forty to fifty *li*, with twenty depots for each ten thousand troops.[114] Chen Zhuo of Shanxi was placed in charge of river defenses and protecting river supply lines. Liu's forces gradually pushed the Nian out of Henan and back through Tong Pass into Shaanxi, sometimes combining riverine and land forces, applying lessons learned in the war against the Taipings. Liu's forces were joined by units moving in from Sichuan. The Nian were forced to range widely for provisions, making it hard for the Qing to force decisive battles.[115] Gao Liansheng and Liu Dian scored victories over allied rebel forces, but the vast front made it impossible for the Qing to completely guard the Yellow River, and rebels slipped across it into Shanxi, almost roaming back into northern Henan.

As these events were unfolding in the south, the Qing commander Mutushan was advocating a policy of conciliation with respect to the Muslim rebels in the west, much to the consternation of Zuo, who thought he was gullible.[116] Zuo complained that Mutushan was relying on persuasion because he feared going into battle with the Muslims with his inexperienced troops, though he did admit that Mutushan's forces were understrength.[117] The court continued to press Zuo to hasten to the front while issuing directives to other officials to take up defensive positions and rush to the aid of Xi'an. Zuo countered that his force was still too small, and he was hamstrung by the fact that Liu Dian had been granted sick leave.[118] Liu Songshan scored an impressive victory over the rebel forces in early 1867, capturing many weapons, banners, and livestock, but the fighting was hard and drawn out. Liu was commended for his troops' discipline and training and for setting an example for his fellow commanders. As Liu and Huang Ding won more battles, Zuo evinced a sense that victory was not far off.[119]

ZUO ENGAGES THE NIAN

Zuo left Hankou on March 29, 1867, at the head of 40,000–75,000 men (sources vary on the number).[120] As we have just seen, some of his subordinate commanders were already in the field battling the Nian. In one letter Zuo praised Liu Songshan for routing a Nian cavalry force with infantry troops, exclaiming, "His [Liu's] troops were not intimidated; indeed it was as if they were cavalry and the Nian were the infantry."[121] But although Zuo believed Nian morale had been damaged by this engagement, he expressed concern over their growing ties with the Muslim (Dungan) rebels. He also noted that the Qing were deficient in troops and supplies. Indeed, Liu Songshan was already facing supply issues. The Qing would have to assume a defensive stance for the time being, protecting the south bank of the Wei River while awaiting the armies of Li Hongzhang and forces from Shanxi. Zuo also cautioned against falling for the Nian tactics of feigned retreat and ambush.[122] He advocated building up a stout defense first, then sending out troops and gradually expanding their theater of operations. Zuo suggested working in concert with local officials to ensure adequate supplies for the armies while simultaneously implementing a *qingye jianbi* strategy to deny resources to the Nian and Hui. If supplies were concentrated in forts and the countryside was barren, the Qing would find it easier to prevail. Zuo blamed some of the supply problems on the pernicious influence of Gelaohui elements in the ranks[123] and also noted that the government forces' military effectiveness was compromised by a dearth of lower-ranking officers.

The Qing had attempted to follow the recommendations of Zeng Guofan and Li Hongzhang since the death of Senggelinqin. Efforts were made to increase the military presence on the Yellow River and Grand Canal, and local militia were recruited and trained. Warhorses and trainers from Manchuria were sent to Zuo in the northwest.[124] Zhang Zongyu had been driven away from the Yellow River by a gunboat patrol in the spring of 1866, though he escaped to raid along the Grand Canal.[125] Fighting intensified along the Wei River in Shaanxi as the Qing opened supply routes from Sichuan and set up depots in anticipation of further campaigns.[126] The Qing were sometimes able to acquire supplies and weapons from defeated rebel forces.[127]

Zuo believed that Qing firearms, if properly deployed, would prove devastating against the Nian lances, especially if used in conjunction with elite cavalry from the north, and made several recommendations for organizing such hybrid forces. Among the first to arrive were Manchus of the Bordered Red Banner from Jilin. Horses and warriors also came from the Mongol tribes of the steppe deployed to the Xi'an area.[128] By early 1867 superior Qing firepower and discipline were starting to carry the day as Taiping Rebellion veterans such as Liu Songshan and Liu Mingchuan took greater charge of field operations. The Nian fled before Zuo's cart formations, though the carts proved difficult to maneuver in certain terrains. Nevertheless the court was still frustrated by the lack of coordinated operations and wanted riverine defenses strengthened still more. Some critics pushed for decisive battles, arguing that "chasing rebels is not a sound plan."[129]

While noting that Henan was vital to national defense and the destruction of the Nian, the court also stressed the importance of continued cooperation from all the neighboring provinces, saying that Henan alone could not bear the burden. The government estimated around 70,000 taels per month would be needed to keep 12,000 troops in the field. Although they numbered only 3,200, the mercenary cavalry cost another 30,000 taels. When draft animals and supply carts were added, the monthly cost for a force of around 15,000 was 115,000 taels. It was hoped that this cost could be met with contributions from Jiangxi (70,000), Hubei (20,000), and Jiangsu (25,000) provinces.[130] The rebel commander Lai Wenguang still led an estimated 30,000–40,000 troops, and Zhang Zongyu had around 20,000 under his direct command. Qing forces defeated Lai near Nanyang in late 1866, killing more than a thousand of his men.[131] Zongyu's younger brother, Zhang Zongzhi, was captured and executed, but Qing officials in the field argued that they needed still more troops and horses to hem the rebels in.[132]

By the ninth month of 1866 Li Hongzhang had moved his headquarters to Xuzhou in northwestern Jiangsu. He was wary of moving west with winter coming on, but that autumn witnessed significant riverine warfare as the Qing moved men and supplies west and the Nian forces tried to cut their supply lines. Zeng Guoquan and his subordinates inflicted several defeats on the Nian but proved unable to maneuver them into a decisive battle.[133] Things worsened toward the end of 1866 when Xi'an was besieged, as noted above, in the west and the Qing commander Zhang Shuce fell in battle against Lai Wenguang near De'an. But Zeng Guoquan sent a river force that checked Lai and Ren Zhu, and Liu Mingchuan then defeated the pair at Anlu.[134] Lai and Ren subsequently fled west, only to be caught in a pincer attack set up by Zeng Guoquan. Nonetheless their force eluded capture and killed more than six hundred Qing troops in a follow-up battle.

As Zuo's main force moved north, the Eastern and Western Nian tried to link up. Both Zeng Guoquan and Li Hongzhang were defeated in successive battles, but Zuo urged them to stand fast and steel their resolve.[135] As Liu Songshan fought the Nian around Xi'an, there were numerous battles in the east where Qing artillery inflicted heavy casualties on the rebels. Li Hongzhang moved to Zhoujiakou to oversee operations in the east. Zhang Zongyu was put on the run by Liu Songshan in the second month of 1867, and Liu kept up steady pressure on both the Nian and Dungan forces.[136]

Zeng Guofan expressed concerns about keeping the supply lines to Shaanxi open. He was worried not only about fighting the various rebel groups, but also about the possibility of mutiny should supplies not be delivered. He stressed stepping up the number of gunboats on the rivers and shore patrols and also recommended using steamers as patrol boats, with customs revenues used to defray the costs.[137] In fact the Qing had sent steamers from Jiangnan to the northwest as early as 1865, directing commanders to train locals in riverine defense, so Zeng's request was not out of line.[138] The battle reports from the spring and summer of 1867 indicate that the court followed Zeng's recommendations. The Qing racked up more victories, though the inability to defeat the Nian once and for all bothered the court. Zeng Guoquan's resignation due to "illness" that autumn may have been the result of these pressures from above.[139] The Qing did manage to kill Ren Zhu, though most of his forces simply attached themselves to Lai Wenguang.

In the third month of 1867 Zuo's forces reached De'an in northwest Jiangxi and established defensive positions. The Eastern Nian were stymied at the Han River and forced to withdraw toward Shandong. In the fourth month Liu Songshan smashed the Nian and Hui at Tongzhou, and Liu and Guo Baochang defeated Zhang Zongyu at Chaoyi in the fifth month.[140] Zuo's forces moved into Shaanxi, and he sent troops east to secure Tong Pass and the river routes. But the men had to stop at the pass and rest when disease struck.[141] Bao Chao himself took ill and was ashen faced when Zuo met with him. Zuo was chilled at the sight because he feared Bao's officers lacked his ability to discipline the troops and there could be a mutiny if Bao died.[142] Allaying Zuo's fears somewhat, Gao Liansheng's men entered Shaanxi in the middle of the month. Liu Dian's men entered Shaanxi about a month later. Zuo gathered information via letters exchanged with his commanders as he moved north. He used this intelligence to keep the court off his back, telling them that "the poison of the Nian was already being arrested" by the triumphs of Liu Songshan and others.[143]

CONSIDERING THE MUSLIM THREAT

Upon his arrival at the front, Zuo also addressed the conflict between the Muslims (Hui) and the Han. He discussed the merits of suasion versus pacification and extermination, emphasizing that dynastic loyalty was paramount. "We don't talk of Han and Hui," he wrote, "but only differentiate between the good [subjects] and bandits. If we have time to resolve the disputes so that all can be happy, then peace will prevail."[144] Zuo understood that the Hui wanted to return to their ancestral lands, but he needed to investigate local conditions before implementing a course of action. He promised to "use the awesome might of the army to excise sickness within the Hui populace," adding that those who then wished to submit would be allowed to stay and a place would be found for them in local society. The recalcitrant would be executed, but the submissive would be resettled.[145]

With this statement Zuo established a precedent. Echoing the position repeatedly articulated by the Qing government, Zuo contended that he was not inherently hostile to Muslims. Rather he believed that certain individuals and sects were leading the rest astray. Once these extremists (to use the modern term) were eliminated peace could be restored, to the benefit of all. The emperor followed the same precept: "Han and Hui alike are my subjects.

Bandits should certainly be killed, but the good folk should be spared. When one employs troops, benevolence and righteousness should be used to control them. One should use both extermination and suasion; rely on both awesomeness and pity."[146]

Meanwhile there were the ongoing issues of funding and supplies. Zuo requested supplies from Hunan, Hubei, Henan, and Jiangnan. As the court put pressure on the governors of those provinces to assist Zuo, he also appealed to the Zongli Yamen to consider obtaining a foreign loan, a solution he would revisit later in his career.[147] While some have viewed these efforts as manifesting a general Qing weakness and the decline of centralized authority, they can also be viewed as creative approaches to solving the problems the Qing faced. The court still had to the ability to reallocate resources, and court approval was required for major fiscal decisions.

Around the same time, Zuo sent the Zongli Yamen a list of recommendations for enhancing the nation's strength and improving its security. His ideas were fairly progressive for his time and bely Zuo's reputation in some circles as an antiforeign curmudgeon. With respect to foreign relations, he advocated actual meetings with foreign leaders and sending diplomats to foreign countries. The government should rapidly establish railways and telegraph lines to facilitate internal transit and communications, which would help both the economy and military operations. They should increase steamship production and other areas of industrialization. Education should be diversified and expanded and applied to every sector of life, most notably the military, to create the basis for a strong empire. Zuo pointed to his own success in working with the French to establish the Fuzhou shipyard as a blueprint.[148]

THE FIRST ENCIRCLEMENT FAILS

Zuo initially hoped to keep the Western Nian bottled up in Shaanxi by hemming them in and defending key points, forcing them to split their forces so he could destroy them one by one, but he badly underestimated their mobility. He also wanted to keep them from crossing the Yellow River and moving east, so he divided the provincial border region of Shaanxi, Shanxi, and Henan into three defense commands to be coordinated by Chen Shi. Because Muslim raiders were now using the rivers, Zuo requested the delivery of another forty gunboats to patrol the Yellow River and additional boats to be sent elsewhere.[149] Chen was in command of five to eight thousand infantry bolstered by a fleet of forty to seventy gunboats. Other boats were deployed in Henan to guard approaches to Zhili on the Yellow River.[150] Early in the seventh month of 1867 the forces of Huang Ding, Liu Songshan, and Guo Baochang defeated the Western Nian at Fuping.[151] More victories followed, though the Qing suffered a few setbacks at the hands of mobile Nian ambushers. Shortly thereafter the Qing bested a Muslim force sent from the north to aid the Nian. Zuo now hoped that he had effectively separated the Nian forces and could pick them off one by one. Plus autumn rains would swell the rivers, further hampering rebel movements. He redeployed his units with these thoughts in mind.[152]

The Qing armies assumed defensive positions, but the fighting extended so that the Nian lines stretched over a thousand *li* from north to south, and the Muslim lines stretched over a thousand *li* from east to west. There was no way the Qing could cover that much ground with the barely 50,000 troops in Shaanxi. They did have some success in reducing and capturing certain cities, such as Suide, which was recovered by Liu Songshan.[153] But they had to wait for new mercenary units to arrive and could not always pursue the Nian they had evicted. Oftentimes they would recover one town only to see another fall within days.[154] The court kept appointing new commanders, and Zuo redeployed his forces, but much of Shaanxi remained in a panic. Liu Dian and Gao Liansheng finally managed to secure the southern part of neighboring Shanxi in order to protect Zhili, where the capital lay, as more supplies were rushed in from the coast.[155]

By the end of the ninth month of 1867 the Nian had broken out of Zuo's encirclement in the north. The 16,000 Qing troops that pursued them were met by Muslim allies of the Nian, and a Qing commander was killed in battle. But the following month there were reports that Qing forces recovered Mizhi and Yulin in Shanxi. In the latter city, local militia were credited with driving off rebel forces with cannon fire. Once bases were secured, the Qing sent out search-and-destroy brigades. The arrival of 2,500 gunners and 3,000 horses from Jilin bolstered the Qing force. But despite these successes the Qing were still unable to contain the Nian. Most alarming from the government perspective were reports that the Nian were obtaining large numbers of firearms from their Muslim allies. Thus, despite reports claiming that rebels were being slain by the thousands, the overall strategic situation was unchanged. Indeed in some cases the Nian would be defeated and flee, pursued by the Qing, only to have Muslim forces move in after the government forces left.[156]

Liu Songshan and Guo Baochang recovered Suide, then followed this victory by killing three thousand rebels at Shijiawan, drowning others, and liberating some three thousand captives. The Qing pursued the rebels northwest, driving them toward Mizhi in Shanxi, capturing more towns along the way, until supply issues forced them to break off the pursuit. Another victory at Qishan followed, and Zuo offered timetables to the court for the arrival of additional forces at the front in Shanxi. But the court was concerned, and with good reason, that considerable Nian forces were pushing east and wanted Zuo to relocate to Zhili.[157] The court also wanted training programs stepped up so that new units from Jilin in the northeast could augment the existing field armies. Some of these programs bore fruit when a crack cavalry force from Jilin defeated the Nian in Henan, with the Qing force of 1,200 killing 1,100 Nian rebels and losing just 100 men.[158]

Reports coming in from all theaters claimed Qing victories, alleging thousands of rebels killed and weapons, banners, and false seals of office being recovered. But the boats requested had not yet arrived, and it was impossible for the Qing to protect all the river crossings. The rebels stole boats to cross rivers and overran isolated communities.[159] The court was also alarmed by reports coming out of Xinjiang, where the Muslim leader Yakub Beg's influence was expanding (more on him later). Meanwhile, supported by the court, Zuo was instituting another purge of Gelaohui elements to improve his forces' discipline and combat effectiveness.[160]

Zuo remained committed to rehabilitating local society as the lynchpin of his policy. Following Zeng Guofan, he contended that if local bureaus dedicated to improving conditions in the community were established, then the good and bad could be separated and prosperity restored. This included improving supplies and food for the military forces assigned to protect the localities. But the nature of the current war made this policy difficult to implement because the battlefield was constantly moving. And as winter set in and rivers froze, it was even easier for the rebels to escape and harder for the already thinly stretched Qing forces to garrison so many places.[161]

As his subordinates battled Nian and Muslim forces across Gansu, Shaanxi, and Shanxi, Zuo was ordered to reinforce the river crossings protecting Shanxi. The Nian were still pushing east as the Qing scrambled to contain them.[162] Zuo redeployed some of his forces as the court issued new orders. He reported that his forces had recovered Jizhou and were besieging Weinan. Liu Songshan and Guo Baochang spearheaded the government efforts on land, and Zuo stepped up his patrols on the Yellow River.[163] Zhang Zongyu was defeated repeatedly but eluded capture. And since the Nian's influence was not based in static control of territory and they had a seemingly endless supply of recruits, these victories were not decisive, demonstrating the problem of using metrics such as body counts and control of territory as the standard for success. Through the autumn of 1867 the Qing scored numerous victories and killed thousands of rebels but proved unable to contain the rebels in the west.[164]

Zhang Zongyu reached out to Lai Wenguang, and the two started making new plans. A combined Nian-Muslim force reached Yichuan in early December and entered Shanxi with Liu Songshan and Guo Baochang hot on their heels.[165] The rebels were smashed there, but some were able to use floating bridges to escape across the Yellow River. Liu and Gao subsequently defeated the Nian again, pushing them into Henan. The Nian took several cities and raided widely, terrorizing the local populace as they pushed back north toward the capital.[166] There were supposedly some 14,000 Qing troops in the area, but most were infantry and had difficulty engaging the mounted rebels. Zuo appointed Liu Dian to oversee military affairs in Shaan-Gan as he went east.[167] Zuo's report concluded on a rather shaky note: "With the fortune of Heaven we should be able to clear the eastern routes and drive the enemy back west."[168]

The Qing court was rocked by this news and was ready to dismiss and possibly even execute Zuo, who hastened east through the winter snows as the court called for him and Li Hongzhang to come to the capital's rescue.[169] The Nian split into three groups as they moved east, striking into Henan and Zhili and advancing all the way to Baoding, approximately one hundred miles southwest of Beijing, in early 1868, throwing the capital into a panic.[170] Another thousand troops were brought in from Manchuria, and the capital's firearms divisions were deployed to Zhili. Foreign weapons were sent to Tianjin, and training in their use was accelerated.[171]

Criticism poured in, and the leading provincial officials were impeached. Many officials lamented the nonarrival of relief forces as their cities were raided or besieged. Others scrambled to repair defenses along the anticipated routes of attack.[172] Zuo requested punishment for his failures and was symbolically removed and demoted, although he still led his subordinates in pursuit of the enemy.[173] The court then offered Zuo, Li Hongzhang, and others the chance to redeem themselves.[174] The emperor expressed concern over the lack of intelligence sent back to the court and demanded that the commanders better coordinate their operations. Zuo and Liu Songshan stepped up their pursuit from the west, and Li moved in from the south. Measures were implemented to solidify supply lines and get the soldiers their pay on time. These quickly proved effective, and the Qing turned the tide, intercepting Nian units, driving others back west, and stabilizing the overall situation.[175] Liu defeated the Nian at Zhanggang late in the first month of 1868. The Qing also scored a victory at Qizhou. The Eastern Nian were crushed around Yangzhou, and their formidable leader, Lai Wenguang, was captured in the battle. More than 20,000 were killed and some 10,000 captives freed in the campaign that led up to Lai's defeat.[176] The Western Nian were now isolated. The Qing soon started demobilizing some regulars and converting them to auxiliaries.

Nian who surrendered were divided into three broad groups. The strong were enrolled in the ranks and ordered to kill other bandits in order to redeem themselves. The old and weak were temporarily placed into special divisions until they could be demobilized and sent home. Those who had deserted the Qing to join the Nian were turned over to their former commanding officers (or new Qing ones), who relocated them. Children freed from the bandits' clutches were sent to their homes if possible. If their homes and families could not be found, they were not to be enrolled in the ranks in the common practice whereby officers adopted boys as sons to be servants and raised as soldiers, though there were provisions to create new divisions of these homeless rescued youngsters. The government set up bureaus for the distribution of famine relief, which included allowances for soldiers, who received silver for food and fodder for their mounts. Roads and infrastructure were repaired in the wake of the defeat of the Nian as well.[177]

Zuo himself reached Baoding on February 22, 1868.[178] He wrote a memorandum to the court explaining his plans and outlining the strengths and weaknesses of his forces versus those of the Nian. As he framed it, his strengths lay in infantry and defense. He could deny cavalry resources to the mobile Nian, but he needed to bottle them up as well. Zuo observed that the Nian relied primarily on lances, whereas the Qing employed cannon and small firearms. The Qing could defeat them easily enough if they could maneuver them into terrain that favored superior firepower.[179] He was confident that the Nian could not stand up to a committed assault, but he could not force a decisive battle because he lacked sufficient troops. The key was to steadily tighten the net around them.

Zuo proposed defending the approaches to Beijing and sending out small strike forces, gradually funneling the Nian into killing grounds. More units could come in from Shandong and Henan to reinforce those already in Zhili. He also stressed pushing the Nian toward the rivers. On receiving this report, the court put Zuo in charge of the military affairs of Baoding.[180] He immediately went about replacing ineffective commanders and cleaning up local administration. By the second month of 1868 his plan was bearing fruit as Liu Songshan laid an ambush and captured fifty-four horses in addition to driving the Nian back.[181] Liu Songshan, Guo Baochang, and Xi Chang came in from multiple directions, "sweeping the rebels before them like sheep or rats" and driving them south and east.

Even with primarily infantry forces Zuo's men won battles both big and small, compelling many Nian leaders to submit, breaking the rebels' spirit, and narrowing their options. The Nian leader Zhang Wuhai, a relative of Zhang Zongyu, was wounded in one engagement and subsequently captured and executed by Song Qing in the second month of 1868.[182] Late the next month the Nian suffered a crushing defeat and lost two major commanders, though many rebels escaped south into Henan. Zuo moved his headquarters to Daming, and Li Hongzhang moved his to Kaihua.[183] Militia were organized across Zhili to deter future incursions.[184] The court also instructed Zuo to garrison key points along the mountain roads leading west into Shanxi.

COOPERATING WITH LI HONGZHANG

The court directed Zuo and Li to hold the Grand Canal, which provided grain for the capital, at all costs. The wily Nian Zhang Zongyu slipped through the Qing cordon, however, and advanced toward Tianjin in late May 1868. But the city was well defended owing to improvements made in the wake of the *Arrow* War, and Zhang was forced back into Shandong.[185] Meanwhile, Zuo sent men to secure the west bank of the Grand Canal. Qing forces arrayed against the Nian now numbered more than 100,000, and the court gave Zuo and Li a one-month ultimatum to crush the rebellion.[186] Zuo moved his headquarters to Dingzhou and assumed oversight of the river defenses of Henan. But he had only one hundred cavalry and five thousand infantry under his direct command, so he could not send out effective offensive units. It fell on Li Hongzhang to engage the Nian units that had already crossed the Yellow River to head east.[187] When the two commanders failed to meet the court's rather unrealistic timetable, the court dispatched the Manchu commander Duxinga into the field to coordinate the armies, countering an earlier decision to refrain from sending out a member of the Manchu aristocracy to oversee the Han commanders.[188] Zuo complained about this appointment, saying having too many commanders and overlapping jurisdictions was hindering operations rather than helping them.[189] The Nian tried to pummel their way out as Zuo and Li moved to cut their supply lines, in effect implementing the earlier containment plan designed by Zeng Guofan.

Learning from their experience battling the Taipings, the Qing commanders put gunboats on the rivers and even sought to redirect part of the Yellow River temporarily to hamper rebel movements.[190] Liu Songshan blasted through a Nian ambush on the Hutuo River, and the Qing repositioned units to guard the north bank of the river and prevent future incursions into Zhili.[191]

Liu smashed through more than twenty Nian forts and killed eight hundred rebels in a battle not far from Wuqiao, where Zuo Zongtang was stationed.[192] Zhang Yao and Song Qing were also put in command of newly reorganized armies. Further implementing their new plans for national defense, in the fifth month of 1868 the Qing established a riverine navy for the Yangzi with command posts at Yuezhou, Hanyang, Hukou, and Guazhou.[193] It would soon come under the command of Peng Yulin.

Zuo also turned the tables on the Nian by employing locals to rebuild and occupy the forts the Qing forces captured from the Nian. As the Qing captured Nian strongholds and seized control of the waterways, the technological balance tipped increasingly in the government's favor. The Qing recovered tens of thousands of guns from the Nian that were used to great effect against them. They also had several dozen gunboats plying the rivers by 1868.[194] As the Qing forces built momentum, killing rebels by the thousands, the court issued proclamations praising the efforts of Zuo and Li in "extending the awe" of the state.[195] Zuo also had to discipline certain commanders, such as Chen Guorui (1837–1883), who was charged with arrogance and insubordination.[196]

Hampered by rainy weather in the spring and summer of 1868, the Nian lost the advantage of mobility. Zhang Zongyu was constantly on the run, scurrying from Shandong to Henan to Jiangsu and back again. In one desperate battle the rebels resorted to cutting fresh bamboo stalks to use as lances because they had run out of weapons, but they fled before even trying to fight.[197] Zuo personally commanded a Qing victory over the Nian at Wulongdu on April 13. By the end of the month, more Nian leaders had been captured and Zhang Zongyu had fled to Wuqiao in Shandong. He kept heading east, but hundreds of other commanders were seeking amnesty and submitting. Zhang tried to menace Tianjin but was deterred by Guo Songlin, who avenged an earlier defeat by the Nian.[198] Even as this was taking place the court issued another directive to bring the campaign to a speedy conclusion. The warfare was disrupting the peasants and harming agriculture, and there were reports of Qing soldiers abusing locals.[199]

The Qing forces won battle after battle. They defeated the rebels at Zhangwei in April. Guo Baochang was wounded in pursuit of Zhang Zongyu but was rescued by Liu Songshan.[200] In mid-May, Liu Songshan, Zhang Yao, and others defeated the Nian at Pingyuan in central Shandong.[201] Government forces chased the rebels in and out of Shandong through the early summer, with the scope of Nian operations steadily decreasing as they fell by the hundreds in skirmish after skirmish. The Qing sent steamers to defend Tianjin and sketched out further plans for coastal defense. Liu Mingchuan, recently recalled from sick leave, clashed with Li Hongzhang over matters of strategy, forcing Zeng Guofan to step in. The Qing finally enacted a comprehensive plan for defending the Grand Canal, and it worked.[202] Zhang Zongyu approached the canal but was driven back. Zhang Yao and Liu Songshan then defeated the rebels at Lijiacun. Through June and into July, Zuo's subordinates won several more battles. Guo Songlin smashed Nian forces at Linyi, Binzhou, and Yangxin in midsummer.[203] They nearly captured Zhang Zongyu at one point, but he escaped into a downpour. The Qing's superior firepower was proving decisive, but the Nian were hard to catch, sometimes traversing two hundred *li* in a single day.

In the meantime, Li Hongzhang had built up an impressive array of moats, ditches, and walls around Shandong to deny resources to the Nian. The rebels roamed aimlessly, slowly starving, as Qing units collaborated with local militia forces. Guo Songlin now took the point position, linking up with forces under Zuo's command. Some rebels escaped into Zhili, only to be driven back into Henan and then forced into Shandong again. In a report to the throne Zuo noted that he and Li differed in their approaches, as Li favored defense over offense and Zuo wanted to pursue both options simultaneously to get faster results. The court let it be known that they were fed up with the petty jurisdictional squabbles of the field commanders and instructed Zuo and Li to put national concerns above their own differences.[204]

Fighting continued to be fierce along the Grand Canal, and the large distances involved meant there were still holes in the Qing defense cordon. When Zuo complained that he had just 5,000 men to hold one 160-*li* stretch of terrain, the court was unimpressed and ordered Zuo and Li to step up their offensive operations, urging Li in particular to be more aggressive. This prompted an increase in search-and-destroy missions with Liu Songshan again at the forefront, usually accompanied by his dashing nephew, Liu Jintang. Zuo reinforced the Grand Canal, and Duxinga also commanded offensive operations. A string of victory reports rolled in, but Zhang Zongyu remained at large, much to the annoyance of the court.[205] But the rebels who did surrender presented a problem. Some were enrolled directly into Qing armies, but many were not in fighting shape and lacked even basic weapons. They had to be demobilized and resettled, no easy task given the local conditions.

On the positive side, the Western Nian were finally defeated, and the Qing could go forward with establishing supply depots and sending troops west to deal with the Muslim rebels. In late July, with Guo Songlin hot on his trail, Zhang Zongyu was repulsed when his force tried to enter a peasant stockade. In a big battle near Shanghe City the Qing killed some two to three thousand of a rebel force estimated at five thousand and freed more than a thousand prisoners. Zhang Zongyu was wounded and thrown from his mount in a hail of bullets but escaped with a few dozen followers.[206] Liu Songshan then smashed other Nian forces around Wuqiao and obtained the surrender of hundreds in subsequent engagements. As more and more rebels capitulated, Zhang Zongyu's remaining followers were mostly blood relatives.[207]

Now that steamboats patrolled the rain-swollen rivers, the Nian were no longer able to rely on waterways for transport. The flooding worsened, and water covered much of the region to a depth of two to three feet, hampering movements by foot or horse. Li Hongzhang repositioned his forces and let Liu Mingchuan and Guo Songlin finish the job. They engaged Zhang's forces, such as they were, at Haihe (Boping), Shandong, along the Grand Canal on August 16, 1868. Song Qing and Zhang Yao were also there, and they crushed the rebels in a pincer.[208] Zhang fled north with a few dozen cavalry, who finally ditched their horses and tried to escape on foot by diving into the canal. Zhang Zongyu was presumed drowned, though his corpse was never recovered. His son was captured alive.[209] Some seven thousand rebels were captured in the course of this final campaign, and four thousand of them were enrolled directly in the armies of Liu Songshan and others.[210] A few dozen other Nian adherents fled south, pursued by Liu Mingchuan.

In its victory proclamation the court praised the united efforts of its appointed officials, especially Li Hongzhang and Zuo Zongtang. Zuo was promoted to Grand Guardian of the Heir Apparent for his efforts.[211] He asked to retire, citing illness, but the court ordered him to go straight back to Shaanxi to deal with the Muslim rebels. Little did he know that this task would occupy him for the next twelve years.

Before heading west, Zuo was summoned to a court audience with Emperor Tongzhi, though the proceedings were dominated by the powerful dowagers, Cixi and Ci'an.[212] They talked about demobilization and the reassignment of the troops that had battled the Nian, but the primary topic was the ongoing Muslim revolt in Shaan-Gan, which Zuo maintained would take around five years to quell.[213] Zuo also expressed his concern about supplies. He estimated that one thousand troops were costing six thousand cash per month in supplies, and the costs for his comparatively elite Hunan Army were even higher. Then there were the costs for horses and fodder. It was exceedingly difficult to get supplies from multiple sources, so Zuo needed the backing of the court.[214] He also wanted to know exactly what his predecessors in the northwest had been doing and why they had failed so miserably. Equipped with this knowledge, Zuo sketched out an ambitious new battle plan.[215] Liu Songshan was to be his major military commander, and many other experienced longtime associates of Zuo would join his retinue. The resulting campaign would prove arduous and would have repercussions that are still being felt today.

Map 4. Dungan Rebellion in Shaanxi and Gansu

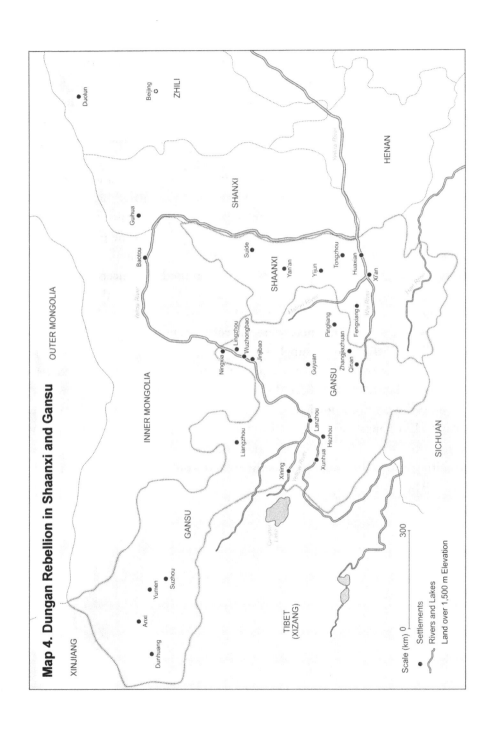

XINJIANG

OUTER MONGOLIA

INNER MONGOLIA

GANSU

SHANXI

ZHILI

HENAN

SHAANXI

GANSU

SICHUAN

TIBET
(XIZANG)

Duolun

Beijing

Guihua

Baotou

Suide

Yan'an

Yijun

Tongzhou

Huaxian

Xi'an

Lingzhou

Wuzhongbao

Jinjibao

Ningxia

Pingliang

Zhangjiazhuan

Fengxiang

Guyuan

Qinan

Liangzhou

Lanzhou

Hezhou

Xunhua

Xining

Yumen

Suzhou

Anxi

Dunhuang

Yellow River

Yellow River

Fenhe River

Malian River

Wei River

Tao River

Yellow River

Qinghai Lake

Scale (km)   0   300

• Settlements

Rivers and Lakes

Land over 1,500 m Elevation

5

"THERE ARE ONLY GOOD AND BAD PEOPLE"

SUPPRESSING THE DUNGAN REBELLION

There is no distinction between Han and Hui; there are only good and bad people.
—Zuo Zongtang

It will be recalled that Zuo's appointment as governor-general of Shaanxi and Gansu (Shaan-Gan) was for the expressed purpose of quelling the Dungan (Muslim) uprising, though the Nian insurgency had necessitated a temporary redirection of his energies. In his court audience Zuo was pressed to act swiftly to bring the Muslim rebels to heel, but he warned the dowagers that the situation was complicated and he did not expect to bring the matter to a conclusion in less than five years. Other officials present thought it might take even longer.[1] Zuo recognized that local resources alone would be insufficient for the task. "The armies of Gansu were unable to protect the people but contrarily misled them," he pointed out. "As for the Gansu officials, they were unable to govern the people and on the contrary, incited the people to chaos."[2] With respect to the local militia, Zuo said, "They resemble troops, but they are not troops. They look brave, but they are not braves. They resemble militia, but are not militia."[3] His troops would be coming from all over the empire. Divided as they were into separate units, command and control would not be easy. Plus command structures and organization differed in Central Asia. Finally, many southern troops were unused to conditions in the northwest, and Zuo was concerned about their ability to operate effectively.

While not pleased at Zuo's assessment, the dowagers understood that Zuo was known for his frank and honest opinions and believed he could be counted on to devote his full energies to the task at hand. Supply was going to be a serious concern. The northwest had traditionally relied on subsidies from Jiangsu and Zhejiang, but these areas were still recovering from the Taiping Rebellion. Shaanxi and Gansu were already operating at a yearly shortfall of 5 million taels, and the coming campaign would add to this. Many resources needed by the army, most notably saltpeter, had to be imported as well because local sources were exhausted.[4] Rations were in arrears, and the advancing armies left starving soldiers in their wake. The government printed more paper money and got it to the soldiers to increase their purchasing power, but the program was not very effective, and inflation rates tended not to favor the soldiers.[5] These problems drove troops to desert and defect to the rebel side, as we shall see below.

Zuo was keenly aware of these problems, and his plans took them into account as he prioritized logistics and supply in his usual fashion. Once he was on the job in the northwest, Zuo observed, "Managing supplies is more difficult than managing the army and managing food in more difficult than managing [other] supplies, but hardest of all is transporting grain." He continued,

When it comes to employing troops in the northwest, grain and transportation are paramount while also the most difficult and managing them takes up three quarters of my time. Even bringing in supplies from the other provinces accounts for barely half our needs. But grain must be transported hundreds or thousands of *li* from outside and one must use camels and mules and donkey carts that have to go in advance of the army and still many problems can arise and one must traverse [terrain] without people or cooking fires, without water or grass, so that one's energy is sapped and upon arrival about half [the men] are already dead. So you cannot use a large force and you must be swift in fixing your plan of operations.[6]

Although Zuo requested 3.5 million taels of silver per year for military operations in the northwest, plus more funds for rehabilitation afterward, the Ministry of Revenue initially gave him just 1 million.[7] He pushed the idea of obtaining foreign loans to subsidize his operations and would eventually take out five loans totaling some 13,700,000 taels, not to mention cutting deals with the Russians to procure cheap grain. As was typical in late Qing reform efforts, Zuo was greatly aided by his extensive network of contacts, as he had banking and foreign connections in Shanghai and elsewhere.[8]

Zuo returned to the west after his imperial audience, and the Qing armies reached Xi'an in the tenth month of 1868. At the time it was estimated that there were perhaps 300,000 rebels altogether in Shaanxi and Gansu. The most prominent leaders were the Muslim Ma Hualong, based at Fort Jinji (Jinjibao) in Gansu, and Bai Yanhu, who operated in southwestern Shaanxi province and was active in the Xi'an area as well.

THE RELIGIOUS AND POLITICAL BACKGROUND

Islam has a long history in China. Muslims arrived soon after the death of the Prophet during the Tang dynasty (618–907), traveling along the famed Silk Road in this cosmopolitan era. As might be expected, most Muslims settled in the northwest and Central Asia, along the trade routes that provided access to goods from the Middle East and facilitated the practice of the hajj by those who could afford it.[9] By the Qing era, approximately 27.5 percent of the population in the northwest were Muslims, though the figure was much higher in some areas. Previous dynasties had exerted little direct administrative control over Central Asia, but that would change in the Qing era (see chapter 6).

In the Qing period most Chinese Muslims practiced Sunni Hanafi Islam, known as Gedimu (Qadim) or Old Teachings (*laojiao*), also known as Khufiyya/Khafiyya, or Old Sect. The Old Teachings emphasized active participation in society, veneration of saints, seeking wisdom at tombs, and silent dhikr, or remembrance; thus, its adherents were sometimes called "the Silent Ones." They tended to concentrate in villages centered on religious practices and were therefore easy for Qing officials to identify and track. With respect to the Old Teachings, each locality tended to have religious and political leaders.

Mosque-dominated villages tended to exclude outsiders. And even in larger cities Muslims tended to keep to themselves and live in designated districts, highlighting their distinctions from the Han. The Mongols, generally being Buddhist, were often hostile to Muslims, for reasons of trade in addition to faith. These underlying religious tensions were exacerbated by natural disasters and tax increases levied to subsidize military efforts in other regions of the empire.[10]

In the seventeenth and eighteenth centuries the Naqshbandi Sunni order of Sufism, which had originated in Yemen, made its way along the trade routes to Central Asia and became known as the New Sect, or Jahriyya. The New Sect emphasized vocalization, wearing shoes at funerals, and a particular style of beards and mustaches. They disapproved of the veneration of saints at tombs, though they apparently had no problem recognizing the inherited charisma of traveling religious figures and their descendants.[11] The Chinese branch was founded in the 1760s by Ma Mingxin, a native of Lanzhou. In the twenty-six years prior to founding his sect, Ma traveled to Bukhara and possibly Samarkand and even Yemen.[12] Sufis in Central Asia, as elsewhere, posed as shamans of a sort, using magic and the curing of illnesses to attract followers and gain recognition as saints. These wandering dervishes had the charisma to unite groups and spread their teachings, especially in the absence of a strong central political or religious authority.[13] Their mobility, compared with practitioners of the Old Teachings, made them more threatening in the eyes of a state ever more sensitive to the potential for dissent among its multiethnic populace. Some saints' tombs became holy sites or shrines associated with curing diseases. Sufi brotherhoods also provided protection and other benefits for their members.[14] Factions would coalesce around khojas, or religious leaders, and these groups would sometimes form alliances with other political or military groups and be drawn into wider conflicts. In the era under consideration, the primary early rebel leader, Ma Hualong, was identified with the New Teachings.[15]

Much like other Muslim leaders in the region, Ma Hualong kept his feet in multiple worlds, purchasing a Qing military title but also telling fortunes, curing illnesses, and restoring fertility for the barren. Ma received tribute and gifts from adherents as far away as Yunnan province, which lends some credence to the notion that his movement was connected to that of Du Wenxiu, though most modern scholars deny such links.[16]

The reasons for the outbreak of these rebellions thus involved a complex amalgamation of long-term and more immediate triggers and grievances. The Qing had first conquered the vast regions of Central Asia in the eighteenth century, effectively ending the threat steppe nomads posed to sedentary China-based empires. And though they now controlled territory vaster than any government in Chinese history, the Qing lacked the manpower to properly administer these far-flung regions. They also had little interest in local governance or resources beyond extracting some tribute and taxes, and their military presence was fairly light, just enough to maintain order in the best of times. For the most part the Qing governed indirectly, appointing Manchu and Mongol overlords to administer vast tracts of territory that were locally managed by an array of officials and figures, most of whom were Muslims and of different ethnic groups. As might be expected, there was ample opportunity for graft and corruption among the ruling stratum, many of whom were regarded as Qing collaborators.[17] Many of the underlings of the appointed leaders were relatives with no practical government experience who saw the posts as simply a means for enriching themselves. Furthermore, because these posts were not especially desirable, people often bribed their way out of them, leaving them to less well connected and sometimes even more unscrupulous officials. One commander of the city of Urumqi stayed in his position for seven years, during which he allegedly never set foot in the countryside and amassed a personal fortune of some 3 million taels.[18] Lower-ranking officials were accused of ravaging Muslim women and forcibly taking them as wives or concubines.[19]

Additionally, and more relevant for the situation in Shaanxi and Gansu provinces, the steady population growth of the high Qing era had encouraged Han Chinese settlers to move to these areas in hopes of starting fresh or improving their lot. Modern studies suggest that by the late Qing there were some eight hundred mosques in Shaanxi, and Muslims made up one-third of the total population, although Han immigration was changing the equation.[20] Though the groups sometimes lived amicably, confrontations between these immigrants and local Muslims, known as Hui or Dungans in the sources, were increasing, even though some modern authors describe the Hui as among the most Sinicized of the non-Han peoples.[21] But because they maintained a strong sense of identity, which included the avoidance of eating pork, a staple of the Chinese diet, the Hui were seen as "fierce, assertive, and combative" by the Han Chinese. According to modern oral histories conducted in the 1950s, Han parents used threats of Muslim boogeymen to scare their children into good behavior, saying things like "Be good or the Hui will come to get you!"[22] David Atwill notes that the "Han antagonism towards the Hui in the nineteenth century was based more on assumptions of behaviors or customs and specific practices (violence, cross-border trading and the like) than on religion."[23]

As disputes increased, local investigators were often charged with favoring one group another, though usually the non-Muslims. There were frequent vendettas between the sides and even massacres. It was suggested that Han officials used the government directive to create militia to guard against the Nian as a pretext for assembling gangs to massacre Muslims.[24] The Muslims returned the favor in a series of incidents in 1862–1866. When Ma Wenlu captured the city of Suzhou in 1865, for example, only 1,100 old and weak people out of an estimated 30,000 in the city survived his massacre. In 1866 dozens of Han dwelling in the city of Taozhou were slaughtered by Muslim rebels.[25] This same pattern was evident in the lead-up to the Panthay Revolt in Yunnan (1856–1873).[26] But in the northwest, massacres were perpetrated by both groups, so the Hui can hardly be considered blameless. As tensions there rose, the Qing government was understandably preoccupied with the massive rebellions in the interior and the rising challenge of the Western imperialist powers, which included the "Great Game" machinations of the Russians and British in Central Asia. It needed only a single spark to set off the powder keg and engulf the entire region in a conflagration.

THE EARLY STAGES OF THE DUNGAN REBELLION

As in many such events, the incident that triggered the Dungan Rebellion was in itself rather minor. Considered within the broader context outlined above, however, it is easy to see how this event quickly escalated into outright rebellion. While specific details vary according to the source, it seems that in the town of Huazhou some Muslims were accused of cutting bamboo trees without permission to make poles to sell.[27] Some versions of the story allege that the poles were to be used to make spears to attack Han. Led by an official named Mei Jintang, a Han mob confronted them, burned down their village, and massacred forty-five Muslim merchants. Seven Han soldiers and eight Muslim troops were also slain.[28] This provoked reprisals, and rumors soon circulated that there would be a massacre of all Muslims in Shaanxi. Some Hui fled into the wilderness to escape, but with nothing to survive on, they formed bands for mutual survival and protection. These bands got swept up in the moment and began participating in the violence.[29]

A Han version of events paints the killing as preemptive: "The Hui are about to revolt so they must be cleansed first." Some contemporary officials claimed that "even though the Han cannot be said to blameless, in reality the crime of the rebellion rests with the wicked Hui."[30] The situation became even more convoluted when another rumor maintained that the Qing were going after everyone, assembling an army to "first cleanse the Hui bandits, then cleanse the Han" (*xian xi huifei, hou xi hanren*), prompting both groups to accelerate militia formation for self-defense. A modern source places the blame squarely on the militia, concluding that "the militia drew the people into revolt and then the Han spurred the Muslims to rebel."[31] Zuo himself placed the blame on incompetent local officials who stoked the violence rather than defusing it. "If the governing officials had been competent," Zuo said, "then the chaos could have been quelled."[32]

Now that it was paying attention, the Qing court learned that there had been other disturbances the previous fall. A modern informant told researchers that the uprising stemmed from Hui sheep grazing in Han fields. The case went to court, and when the official ruled in favor of the Han, the Muslims revolted. Others claim the immediate dispute was connected to melon prices. Still another local history asserts that Han digging a well found hidden weapons, which they presumed were buried there by Hui plotting a revolt.[33] Similar stories have emerged from other locations in Shaanxi, such as one from Zhouzhi County that notes the presence of Hui bandits ransacking villages and temples, prompting the Han to gather in forts and stockades for self-defense.[34] Given the volatility of the situation, it is likely that unaffiliated petty bandits took advantage of the existing tensions to enrich themselves, much as modern looters do when social unrest or natural disasters afford them the opportunity. In fact, Zhouzhi would later become a center of Nian activity until the rebels were eradicated by Liu Songshan and Guo Baochang.[35]

In any event, the Ministries of War and Revenue understood the rising threat. Among other things, they called for the creation of *tuanlian* (militia) by both Han and Hui groups.[36] But this only intensified the processes of local militarization already underway and fueled the fire, as evidenced by the response to the Qing bolstering defenses around Hezhou, which would become a hot spot in the resulting Dungan Rebellion.[37] In fact, Gansu and Shanxi residents were among the only groups allowed to legally own firearms under the Qing Code, explicitly because these regions were prone to ethnic conflicts.[38] As historian Lei Duan observes, "The diffusion of firearms in local society thus not only deteriorated social and political stability in the late Qing, but also spurred more ordinary people to pursue comparable or more powerful weapons for self-defense. Village elites, too, who had enhanced their status through the holding of degrees, started exercising their power through the procurement of guns in their functions in local defense."[39]

The violence spread across the region, and some officials were cashiered for dereliction of duty in not stopping it. The Qing authorities hoped that a show of force could overawe the rebels and restore order. But rebel groups were already digging ditches, reinforcing stockades and blockhouses, and taking other measures to counter Qing relief columns.[40] This provoked more aggressive reprisals. As killings increased by the day, local officials were confronted with a refugee crisis. Entire Hui villages were razed by Han gangs, and large forces of mounted Hui bandits roamed and looted the countryside. The central government earmarked more troops and supplies to restore order, including sending Manchu troops from Heilongjiang. But before they arrived more Han villages were torched by Hui, prompting government officials to highlight the supposed savagery of the Hui, comparing them to dogs and sheep who understood awesomeness (*wei*) but not virtue (*de*) and might require overwhelming force to compel them to submit. Nonetheless referencing the ongoing crisis in Yunnan with the Hui, some Qing officials still hoped a more conciliatory approach might work (*fulun yi an qi xin*).[41] They also noted that this region was isolated and rugged, making it difficult to move troops and supplies, so a policy of suasion might be best at this juncture.[42]

When persuasion failed, the government responded by sending more force. One report noted, "The poison of the evil Muslims in spreading so that now the good Muslims are [also] terrified." It continued ominously, "If we are not able to soothe them, then we must punish them." But the Qing still lacked a workable plan, and it was important to distinguish the good from the bad Muslims.[43] This report stressed that it was unfortunate that a few traitors had stirred up things so badly. Yingqi was distressed that extra troops had not yet arrived and pressed the court for aid. For their part, while acknowledging that the Han had also played a role in exacerbating tensions, the court noted that those who refused its directives would be severely punished.[44]

Reports from the front continued to roll in chronicling widespread Hui looting and pillaging that resulted in many Han deaths. It seemed that the Qing were under siege everywhere. There were also reports of isolated Qing forts and garrisons holding out, and special attention was drawn to the efficacy of Qing artillery. The fact that the rebels also possessed a fair amount of firepower attests to the level of militarization in the region. As Qing forces moved through Tong Pass and advanced from Ningxia, there was talk of sending a trusted Muslim official to the front to open negotiations, but it was admitted that even Hui officials would have difficulty curtailing the violence. More than two hundred isolated towns and hamlets were imperiled, and there was no place for refugees to flee, as fires were literally and figuratively erupting all around and roads and water transportation nodes were severed.[45]

EFFORTS AT CONTAINMENT

Over the next six years, Shaanxi and Gansu were wracked by rebellion as control oscillated between rebel and government forces. The court was preoccupied by the more serious Taiping and Nian uprisings in the heartland as well as hamstrung by the need to address the ongoing Muslim unrest in the southwest and Central Asia, meaning their resources were seriously overstretched.

Nevertheless, throughout these years they threw commanders, troops, and financial resources at the Dungan rebels. While the results were certainly mixed, the Qing realized their overriding goal of containment, albeit with significant local costs.[46] Indeed, the court was well aware of the rumors about "cleansing the Hui" and had even helped stoke them. Actions and reactions in the field developed their own self-fulfilling logic. When new armies arrived, some Han thought they were there to help cleanse the Hui. As a result, many Hui were terrified, and even those who had formerly been neutral or even pro-Qing joined the rebels in order to survive.[47] The court reiterated its neutrality, stating, "His Majesty's grace only distinguishes between good and bad; not between Han and Hui."[48]

The general state of affairs precluded easy solutions. The well-armed rebels hunkered down in fortified positions that were exceedingly difficult to capture, and assaults resulted in heavy casualties. When positions were finally taken, the government forces were in no mood for lenience, and massacres often resulted. And there were also cases of false surrender. Qing commanders brought larger forces, and since battle rewards hinged on concrete metrics of success like body counts, the excesses continued. Larger forces required more supplies from other provinces. And the endemic warfare, coupled with the winter weather, put greater stress on the local economy, making the rebels more desperate. Disease swept through the Qing troops at all levels. The Manchu commander Duolonga complained about supply problems as well, claiming he had received just one month's worth of supplies over the previous five months. This prompted an increase in riverine patrols and a new effort to negotiate with some rebel leaders.[49] The court ordered the shipment of additional supplies and the dispatch of more Mongol auxiliaries.

The mounting Qing triumphs sparked offers to surrender. Qing officials remained dubious, but when the old, the weak, and women and children came forth, the officials considered making provisions for "good Hui."[50] But the capture of Lingzhou, south of Ningxia, by Ma Hualong and his allies, strengthening their hold on Jinjibao, belied any apparent softening. Ma allegedly killed more than 100,000 people when he took Lingzhou and assumed the title of grand marshal.[51] One official accused the Muslims of perfidy, saying they "overtly feigned submission but inwardly plotted rebellion."[52] The Qing struck back with ferocity, killing some 20,000 rebels in a series of battles as they used heavy artillery to recapture areas around Jingzhou.[53] But this, coupled with other Qing excesses near Ningxia, simply drove more of the formerly neutral Hui to the rebel side as Ma Hualong stepped up his activities around Lingzhou.

While officials continued to submit plans for recovering the region, they were well aware of the devastation caused by the ongoing conflict. It was estimated that more than a million *mu* of arable land had either fallen into rebel hands or been abandoned. Officials were dispatched to assess the damage caused so far and make new assessments for tax rolls after order was restored. They were also instructed to determine if military farming, often proposed as a solution to supplying troops, was a viable option. Significantly, officials also discussed relocation and segregation plans for restoring local order and prosperity after the fighting ended.[54]

As fighting raged across the region, Ma Hualong tightened his hold on Jinjibao and Lingzhou. The Qing debated various courses of attack but were daunted by the scope of the uprising; there were simply too many fires to put out. Harrowing accounts of Qing reverses and martyrdoms trickled in along with reports of victories, and finger-pointing ensued as officials sought to escape blame. The Qing focused on establishing supply lines by setting up depots. They also issued proclamations encouraging locals to stand pat and defend their areas, promising help from multiple quarters.[55] But this just seemed to encourage more violence between Han and Hui militia, too often resulting in massacres that escalated existing tensions.[56]

The Qing were in an enormously difficult position. The region was isolated, with few roads and waterways to bring the needed troops and supplies to the front. There was a vast territory to cover, and the Qing lacked the manpower even to garrison key chokepoints.[57] In the rugged mountain environment it was easy for rebels to slip through holes in the attackers' lines. The fighting itself was fierce, and the rebels were well armed and experienced. They inflicted heavy casualties, and the Qing were often forced to await reinforcements before pressing any campaigns. As had been the case with the

Nian, the enemy was mobile and easily blended in with local populations. The fluid situation made it difficult to direct the campaign from Xi'an. The supreme commander needed to be closer to the action. There was also the fact that the court was overeager for positive results and inclined to shuffle appointments and responsibilities, so a given commander seldom had enough time to formulate and execute a plan.[58]

THE STRUGGLE FOR SHAAN-GAN INTENSIFIES

The spring of 1865 witnessed more of the same, with Qing victories countered by scattered defeats in Shaanxi and Gansu and ever more concerning news from Xinjiang. Manas, Turfan, and other important trade cities fell because there were not enough Qing troops in the region to guard them and distances were too great to relieve besieged towns. Even Mongol troops had been forced to flee in some places. As the court made its usual appointments and issued sweeping calls for concerted action, reports detailed just how fast matters were spiraling out of control. The rebels attacked seemingly everywhere. The attacks were uncoordinated, however, and in at least a few places the Qing defenses were holding, though food and ammunition stores were being swiftly depleted.[59] Even worse, the clearer it became that the Qing relief forces could not arrive in a timely fashion, the faster the uprisings spread.

It was against this backdrop that Yang Yuebin of Hunan was named governor-general of Shaan-Gan. The reader may recall Yang's role in creating the riverine navy that battled the Taipings in the 1850s. Coming to the theater from Jiangxi, Yang was struck by the stark landscape, which was "cracked dry and red for more than 1000 *li*."[60] Upon his appointment, Yang received a prescient assessment of local conditions from Liu Rong. Liu listed several key problems:

- Officers chased the enemy around aimlessly and reported exaggerated victories.
- Officers lied about battalion size in order to get more supplies and/or indiscriminately took everyone into their ranks. Some of these thugs preyed on the locals.

- Too many officials accepted bribes in exchange for recommendations for promotion.
- Troops often shook down locals for military "contributions."
- Poor leadership was amplified by the problem of overlapping jurisdictions and responsibilities.[61]

Qing troops were numerous on paper but could not fight, whereas the Muslims were forging alliances both with one another and with local bandits, including Yakub Beg in Central Asia.

There was also the issue of prioritizing different theaters of war. The Dungan Rebellion remained less important than the Nian in the eyes of the court. Heavy cannons were held back in Zhili to defend river approaches to the capital. A variety of firearms of different calibers were requisitioned for use in the northwest, however,[62] and these helped the Qing to capture rebel redoubts across Shaanxi and Gansu, even though the bases of Ningxia and Jinjibao held out.[63] Gunpowder supplies were deemed especially important, and new orders were requisitioned from Shanxi and Henan.[64] Seeking to emulate the successful tactics used against the Taipings, the government forces tried to improve their coordination with local militia, using the latter to garrison key points and protect supply depots, freeing up regular troops for search-and-destroy operations and the prosecution of sieges.[65] Key to Qing efforts was keeping their supply lines open and foiling efforts by rebel groups to support one another.

Some efforts were still made to smooth over Han-Hui disputes. One official likened their differences to those in a marriage. Problems might arise, but they could be dealt with.[66] But it was nevertheless clear that the current scenario was emboldening the Hui to expand their operations, so extermination was more likely to succeed in the long run. The problem was finding a way to hold out until the Qing could bring their full force to bear against the rebels, and that included bringing experienced troops to the front and defining a clear policy. It was believed that if the roots of the rebellion at Ningxia, Lingzhou, and Jinjibao were pulled out, the rebel movement would wither and die.[67] These assessments were valid, but it would take a few more years before the Qing could send its best troops and commanders to deal with the rebellion, and in that interim the rebels gained influence and experience. Nevertheless, the ability of the Qing to maintain a foothold in these areas is noteworthy, even if it was partly because the various rebel leaders did not coordinate their activities in the pursuit of a central goal.

The court continued to receive allegations of indiscriminate killing of Hui by the Qing forces and reiterated that Hui who peacefully returned to their former occupations would be spared. Moreover, "cleansing operations" were strictly prohibited, and troops were ordered not to loot, burn, or pillage, on the possible penalty of death.[68] The Qing tried to convince loyal Hui to create militia to help restore local order. They considered various approaches to distinguish the good Hui from the bad, such as adopting registration cards. And they were leery of sending Han officials back into these areas lest they trigger more violence.[69] Indeed there was considerable concern on the part of the central authorities that the officials in the provinces were unable to properly coordinate operations, as evidenced by the mutinies and ongoing supply woes. These concerns were what prompted the court to finally appoint Zuo Zongtang, because those weaknesses were precisely Zuo's strengths.[70]

The court meanwhile was busy funding and coordinating the campaign. In true bureaucratic fashion, gallons of ink were spilled putting forth plans for sending supplies and collecting campaign funds. Officials were appointed to staff every level of the logistics hierarchy. Various ways to sell offices in Sichuan and other provinces were explored.[71] The throne pressured the interior provinces to meet their obligations.[72] Li Hongzhang was pressed for the delivery of 40,000 taels he had pledged, and there were delinquent orders from Hunan.[73] The court also looked for more saltpeter, tapping Tianjin as one source. Rising grain prices and transportation costs, not to mention the logistical challenges of getting camels, carts, and the like all the way to further complicated Qing calculations.[74]

TRYING TO STABILIZE THE EAST

Ningxia surrendered to the Qing in late January 1866.[75] Mutushan reported that the leader in Ningxia, Ma Wenxuan, had climbed down the city wall using a rope to personally open talks. The Qing sent in civil and military officials to assume control of the city and the weapons, including firearms of all sizes, the rebels surrendered. Eleven Hui ringleaders were executed, but the rest were spared.[76] When the army entered, however, rumors spread that the troops were going to massacre the inhabitants and torch the city. The people became restless, and the army withdrew to allay their fears, only to return and run amok, killing thousands and plundering much wealth, undermining the credibility of the state in the process. The court was furious on hearing this news and dispatched an official to investigate. The Qing soldiers tried to claim that the Muslims were plotting treason and had not really surrendered. Some claimed Duxinga ordered the massacre because he suspected that the Muslims were still hiding weapons in their homes, but the court was unconvinced.[77] Nonetheless, they increased Mutushan's authority because he was credited with punishing the instigators of the slaughter.[78]

When Duxinga and Mutushan clashed over subsequent policy, Duxinga was dismissed and transferred to Manchuria. With the bellicose Duxinga out of the picture, Mutushan implemented the appeasement policy he preferred (see chapter 4).[79] Mutushan negotiated a deal with Ma Hualong in May 1866 whereby Ma turned over twenty-six cannons, one thousand foreign guns, and more than ten thousand spears and swords in exchange for a clean record and a more or less free hand in Gansu, along with a vague pledge to aid the Qing in quelling other rebels. Ma accepted a vice-commander post from the Qing and symbolically changed his name to Ma Chaoqing, which literally translates as "clear morning," meaning he was making a fresh start.[80] In fact, the rebellion quickly spread back into Shaanxi under Ma's "watch."[81] The Muslim leader Ma Shiyuan led ten thousand rebels in an attack on Yan'an. More fighting erupted in Xining and Taozhou.[82] Ma Chaoqing defeated Lei Zhengwan and Cao Kezhong at Jinjibao. This site would evolve into one of the lynchpins of the campaign.

Meanwhile, owing to grain shortages, rising prices, and irregular pay, a mutiny erupted among the Green Standard (Han) troops of Lanzhou on April 17, 1866. In its wake, rebels seized many places around the city, and there were concerns that Lanzhou would be lost entirely to them.[83] Matters were eventually settled, but Zuo criticized Governor Yang Yuebin for his poor handling of the situation, stating, "The army of Gansu was unable to protect the people, but to the contrary, stirred the people up. The officials of Gansu were unable to manage the people, but to the contrary incited them to rebellion."[84] Liu Rong managed to calm things down by restoring food supplies, and Cao Kezhong restored military order by securing the city in June, but he soon resigned due to illness. Yang Yuebin tendered his resignation in September 1866, around the same time Zuo Zongtang was appointed to manage the growing crisis in the northwest, with Mutushan assigned as acting governor-general, stationed at Lanzhou.[85]

ZUO'S PREPARATIONS

One of the few rays of hope in the northwest was the impending arrival of Zuo Zongtang, who was in Hankou at the start of 1867.[86] Officials currently at the front were optimistic that Zuo could turn the tide. As outlined in the previous chapter, Zuo was making his usual extensive preparations in advance of his deployment in the field. He dispatched his own trusted underlings to get the lay of the land and started calling in favors and pulling strings to amass supplies and funds for the campaign, augmenting the initiatives of the central government in setting up supply and logistics bureaus. Significantly, one of the relief corps dispatched was designated the "foreign gun corps" (*yangqiang-dui*).[87] Zuo also said he planned to bring in more mercenaries, organize local militia, and work more closely with local officials in tapping and exploiting local resources, a policy he referred to as "Self-Strengthening." The Qing had to "first defend the perimeter in order to restore their awesomeness." If the *qingye jianbi* strategy was properly employed and the people were secure, there would be nothing for the bandits to plunder. The infusion of fresh troops, including Manchurian cavalry, to replace the old and weak soldiers of Mutushan would further invigorate the Qing side.[88] Mutushan's governance came under heavy criticism, notably by Yang Yuebin, who judged the Manchu commander's policy of accepting false surrenders an abject failure.[89]

Zuo announced that he planned to use war carts in conjunction with cavalry and would implement *tuntian* (military farms) to help feed his troops, noting that "since ancient times the establishment of *tuntian* has been essential to military affairs along the frontiers."[90] But "prior to going into Shaanxi we must clear the bandits from outside [Tong] Pass. Prior to moving troops into Gansu, we must first clear the bandits from Shaanxi. Before stationing troops in Lanzhou we must clear the roads of bandits. Afterward, once the supply lines have been established, then we can advance to annihilate [the enemy] without hindrances."[91]

He also suggested increasing taxes in other places to help pay for the post-war rehabilitation process, though he knew how hard a sell this would be. In what might be interpreted as proto-nationalist sentiment, Zuo made the case that the problems of Shaan-Gan were those of the empire. Shaanxi was running 1.5 million taels in arrears in taxes annually, and Gansu, 2 million. With the rebellion in the interior now quelled, it was time for those provinces to help their counterparts in the northwest. The central government's immediate solution was to transfer 1 million taels from maritime customs revenue to Zuo.[92] At the local level, Zuo discussed the need to break the cycle of rebellion by restoring local institutions and infrastructure and keeping "evil elements" from aiding traitors.[93] With his usual self-confidence, Zuo cited his prior successes in the southeast as a reason to apply his methods.[94]

The court replied positively to Zuo's plan amid accounts of Nian raiders joining with the Hui and Hui men raping Han women.[95] Gao Liansheng was summoned to secure Zuo's rear supply lines. Large shipments of guns, powder, helmets, and armor were on the way from Hong Kong.[96] Zuo's supply depots were already being constructed.[97] Liu Dian had also arrived to help stabilize the situation in advance of Zuo.

Meanwhile, Xinjiang and northern Gansu were slipping further into chaos. In the spring and summer of 1867 Liu Songshan, Guo Baochang, and Huang Ding kept the Qing pressure on the rebels. Even though the Dungan forces numbered in excess of 40,000 in certain engagements, they were consistently driven back by the better equipped and trained Qing units. Hami was recovered, and supplies were sent there to stabilize the situation. Keeping the Nian away from the Dungans remained a priority. Zuo set up additional guard forces along the Yellow River, hoping to pin rebel forces against it and annihilate them. He wanted them cleared from Shanxi first due to its proximity to the capital and then moved back to the west.[98] While Zuo favored military suppression over negotiation, the court feared he lacked the troop strength to follow through and argued that some of the rebels y might still "return their allegiance and cleanse their hearts."[99] Not all Hui were bad, though force would still be required to coerce the wicked. Any policy might fail, as the hatreds between the Han and Hui ran deep in Shaanxi,[100] but the court favored a resettlement plan and authorized Zuo to pursue it once he arrived at the front.

HANGING ON

As Zuo was making his final preparations, the siege at Suzhou was still dragging on. The Qing forces prevented collaborators from breaking the siege but could not make much headway in taking the city owing to lack of troop strength.[101] Mutushan arrived and was informed of the ongoing supply and troop shortages that had hampered the Qing efforts.[102] He reported that there were also acute shortages of officials and trainers for the soldiers. Qing forces in the region were spread thin, making it hard to attack or defend and further compromising resupply efforts. He was trying to improve discipline to stem desertion.[103] But there were also concerns that bringing more troops in would create still more problems. They would have to be supplied and fed, and failure to do so would result in trouble with the locals. The central government put more pressure on other provinces to deliver pledged supplies and funds.[104]

As the calendar turned to 1868, the Qing continued sending troops and supplies into Xinjiang as well, desperately trying to arrest the deteriorating situation.[105] But this was precisely the time when the Nian broke through the Qing encirclement and threatened Zhili. The spring witnessed fighting across the region, as Qing troops came in from Sichuan to the south and Manchuria to the east. More networks of supply depots were established.[106] Suzhou remained under siege, but Zuo had managed to prevent the Nian from escaping back to the west. Liu Dian and Lei Zhengwan reported significant success with their firearms, as did Mutushan, who credited modern guns with enabling the recapture of several forts.[107]

But reconstruction remained a core problem in the war-torn land. Mutushan observed that nine of eleven homes remained empty in the wake of the "soldier calamities" in some areas.[108] Basic living standards had yet to be restored. Reports of widespread Muslim looting attested to the difficulty of simultaneously prosecuting sieges on multiple fronts, ferreting out rebels, and attempting to restore public order. Mutushan and Chenglu repeated their mantra that they were close to victory at Suzhou if they could just get the funds already pledged to them, eliciting promises from the court to follow through.[109]

As increasingly dire reports came in from Xinjian, the battle fronts in Shaan-Gan shifted through the summer, with both sides claiming victories but the overall situation remaining the same. Again demonstrating their prioritization of foes, the Qing officials in Beijing were content to send officials and a trickle of supplies to Xinjiang to buy time while they focused on crushing the Nian and retaking Suzhou. They suggested *tuntian* as an expedient to augment supplies and also dispatched Chahar Mongols to the west.[110]

ZUO'S RETURN TO THE NORTHWEST

Upon arriving at Xi'an in the middle of the tenth month of 1868, Zuo Zongtang followed his usual procedures. He evaluated possible supply routes and ordered supply depots and warehouses built at critical junctions. He made use of multiple supply routes to deliver more supplies and men safely. He carefully checked weather patterns and local geography and personally supervised loading, unloading, and transport of supplies whenever he could. He also continued to pursue various avenues for funding, including calling in personal favors and securing *lijin* from southeastern provinces. The 4 million taels he got for operations was soon boosted by funds coming from customs receipts, the other provinces, and the Ministry of Revenue. And beginning with this campaign, Zuo sought and received foreign loans to pay for supplies and arms.[111] Interestingly, he tried to close down one revenue stream, requesting that the sale of offices to raise funds for the campaign be stopped because he believed it watered down the quality of officials. Zuo himself would eventually adopt the practice when he set up bureaus for selling offices in Henan.[112] He also took steps to quell mutinies at Suide and Yijun provoked by supply problems.[113] As Zuo put it, "In military affairs, feeding the troops is foremost."[114]

Supply problems aside, Zuo was concerned that he had only 30,000 troops at his immediate disposal to cover both offensive and defensive operations.[115]

In terms of recruitment, Zuo tried to have trusted subordinates recruit and lead the troops. He also made the critical decision to emphasize quality of men over quantity, realizing that a smaller force of crack troops could be much more effective than a larger force. They needed fewer supplies and were just as lethal when properly trained and equipped. He was keen on bringing firearms and heavy artillery into the field, and he hired many foreigners as trainers and technicians. He quickly conceived a plan to establish arsenals in the region to better equip his forces.[116]

And he decided to pursue his familiar divide-and-conquer strategy as opposed to the "kill them all" approach favored by his Manchu predecessor, Duolonga.[117] In essence, he resolved to pursue the stated Qing policy of distinguishing between good and bad, not Han and Hui, though he seemed to favor a more aggressive policy on the whole.[118] Extermination had the potential to expand enmity toward the Qing and perpetuate the cycles of violence that originated as much with the Han as with the Hui. As Zuo put it in one note, "Shaanxi's gentry manifest a profound hatred for the Muslims. When they are asked their views about the Hui they are always of the opinion that all Muslims should be killed. . . . I fail to understand their reasoning."[119] Showing his awareness of the international situation, in one letter Zuo expressed concern that the Hui might regard Turkey rather than China as their "ancestral country" (*zuguo*) and suggested the Qing take steps to prevent that from happening.[120]

Zuo's study of history had also instilled a sense of the importance of the northwest to China's development and culture. A region that had once been a wellspring of culture and international exchange had fallen on hard times. He believed he could restore it through bringing Han culture back, introducing new methods of sericulture and industry, building schools, and better integrating the northwest and Central Asia into the regular administrative structure of the empire. Sincere in his conviction that Confucian values lay at the core of superior Han civilization and had the potential to transform anyone into a productive member of (Han) Chinese society, Zuo viewed the establishment of concrete infrastructural and cultural improvements as the vital first step in pacifying and civilizing the region. In this respect Zuo's

views bear more than a passing similarity to the American policy of "benevolent assimilation" that proponents of colonizing the Philippines would cham-
pion a few decades later.[121]

He was also sensitive to the designs of Russia and Great Britain and appreciated the interconnectedness of Xinjiang, Mongolia, and Beijing. It would be
a shame to cast aside everything their ancestors had fought for.[122] Along these
lines, Zuo was quite critical of his predecessors. "If the [previous] governors
were all so ordinary in talent, how could they be expected to quell disorder?"
he asked.[123] Some officials forcibly took local women, including Muslims, as
wives or concubines. Others indulged in lavish dramatic performances accompanied by huge banquets featuring live fish imported from distant regions and
hundreds of taels' worth of liquor.[124] Soon after Zuo took charge in Shaanxi he
reported that the Manchu commander Chenglu had supposedly not set foot
outside his yamen during the entire seven years he was posted in Urumqi.
He reportedly amassed a personal fortune of 300,000 taels and when finally
pressed to deal with rebellion killed just two hundred old and weak peasants
while sending a victory report to the throne.[125]

Zuo estimated there were perhaps 200,000 rebel troops in some 18 battalions with a central base at Fort Zhenjing, whence they could strike easily
at locations across three provinces. Zuo invited his commanders to Xi'an to
discuss war strategy and assigned jurisdictions.[126] As noted above, Zuo brought
many of his old subordinates with him, and his core units were veterans of
the old Xiang Army, also known as the Chu Army, and were similarly organized. An infantry battalion comprised 500 men with 200 officers, and a cavalry battalion had 250 troops and 50 officers. Officers were also attached to
handle food, fodder, salt, firewood, and other essentials, and paymasters were
expected to purchase items from local traders, not forcibly requisition them
from commoners. Foot soldiers received a salary of 4 taels, 2 copper cash per
month. Officers received an extra 3 taels. Squad leaders of 12 received still
more, and pay rates rose up the chain of command to battalion commanders,
who received 50 taels per month, plus 150 to distribute as incentives, with
bonuses for combat exploits. Noted for its discipline, the Chu Army had five
major prohibitions, all punishable by death: rape, plunder, looting, arson,

and murder.[127] Forcible seizure of livestock, women, and property was also forbidden. As a means of combating Gelaohui influence in his ranks, Zuo also forbade strict and excessive deference to elders.[128]

Troops were exhorted to pity and respect the common people and regard themselves as their protectors. Fair prices were to be paid for all things bought and sold. Zuo kept tabs on his officers and sought to curtail graft through regular inspections and investigations. In one case when he found out that a unit was short on men but the commander and been requisitioning supplies for a full unit, he had him disciplined in front of the whole battalion as an example.[129] As in the southeast, he stressed the importance of agriculture and infrastructure for the people, soldiers, and society in general. His men were often assigned to engage in public works projects, building roads and bridges, repairing waterworks, and planting trees. These efforts raised morale and helped build a sense of community.[130]

In terms of personal conduct, Zuo sought to forge positive relationships with his troops. He interacted and joked with the men while on campaign and shared their hardships. He treated soldiers like family, sending medicine to sick subordinates and giving or lending money to those in need.[131] These attitudes clearly stemmed from his upbringing and personal experiences in Hunan. Finally, Zuo placed emphasis on intelligence, following Sunzi's maxim about knowing as much about one's enemy as possible. He would not advance until he felt that he had every salient detail and would not strike until the time was right and victory was nearly assured. This meant that he was also very cautious when it came to military orders and communications. As he put it, "One misplaced or false character could determine [the outcome of] a battle."[132]

Zuo decided to first send reinforcements to the Wei River Valley to secure its vital artery while he prepared to clear out the north part of the province. He envisioned a four-pronged advance under six commanders. He again stressed that good Muslims should be allowed to submit, while the wicked, whom he consistently identified as adherents of the New Teachings, were to be punished. Zuo wanted to stamp out Ma Zhenghe's resistance at Dongzhiyuan first, then go after Ma Hualong/Chaoqing at Jinjibao, then recover Hezhou to the west. Attacks on Xining and Suzhou would follow.[133] Zuo would oversee the central army, Liu Songshan would strike north, and other commanders would move south and west. But Zuo's insistence on amassing supplies before acting brought criticism from the court that he was acting too slowly. An unrelated Gelaohui uprising also gave Zuo pause. And his upcoming venture was drawing the attention of Westerners in China as well. His critics included the German Baron von Richtofen. Zeng Guofan supported Zuo, however, and the throne ignored their criticism. Zuo's campaign was in full swing by January 1869 as Zhang Yao and the Manchu commander Jinshun joined him.

Liu Songshan started the campaign off impressively, smashing a large rebel force near Suide, killing 6,000, liberating 20,000, and getting one of their leaders to surrender as he took more than 100 fortified redoubts in a single day.[134] Thousands more were slain around Dongzhiyuan.[135] Some tried to flee south into Sichuan province but were crushed by another Qing commander. The Muslim leader Ma Guangfu was captured in battle at Yan'an. But even as he was issuing victory reports in the autumn of 1868 Zuo noted that he was facing supply shortages exceeding 15,000 taels per month.[136] Liu Dian, for example, had barely received enough from Sichuan to sustain his army for one month. Once more Zuo suggested foreign loans to make up shortfalls.

Through the final month of 1868 and into 1869 the Qing forces made impressive progress, often working in tandem with local militia as Zuo's forces had done in the southeast. More than 100 rebel redoubts and stockades were taken, resulting in an estimated 5,000–6,000 dead, the freeing of 20,000 POWs, and the capture of around 3,000 livestock.[137] Rebels who fled into the mountains were pursued and killed. It is highly possible that some of those massacred were noncombatants. Liu Songshan reported the outrageous figures of more than 10,000 dead against just 27 losses himself. Qing firepower was clearly overwhelming, and the weaknesses of the rebels in open-field battle were exposed after years of irresolute action on the part of previous Qing commanders. As Qing victories piled up, the rebels at Dongzhiyuan offered to surrender.[138] The court was dubious, urging its military commanders to go forth and "use the awesomeness of the army to rectify their hearts," observing that it would be regrettable if they submitted and then later reneged.[139]

162 *Chapter 5*

The foreign press in China was also closely monitoring the campaign. The *North China Herald* noted the rebels' possible links to the ongoing rebellion of Yakub Beg and speculated that the rebels might strike north, going around Qing defenses in central Shanxi to threaten Beijing. The article added that the government was very concerned about losing control of Shanxi, which was considered "the most wealthy" part of China because many bankers were from that province. Still, the *Herald* expressed confidence that matters would be settled by spring. But there were many outlandish rumors circulating in the foreign settlements; for example, "that a woman, a widow, is the head of the [rebel] body; and . . . they have Chinese from all parts of the north of China in their ranks."[140]

Though surrounded, Gao Liansheng fought his way free in another battle, prompting the rebel leader Bai Yanhu to offer submission.[141] Thousands more were killed in follow-up engagements as the Qing pushed the rebels back toward Jinjibao. Lei Zhengwan defeated the rebels near Taichengzhen and distributed captured supplies and livestock to the freed prisoners. Liu Song-shan's units were experiencing supply difficulties as they battled their way north and were allegedly forced to kill their draft animals for food—which is surprising given the number of livestock they had reported capturing. The Gelaohui-inspired uprising in Suide in the second month of 1869, inspired by supply shortages, was quelled in less than two weeks, with seventy-seven ringleaders being executed.[142] Though the mutineers had sent out calls to join them, Liu Songshan and Song Qing approached the city from multiple routes, infiltrated the mutineers' ranks, and effected a quick resolution. Other mutinies, including one by Gao Liansheng's troops, erupted but were handled swiftly, though Gao himself died as a result of wounds incurred during the mutiny.[143] Lei Zhengwan was tasked with restoring Gao's troops to order.

Zuo advanced to Jingzhou to direct the campaign about the same time as the mutinies occurred.[144] Not long after the events described above, another mutiny erupted at Yijun, north of Xi'an, where members of the Gelaohui killed a local commander. Zuo quelled this revolt and executed the ringlead-ers. Though the mutinies were apparently unconnected, the involvement of the Gelaohui in both reified Zuo's concerns about their influence within his forces, prompting him to reiterate his calls for steadier supplies and better junior officers.[145] The Gelaohui were hard to identify, and their numbers were constantly renewed as new mercenaries and militiamen were incorporated into the Qing ranks.[146] The problem was considered especially serious in the troops from Sichuan, where it was suspected that eight or nine of every ten soldiers had Gelaohui ties.[147]

Many people left homeless by the long fighting were inclined to rejoin the rebels as soon as Qing forces moved on from liberated areas. Zuo wanted more relief sent and additional measures implemented to succor the people as well as to ensure his troops' supplies. He pressed the southeastern provinces in particular, prompting the court to issue a directive to tap more *lijin* funds.[148] He asked the court to dispatch officials tasked specifically with logistics. For their part, the rebels divided their forces in smaller bands ranging in size from ten to one hundred and looted Qing camps and supply trains to sustain themselves.[149] Bai Yanhu proved especially crafty, but like the others, he preferred hit-and-run tactics and almost never engaged the Qing in a frontal attack that he knew he would lose.

Zuo captured his first goal, Dongzhiyuan, on April 4, 1869, annihilating 20,000–30,000 Muslim rebels. He reported some 20,000 horses captured and more than 10,000 prisoners liberated.[150] Zuo was deeply affected by what he saw there, remarking that "one could only see white bones and discarded spears and there was no smoke from cooking fires. Surely nowhere in the world was as horrid as this?"[151] Such sights convinced him that the government must eradicate the rebels at all costs. As usual, Zuo expressed his desire to restore the local economy. He ordered wells dug and seeds and tools provided to locals to restore agriculture and encourage them to return to their old livelihoods, seeing this as a way to foster goodwill between the people and his troops, always a hallmark of his policies—and not coincidentally one that would be adapted by the Chinese Communists in the same region several decades later.[152] Immediate measures included the release of 100,000 taels for famine relief. In each place his troops captured, Zuo sought to appoint officials of high moral caliber. Liu Dian was integral in shaping these policies.[153] But in some cases so many people were liberated or surrendered that the government could not keep up with the need for establishing pacification bureaus to enable reconstruction and rehabilitation.[154]

As Qing victories mounted under Zuo's invigorating command, central Shaanxi was considered pacified, though sporadic fighting persisted. The Muslim rebels now split into two major groups. One sought to cut the routes to Lanzhou from Hezhou and Dizhou; the other was based in northern Gansu and conducted raids into the lands of the Alashan Mongols. Zuo sent multiple columns north so he could divide and conquer his foes. Advances were interspersed with breaks while the troops farmed and reopened transit routes. The three main foes were now identified as being Ma Hualong/Chaoqing in Lingzhou and Jinjibao, Ma Duosan at Xining, and Ma Zhan'ao at Hezhou.[155] Since Ma Hualong was clearly the strongest of the three and had the largest network of followers, Zuo resolved to take him out first, regaining strategically placed Jinjibao in the process.[156]

Rebel stockades and forts dotted the mountains, making advances dangerous. The Qing employed local guides to scout routes of advance. Whenever possible they softened up defenses with their mountain-splitter cannons, a favorite of Zuo's since his days campaigning against the Taipings. Mutushan would later explicitly request delivery of these formidable weapons from Hubei.[157] All the while, the court was pressuring Zuo to speed up his operations, and Zuo was pressuring the court for more funds and supplies.[158]

APPEALING TO THE HUI

Zuo tried to cultivate relations with the "good Hui," assuring them that it was his goal to ensure "peace for a thousand years." Such a lasting peace could be achieved only by completely restoring local order. Otherwise, the violence would continue as soon as the Qing troops moved on. This involved county-by-county restoration, reconstruction of tax rolls, and clear registration of inhabitants, aided by his proposed relief measures. The crux of this lay in settling the Muslims and smoothing over their disputes with the Han.[159]

Although some officials suggested that "superior Han culture" would eventually win the Muslims over, Zuo seemed more inclined to favor relocation, though he remained committed to infrastructural improvements and cultural assimilation efforts as well. Zuo argued that the Han and Hui were innately different, had different customs, and did not intermarry, so separation was both proper and feasible.[160] At least some Muslims seemed prepared to overlook Zuo's chauvinistic approach and appreciated his genuine concern for their welfare, bestowing the name Zuo Ahong (Muslim Teacher) on him.[161]

Zuo was convinced that the Hui could be selectively plucked and nurtured like flowers to spread the good seeds and eliminate the bad, represented by Ma Hualong and the Old Teachings.[162] Zuo acknowledged that the Hui possessed human hearts and simply wanted to survive but needed somewhere to go, so he had designated areas around Pingliang for their settlement, promising land, seeds, and tools, and expressing hope that they could embark on fresh starts and enjoy imperial benevolence. In yet another letter, however, Zuo noted that the Hui had been troublesome ever since they came to China, but it was both impolitic and impractical to wipe them out. "The way to deal with the Muslims is not like the way we dealt with the Taiping and the Nian," he insisted. "They have accumulated deep enmities with the Chinese. Their marriage customs differ and when they see each other, 'murderous intent' immediately arises, which is very difficult to get under control. Moreover, their races are distantly separated, so they differ even in appearance. . . . Furthermore I fear that Chinese subjects' reactions will redouble the enmity."[163]

The court approved of Zuo's resettlement plan while also declaring its commitment to universalism.[164] In choosing sites for relocation, Zuo looked for uninhabited wastelands that could be irrigated and settled by large numbers of people who could eventually attain self-sufficiency. These places should be on comparatively flat land that was not too close to Han settlements or major roads, but not so far from them as to preclude government intervention in the case of trouble. Zuo devised different means of allocating lands. In some places people were given homes and land and wells were dug. In others each family was given food, tools, animals, and supplies to use as they saw fit. In some places *baojia* were organized to help each other. In still others a headman, generally a Muslim, was appointed to manage affairs, much as was the case in Central Asia. Officials who abused the people were to be executed. Fodder was provided for livestock, and food supplies were allocated in accordance with the age of recipients.[165]

FURTHER SUCCESSES

The Qing won a series of engagements under Jinshun, including the capture of Kangpingbao, which helped open the route to Lanzhou. Lei Zhengwan and Huang Ding secured the northern route via Guyuan, and others secured the south. The *North China Herald* even suggested that the campaign might be finished much faster than the five years Zuo had predicted it would take.[166] The *Herald*'s writer noted that "for several years this region had been miserably desolated by these ruthless insurgents, who from the reign of Shun-chi [Shunzhi] have at brief intervals given trouble to the government." Zuo's efforts, the writer added, have "every promise of complete success."[167]

Liu Songshan, accompanied by his nephew Jintang, made steady progress north from Huamachi through the summer months, with Zuo crediting Liu's success to better supply and coordination.[168] The court was pleased but urged Liu to keep up the pressure. He did, reporting many victories with many enemy dead.[169] Some Manchu commanders accused Liu Songshan of indiscriminately slaughtering Muslims in these battles, but Zuo blamed the Muslims, specifically adherents of the New Teachings. Mutushan continued to argue that a policy of conciliation would better serve both the Qing and the people, and contended that Ma Chaoqing (Hualong) had sincerely repented and was now serving the Qing. He also reported that grain prices were so high (thirty taels for one-tenth of a *dan*) that people were reduced to cannibalism in many areas.[170]

For his part, Zuo regarded the New Teachings Muslims as a cancer and never trusted their offers to surrender. He wanted Ma handled by military means, telling the court that many of the "submissive" rebels, including Ma Hualong, were still secretly rebellious. The rebels still occupied some five hundred forts and stockades around Jinjibao and were stealing supplies and ravaging Han women within a hundred-*li* radius around their base.[171] In a letter to his son Zuo expressed his outrage that Mutushan had the temerity to refer to Ma Hualong as a "good Muslim" after what had transpired over the past several years. Zuo claimed that Ma was cultivating Mongol allies even as he accepted ranks and rewards from Mutushan, using the money to restore forts, buy horses, and manufacture weapons while retaining his links to the rebels across Shaanxi.[172] Zuo and Liu were convinced that Ma was simply preserving his wealth and position to buy time to reinforce his hold on certain cities. Ma's surrender, Zuo said, "did not reflect his true heart [*fei qi zhen xin*]."[173]

This would be a recurring pattern over the next several years as various proponents of persuasion pled their case, only to have Zuo reject them on grounds of rebel duplicity while reiterating that he had no quarrel with Muslims in general.[174] Indeed, Zuo tried to reassure the locals by telling them that he was merely following the emperor's instructions to "punish bandits and protect good people." Hui and Han alike had nothing to fear so long as they were loyal and did not aid the rebels. Those who did not aid the bandits "need not fear the thunderous power of the army."[175] The Qing were not out to exterminate the Muslim people (*jin jian Huizu*), he said, adding "those who are loyal and good will be protected without discrimination."[176]

In fact Ma Hualong/Chaoqing had strengthened his hold on Jinjibao and extended his influence across the region. Ma owned a couple of trading firms and invested in Muslim businesses from Shaanxi to Mongolia to Gansu. He also supplied other New Teachings Muslims with arms purchased in Central Asia and traded extensively with the Muslims at Dongzhiyuan. Zuo was well aware of Ma's perfidy and chose him as the next major target.[177] Considering the broader strategic situation, Zuo reasoned that if the rebels in Shaanxi were defeated first, the Qing could cut off support to Gansu and recover stolen supplies, arms, and battle mounts.[178] But the main leaders were hunkered down along the Yellow River in the northernmost part of Gansu.

THE CAPTURE OF JINJIBAO

Zuo pressed toward Ma's central base at Jinjibao in multiple columns in the summer of 1869 while Liu Songshan advanced to attack Zhenjingbao in August. The latter was defended by Dong Fuxiang, who sent out his father and brother to negotiate. Trying to force the issue, Liu's armies attacked and defeated Dong's forces and convinced them to surrender. In this operation Liu cleared hundreds of bandit strongholds and brought some 170,000 to the Qing side. More than 40,000 of these were Muslim troops loyal to Dong Fuxiang who would serve in key roles over the next several years, providing valuable combat service and helping the Qing attract other Muslim allies.[179] Giving Dong a central command position, Liu then advanced north. The arrival of Mongol and Manchu troops from the north and east further bolstered the strategic position of the Qing, affording them greater mobility in pursuing fleeing rebel units and helping secure their supply lines. They also severed some of the communication lines between rebel groups in Shaan-Gan and Xinjiang.

Zuo moved his headquarters to Pingliang as Qing forces closed in on Lingzhou. The Muslim forces put up spirited resistance, but with their superior firepower the Qing reduced their forts to ashes.[180] These defeats prompted Ma Hualong to send another letter to Zuo offering to surrender, which Mutushan was unsurprisingly inclined to accept, but as Ma simultaneously sent troops to fight the Qing at Lingzhou, Zuo instructed his field commanders to step up their assaults, hoping to overawe the rebels.[181] Liu killed more than ten thousand in subsequent operations, and on October 7, 1869, Ma again offered to surrender. The court was inclined to listen but ordered a thorough investigation because Zuo and Mutushan had completely different opinions on Ma's sincerity.[182] As negotiations continued, Liu captured outlying defenses and Ma sent out secret dispatches hoping to summon relief columns. The Qing plowed through the rebel defenses, abetted by their heavy artillery, as offers to submit were renewed. Meanwhile, Huang Ding defeated Bai Yanhu, and Qing forces secured Guyuan, which was centrally located astride the route to Lanzhou. Lei Zhengwan pushed other rebel forces back toward Jinjibao as Zhang Yao and his forces smashed through rebel redoubts, clearing out the Ning–Ling corridor.[183]

The Qing forces advanced on Lingzhou from all directions, fighting day and night, working their way through fortified defiles. Liu's army occupied Lingzhou in November 1869, allegedly massacring the populace indiscriminately, though Liu claimed many escaped and continued to raid the countryside.[184] Zuo reported that 1,400–1,500 rebels were killed, 273 were captured, and 700 prisoners were freed. Another 1,500–1,600 were killed and hundreds more rescued when the Qing secured the nearby forts. Many false seals of office were recovered as well.[185] Zuo described the land around Lingzhou as "a barren wasteland, nearly bereft of people. As far as one can see, white bones cover the yellow sand; it's as if people haven't lived there for generations."[186] Moving to secure rivers and bridges as they pushed southwest from Lingzhou to Jinjibao, Liu's forces repeatedly used their modern artillery to reduce rebel defenses.[187] Liu advanced to within fourteen *li* of Jinjibao as Lei Zhengwan skirmished with Ma Chaoqing's forces to the south. Liu Songshan continued to receive surrender offers from Ma Chaoqing as the court asked Zuo to clarify his position on the matter. Zuo was ordered to assume full command over Mutushan, though the current conditions delayed the transfer of authority. Meanwhile, Liu Jintang was tasked with intercepting rebel units attempting to rescue Ma.[188]

The Qing blasted on toward Jinjibao, reducing rebel fortifications as they went. The main fortress itself was encircled by a ring comprising literally hundreds of outlying bastions and stockades, some built of wood, others of stone and earth. These were further buttressed by flanking towers, lookouts, and ditches and moats.[189] Attackers had to wind their way in, constantly exposed to harassing fire, while the defenders had ample locations where they could fall back and defend. In order to weaken the defenders' capabilities, Zuo divided his own forces. Liu Songshan was entrusted with approaching Jinjibao from the northeast, while Zhou Kaixi, a logistics specialist who had worked with Zuo in Fujian, was detailed to approach from the south. Having cleared the area between Ningxia and Lingzhou, Zhang Yao was to move south from Mongolia along the west bank of the Yellow River.[190]

Through the autumn of 1869 there was sharp fighting on all fronts as the rebels alternately sallied forth and then dug in, while also sending out small commando units to sever Qing supply lines. But Liu and Lei kept up their steady pressure, bombarding the rebels' defenses faster than they could repair them. Liu also rebuilt previously destroyed Qing fortifications as he advanced.[191] Rivers and canals were diverted to flood rebel bases, and heavy cannonballs smashed through walls. The northern defenses were especially stout, and those assaulting from that direction were exposed to blistering fire from all sides. Qing casualties were heavy and further mounted when Ma Hualong personally led sorties of crack cavalry, hoping to clear space for his defenders to forage. Ma's allies had enjoyed scant success in their attempts to relieve the siege. Bai Yanhu, for example, was repulsed when he attempted a relief attack from the north toward the end of the year, and Ma Duosan had also been bested. Bai's decision to flee west weakened the defenders' position.[192]

Despite his triumphs Zuo remained of two minds on the best approach. In a report on Liu Songshan's progress Zuo said, "The nature of the Hui is that of beasts; they know to fear awesomeness but not to love virtue so using principles is secondary in managing them." But then he added, "They are not the same as other bandits. With other bandits you'd exterminate them first, then resort to suasion, but in managing Hui one should first employ suasion [as a ruse?]."[193] If the Qing resorted to persuasion, though, Hui bandits would certainly accept it to buy time while they "secretly form[ed] factions to swallow the Han," so ultimately the policy of suasion was a dead end, with the ongoing Muslim rebellion in Yunnan being proof of that.[194] Zuo decided to keep both policies on the table. The Qing might still emphasize suasion but should not discard the possibility of extermination.

The increasingly desperate Ma tried to summon help from his compatriots in Shaanxi. But Liu Songshan's men dug their own rear defenses, expanded their siegeworks, and captured positions north of Jinjibao. A satisfied Zuo said, "If Liu Songshan had lightly accepted surrender [before], then calamity would have ensued later."[195] Lei Zhengwan detailed his troops to hold key passes in the mountains and captured rebels trying to smuggle supplies to the defenders.[196] The Qing capture of Shijiazhuang further frightened Ma, and he attempted another cavalry charge but to no avail. Relief efforts by Ma Zhan'ao also proved fruitless. As Liu's cannon continued to rain death on the rebels, more defenses were reduced and several leaders were captured.[197] Zuo realized the Qing would have to cut the irrigation canals leading into the city and started making plans accordingly.[198] Deserters warned Liu of an impending counterattack, and he used this intelligence to lure the defenders into an ambush, killing 800–900 while sustaining just 134 casualties.[199]

Zuo kept up his meticulous planning, and the Qing made steady progress toward Jinjibao from all directions. The court pressured Zuo to seal the deal, and he sent Gao Baochang to reinforce Liu Songshan, who had to deal with a minor mutiny among the mercenaries occupying Lingzhou. Battle reports indicated heavy fighting punctuated by alternating attacks and withdrawals in conjunction with the supply situation.[200] The rebel forces that rode out seeking supplies were driven back. They often retreated to fortified temples or mosques, forcing the Qing to bull their way through these as well. Corpses lined the roads leading south from Jinjibao. The Qing arrayed cannons and dug trenches around their camps to deter raiders.

With each minor fort taken, upward of a few hundred rebels were killed. Mongols were brought in to counter the raids of Ma Zhenghe, who was still trying to assist Ma Chaoqing.[201] In the opening month of 1870 more than four thousand rebels were reportedly killed.[202] The Qing were using everything at their disposal, from cavalry attacks to heavy artillery, from siege tactics to fire arrows. The rebels maintained their own desperate efforts to loot supplies and attract allies to harass the besiegers.[203] Zuo became concerned about supplies again and urgently requested deliveries. The Qing put more gunboats on the rivers to protect their supply trains.[204] Efforts were made to secure supply lines from all directions as the net closed around Jinjibao.[205] More cavalry on the way from Manchuria were expected to improve the government forces' ability to pursue defeated rebel units.

The Qing were assisted by "good Hui" acting as scouts and guides. Placards of allegiance were erected outside the homes of such loyal subjects as the Qing added propaganda to force. More Hui submitted, bringing large numbers of weapons with them. Relief columns were intercepted time and again. But just as the Qing seemed on the verge of victory, disaster struck.

In a series of clashes Liu Songshan moved closer to the inner defenses, but he was forced to pull back when he met heavy resistance. He knew the walls were stout and the ditches his men would have to cross were deep, so he commenced building more siege weapons, detailing subordinates to focus on deterring relief columns. Liu dislodged the rebels at Hujiabao and pursued them, killing more than a thousand as they battled on the icy ground. Liu next attacked Mawusai and other forts, raining fire down into the structures and hitting the walls with scaling ladders.[206] But the assault came to an abrupt end on February 14, 1870, when Liu Songshan was hit in the chest by artillery fire.[207] As he was dying, he allegedly said, "I've long received the grace of the state. If I die don't worry about retrieving my body; just kill more bandits!" He also allegedly wanted his corpse left in the field so that his ghost could continue the fight.[208] Honoring his uncle's wish, Liu Jintang put Songshan's corpse in a coffin and carried it with the troops for some time after his death. Zuo said of Liu, "He was righteous and loyal; men such as him do not come along twice in one generation. . . . It is like losing my right arm."[209] Zuo ordered the construction of a martyr's shrine for Liu, citing his distinction in battling the Taipings, Nian, and Hui across ten provinces on behalf of the Qing. He would subsequently be canonized as "Loyal and Stout."[210]

Following Liu's death, the Qing forces suffered a series of setbacks that delayed the capture of Jinjibao for more than a year. Taking advantage of the situation, Ma Hualong sent his lieutenants Ma Zhenghe and Ma Wanchun back on the offensive, and they recaptured several forts as well as securing the gorge at Longwangmiao where Zuo had hoped to cut their irrigation lines.[211] The Qing columns immediately pulled back, losing their strategic advantage. Other Qing commanders had also died in the previous several months, so this was a potentially catastrophic reversal.[212] Zuo received an additional personal blow when his wife, Zhou Yiduan, died a few weeks later.[213]

When news of the disaster reached Beijing, some foreign sources predicted that Zuo would be dismissed and replaced by Li Hongzhang. The foreigners took the opportunity to criticize the state of the Qing military and its training, contending that the Qing could not yet think of acting against a foreign power, "even in its dreams."[214] Similar sentiments would prevail over the next several years until Zuo defeated the Muslim rebel Yakub Beg. Indeed, an article published two months later about Yakub Beg's rebel movement, while downplaying its scope, added "we know from much experience how ill-qualified Chinese soldiers are to oppose an energetic foe."[215]

As the Hui forces regained the initiative, Zuo petitioned the court to appoint Liu Jintang, Songshan's young but experienced nephew, to assume command of his troops.[216] Zuo argued that the men already knew and trusted Jintang, and vice versa. His experience was the equal of nearly anyone currently in the field.[217] Liu Jintang's appointment was authorized, and he was promoted three grades.[218] It would prove to be one of the best decisions Zuo ever made.

The rebel forces that had broken through Zuo's encirclement and ranged east into Shaanxi were driven back, and within six weeks Zuo's forces were renewing their attacks on the outer defenses of Jinjibao.[219] The veteran commander Xu Zhanbiao defeated Ma Zhenghe, killing him in battle, and Ma Hualong retreated back north before Liu Jintang's army.[220] Through much of April the Qing checked the southern rebel forces and the two sides fought for control of the canals, with the Qing emerging victorious at channeling the waters into the Yellow River.[221] They then went about securing the corridor between Shaanxi and Gansu in the north and scattering Ma Hualong's erstwhile allies.[222]

The Qing also accelerated efforts to get Western guns and ammunition into the hands of the troops. Western gunpowder was purchased in large quantities in Tianjin. The emperor instructed Ding Richang and officials in the southeast to get firearms to the northwest as fast as possible. Control of the waterways was essential to success, both to facilitate the delivery of supplies and to contain the rebels.[223] Along these lines, much planning was devoted to redeploying Qing troops around Jinjibao and augmenting regulars with militia. The court also wanted investigations into the state of training, believing, as Zuo did, that simply throwing more soldiers at the problem was not the solution.

After capturing rebel forts around Lingzhou in a series of engagements, Zuo sent Lei Zhengwan and Huang Ding out from Guyuan. They captured several forts west of the Yellow River, thereby cutting off aid from that direction. The rebel fortifications at Xiakou Gorge were breached and five more barriers were smashed, with all the defenders slaughtered.[224] The Qing maneuvered the enemy into situations where they could deploy their big guns, also endeavoring to keep their supply lines secure. Ma Zhenghe was ambushed and killed, and Zuo reported that more friendly Hui leaders were aiding the

Qing, often at considerable risk to themselves.[225] Xu Zhanbiao retained his position of mobile commander and prevented many of Ma Hualong's former allies from returning to Jinjibao, though other places fell to the rebels. But over the spring months the Qing stabilized central Shaanxi and steadily regained the initiative.[226]

The refugees clogging the roads hampered Qing operations, because the troops had to both defend them and be sensitive to potential fifth columnists in their ranks.[227] In some places local Hui leaders continued to fan the flames of dissent, bringing new rebels into the cause. Starvation forced some hapless commoners into rebellion or banditry. Zuo repeated his admonition for troops to distinguish between good Hui and bad Hui and tried to draw attention to the exploits of the former while still warning of the "evil teachings" of the New Teachings sect.[228]

Although Liu Jintang had recaptured Lingzhou, scattered fighting continued to the south and there were widespread reports of cattle rustling by the rebels. Qing forces now advanced deliberately, with only a few skirmishers going ahead to investigate the situation. This approach, while apparently necessary due to the supply situation, afforded Ma Hualong the opportunity to rebuild his defenses around Jinjibao, digging wells and ditches and repairing walls that had been reduced the previous year. Once he gained his footing as commander and got his supply train in order, Liu Jintang followed his uncle's example and brought his big guns to bear. His forces alternated fierce assaults with periods of scouting and retrenchment as they methodically pushed toward their goal. Liu also kept up lines of communication with Ma Hualong, telling him that the Qing would entertain surrender offers only if all weapons and horses were surrendered first.[229]

Rebels sheltering inside the fortifications slipped out at night to dig trenches and reinforce walls. They also diverted waterways around the fortress to inundate the ground. Qing forces countered by sending scouts ahead with poles to gauge water depth. Rebels who left the city to scavenge for food were captured and questioned for information on the situation inside the walls. By late summer the Qing estimated that only about thirty of the original five hundred or so fortifications remained, and tens of thousands more rebels had been slain. Some reportedly immolated themselves rather than be captured by the Qing.[230] But still the city held. The inner walls of Jinjibao were four *zhang* high, three *zhang* thick, and nine *li* in circumference. There was an inner bastion and a moat in addition to these defenses.[231] The Qing built platforms for their cannons to fire down into the defenses. The rebels countered by breaching dikes to flood the ground and slow the artillery advance.

Zuo meanwhile continued to consider enacting measures aimed to end the discord between Han and Hui, including forbidding intermarriage and enforcing separation of the groups. He also offered a particularly sobering assessment of the human costs to date. Whereas before there had reportedly been 100,000 Muslims in Shaanxi, and perhaps 20,000–30,000 in Xi'an alone, only a few thousand remained. Perhaps 90 percent had died from warfare, disease, or starvation. But even with that smaller number, resettlement would be difficult. Shaanxi was devastated, and Gansu was scarcely in better shape. Zuo hoped that a combination of military farms and the distribution of animals, seeds, and tools could at least provide a start in rejuvenating the countryside.[232] But the fact that Qing officials sometimes executed Hui who surrendered because they did not trust them undermined the government's credibility.

By the autumn of 1870 the Qing had encircled Jinjibao again, with Liu Jintang's forces in the east and south, those of Jin Yunchang to the north, those of Xu Wenxiu to the northwest, Huang Ding's in the west, and Lei Zhengwan's to the southwest. In the tenth lunar month of 1870 the Qing took Hanbao. At this point only five of the outlying forts had not yet been attacked.[233] The rebels responded by flooding the area around Jinjibao, strengthening their walls, and temporarily cutting Qing supply lines from the west. They also sent more pleas to their allies to come to the rescue. These measures only delayed the inevitable. Superior Qing firepower again turned the tide, and rebel stockades fell. The Qing were now just a few miles outside the inner defenses in the west. Over thirty consecutive days of fighting the Qing hammered away.[234] Liu Jintang was camped to the southeast, but because the rebels had severed many of the bridges around the city, the Qing armies could not link up. Xu Zhanbiao and Lei Zhengwan captured another twenty defensive positions to the southwest.[235] Another Muslim sally was thrown back by Liu Jintang.

Liu's counterattack resulted in the incineration of more than three thousand structures and the capture of twenty outlying forts.[236] The Qing also stepped up their cooperation with local militia elements.

Ma offered to surrender, still hoping to buy time to shore up his faltering defenses. His pleas fell on deaf ears. The Qing killed at least six thousand more rebels over the next month as they tightened the siege. Zuo circulated letters to other Hui leaders telling them that Ma Hualong was in the process of negotiating his surrender, and this prompted a few more defections and the surrender of weapons, including dozens of heavy cannon.[237] In all cases the troops had to formally surrender, and the Qing authorities secured and inspected the fortifications for hidden weapons caches.

There were now thirty Qing camps around Jinjibao, with supplies streaming in day and night via horse, mule, and camel.[238] To speed things up, the court authorized provinces to deliver revenues directly to the front. They also pressured the various provinces to honor their pledges and explored alternative options for getting more camels to the troops, seeking to bring them in from Mongolia.[239] But the court remained frustrated that Zuo had not yet captured his objective, noting that the costs in the last year alone had exceeded 8 million taels. Zuo explained that there were more than 450 smaller forts and stockades that had to be breached in addition to 100 structures closer to Jinjibao, plus the rugged mountain terrain to contend with. Nonetheless, the Qing forces burned through twenty-three positions in the late summer under a constant barrage of defensive sniper fire, taking heavy casualties with every fort they captured. Each captured fort then had to be secured and the areas around it patrolled. The Qing lacked the manpower to perform these tasks, and supplies were still barely adequate.[240] Summer reports repeatedly referenced delayed or missing supplies, and the court sent dozens of directives to the provinces to send more provisions or funds. Zuo requested more Western artillery to help finish the job and noted that his Xiang Army was already fighting its way through the outer defenses, having made significant progress despite the heavy casualties.[241] Zuo thought they might be able to soften up the rebel defenses with steady bombardments but was disturbed by reports that arms dealers in Lanzhou were selling weapons to the rebels.[242]

NOTE ON THE IMAGES

In 1874–75, the Russian government sent a research and trading mission to China to seek out new overland routes to Chinese markets, report on prospects for increased commerce and locations for consulates and factories, and gather information about the Dungan Revolt then raging in parts of western China. Led by Lieutenant Colonel Iulian A. Sosnovskii of the Army General Staff, the nine-man mission included a topographer, Captain Matusovskii; a scientific officer, Dr. Pavel Iakovlevich Piasetskii; Chinese and Russian interpreters; three Cossack noncommissioned officers; and the mission photographer, Adolf-Nikolay Erazmovich Boiarskii, credited with all photos in this section, taken in 1875. The mission proceeded from St. Petersburg to Shanghai via Ulan Bator (Mongolia), Beijing, and Tianjin and then followed a route along the Yangzi River, along the Great Silk Road through the Hami oasis, to Lake Zaysan, and back to Russia. Boiarskii took some two hundred photographs, which constitute a unique resource for the study of China in this period. The photographs later became part of the Thereza Christina Maria Collection assembled by Emperor Pedro II of Brazil and given by him to the National Library of Brazil. The photographs reproduced here reside in the Library of Congress in Washington, DC.

Zuo Zongtang as governor-general of Shaan-Gan

Governor-General of Shaan'gan, Zuo Zongtang, in Military Garments with Long Court Beads. Lanzhou, Gansu Province, China.

Zuo Zongtang in civilian dress in Lanzhou

Governor-General of Shaan'gan, Zuo Zongtang, in Civilian Dress with a Peacock Feather in His Hat. Lanzhou, Gansu Province, China.

Chinese artillery cart in Lanzhou

Three-Wheeled Wooden Vehicle with Chinese Artillery. Lanzhou, Gansu Province, China.

Chinese dragon artillery piece, Lanzhou

Three-Wheeled Wooden Vehicle with Chinese Dragon Artillery Longshen Pao. Lanzhou, Gansu Province, China.

Mosque in Lanzhou showing lunar pavilion

Muslim Mosque in Lanzhou, with a Lunar Pavilion. Gansu Province, China.

Mosque in Hami's Muslim district showing dome

Mosque in Hami's Muslim District, Showing the Juxtaposition of Chinese Roof and Islamic Dome. Xinjiang, China. (China Xinjiang Uyghur Autonomous Region Hami)

Mosque in Hami

Mosque in Hami's Muslim District, Xinjiang, China. (China Xinjiang Uyghur Autonomous Region Hami)

Mosque destroyed in Hami during rebellion

Minaret in the Muslim Quarter of Hami and Ruin of the Mosque Destroyed by Rebels in Hami, Xinjiang, China, 1875. (China Xinjiang Uyghur Autonomous Region Hami)

Suzhou after its recovery by Zuo Zongtang in 1872

*Town of Suzhou Fu, Which Was Razed to the Ground during the Uprising.
Jiuquan, Gansu Province, China, 1875.*

Qing barracks in Gansu

Quarters for Chinese Troops. Gansu, China.

Qing battle formation in Gansu

Troops Carrying Flags in Military Formation, Preceded by Four Cannons.
Gansu Province, China.

West gate of Lanzhou

West Gate of City Wall of Lanzhou, Gansu Province, China.

Muslim woman in Hami

Hami Muslim Woman. Xinjiang, China. (China Xinjiang Uyghur
Autonomous Region Hami)

Zuo also continued to complain that the local officials were "greedy and covetous," observing, "There is no evil they do not commit. Not only Han subjects hate them; Muslims hate them as well."[243] This was problematic as Zuo was actively working to foster better relations between the "good Hui" and the Han. He dispatched officials to the localities to assuage Hui fears and try to convince them that not all Qing officials were evil exploiters. Plans were sketched out to clean up local administration with an eye toward curbing future rebellions and eradicating systemic problems. Corrupt officials were sometimes executed for crimes such as skimming supplies.[244]

Over the last few months of 1870, the Qing assaults on Jinjibao continued in tandem with negotiations. Some six thousand rebels were killed in battles in the tenth month as the Qing secured most of the areas to the east of the rebel base and forces approaching from the south killed another three thousand. Just over one hundred of the more than five hundred original defensive structures remained.[245] Defectors informed Zuo that many inside the city were starving even though Ma Hualong was distributing food daily. People were eating seeds, grass, and shoe leather.[246] Some came out and begged to surrender. Liu Jintang authorized it on the conditions that their particular bastion was abandoned and all weapons and population registers were turned over. This prompted others to submit, though dozens of leaders remained intransigent.[247]

On December 18, 1870, Ma Hualong and others started turning over weapons to the Qing, hoping to cut a favorable surrender deal. Liu was now close enough to the inner stronghold to bring his big guns to bear and inflict serious damage. Some eight thousand old and weak Muslims submitted to the Qing on January 1, 1871.[248] The men were put into army units, and the women were escorted outside the attack perimeter. Zuo ordered that food be given to these refugees, and many were resettled in Pingliang. A vice-prefect was appointed in Pingliang specifically to oversee the peaceful assimilation of the Hui. Zuo remained suspicious of the pernicious influence of the *ahong*, so he urged the establishment of schools to "encourage the Muslims to read the books of Confucius and Mencius" to make the meaning of propriety and righteousness clear. He also discussed the need to introduce the Sacred Maxims of Kangxi and other edifying texts.[249] Still convinced of the superiority of Han culture, he sincerely saw cultural assimilation as the key to long-term peace and prosperity.

Ma continued to dangle the possibility of submission, but the fighting did not abate. Liu reiterated that all arms must be turned over as a precondition and not one scrap of iron could be retained. The Qing also wanted to see the *hukou* (population) registers. An estimated four to five thousand people remained inside Jinjibao proper, but hardly any were fit for combat. As more guns were turned over and refugees streamed out, Liu Jintang selected 1,800 sturdy men for a final assault.[250] Ma finally agreed to meet Liu Jintang in person, but when the gates were opened, the embittered Qing commanders seized him and his retinue.[251]

Liu wanted to kill Ma at once but held off, hoping that Ma could be used to persuade other rebels to surrender. He also wanted to make sure all the weapons were turned over.[252] More than two thousand guns, many of foreign provenance, were recovered. The court authorized Ma's execution on February 7, and Ma Hualong and some eighty of his followers were killed by slow slicing on February 21, 1871.[253] Ma was initially spared as Zuo tried to get him to write letters encouraging other rebel leaders to surrender, but the Qing decided he was simply too dangerous and untrustworthy. The Qing had discovered a hidden cache of 1,200 guns when they searched Jinjibao. In an act eerily presaging the search for weapons of mass destruction in Iraq in the early twenty-first century, Zuo said that he knew the rebels had more arms hidden and authorized the execution of the leaders as a preemptive measure.[254] Nearly 200,000 taels in rewards were distributed among the victorious troops, amounting to about 2,000 per battalion.[255]

Mop-up operations were brutal. Hundreds were killed in nearby strongholds, and hundreds more reportedly immolated themselves to avoid capture. As many as nine thousand more rebels were slain as the fighting continued, hundreds were captured, and hundreds of weapons were recovered.[256] Massacres were reported in various localities, but perfunctory investigations tended to accept the explanations of Qing officials who argued that those killed were had not sincerely surrendered.[257] Local officials were brought into the process of pacification, and it seems likely that some took the opportunity to settle old scores. Many of the Qing forces from the east had finally reached the front, and they were detailed to assist in the pacification process.[258]

Just 11,000 Muslims were said to be left in Shaanxi.[259] In a letter to Jinglian, then the Manchu commissioner of Urumqi, Zuo said, "Because the region has long been subjected to the devastation of military operations, gazing over the landscape for hundreds of *li* one sees only white bones amidst the yellow weeds and human habitation has been cut off. I want to extend relief but in these conditions there are many obstacles and . . . it's going to be very difficult to accomplish anything fast."[260]

EFFORTS TO REHABILITATE SOCIETY

Some of the recovered supplies and loot were redistributed to the people, though the army requisitioned some as well, notably horses that could serve as war mounts.[261] Reports indicate that many of the women were given to Zuo's soldiers to become concubines or servants. Other young family members were relocated to Fujian or Guangdong to be indentured servants to soldiers. Some confiscated funds were used to enroll soldiers into Qing units, including to boost the strength of the Xiang Army, though only around 20 percent of those who surrendered were deemed combat worthy. There were debates over how many troops to station in these areas. On the one hand, the court was worried about the rebellion reigniting, but on the other hand, they were sensitive to concerns that a heavy military presence might provoke lasting resentment; and of course, the cost was a factor. Funds were needed to repair fortifications and waterworks.[262] Around 20,000 noncombatants were resettled in refugee camps, most around Pingliang in accordance with Zuo's plan noted above.[263] He also had primary schools built in Pingliang for the edification of the masses.[264]

Zuo prohibited opium cultivation, though the populace resisted the edict in both active and passive ways. He expressed concern that some officials sent to investigate reports of opium cultivation were bribed by the cultivators with their crops.[265] In an effort to get his message across to the masses, Zuo had his opium ban promulgated in rhyming four-character phrases.[266] At the start of 1873 Zuo again tried to enforce opium bans, though foreign sources claimed the directive came from the court rather than Zuo himself.[267] Zuo wanted cotton to replace opium cultivation, arguing that cotton prices had been rising and it was a viable economic alternative. He also pushed for expanded cultivation of rice and mulberries for the silk industry. Books on cultivating all these crops were printed and widely distributed, but results were mixed. The climate was not necessarily suited to these southern crops, and opium was still apparently more profitable.[268] And equally important, the Qing state had come to rely on opium taxes. Foreigners criticized the efforts as both improbable and impractical.[269] Zuo eventually relented, arguing in 1881 for a higher tax on opium since it had proved impossible to curtail its cultivation.[270]

As promised, Zuo provided the Hui with seeds, tools, and livestock and allowed them to follow their cultural and religious practices, at least those of the Old Teachings. He even authorized the construction of new mosques.[271] A modified version of the *baojia* mutual security system headed by trusted local Hui was set up to ensure order and prevent the transmission of heterodox teachings.[272] Zuo petitioned the court to officially ban the New Teachings, arguing that "this can really be thought of as separating the good from the bandits" and also that Muslim unrest in the Qing since the Qianlong reign could be traced to them. He likened heterodox doctrines to the White Lotus doctrines in their ability to delude and inflame the masses. Along these lines, he pointed to how Ma Hualong had styled himself the supreme (*zongda*) ahong (*imam*), an explicit challenge to Qing legitimacy that could not be countenanced.[273]

Moreover, Zuo wanted the ban implemented quickly to nip future rebellions in the bud. The bad Hui would be angry, but the good Hui would admire the government for bringing lasting peace and stability. Like misguided children, the Hui could not easily distinguish between good and bad, so it was best to simply prohibit the New Teachings, which would also obviate the need to keep large garrisons in the region to preserve the peace.[274] He concluded his appeal to the court by saying that such an act would reveal the benevolence of the monarch in the tradition of the august founder of the dynasty.

Zuo's proposal met with mixed results. The court did authorize the New Teachings ban for implementation in Gansu.[275] The notice was to be posted in all mosques in the province and promulgated by all the *ahongs*. Religious leaders could be executed for preaching the New Teachings, but punishment would not be extended to their followers so long as they promised to change their ways. The good Hui need not fear and could continue their lives and practices as before. While acknowledging that Qianlong himself had correctly recognized the dangers of the New Teachings, the court nonetheless rejected implementing Zuo's petition empire-wide on the grounds that it would be difficult to enforce. Local officials were often ill-informed and had only a faint grasp of doctrinal differences among the Hui.[276]

The violence had severely affected the local infrastructure and economy, so Zuo prioritized restoring both. He ordered the construction of boats and restoration of bridges to restore all lines of communication to Lanzhou. He stressed the need to ensure adequate gunpowder supplies for the armies while also encouraging local commerce. He established a publishing house in Xi'an to print edifying Confucian texts for distribution among the populace and supported building more local schools, demonstrating that he sincerely believed in the transformative power of education, particularly a proper Chinese education.[277] Restoring the tea and salt trades was a priority. Another measure adopted was investigating local appointments and putting more responsible local officials into positions of authority. Muslim leaders were given extra rewards and promotions for getting fellow believers to submit to Qing authority.[278]

Jinshun reported that *baojia* had already been established in several areas, and local leaders were cooperating with Zhang Yao to implement the laws and keep order. Roving Qing cavalry patrols were deterring bandits. Many weapons had been turned over or confiscated. Relief bureaus were being set up across Gansu at a cost of around 20,000 taels per month to get them up and running.[279] As they restored the devastated countryside, the Qing were also rebuilding the infrastructure they would need to supply and prosecute the war to defeat Yakub Beg.

THE STRUGGLE FOR HEZHOU

The Qing now turned their attention toward Hezhou, located southwest of the Gansu provincial capital of Lanzhou and defended by the formidable Ma

Zhan'ao. Like Jinjibao, Hezhou was well defended by an elaborate network of stockades and bastions that made adroit use of the rugged terrain. Ma Zhan'ao was a savvy leader whose lineage had held sway in the region since the Jin dynasty (1115–1234). As had been the case with other districts in the northwest, the economic ripple effects of the Taiping Rebellion had affected Hezhou in that its subsidies were curtailed. People formed militia to survive in the poverty-stricken, polarized environment. Gangs and factions emerged. The Qing troops exacerbated tensions by pursuing rebels into the mountains to collect noses and ears for rewards and by indulging in rape and plunder. Mass starvation and cannibalism were not unknown.[280]

Ma Zhan'ao's solution was to facilitate trade and commerce but discourage private profit-seeking in the tradition of the Koran. He set up trade consortiums with some close allies and discarded the rotten local leadership established by the Qing state.[281] Over time Ma Zhan'ao emerged alongside Tuo Ming, Ma Hualong, Ma Wenlu, and Bai Yanhu as one of the key Muslim leaders. He was arguably the most militarily capable of them and cleaved most closely to the true spirit of his teachings, particularly with respect to his concern for the people under his charge. Zuo apparently recognized this quality and was more amenable to negotiations with him than he had been with Ma Hualong.[282] He was also eager to play up the "good Hui being spared" angle, as rumors of full-blown cleansing of the Hui were still circulating, no doubt prompted by the Qing troops' atrocities in the wake of the capture of Jinjibao.[283]

Zuo ensconced himself at Anding, some eighty miles to the east, and concentrated on mustering supplies, although the death of his logistics expert, Zhou Kaixi, in a mutiny in the spring of 1871 slowed the process.[284] He followed his usual practice of drawing up careful plans, and his forces set forth in the seventh month along three routes, led by Fu Xianzong, Xu Wenxiu, and Yang Shijun.[285] His total troop strength was only around 35,000, so defeating the enemy with brute force was not an option. Zuo moved to Jingning to oversee the campaign. In the late summer Zuo's forces steadily advanced, capturing Kangjiayan (also called Kangjiaji) at the end of the eighth month.[286] Around this time the court got concrete news that Russia had occupied the Yili Valley in the name of "securing" it for the Qing and "preserving regional order." Concerned by this news, Zuo decided to go after Hezhou and Suzhou simultaneously and dispatched Xu Zhanbiao to scout conditions at the latter city.[287]

The Qing steadily marched southwest, taking the forts that protected the strategic corridor into Hezhou. Government forces hacked their way through the mountain passes starting in the early fall.[288] Qing reports indicate that they fought more than a hundred battles in the autumn of 1871 alone, with Zuo noting, "There is no day without a battle."[289] Despite these successes, Zuo admitted in a letter to his son that the terrain favored Ma Zhan'ao. And the constant fighting created serious attrition, with battle deaths accompanied by desertion despite Qing efforts to keep discipline and morale high. It was estimated that barely half the original Huai Army troops were still present. "What is called the Huai Army is not really the Huai Army," one official observed.[290] Several Qing commanders had been slain as well.[291] Supply issues also continued to bedevil the Qing, as Gansu had allegedly received just 300,000 of 7 million pledged taels in supplies.[292]

The fighting was much like that around Jinjibao, with the Qing taking heavy losses as they bulled through rebel defenses by relying on artillery superiority as well as engineering skills.[293] By November 17, 1871, they had crossed the Tao River on rafts and floating bridges built by their engineers.[294] Fu Xianzong smashed a Hui army at Heishan. As they closed in, the rebels tried to cut the Qing supply lines, achieving some success.[295]

The Qing stepped up their attacks on the outer defenses of Hezhou in early 1872. The rebels had dozens of bastions in the area and sallied forth to cut Qing supply lines. The government troops attacked the newly erected defenses for several days but could not bring them down.[296] The rebel leader Ma Haitan led five hundred "expendables" (*gansidui*) forth in a commando raid, trying to drive the Qing back with guns. The Muslims followed up their successes with more triumphs, advancing all the way to Dongjiashan and capturing seventy Qing forts along the Tao River. Supply woes continued to bedevil the Qing, and there was talk of a temporary withdrawal. Qing forces lost discipline as they retreated through the spring mud. Hannah Theaker calls this the "worst loss of Zuo's career."[297] The retreat turned into a full-blown rout at Xinlupo. Zuo's forces were defeated at Dongjiashan in February, and the commanders Fu Xianzong and Xu Wenxiu were killed there. Ma Zhan'ao and Ma Haiyuan recovered the corpses of the Qing commanders and returned them to Zuo. The foreign press covered these reverses and promulgated a rumor (once again) that Zuo was about to be replaced. The *North China Herald* concluded that rampant peculation had undermined Qing effectiveness, and one writer speculated that "soon most of north China will be under the rule of the Mahomedans."[298] The *Herald* also charged that subordinates of Li Hong-zhang had deliberately held back in order to make Zuo look bad because Li desperately wanted to be viceroy of Gansu and Shaanxi, presumably due to the potential for lining his pockets.[299]

Fearing a repeat of what happened at Jinjibao, Zuo quickly replaced the fallen officers and kept up his pressure. Zuo then appointed Wang Debang, a decorated veteran who had been working in a support role, to assume command of the armies. He also executed six other officers for their failure in battle, though he blamed the defeats to a combination of supply woes and tactical errors by troops that were not his best.[300] He called for the supply and pay rates to be set at the level of those paid to the Huai Army to improve morale and performance.[301]

But it was only a matter of time before Zuo's superior resources would carry the day. Ma Zhan'ao decided to submit despite his victory, reasoning that he could hold out for only so long, and to resist would eventually result in the annihilation of his family and followers.[302] "Even if we accumulate ten victories," Ma said, "it won't be enough. One defeat will bring all to naught. . . . If we seek pacification from a position of strength and presuming the court is sincere about wanting to receive our submission, we can all return to our bygone days of peace."[303] His associate Ma Haiyan agreed, seeing this as their best chance to gain lenience after ten years of rebellion. There were some who still wanted to fight and plotted to attack the Qing at Anding, but Ma Zhan'ao warned them that it would result in their total annihilation. He pointed out that even Hong Xiuquan, who had conquered more than six hundred towns and cities, was pacified in the end by the Xiang Army. Things had been bad in Gansu between the Han and Hui for more than a decade. How could they not want this to end? In what is likely an apocryphal flourish of Han historians, he allegedly added, "How can Hezhou resist All Under Heaven? The superior man sees his opportunities and acts, not waiting for the end of the day. Now matters have transpired to allow us to submit and no viable options remain. I've already made my decision and wish to hear no more words from the rest of you."[304]

Zuo accordingly sent envoys to Sanjiaji to say that he would permit surrender if weapons and horses were turned over. Ma gave the Qing some 4,000 horses and 14,000 weapons in addition to his troops.[305] He also asked for assurances that his people would not be relocated. Zuo acceded to that request because moving them would have been costly and inconvenient.[306] Ma's descendants remained influential in the region until the communist takeover. Although a Han official was appointed governor of Hezhou, the Muslim *ahongs* retained their posts and powers. This trade-off suited Zuo well and proved a great windfall for the Qing.[307] The Muslims from Hetao gave Zuo a Tang painting of men on horseback titled *Pingrong jun* (Pacifying the Rong on horseback), which he sent home to his grandchildren in Hunan.[308] Though some Qing officials voiced their distrust of Ma, Zuo argued that having loyal Muslim allies in such a strategic place would open up Qing operations in both the east and west without forcing them to expend valuable resources forcibly pacifying Hezhou.

THE CAPTURE OF XINING

As Zuo was taking Hezhou, Xu Zhanbiao was guarding the approaches to Suzhou and coordinating defense efforts with Chenglu and Liu Mingchuan. On his way to Suzhou, Xu defeated Bai Yanhu in a river battle. Bai fled to Xining, northwest of Lanzhou on the Yellow River, and sent out peace feelers.[309] Xining had been one of the hotbeds of the rebellion since its inception because it was one of the places where rumors of ethnic cleansing originated. There had been heavy fighting there in the spring of 1871 as Ma Zhan'ao made common cause with Bai Yanhu. Ma had also welcomed refugees from Jinjibao, prompting Zuo to step up the pressure.[310] Zuo steadily amassed supplies through the summer of 1871 while keeping tabs on the developing situation in Xinjiang. Chenglu skirmished with Bai Yanhu at the same time, though his actions were primarily reactive.[311] The overall Qing strategy was to prevent the various rebel groups from aiding one another. To this end, they brought in Mongol troops to serve as mobile strike forces.[312]

Xining could be approached by just one road, and fortifications extending out some eighty *li* around it made the city a miniature version of Jinjibao.[313] Liu Jintang mounted his assault in the final three months of 1872, cutting his way through the fortified gorges and fighting more than fifty battles in a bloody campaign. The rebels gathered by the thousands in the passes and gorges, launching hit-and-run attacks, but the Qing forces pounded them relentlessly with artillery and advanced toward Xining in multiple columns. They continued to build way stations and towers to facilitate the transportation of supplies. Rebels were enticed into ambushes by feigned retreats and then flanked by Qing units.

Xining proper was defended by former partisans of Bai Yanhu.[314] As the Qing cordon tightened, the rebel leaders sued for peace. Seeing this as a delaying tactic, Liu had a subordinate set the outlying towers ablaze. The Qing killed four thousand in their final assault. When the city was liberated, some 30,000 prisoners allegedly came forth to burn incense in welcome.[315] The ringleaders fled to Datong with Liu in pursuit. While others got away, Ma Yongfu eventually surrendered to Qing forces at Bacheng. Liu reported that he recovered more than 4,000 guns and 1,600 horses from the rebels at Xining. Many of the weapons were of foreign manufacture, attesting to the extent of Central Asian trade networks.[316] Though Liu Jintang and others were dubious about the sincerity of Xining's surrender, when Bai Yanhu later returned to the city the people reportedly shut the gates and refused to admit him and his followers.[317]

Zuo established rehabilitation bureaus staffed by Han, Hui, and local ethnic groups, making good on his pledge to restore the local economy.[318] Such bureaus were only loosely organized and issued broad—and sometimes contradictory—directives. In a letter to a local Qing official there, Zuo warned that even though the Muslims had capitulated before the awesome might of the Qing, the Hui were prone to duplicity, and it was hard to distinguish the good from the bad. The victors should not be too indulgent toward the Hui, Zuo said, lest some return their allegiance to the rebel side.[319] Nevertheless, he told the central authorities that he trusted in the sincerity of Ma Zhan'ao and predicted that if land registers were cleared up and the infrastructure restored, local prosperity could return within a decade.[320] Local officials were not always so positive. Wang Shengyuan, the prefect of Xunhua, noted, "From the rebellion onward, there have been no officials in the city and so ten years have passed where [the people] did not know law, discipline officials, nor punishment, and did not know etiquette, righteousness, honesty, nor shame."[321] Once more, the Han paternalism directed toward the Hui and the American paternalism directed toward Filipinos and Native Americans are strikingly similar, right down to the use of carrots and sticks to encourage cooperation and assimilation.[322]

FINISHING THE BATTLE FOR SUZHOU

As Zuo was restoring Xining, Bai Yanhu struck out for Suzhou to join the rebel forces there. Suzhou had been held by rebel forces off and on for years. It was well defended by artillery, and many defeated Muslims had fled there, bolstering the city's troop strength. Suzhou had also served as a base for Muslim raids on Dunhuang and other places beyond the Great Wall. As noted above, Xu Zhanbiao had been actively fighting for the Qing in the area since the spring.[323] Other cities in the region remained in rebel hands, and struggles raged through the year.[324] Qing troops fought a four-day battle with Bai's forces outside Lanzhou in the seventh month of 1872, but he eventually fled west, skirmishing with them intermittently over the next two months. Liu Jintang pushed for mobilizing all available resources to crush Bai once and for all, but the Qing were hampered by the presence of local bandits and uncertainty about the loyalty of the recently surrendered Ma Zhan'ao.[325]

In a letter to Xu Zhanbiao, Zuo expressed cautious optimism that holdouts in Suzhou might submit, noting that he would allow them to redeem themselves through meritorious service if they did so.[326] But he was concerned that Muslims who submitted might not be trustworthy, as had been the case elsewhere, so they should carefully consider whether any would be allowed to keep their weapons. In other letters, however, Zuo stressed the sincerity and assistance of Ma Zhan'ao, so there was also a clear precedent for Muslim loyalty.[327] And he reminded Tang Zhanglin, a Hunanese then serving as governor of Shaanxi, "The completion of affairs in the west lies in grand strategy; it cannot be decided solely by troops on the battlefield."[328]

Liu Jintang also joined the assault on Suzhou. He occupied Luotuobao and Nanchuan in the autumn of 1872, killing more than ten thousand rebels in a battle in a snowstorm. His army continued its progress through rugged mountains and gorges, trusting artillery to blast through defenses as he advanced toward Dongguan.[329] Ma Guiyuan, who had been defending the area, fled but was subsequently captured and executed by Liu Jintang and Ma Zhan'ao.[330] The Qing recovered mounts, eight hundred guns, and six thousand spears that later proved useful in the siege of Suzhou.[331] Zuo sent three thousand men from his Xiang Army to the siege in late 1872, along with his commanders Zhang Yao and Song Qing. Siegeworks were constructed like those used at Jinjibao. Fighting throughout the fall brought some progress, but the rebels remained stubborn. Zuo reported that multiple relief columns had been thwarted and the rebels inside were reduced to eating their horses.[332] But his own men were suffering too as the winter weather set in, and he urged the delivery of winter uniforms.

In the first month of 1873 Du Wenxiu and other ringleaders of the Muslim rebellion in Yunnan were captured and executed.[333] Although the Yunnan movement was entirely separate from the rebellion in the northwest, this was an important symbolic victory for the Qing. In the next month Liu Jintang secured the forts at Datong and Xiangyang, and Jinshun's army advanced to the outskirts of Suzhou. The Qing brought in their mountain splitters to smash through the outlying defenses, simultaneously attacking from multiple directions to divide the rebels' strength. Corpses piled up as the rebels withdrew through the northern defenses. Xu Zhanbiao moved closer to the three forts west of the city, using protective carts and tunneling under the walls to lay fuses. Some rebels burst out to contest the Qing but were ambushed. The charges went off and the Qing captured the first fort.[334]

In a letter to the Zongli Yamen written at the same time, Zuo stressed that Qing power was still not sufficient to control the Muslims in the northwest, so it was no wonder that the Russians had taken advantage of the situation and moved into Yili. With more troops and supplies and the proper cultivation of resources, he was sure he could alter the balance of power. He advocated sending a forceful envoy to settle a treaty with Russia and restore the border. If the Qing did not tie them up in Yili, he warned, the Russians would seize Urumqi next. He also inquired if the Zongli Yamen had come up with their own comprehensive plan.[335]

Ma Zhan'ao succeeded in drawing some regional leaders over to the Qing side, but Zuo remained cautious of their loyalty even while praising their contributions to the Qing cause. For example, when one Ma Shouqing surrendered, bringing three thousand horses, two thousand guns, and five thousand spears to the government side, Zuo wanted the figures verified. He also cautioned other officials that Hezhou remained unstable due to local bandits.[336] And he remained concerned about the potential for local unrest provoked by those who fled Suzhou.[337] Furthermore, he was troubled by ongoing unrest in Xining, where local bandits and rebel holdouts still raided. Bai Yanhu was in the area stirring up trouble, so Liu Jintang was detailed to contest him.[338] When Bai was eventually driven beyond the Great Wall the court ordered Zuo to pursue him.

Song Qing reached Suzhou from Ganzhou in the early summer.[339] The Qing forces arrayed around Suzhou numbered around 32,000 by this point. Ten regiments were detailed to keep pressure on the defenders as others tried to grow food and to fight off those trying to come to the aid of the rebels. Others were deployed in mobile operations outside the city. Xu Zhanbiao took another fort in early spring, opening Qing supply lines to Jiayuguan in the west, and also managed to link the siegeworks from the southeast to the southwest of the city. By the sixth month the Qing had taken another key bulwark of the outer defenses, had captured the *ahong* Zhang Jingfu, and had built towers from which to fire down into the city.[340] Xu kept attempting to lure rebel groups out while also intercepting relief columns, personally leading the troops in many of these actions.[341] As the Qing tightened their siege, Zuo wrote to Xu that the defenders were "like a fish about to be gutted."[342]

Nevertheless, Zuo realized that he was by no means ready to lead troops deep into Central Asia until Suzhou was secured and he had established more stable supply bases. If the Qing were serious about recovering Yili, they first had to seize Urumqi. And in order to retake Urumqi they would need to set up *tuntian* to supplement the armies' food. This would have the bonus of keeping the soldiers occupied while they waited to move and would avert potential problems with the locals. These considerations also convinced Zuo that bringing smaller numbers of better trained and supplied troops was the key to establishing and maintaining control of Xinjiang.[343] Further, if the siege of Suzhou went on much longer, deserters from the city would flee beyond the pass and create still more problems in Central Asia.[344]

The fighting dragged on through the summer as the Qing battered away at Suzhou's defenses. Xu Zhanbiao tried sapping the walls but was repeatedly thwarted by countermeasures. He extended his own ditches, arraying additional cannon platforms around them. Troops were rotated in and out so that the gunners could maintain steady barrages, but the defenders remained intransigent. Nonetheless, their own efforts to sally forth were met by a "wall of death" in the form of Qing artillery barrages.[345] Xu Zhanbiao detailed subordinates to expand their patrols farther from the city to intercept partisans who might bolster the defenders' morale. Probing attacks by Bai Yanhu and other rebel partisans had little strategic value, but troops and resources had to be diverted to drive them off. Bai himself was reportedly wounded in one engagement.[346] The Qing concentrated on shoring up their supply lines, with Zuo exhorting local officials to step up their efforts.[347]

By late summer only the innermost defenses remained. But as was the case in many Chinese cities, the walls were made of densely packed earth and reinforced with brick on the outside. They were also sloped inward, which helped deflect projectiles and reduced the force of impact, making them practically impenetrable even to artillery.[348] The walls were more than thirty-five feet high and were encircled by a moat ten to twenty feet wide and ten feet deep. When Xu deemed direct assaults impractical, he decided to try sapping the walls and starving out the rebels, whom he knew to be short on supplies.[349]

Seeking to bring a conclusion to the long siege of Suzhou, Zuo himself went to the front in the eighth lunar month. Two of his commanders had been killed by enemy fire, and he wanted to assess the situation firsthand. The rebels' morale plummeted when they saw the supreme commander's banner.[350] Zuo inspected the defenses, conferred with his commanders, and set up a rotating attack schedule that would keep steady pressure on the defenders.

Zuo camped outside the south wall, increasing the number of troops on the south, west, and north, and ordered an all-out assault. Xu Zhanbiao's forces breached the moat that evening but didn't penetrate the city walls. The next morning shots rang out as the defenders rallied, and some Qing petty officers fell while trying to scale the walls. The Qing kept up dual sapping and bombardment efforts, attacking from all sides simultaneously. A few rebels emerged and begged to surrender but were refused. Zuo built two more siege towers to fire down into the city. Half the defenders were killed, and corpses piled up as others came out to submit. The rebels remaining inside were now reduced to eating mules, camels, and leather. But their spirited defense had inflicted more than five hundred casualties on the attackers in just four days.

Bai Yanhu's efforts to aid the rebels in the spring and summer of 1873 were repeatedly stymied.[351] The arrival of Liu Jintang further disheartened those inside the city, and more envoys were sent out to negotiate, but Zuo was disinclined to offer favorable terms because he knew the fall of the city was imminent. The defenders then offered to turn over 1,100 guns and 1,000 swords and other weapons, and some came out to surrender to commanders at checkpoints outside the city. But the fighting continued, and the corpses piled higher in the streets. News that Bai Yanhu was raiding widely outside the Great Wall added urgency to the attackers' efforts. The court authorized more supplies and the livestock needed to carry them.[352] The defenders sallied forth in desperation, but a force of five to six thousand was beaten back through the south gate. An even larger force burst out after that with similar results. Some then sought to negotiate, but Xu, like Zuo, felt that victory was nigh.

The fighting and negotiating continued, and rebels slipped out of the city nightly to scavenge for food. The defenders kept sallying forth, but their efforts weakened as the Qing artillery reduced their numbers. The rebels still had a fair number of guns, however, and Zuo knew retaking the city would not be easy. The inner city had high, thick walls and a deep moat. And of the 1,500 or so cannons the Qing had brought in, only about 900 were still operational. Escaped prisoners told the besiegers the rebels knew they had no chance of surviving and were resolved to fight to the death.

The Qing arrayed large batteries to direct artillery fire at specific places and filled in ditches and moats to get closer to the walls. The rebels pulled back inside the inner defenses, taking food stores with them and torching buildings behind them. The Qing hit multiple towers and gates, prompting a small rebel force to sally out, but Qing cavalry smashed the force and captured a leader. Some of the gates were breached and a street fight ensued, but the rebels still held out. But Qing firepower drove them further inside, and the heavy guns were pulled to within the shadow of the walls. New cannon platforms were erected to fire into the inner city.[353]

In the end, Zuo's Krupp guns and explosive mines proved too much for the walls of Suzhou, and Qing forces broke through, killing an estimated 5,400 as the city burned around them. Jinshun and Song Qing entered simultaneously through different gates, and defenders who came forth to contest them met only death.[354] They captured the remaining outer defenses at the same time. Ma Wenlu surrendered on October 24, 1873,[355] and was sentenced to decapitation. Zuo had all the prominent commanders executed eight days later, along with 1,573 soldiers.[356] Another 7,000 Muslims were executed on November 12. According to Zuo some 2,000 old people, women, and children were resettled in Lanzhou, although other sources claim that just 900 of these people survived.[357] Zuo claimed that of the 30,000 Han formerly resident in Suzhou, barely 1,100 survived, and many of these had been plundered by the Hui.[358] Some modern writers blame Zuo Zongtang for the massacres; others charge that Xu Zhanbiao did not have adequate control of his men. In terms of supplies, the Qing recovered more than two thousand weapons, though only seventy horses.[359] Public stele were erected commemorating the Qing victory over the rebels and serving as a warning to others who might attempt rebellion.[360]

With Suzhou taken, Zuo dispatched Xu Zhanbiao west to aid the belea-guered Qing forces in Yili.[361] Zuo himself had already been ordered to head west, but as was his custom, he planned to amass sufficient supplies before embarking on such a major operation. Jinshun was ordered to get out there in the meantime and apprehend Bai Yanhu if possible. The government also wanted to secure Hami as the embarkation point for subsequent operations.

The victorious Qing enacted recovery plans in Suzhou as they had done elsewhere, including setting up *baojia*, digging wells, opening mines, setting up *tuntian*, and opening barren lands for cultivation by the impoverished and dispossessed. Zuo estimated that barely 10 percent of the original landowners still had their plots after the long-term unrest. He also freely admitted that the violence did not emanate solely from the Hui side, so it was imperative that local officials smooth over relations and bring the people close again. Zuo was adamant that only the Old Teachings would be sanctioned henceforth.[362]

Realizing he would need more arms for his westward campaign, Zuo built a new arsenal at Lanzhou, primarily to make ordnance, and placed it under the oversight of Lai Chang, a native of Guangdong who had served Zuo in Fujian. Lai would later help Zuo establish another arsenal in Suzhou itself, where they made Prussian-style breechloading rifles and field guns.[363] In a letter to the Zongli Yamen, Zuo bragged that they could manufacture copper caps and fuses, large and small bullets, and Prussian seven-shot breechload-ers. Workmen were brought in from Ningbo, Guangdong, and Fujian. The arsenals at Lanzhou and Suzhou would prove critical in Zuo's campaign in Xinjiang.[364] Zuo stockpiled cannon and ammunition at Lanzhou and put aside funds that could be used for subsequent operations. Huai Army elements trained there, preparing the troops for subsequent actions in Suzhou and far-ther west. Supply depots were set up and plans sketched out for building more and bringing in porters, camels, and other support staff to facilitate a lengthy campaign in Central Asia that would use Suzhou as the embarkation point.[365]

In the following months Zuo and his administrators combined rehabilita-tion efforts with bandit suppression.[366] They investigated the lands themselves with an eye toward estimating the viability of newly opened wastelands. Offi-cials grappled with various issues as they tried to implement new registration requirements for the Hui. Local administration in the region had always been rather ad hoc and not in line with empire-wide standards, and the devastated infrastructure further hindered rebuilding efforts. The Qing officials realized that local militia were still necessary for defense against bandits but expressly forbade the Hui from constructing stockades lest they restart the cycle of violence. Indeed, it appears that the Hui needed permission for a variety of building projects. Private militia were forbidden. At the same time, Zuo allowed some local flexibility in implementing regulations, realizing the need to restore economic stability above all else.[367] Efforts were taken to prohibit soldiers from exploiting the local populace. Soldiers were expected to grow at least some of their own crops.[368] Requests were sent to the central government to send more seeds for distribution to the people. Soldiers were also encouraged to spend their earnings in local markets to support the economy.

Zuo was promoted to Grand Secretary for his efforts, becoming the only Han official in the entire history of the Qing to hold this prestigious rank without having a *jinshi* degree.[369] He was also promoted to governor-general. Some modern scholars are highly critical of Zuo's actions at Suzhou and elsewhere in these campaigns, contending that he abandoned his cherished Confucian principles when it came to protecting ordinary Muslims.[370] These charges are not entirely without merit, though it seems that his actions were calibrated in accordance with immediate military circumstances. Obtaining the surrender of Ma Zhan'ao was doubly advantageous as it saved Qing lives and brought a potentially valuable and resource-rich ally into the fold. In the case of Suzhou, assuming that many of those in the city were in fact escapees from Shaanxi and elsewhere in Gansu, the massacre represented the opportunity to stamp out key elements in the ongoing rebellion, likely leading to the long-term peace Zuo craved.

THE PURSUIT OF BAI YANHU AND PREPARATIONS FOR THE WESTERN CAMPAIGN

Bai Yanhu, the slipperiest eel of all, escaped beyond the Great Wall and allied himself with Yakub Beg. His troops raided freely across the region and he cultivated ties widely, but he was generally an untrustworthy ally and a middling field commander. Even relatively small garrisons proved able to repel his assaults, as was the case at Jimusa in the summer of 1874.[371] But his role in spreading the rebellion was significant to the Qing, and Zuo identified him as public enemy number one in later years, noting that he could not be controlled and had to be "snuffed out."[372]

Following the fall of Suzhou, Zuo continued amassing supplies for his planned recovery of Xinjiang. The government had already transferred some troops from Uliastai and Barkol south to the region around Hami and Dunhuang to secure the trade routes.[373] Mongol cavalry were sent south. One of the first orders of business for Zuo was to release units from Suzhou to aid Hami, which would be the springboard for the forthcoming campaign. Next, he wanted to spread word of the Qing victory at Suzhou to boost morale and reassure those hanging on in Central Asia that help was on the way.[374]

Over the next several months, Zuo refined the plans he had already sketched out for the recovery of Xinjiang, pulling all the strings available to secure an ample supply reserve. As he wryly noted, one does not lightly mount a campaign into Central Asia without adequate preparations.[375] Drawing on his extensive knowledge of previous campaigns in the region, Zuo devoted his considerable planning powers to mapping out each stage of the operation. In addition to troops, porters, weapons, ammunition, and funds, he needed camels, donkeys, and other draft animals. Water sources had to be identified and, if possible, wells dug in advance and supply depots set up. The death of the nineteen-year-old emperor at the end of 1874 threatened to derail all Zuo's careful plans. Li Hongzhang, who had recently been given oversight of coastal defenses, vigorously argued that strengthening those defenses was far more important than pursuing a western campaign. This debate, discussed in the following chapter, had repercussions that are still being felt today.

ASSESSING THE CAMPAIGN AGAINST THE DUNGANS

True to his character, Zuo was the first to pat himself on the back after his victory over the Muslims, which he credited to his ability to stay the course and not get discouraged by early reverses. As he put it, "The affairs of the realm are all in the hands of important people. There would be no country with Shaan and Gan. There would be no Shaan and Gan without me."[376] He was especially proud of the schools he established afterward and the publishing ventures that produced works such as the *Five Classics,* the *Four Books,* and *The Classic of Filial Piety* for dissemination to the masses, noting that officials in some localities were requesting these books for their eager students.[377] Other officials wrote flattering letters praising the success of Zuo's programs in opening up lands for cultivation and restoring the infrastructure of ravaged places such as Suide.[378]

Modern Chinese scholars focus on Zuo's efforts in Lanzhou, crediting him with introducing Western ideas as well as advancing the overall educational and cultural level of the people during his tenure there. Prior to Zuo's arrival, one supporter notes, everything was run through Xi'an, which was too distant from Lanzhou and Xinjiang. It was difficult for locals to sit for exams, and it cost hundreds of taels for would-be officials to travel to Xi'an. Perhaps only 20 percent of qualified subjects had the opportunity to sit for the exams.[379] Zuo sponsored primary education at all levels, including free public elementary schools, mosque-based schools, and provincial examination study halls, some of which received edifying texts produced by the publishing houses Zuo set up in Lanzhou. In addition to their educational benefits, the publishing works stimulated the local economy by employing hundreds of workers and brought scientific and technical knowledge to the northwest and Central Asia.[380] He also rebuilt the city's walls and infrastructure, assuring its continued preeminence in the region.[381]

Zuo himself pronounced the defeat of the Dungans his greatest achievement—until his next one, of course, which would be the surprisingly swift dispatch of the formidable Yakub Beg, self-proclaimed "Defender of the Faith" and emir of Kashgaria. But even Zuo admitted that the cost of the western campaign had been devastating to the inhabitants, with barely 60,000 of the 700,000–800,000 Muslims previously residing in Shaanxi surviving to be resettled in Gansu.[382] One modern scholar estimates that the Hui population in Shaanxi was reduced from 1.5 million to fewer than 100,000.[383] Writing in the early years of the People's Republic, Cui Ji'en called Zuo's policies outright butchery, arguing that while Zuo's ostensible philosophy was "submission then extermination," in fact this was just a ploy to get the Muslims to surrender their weapons so he could slaughter them.[384] Cui accused Zuo of repeating this pattern in every campaign from Jinjibao through Suzhou. In true communist fashion he also claimed that Zuo used the plundered wealth of the slaughtered Hui to financially benefit himself and his family.[385] Based on what we know about Zuo's general austerity and lifestyle, this charge, at least, seems absurd.

But there is no doubt that the Dungan Rebellion and the suppression of the Dungans caused tremendous local destruction and dislocation. The gazetteer of Hu County states that by the Guangxu era virtually all the mosques there had been destroyed and there were no more Hui teachers, though there were still some six hundred Catholics residing in the county.[386] Indeed, combined with the operations in Xinjiang discussed in the next chapter, the Dungan Rebellion lasted more than 15 years, covered more than 25 percent of the Qing empire, and affected more than 10 million people. Some accounts claim that the total population of Gansu dropped from 15 million to just 1 million over the course of the rebellion.[387] Recalling other accounts of the destruction attributed to the rebels, Cui Ji'en cited a British colonel named Bell who reportedly said, "For 1000 *li* it's a barren wasteland. All one sees in the distance are white bones and yellow spears; there's no smoke from cooking fires."[388]

These figures are confirmed to a significant extent in the official Qing campaign history of the rebellion, *Pingding Shaan-Gan Xinjiang huifei fanglue*, compiled under the direction of Prince Gong soon after the events in question. This collection encompasses thirty volumes in the modern reprint and is one of the major primary sources for this chapter and the following one. These detailed and unaltered accounts are replete with records of massacres that attest to the "body bag mentality" that animated many Qing officials while also illuminating the mindset of the court as it struggled to appear unbiased in governing the disparate peoples under its rule, realizing that it was "bad press" to be viewed as protecting the Han over the Hui. Eric Setzekorn credits this to the Qing propensity to create purely military victories that favored certain metrics but did little to create lasting peace, though Zuo himself was more sophisticated in his approach.[389] Certainly there were Han and Manchu officials sympathetic to the Muslims' plight, but the fact that rumors of wholesale massacres gained enough traction to spark preemptive revolts speaks volumes concerning the state of race relations in these regions. The Qing may have conquered these areas, but the ad hoc nature of local administration and the degree of favoritism and corruption present almost ensured unrest.

Echoing accounts of the destruction wreaked by endemic warfare in the Ming-Qing transition era, Lavelle notes the presence of massive packs of wolves roaming the countryside of Gansu. He suggests that the overall population of the province declined by 75 percent and by as much as 90 percent in some places, such as Pingliang.[390] Gansu's population did not reach prewar levels again until the start of the communist era.[391] As seen above, Han immigration as a result of the Taiping Rebellion had heightened existing tensions in the 1850s and 1860s. During the wars themselves, many minority peoples fled the strife for interior provinces, but postwar famines spurred further migrations.

After all the campaigns were over, the Qing state encouraged Han migration to the northwest and Xinjiang to help rebuild these regions and better integrate them into the regular structure of the empire. Government settlement programs offered land, tools, clothing, and other incentives. Many Hui were resettled there as well, so that by the end of the Qing an estimated 80–90 percent of the population in many counties in Gansu were recent migrants.[392] In Xinjiang this figure may have been as high as 40 percent, as migrants from all over the empire sought fresh starts there and many soldiers elected to stay as well. This demographic shift laid the groundwork for tensions that still grip the region today. As Nailene Chou rather laconically notes, Zuo could have "found a more positive way to deal with multi-ethnic society," though given Zuo's upbringing and the circumstances of the rebellion, such critiques smack of presentism.[393]

On the positive side, Zuo did attempt to live up to his pledges to rehabilitate local society. Residents were enrolled into population registers and given official seals confirming their status as loyal subjects. They were given seeds, draft animals, and tools. Adults received eight taels per month in relief funds, and children received five taels. Even in the midst of the fighting Zuo set up aid stations for disaster relief. He continually encouraged planting new fields to feed the troops and locals. Indeed, his efforts on behalf of the Hui are noteworthy in that they were opposed in some places by local Han gentry who claimed that the Muslims were troublemakers and requested the dispatch of "extermination troops." Others resisted Zuo's directives and tried to stop Hui from receiving their tools, grain, and subsidies. Zuo was forced to send out his most trusted subordinates to ensure compliance. Unsurprisingly, these were usually men from the Chu Army.[394]

It should also be noted, however, that Zuo remained adamantly opposed to the New Teachings and strictly prohibited them where possible, treating them as heterodox. And to prevent mosques from being used as defensive structures in case of rebellion, Zuo issued strict regulations for their size, height, moats, and the like. Altars could only be a certain height, and tall towers could not be built or repaired inside walled structures. He also set up his own system of *ahong* (local imams) to regulate local affairs and smooth over potential misunderstandings. Overall, these measures were reasonably effective, and within five or six years, agriculture had greatly improved and much of the economic prosperity of Shaanxi and Gansu was returning.[395] Finally, the destruction of the rebellion undermined the traditional power of the Sufi *shaykhs*, paving the way for the rise of Muslim warlords in the region.[396]

Map 5. Reconquest of Central Asia

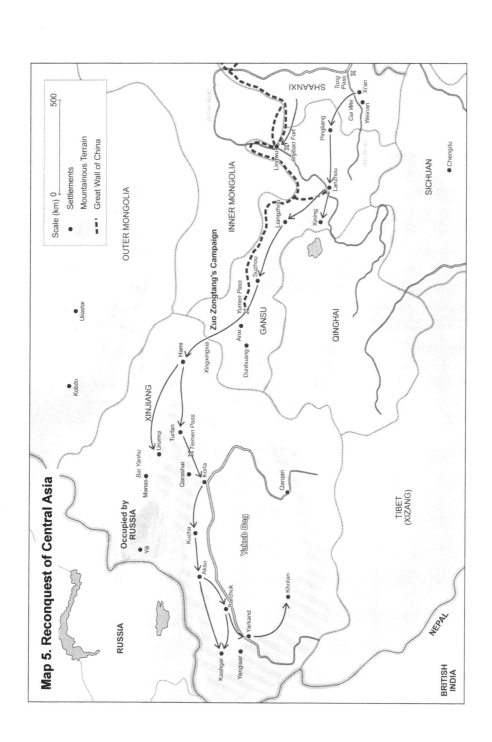

6

PLAYING THE GREAT GAME

THE RECOVERY OF XINJIANG AND THE YILI CRISIS

I'm finished with empty words. It's time to unleash the awesomeness of the army!
—Zuo Zongtang

The conquest of the Dungans had been a long and bloody campaign to be sure, but Zuo finally managed to bring the rebels more or less to heel, paving the way for his next great enterprise, the recovery of Xinjiang. As noted in the previous chapters, Zuo had been envisaging the recovery of this vast region from the time he was first appointed to contest the Muslim rebels in the northwest. He was no doubt heavily influenced by the example of Lin Zexu, whose works Zuo consulted closely both before and during his campaign and with whom he had discussed frontier affairs. Indeed, Zuo can be credited with fulfilling the dreams of the early nineteenth-century Qing statecraft scholars who saw Xinjiang as a "promised land"—an outlet for Han settlers and a potential resource base.[1] Victory there would bring Xinjiang into the empire as a regular province, something Zuo also desired for Taiwan. Zuo's campaign marked the culmination of Qing imperial practices and also laid the groundwork for a new envisioning of the Qing empire as growing Han nationalism became integrated into the Qing imperial project, a process that would soon overwhelm the empire itself.[2] Furthermore, Zuo's efforts to more closely bind Xinjiang to the rest of the empire marked the apex of the influence of his "Hunan mafia." From 1884 to 1911 some 55 percent of the men who held office in Xinjiang were from Hunan, and most of them lacked even the lowest civil service degrees.[3] Zuo's commander Liu Jintang went on to serve as the province's first governor. The demographic and cultural changes wrought by virtue of Zuo's campaign had repercussions that still resonate as various modern actors choose different aspects of the story to support their preferred narrative.

AN OVERVIEW OF QING ADMINISTRATION IN XINJIANG

The Qing conquest of Xinjiang and its formal integration into the administrative structure of the empire was one of the great events of Chinese history.[4] The various steppe nomad groups had been the eternal foes of sedentary "China proper," and though periods of warfare were interspersed with times of mutually profitable peaceful trade, the dynamics and rhetoric tended to be confrontational. The defeat of the Zunghar Mongol confederation in 1757 therefore represented the end of an era, as the Qing combined their own steppe warfare prowess with their logistical and technological capabilities to create a military machine capable of projecting power into Central Asia to an unprecedented degree.[5] Never again would the Mongol tribes or confederations present a serious threat to the centralized government of China.

Emperor Qianlong, who presided over the final victory over the Zunghars, was well aware of the significance of this achievement, considering it integral to the establishment of a forward defense network by the Qing.[6] For that reason the Qing attempted to create an administrative framework for the region that would safeguard the interests of the empire and yet allow for regional cultural differences.[7] James Millward, one of the leading scholars of Qing Central Asia, notes that "Qing administration in Xinjiang . . . was complex, multi-layered and more sophisticated than any imperial government in the region that had preceded it. It permitted a degree of local autonomy while maintaining a monopoly on military force and employed a cadre of local officials under the supervision of imperial officers. It managed ethnic diversity through multiple administrative and legal systems and did not attempt to proselytize or culturally assimilate."[8]

Qianlong established the post of military governor of Yili in 1761 to administer the vast region. In the regions south of the Tianshan Range imperial agents were stationed in Kashgar, Yarkand, Yengisar, Ush, Aksu, Kucha, and Karashahr. The job of these agents was to collect taxes and oversee begs (a generic title for Qing appointees).[9] A councilor stationed at Kashgar presided over all of these agents. There were no permanent Manchu garrisons.

The post of Hakim (or Akim) Beg, rank 3, was given to Muslim leaders. Initially, the highest-ranking begs were selected from families who had joined the Qing in crushing the Zunghars.[10] Eventually all native bureaucrats held the title of beg, as it came to designate an "official" rather than a hereditary noble.[11] Over time the Qing grafted all manner of beg titles to different elites, and their responsibilities varied greatly. The councilor at Kashgar recommended men for this post, and they were formally appointed by the Ministry of Personnel.[12] Some local notables also received princely titles from the Qing, though most such individuals had other ties to noble status within their own communities.[13] The highest ranks dressed in Chinese fashion, and some even wore queues. The begs were given servants and various perks rather than regular salaries. This afforded them considerable local influence and was a virtual invitation to institutionalized corruption.[14]

At the highest level, Qing Xinjiang was divided into three military circuits (*lu*). These were divided in the north and south by the Tianshan Range, so that the old territory of Zungharia was designated Tianshan beilu. Kashgaria, located in the south, was designated Tianshan nanlu. To the east was Donglu, which encompassed the territory around Turfan, Hami, Barkul, and Urumqi. Unsurprisingly, the closer one got to China proper, the more the administrative structure resembled that of the rest of the empire. Turfan and Hami were designated subprefectures. Urumqi was an independent department with three counties: Changji, Fukang, and Suilai. In 1773 a circuit intendant (*daotai*) answering to the governor-general of Shaan-Gan was placed in charge of Urumqi. Nonetheless, there were military officials with overlapping responsibilities and semi-independent princedoms in some areas, including Hami and Turfan. The overall commander was the supreme general stationed at Yili. Prior to the late nineteenth century all the high officials were Manchus or Mongols. The northern and eastern circuits had resident garrison troops, while the southern circuit had rotating troops who served three- to five-year stints. Rebellions to the south and west thus had the potential to fester owing to the lack of troops and the great distances involved in dispatching military force.[15]

While the rebellions we are about to discuss suggest that the Qing administration of Xinjiang was compromised by serious shortcomings, and certainly it was, there is no evidence that it was any more effective, malevolent, or benevolent than other contemporary empires. So while the general level of the government was not great in Xinjiang, the administration functioned more or less for decades with only minor irruptions.[16] From its inception the government in Xinjiang required heavy subsidies from the central authorities, and local administrators were forced to be creative in devising means to stimulate the regional economy such as opening mines, building up the infrastructure, establishing *tuntian*, expanding cotton production, and trading with local nomads to acquire much-needed livestock. The unprecedented scope of the Qing implementation of *tuntian* presaged Chinese Communist Party efforts to create state farms (and labor camps) in the region.[17] Some of these farms were so successful that grain could be cheaper and more plentiful in Xinjiang than in China proper, especially during the periods of civil war. But disturbances elsewhere in the empire compromised the Qing ability to provide subsidies to Xinjiang. By 1860 silver stipend payments to Gansu and Xinjiang were an enormous 10–20 million taels in arrears. This opened the door for an array of would-be conquerors to try their hand at expansion.[18]

The region was also affected by broader global trends, including the so-called Great Game for empire being waged between Great Britain, Russia, and the Ottoman Turks in Central Asia.[19] Inns, water depots, and post stations opened initially for military purposes also facilitated long-distance trade. Cities like Kashgar and Yarkand attracted merchants from India, Russia, Central Asia, and Turkey bringing gems, silver, silk, livestock, hides, furs, medicine, and, of course, opium. Kwangmin Kim suggests that these various ties facilitated the creation of "oasis capitalism," thereby integrating this region more closely into the wider world and subjecting it to influence from competing powers in a complex process that offered significant opportunities to local power brokers.[20] Initially, Chinese immigration to the region was restricted. In fact, some policies favored the Uighurs, even if these were practical measures designed to increase revenue rather than to support the position of the latter.[21]

CENTRAL ASIA AS A POWDER KEG

The Khanate of Khokand (Khoqand) is a prime example of how global forces contributed to the development of Central Asia and the rebellions of the nineteenth century. Khokand was a city-state located in the central Fergana Valley that flourished between 1709 and 1876. It attained its independence from the Khanate of Bukhara in 1709 and was more or less independent until forced to become a Qing protectorate during the reign of Qianlong. It was restyled as a khanate under the reign of Alim Khan (r. 1799–1811). Khokand benefited from the Qing defeat of the Zunghars and expanded in part due to the brisk rhubarb trade in the region.[22] Its leaders embraced the interests of multiple constituencies, including local tribes, the military, and *ulama* Sufi orders, which allowed the polity to greatly expand its territory and influence. They also sheltered the Afaqi (White Mountain) Khoja clan, a Sufi group connected to the Dalai Lama and opposed to the Ishaqi (Black Mountain) clan.[23] These ties embroiled Khokand in many of the conflicts of the nineteenth century as Afaqi revanchists repeatedly sought to retake control of territories they had lost to the Qing and others.[24]

These Khokandi invasions helped stimulate the court to lift the ban on Han immigration to the region. They also convinced the Qing to grant Khokandi merchants the right to trade tax free in Xinjiang, a deal that marked the zenith of Khokand's power.[25] Some scholars suggest that this 1832 treaty thereby set the precedent for new types of trade agreements that would become the norm for the Qing following the First Opium War.[26] But they can also be viewed as simply another manifestation of the inherent Qing flexibility and pragmatism in such matters. The so-called tributary system of foreign relations was in fact very flexible, allowing for multiple interpretations and implementations of policy according to local situations. It was designed to create an image of Qing supremacy, to be sure, but that was a veneer that most contemporaries were undoubtedly savvy enough to see through, even if many modern scholars are blinded by misguided and facile contrasts between "traditional" Chinese diplomacy and supposedly "modern" Westphalian ideas. In fact, as Laura Newby adroitly points out, the tribute system was a "diplomatic toolbox, a toolbox replete with a vast range of instruments, all of which had been tried and tested by the rulers of China over the centuries." The system "allowed the Qing court to exercise a range of concessions (and punishments) that enabled it to achieve its greater purpose—the integrity of the empire and increasingly its own legitimacy to rule."[27]

In the wake of a holy war between Khojas in Khokand, the Khoja leader Wali Khan, son of Jahangir, invaded Kashgar multiple times between 1847 and 1857.[28] The Qing finally defeated Wali's force of 20,000 with their own army, estimated at 12,000 in the summer of 1857, using superior firepower. Wali survived and fled but was later arrested and poisoned by Yakub Beg (1820–1877).[29] In response to Wali's incursions the Qing set up additional watchtowers, increased the number of cavalry units, firearms, and cannon, and considered plans for appointing new officials in places such as Aksu.[30] The Qing also encouraged the "good Muslims" to join with the Han in creating militia for mutual defense.[31] They eventually set up eighteen signal towers between Aksu, Yarkand, and Yili, each with fifteen to twenty horses, for relaying messages and to serve as bases for patrols.[32] Efforts were also devoted to restoring local administrative efficiency and working more closely with the begs, though the latter's peculation continued to stoke unrest.[33]

Scattered minor uprisings erupted over the next few years, but these were handled, often with the aid of mercenary troops that included Han, Mongol, and Muslim units. Local begs were also credited with assisting government forces.[34] Qing records indicate that superior firepower allowed them to prevail most of the time but also draw attention to the fact that the rebels also had access to advanced weaponry, attesting to the level of militarization of the frontier. These uprisings exposed the underlying weakness of the Qing, who lacked sufficient troops and were further hamstrung by supply difficulties. Despite troop increases in the Daoguang era, many garrisons were operating at 70 percent or less of prescribed strength, necessitating the assignment of Green Standard troops to make up the shortfalls, a practice previously eschewed by the Qing.[35] The frontier disturbances sometimes spread into Gansu and farther east. But the various Muslim groups were far from united. While they might all denounce the Qing as infidels, the interests of Uighurs, Khojas, and Dungans differed as often as not, and these differences would facilitate Zuo's efforts at reconquest.

THE RISE AND SPREAD OF THE REVOLTS

We have noted how rumors of the massacre of Muslims in Shaanxi and Gansu helped incite and spread the Dungan Rebellion. The same rumors played a key role in Central Asia, with some sources suggesting that they spread through mosques and provoked the Han to create militia for self-defense.[36] The Dungans revolted first in Kucha, then in Urumqi, Yarkand, Kashgar, Yengisar, Manas, Changji, and Gucheng. The rebellions spread to Turfan and Hami and north and east from there.[37] The circumstances of the uprising in Kucha mirror those in Shaanxi discussed in chapter 5. Amid rumors of an impending Han massacre of Dungans, the locals worked with Turkic Muslims to defeat the small Qing garrison. It is highly likely that the rumors in Kucha had spread there from the east.[38] Exacerbated by tensions stemming from the conflicts over the previous decades, and abetted by the contemporary weakness of the Qing in the region, rebellion spread fairly easily. But despite Yakub Beg's later declarations, the rebellions do not appear to have been part of a systemized jihad against the Han and Manchus, as some modern Chinese sources suggest. In fact, contemporary records note that merchants were often targeted, lending credence to Kwangmin Kim's observations about economic disparities driving strife in the region.[39]

The revolt in Urumqi started on June 26, 1864, led by the Dungans Tuo Ming and military commander Suo Huanzhang.[40] As elsewhere, its underlying causes included new taxes, Manchu abuses, and ongoing strife between the Dungans and Han immigrants. The latter conflict precipitated the rise of gangs, not unlike the situation in Shaanxi and Gansu. Sources suggest that Suo and Tuo had been plotting for years and likely spread the rumors of impending Han massacres of Muslims themselves. Tuo was most likely an adherent of the New Teachings, which bound him to Suo Huanzhang and Ma Hualong.[41] Tuo declared himself king and appointed generals in various regions.[42] Suo was named grand marshal. These appointments were primarily symbolic at this point, but in the eyes of the Qing government they linked the uprisings in Xinjiang to those farther east. Yarkand saw revolt in late July, and some two thousand Qing troops and seven thousand Chinese residents were massacred there. Kashgar erupted around the same time, allegedly because the Qing killed Dungans there.[43] From Kuche the rebels launched campaigns to the east and west. Turfan was taken in March 1865 after an eight-month siege. In the meantime, many other cities were captured and many Han were massacred.

In the west, the unrest spread to Karashahr, Ush Turfan, Bai, and Aksu. The revolt reached the Yili Valley in November 1864, though Yili did not fall until March 1866.[44] In most of these early rebellions the Dungans revolted first, followed by the Turkic Muslims/Uighurs, though in most cases the latter assumed leadership roles. Some of the rebel leaders proved quite savvy, cutting trade deals with the Russians and making other changes to local sociopolitical arrangements to advance their personal agendas. This demonstrates the fluidity of local situations and the degree to which even relatively isolated cities were plugged into regional and global processes.

In a few cases the Qing forces held out and holed up in the inner Manchu cities; in others their heroic sacrifices were later honored. Records indicated that more than ten thousand Qing were massacred in Yili, and in some places the rebels piled severed hands and feet outside the city walls.[45] In his usual florid style, D. C. Boulger describes the heroic deaths of the Qing defenders of Yengisar as evincing "their superiority over the semi-barbarous races under their sway even when all hopes of a recovery seem to be abandoned."[46] The rebellion was not a coherent movement, nor was it a Uighur separatist movement, despite modern nationalists' claims.[47] Many of the rebel groups were mutually antagonistic from the start, and cities changed hands repeatedly. Reading the primary sources can be especially challenging because reports reaching Beijing were often badly outdated by the time they arrived. The imperial responses likewise often referenced situations that had long since changed. Matters improved significantly with the establishment of telegraph communications toward the end of Zuo's tenure in the northwest.[48]

THE RISE OF YAKUB BEG

In 1865, Alim Quli, then the ruler of Khokand, sent Buzurg Khan to attack Kashgar, with the Muslim adventurer Yakub Beg as his military commander. Yakub soon displaced Buzurg Khan and seized Yengisar, returning tribute to Alim Quli. He next seized Kashgar with Dungan assistance, killing thousands of Han and compelling many Manchu guards to commit suicide. This was not the only time Yakub would form common cause with the Dungans, though such alliances of convenience did not last. In fact, the militia leader and guerrilla fighter Xu Xuegong, who would later receive many honors from the Qing court, had helped Yakub Beg attack Urumqi in 1870, forcing Tuo Ming to surrender. This was despite the fact that Xu himself had raided Hui stores and formed bands against Dungan rioters.[49] Xu and Tuo later joined forces to resist Yakub after Xu had a falling out with him. Xu was also involved in the fighting around Turfan. Yakub embodied the kind of semiofficial adventurer who could prosper in such an environment, playing both sides to his own benefit.[50] Nonetheless, most of Yakub's troops were Andijani mercenaries and others animated by his seemingly orthodox Muslim faith.[51] This would create problems for him later.

Yakub's background is colorful and has been highly romanticized. Some stories say that he worked as a dancer or entertainer before joining the military. Several popular books and even a novel were written about him during his lifetime, and numerous accounts from contemporary Western observers survive. He was born around 1820, but his racial background is unclear. He was most likely Tajik. He spoke multiple languages, including Persian and Turkic. His father and grandfather had some religious and political standing, and his sister was married to the governor of Tashkent. Around 1840 he got a job as a minor official, and over the next decade, through the combination of his own talents and his family status, he advanced to beg status, commanding a force of five hundred men.[52] He was involved in a series of local power disputes that gained him notoriety, including clashes with the Russians over a place known as the White Mosque.[53] Over the next dozen years he was embroiled in assorted frontier intrigues, alternately supporting and opposing petty local potentates.

As noted above, he was eventually appointed by Alim Quli to aid Buzurg Khan, another son of Jahangir, in reestablishing Khokandi influence in Kashgaria. After his initial exploits in the service of Buzurg Khan, he captured Yengisar from the Dungans in April 1865, allegedly massacring some two thousand Chinese when he took it.[54] He spent the summer of 1865 battling other regional power contenders. With better guns and more experienced commanders he bested his rivals and took Yarkand and Kashgar, killing most of the Chinese in the latter city.[55] The Qing *amban* of Kashgar and his family allegedly committed suicide by detonating a mine under their residence rather than be captured by Yakub. He picked up seven thousand more troops from a defeated foe, lost control of Yarkand, and later recovered it. After taking Khotan, Yakub went after Kucha, where internal strife facilitated his conquest on June 5, 1867, giving him effective control over all of Kashgaria.[56] But he had foes on all sides. There were nomadic raiders to the east. Chinese guerrillas and *tuanlian* forces distributed across the region also created a fluid situation. Nonetheless, Yakub seized Turfan in November 1870 and Urumqi soon thereafter, also defeating a Mongol force near Kurla as he implemented his policy of blood and iron.[57] While his successes in these early years were certainly impressive, they drained his resources and created many enemies, most notably among the Dungans, who might have been his strongest allies.

The Russians initially adopted a policy of nonintervention, but frontier raids and streams of refugees prompted them to reconsider. Fearing that Yakub might decide to occupy the Yili Valley on behalf of Britain, they instead decided to occupy the fairly rich area themselves, ostensibly on behalf of the Qing, to help preserve order in the region.[58] In June 1871 the Russian commander G. A. Kolpakovskii defeated a Muslim force and occupied Suiding, where a local sultan submitted to him.[59] The Russians officially assumed control on July 4, 1871. Some locals continued to resist Yakub, and assorted militia were organized in hopes they could hold out until Qing assistance arrived. A few of these intrepid bands even managed to kill Muslim commanders, gaining valuable combat experience that would avail the Qing down the road. The Qing sent the official Yongquan to negotiate

Yili's immediate return, but he was hampered by poor weather and a lack of troops and did not meet with his Russian counterparts until May 1872. The Qing sought to buy time and maximize resources by encouraging the creation of militia.[60]

By the summer of 1871 Yakub Beg controlled southern Xinjiang from Kashgar to Turfan. Within two years Urumqi was fully under Yakub's sway, and his realm was nearing its apex. His startling successes prompted the *Times* of London to hail Yakub as "the greatest man Central Asia has produced for many a generation."[61] Such proclamations, along with their own intelligence reports, greatly alarmed the Qing, who were afraid that their recent victories in Shaan-Gan might be undone. They considered various countermeasures, but as of 1871 this mostly involved reinforcing Hami and creating another forty-four supply depots stretching west from Gansu.[62] The government would soon authorize Zuo to go beyond the pass to restore order, though as we will see, the implementation of this directive was delayed and later contested.[63]

YAKUB BEG'S STATE

Yakub never assumed the title of khan, though he was pressured to do so. He allegedly preferred to be called "the Fortunate One" or "Fatherly Holy Warrior." The Ottoman sultan gave him the title emir in 1873. Qing reports make vague references to Yakub's declaration of overlordship of the Muslims of the region. Whatever his pretensions concerning an official title, Yakub had few secretaries and almost no advisers. He wanted no potential challengers to his rule, probably because he had witnessed the endemic squabbling between potentates in the region in his younger days.[64] He did split his realm into provinces, known as *vilayet*, with their own governors.[65] Each province also had a judge specializing in sharia law.

Yakub's military force totaled about 40,000 troops. There were three main categories: mounted infantry (*yigit*), infantry (*sarbaz*), and artillery (*taifurchi*). The ratio of horse to foot was approximately three to one. Soldiers were both recruited and conscripted and paid in cash and in kind, though rates varied greatly and declined over time. Most of his high officers were not Kashgarians, and he appointed people of different races and backgrounds to deter plotting. Both practices undermined morale and stoked resentment among his followers, compromising his military effectiveness when the final showdown came. Provisions were supplied to commanders by central controllers. Tracts of land were given to laborers and soldiers to produce food supplies in an arrangement similar to *tuntian*. He tried to procure modern weaponry from the Russians, Ottomans, and British to gain an advantage against the Qing. He got some weapons from Britain and the Ottomans and started producing his own rifles in Kashgaria. Most of his rifles were muzzle-loading Enfields produced between 1853 and 1867.[66] His nominal overlord, the Ottoman sultan, provided two thousand arms, including heavy cannons.[67]

Yakub's military was very much of the times in being a hybrid organization that mixed the latest weapons with traditional ones and combined modern formations with those favored by the entrenched hereditary elites. He emphasized drill and training in the Ottoman style while adapting elements from the Afghan, Indian, and Russian militaries.[68] But the diverse groups did not mesh or train well together, and their skills varied. They also had difficulty communicating. Moreover, Yakub fancied himself a gifted commander and often ignored the advice of his Ottoman advisers. His troops also resisted wholesale military reforms, most notably his Khokandian cavalry, who remained rooted in their native traditions, not unlike their counterparts elsewhere in the Ottoman Empire.[69] Over time Yakub's army became bloated and expensive, but he dared not reduce its size because he feared the Qing response.

In some ways, Yakub's most striking achievements were in the diplomatic sphere. When he first seized power, the Russians were cautious. They tried to stir up trouble with Khokand while also sending out diplomatic and trade feelers. Yakub played coy, refusing to entertain requests until the Russians acknowledged his status.[70] They finally dispatched Baron Kaulbars to Kashgar, and in June 1872 Yakub signed a treaty with Russia.[71] Mostly trade oriented, it involved Russia recognizing Yakub as the de facto ruler of Kashgaria and Urumqi in exchange for generous trading privileges. This gave him the leverage to cut an even better deal with Britain in 1874.[72]

Yakub's relationship with the Ottoman sultan solidified his legitimacy among Central Asian Muslims and coincided with the Ottomans' efforts to extend pan-Islamic ideology in hopes of reviving their fortunes.[73] Yakub further curried favor with the Ottomans by minting coins with the sultan's name on one side. For Yakub it was a win-win situation: his nominal overlord was largely unable to affect his policies, while he could press the sultan for weapons, supplies, and advisers.[74] But at the same time, his vacillation in other areas allowed the Russians to absorb Bukhara in 1868, Khiva in 1873, and Khokand in 1876.

HANGING ON IN XINJIANG

Through the early 1870s, as Yakub sought to consolidate his position, the Qing strove to hang on. They were concerned about their lack of troop strength in the region and tried to ship firearms and artillery to loyalists to serve as force multipliers.[75] They augmented these efforts by sending mobile strike forces, often of Alashan Mongols, to sever the rebels' supply lines and raid their cities and camps.[76] The government sent funds west to procure more horses and camels. More officials were sent to stabilize pockets of resistance. Priority was placed on stabilizing Barkol in order to protect Suzhou, still under siege by the Qing.[77] Manchurian troops and livestock began trickling into the front in the spring of 1873, with reports from field commanders underscoring the importance of firearms.

Hami was besieged again, and Zuo was tasked with getting supply depots established around Anxi in order to send assistance.[78] The court sent more Mongol and Manchu Banner troops to guard the strategic throat between Xinjiang and Gansu.[79] The siege of Hami intensified in the autumn of 1873 and stretched to more than forty days as supplies dwindled. The Qing scrambled to lift the siege while simultaneously delivering supplies farther west to Yili.[80] The court pressured Zuo to finish the siege of Suzhou so they could divert forces to rescue Hami, which Zuo did in early November.[81] Though matters briefly took a turn for the worse, Bai Yanhu and his followers were eventually driven away from Hami and toward Turfan.[82]

With Bai no longer a major threat, the Qing were able to more actively harass Yakub's forces. Though the battles were mostly skirmishes, the Qing forces freed prisoners and captured weapons and supplies while dislodging the rebels from some isolated forts.[83] These seemingly minor triumphs were important for several reasons. It became increasingly obvious to Zuo that professional, well-led troops in smaller numbers could prevail over Yakub's polyglot, unevenly trained minions.[84] Indeed, the fashion in which the Qing won many of these battles suggested that terrain and weather were more formidable opponents than Yakub Beg, so Zuo planned accordingly. As the Qing continued to gather intelligence, build militia forces and supply depots, and skirmish with the rebels, Zuo took a brief holiday.

ZUO ASSUMES COMMAND

Upon returning from his vacation, Zuo resumed his planning for the next campaign. He knew that the steppe could not accommodate an overly large force, so he issued directives to remove old and weak troops from the ranks and improve accounting methods to determine supply and equipment needs. He decided that some troops would stay and drill around Suzhou because that region could better support *tuntian*. He ordered more cannons from the east. Zuo estimated it would take at least two years to restore productivity to the region, but the more settlers the Qing could attract, the faster this would happen. He was also concerned about supplies, though he predicted a good winter wheat crop that would help the situation. The number of draft animals arriving in the form of mules and camels likewise gave him cause for muted optimism, though transportation costs were not cheap. As for the Dungan rebels, Zuo claimed that their previous force of 700,000–800,000 had been reduced to 60,000, with Bai Yanhu himself leading just over 2,000 raiders.[85] One presumes Zuo's estimates included all the Muslim rebels from Shaan-Gan, since Yakub's forces never came close to these figures.

It is worth noting at this point that Jinglian was technically the overall commander of the forthcoming expedition, with Zuo being the logistics officer while he continued to oversee reconstruction efforts in Gansu.[86] When Jinglian pressed the court for additional troops and supplies, the central authorities responded by pressuring the interior provinces and sending more Chahar Mongols into the fray.[87] They also placed stock in the ability of Xu Xuegong to keep thwarting rebel efforts. As Zuo pursued his reconstruction measures around Suzhou, the court pressured him to extract more from local officials for the war effort.[88] By the summer of 1874 there were Han and Banner troops in Barkol, Anxi, Dunhuang, and Yumen, and three thousand of these were detached to Gucheng. Zuo continued to build supply depots to assist these troops as Jinglian kept the court abreast of the strategic situation.[89]

Always in need of money, Zuo pushed the court to divert more revenues from foreign trade and the tax revenues that trade brought into the maritime provinces. At this time Zuo was officially promoted to grand secretary and governor-general of Shaan-Gan, paving the way for his assumption of command over the whole Xinjiang operation.[90] Additional funds were indeed transferred from maritime customs revenues, and the Ministry of Revenue was instructed to verify the estimates provided by field commanders for their respective upkeeps. Once all the figures were calculated, the court agreed to earmark another million taels in maritime tax revenues in addition to the 2 million already collected.[91]

Qing officials vigorously debated supply routes and procedures through the autumn of 1874 and into 1875, with Zuo offering his detailed plans and the court countering with questions and requests for clarification on nearly every point.[92] Even with more troops and supplies coming in, Zuo estimated that it could take two to three years to amass the resources needed for a full campaign. Delays in troop movements caused by lack of supplies and draft animals coupled with Zuo's realization that smaller elite units would be more efficient drove him to scale back the campaign. Zuo's obvious expertise, set against the backdrop of the Great Policy debate outlined below, finally resulted in his appointment as supreme commander of military affairs in Xinjiang in the third month of 1875, with Jinshun as his deputy, replacing Jinglian as commissioner of Urumqi.[93]

As might be expected, the Western press in China seized on reports—accurate or not—of Qing reverses, confidently predicting the end of Qing rule in Central Asia. A report from late 1874 chronicled rebel victories in Urumqi and Tarbagatai and noted that almost all the lands south of the

Tianshan were in rebel hands, though Hami still held out. The report suggested that fighting would be much harder than it had been in Gansu and that the "Amir of Kashgaria" clearly had the upper hand.[94] Subsequent stories in the *North China Herald* chronicled the appointment of Zuo Zongtang, noting he was the first *juren* in the history of the Qing to hold such an exalted post. The *Herald*'s writers viewed the decision to march into Central Asia and contest Yakub as possibly suicidal for the Qing because it practically invited the intervention of Russia, which already had a military presence in Yili. One writer even argued that a victory by Yakub would be best for the Qing.[95] Reflecting the social Darwinism of the era, another story maintained that Zuo's troops were ill-trained and poorly equipped compared with those of Yakub, concluding, "In a fair fight there is little reason to believe Chinese could stand against their more energetic opponents."[96] The same story also criticized the Qing for wasting money on arsenals and gunboats.[97] Similar articles and editorials continued through the end of the year as even those who credited Zuo with being "a capable commander for a Chinese" criticized China's "utterly unscientific" practices in logistics and other military matters. One report called the whole enterprise "an exercise in sheer folly" as it repeated erroneous information that Zuo's force was already cut off and possibly destroyed.[98] By contrast the rebels were praised as "exact specimens of the horsemen under Genghis Khan."

THE GREAT POLICY DEBATE

While Zuo had envisioned a campaign into Central Asia from the time he was appointed to battle the rebels in Shaanxi and Gansu, not everyone saw the value in it. His old rival Li Hongzhang was a particularly vociferous critic, deeming the territory "useless," calling it "several thousand *li* of empty land vainly acquired," and citing the great expense required to simply keep the region in the Qing orbit.[99] Adding that Yakub had the support of the Ottomans, Russia, and Britain—which was not true—Li argued in favor of recognizing the independence of the Muslim chiefs in Central Asia and cited the late Zeng Guofan as supporting his position.[100] Although Li was most concerned to protect his own interests and his dominant position at court as an advocate of coastal defense, he contended that allowing Muslim leaders to build up their own independent states would deter both Russia and Britain in Central Asia. Surviving sources indicate that the opposite was more likely to be the case.[101]

The resulting debate between Zuo and Li and their respective supporters has been characterized as a progressive and forward-looking Li facing off against a conservative Zuo hopelessly clinging to outdated notions of Confucian propriety and enslaved by an "Inner Asian mentality" in his foolish and shortsighted bid to prop up the declining Qing empire.[102] But the debate must be understood against the backdrop of contemporary Qing political discourse, which was informed by the *qingliu* strain of public debate, usually translated as "pure discussions." As in politics everywhere, this was often performative, whereby officials articulated extreme positions as a means of gaining attention and advancing their careers. It is noteworthy that in the 1870s *qingliu* speakers became increasingly bellicose as Qing policies of conciliation seemed to be backfiring, with wolves gathering on all sides of the empire.[103] This forced some to take perhaps more inflexible stands than they might otherwise have in order to protect their own spheres of interest and influence. Indeed, Western reports from the time are replete with references to Li's rivalry with Zuo and its implications for Qing policies, with most leaning toward Li as the "more progressive" reformer. The vainglorious Li may have sincerely believed that he was the key to saving the empire and that what benefited him personally was therefore good for the empire as a whole.[104]

Zuo's arguments centered on both strategic and sentimental grounds. Concerning the former, Zuo invoked the common metaphor of diseases of the limbs versus diseases of the heart.[105] He played up the potential for escalation if he did not act immediately. Bai Yanhu alone was not a formidable threat to the Qing, but if he joined forces with Yakub Beg, both would be empowered. And Yakub was already treating with the Russians, British, and Turkey.[106] The Russians were interested in territory, and the more they gobbled up, the more they would want. If Xinjiang fell, then Inner Mongolia would be next. When that fell, Beijing would be next. The

Western European powers and Japan, on the other hand, were primarily interested in extracting more trading concessions.[107] This could be dealt with in due course simply by calibrating arrangements already in place. Zuo further argued that his campaign was not siphoning funds from Li's coastal defenses because those allocations came from other sources. Playing up the sentimental aspect, he brought up the issue of honoring the ancestral achievements of Qing imperial forebears—an interesting argument coming from a Han official.[108]

Matters were further complicated by Japan's intrigues in Taiwan and the "Margary Affair."[109] The latter involved a junior British diplomat named Augustus Raymond Margary who had been dispatched from Shanghai to southwest China to research overland trade routes between China and India. On his return trip he altered his route to avoid rumored trouble in the area and headed for the city of Tengyue in western Yunnan. Margary and his Chinese staff were killed in a clash with local guerrillas on February 21, 1875, creating an international diplomatic incident, even though international law held China not culpable for the deaths.[110] Thomas Wade, chargé d'affaires of the British Legation, demanded restitution from the Chinese government. After more than a year of diplomatic wrangling, Li Hongzhang and Song Guangtao settled the matter via the Chefoo (Zhifou) Convention. Zuo was particularly annoyed at Li's handling of the affair and its outcome. So he couched his argument in Self-Strengthening, writing to the governor of Liang-Jiang, "If we self-strengthen, then what can England and Russia do to us? But if we aren't able to self-strengthen, we'll be the object of bullying from both England and Russia and then what kind of country will we be?"[111]

Rather than taking one side or the other in the Li-Zuo debate, some noted that coastal and interior defense were in fact interrelated. Interestingly enough, one such official was none other than Li Hanzhang, Hongzhang's younger brother, who called for first crushing the Muslim menace, then releasing the old and weak troops and using surplus funds thereby gained to bolster coastal defense.[112] Wang Wenshao (1830–1908), then the governor of Hunan, vociferously supported Zuo, stating,

If our troops fall behind a step, the Russians advance a step. If our troops lose a day, the Russians gain a day. There is nothing more urgent than this affair. The several nations of Britain, France, and the United States also may exploit the situation to their advantage and take action. Any progressive worsening of the Russian affair will inevitably bring on the maritime problem and our defense will be hard put to the double challenge. As a result the general state of Chinese foreign relations in the future will be unthinkable.[113]

Qing intelligence operations in Central Asia were becoming increasingly sophisticated. More Chinese had direct experience of the Central Asian frontier now, and a few even spoke Central Asian languages. Others were informed by their contacts with Europeans.[114] Zuo had tasked Zhang Yao and Song Qing with sending spies into Central Asia to gather information, particularly south of the Tianshan.[115] In a long letter to the Zongli Yamen, Zuo laid out his overarching plan, discussing Russian trade, the Yili situation, and his plan for buying grain from Russia, noting that gaining Russia's support now would help China in multiple ways later.[116]

Zuo's strongest supporter at court was the Manchu Wenxiang (1818–1876), a member of the Plain Red Banner who was grand secretary and special assistant to Prince Gong for the conduct of foreign affairs.[117] Wenxiang had played a key role in negotiating the treaty with Japan that defused the crisis in Taiwan. His mindset also matched Zuo's in that he was an ardent believer in the need for educational and military reforms. He helped set up the translation bureau (Tongwenguan), took command of training riflemen in the capital, and came up with the idea of sending Anson Burlingame (1820–1870) to the United States in 1867 to serve as China's ambassador at large to Western nations. He was also widely regarded as incorruptible, living simply and eschewing opportunities for graft and enrichment, yet another quality he shared with Zuo. Wenxiang's support helped sway the debate in Zuo's favor, and Zuo was placed in charge of military affairs in Xinjiang on May 3, 1875.[118]

ZUO'S PREPARATIONS

Zuo had been preparing for his Central Asia expedition for years; one might even argue that he had dreamed of such an exercise for decades given his long-standing interest in Xinjiang. He envisioned mounting the campaign in five major phases: (1) reorganize and equip his army; (2) create a stable base in western Gansu; (3) prepare additional bases at Suzhou stretching out into Central Asia via Yumen and Anxi; (4) occupy Hami, Barkol, and Gucheng to use as advance bases for the further penetration of Yakub's realm; and (5) advance from Barkol and Gucheng to take Urumqi and Manas, followed by Turfan and Korla, eventually converging on Yakub's stronghold at Kashgar.[119] Zuo's decision to move north first was based on his knowledge of the terrain, gleaned from consulting recent maps as well as historical ones; his assessment of Yakub Beg's strength, obtained from Russian spies; as well as his knowledge of previous Qing campaigns in the region.[120] He was not overly impressed with Bai Yanhu, who held the north, and felt that morale-building victories there would accelerate Qing progress later in the campaign. He also hoped to divide the enemy's strength by making his plans known, possibly opening Yakub up for a pincer attack from the north and east later in the campaign. As of 1875 Zuo had some sixty brigades under his purview. He deemed this number a bit excessive and was of a mind to detail smaller crack units for the foray into Xinjiang, which he explained in a secret letter to the court in which he also delineated his proposed supply lines and route of attack.[121]

The vast distances involved remained a problem. It was 900 *li* from Liangzhou to Suzhou, another 360 *li* from Suzhou to Jiayuguan, and another 200 *li* to Anxi. The terrain was rugged, and roads were poor. Livestock were in short supply, so he would have to rely on human-powered carts, echoing a solution reached by the Ming centuries before in the war against the Japanese in Korea.[122] Each human-powered cart could transport one hundred *jin* of supplies at a cost of four copper cash per one hundred *li*, which was significantly cheaper, but slower, than using mule or camel transport. Zuo pushed the central government for additional funds while simultaneously pressing merchants in Lanzhou to get him more camels, by far the preferred option for transporting goods. He also worked through merchants to buy sheep and other foodstuffs from Mongol tribes to help feed the armies.[123]

By the eve of his offensive he had amassed around 60,000 troops and reserves, 5,000 wagons, 5,000 donkeys and mules, and 29,000 camels and had more than 16 million kilograms of grain stored in depots stretching from Lanzhou to Barkol.[124] Nineteen of his brigades were from Xinjiang; fourteen were from Henan under the command of Zhang Yao; twenty were led by Jinshun; twenty-four hailed from Hunan under the command of Liu Jintang; and five were from Sichuan under the command of Xu Zhanbiao. Each brigade included two support staff for every five soldiers.[125] In terms of finances, Zuo had secured another 8.5-million-tael loan from the Hong Kong and Shanghai Banking Corporation (HSBC), though the terms were criticized then and have been since.[126] He also wrangled 3 million taels in maritime customs revenue from the emperor.[127] Zuo demonstrated his own diplomatic acumen in concluding a deal with the Russians to buy grain, which significantly cut down on transportation costs.[128] He also discussed his plans with Russian officials to ensure that they were aware of the Qing campaign and would not interfere. Zuo beseeched the Ministry of Revenue and colleagues all over the empire for additional funds, arguing that current subsidies to Xinjiang barely covered one month of military expenses.[129]

Zuo remained concerned that his troops were undertrained and was also worried that the Qing garrisons remaining in Central Asia were understrength, so he tasked Liu Jintang with stepping up training, notably with artillery, including the new mountain-splitters that had been manufactured in Gansu.[130] Some one thousand German smoothbore cannons were brought in, and an artillery division was set up under the direction of Hou Minggui. Zuo also expected thousands of guns from Fujian. He continued to press the court for all manner of supplies, from clothing to tents to draft animals.[131] He also carefully calculated consumption rates and considered ways to avoid overburdening the locals in corvée and extraction, establishing grain reserves that could be used for both the armies and the locals.[132]

The force reportedly made a positive impression on European observers. One Englishman said that "this Chinese Turkestan army has the appearance of one of the strongest European armies."¹³³ Others voiced their appreciation of Zuo's arsenal at Lanzhou. Zuo communicated regularly with Liu Dian to ensure his troops had adequate firearms and supplies of gunpowder.¹³⁴ In a letter to Liu Jintang, Zuo said that more than 20,000 guns had already been delivered to Hami and stressed upkeep and maintenance of these weapons, including the use of proper lubricants to keep them operating in the dry climate.¹³⁵ Zuo's emphasis on having superior weaponry is evident in his assessment of Yakub Beg's capabilities, where he noted that Yakub had significant numbers of firearms, but they were not as state of the art as his own.¹³⁶

Zuo clashed with some of his commanders over the route the Qing forces should take. Inspired by the earlier campaigns of Kangxi and Qianlong, Zuo wanted to take the shorter northern route. Jinglian and Yuan Baoheng favored the southern route. To support his position Zuo noted the lack of draft animals, a result of the recent war in Gansu and its attendant famine.¹³⁷ Zuo's view carried the day.¹³⁸ In the summer of 1875 Zuo held a council of war with Liu Jintang and his other field commanders in Lanzhou. In addition to appointing his military commanders, Zuo designated officials for other duties. Jinshun was charged with coordinating militia activities around Urumqi. Liu Dian was posted to Lanzhou to coordinate affairs in Shaan-Gan and facilitate the delivery of supplies to Zuo's forces farther west. Zuo himself advanced to Suzhou in the third month of 1876 to coordinate the campaign.¹³⁹

Zuo regularly sent out spies to gather information about the ever-changing conditions in Xinjiang and cultivated allies, bringing the formidable Xu Xuegong to his side in 1875. He was especially concerned about the positions of Russia and Britain with respect to Yakub. He also warned Liu Jintang about the dangers of Bai Yanhu working closely with Yakub.¹⁴⁰ He considered the possibility of an attack from Tibet or some other southern place that might sever his supply lines and took measures to deter that. Once he received his intelligence Zuo was confident that he could take Urumqi quickly. This victory would spread awe of his army, facilitating the recovery of the south and impressing China's imperial rivals.¹⁴¹

Zuo was not entirely positive about his prospects, citing the difficulties experienced by Qianlong's armies the century before, but he also thought that he might be able to simply overawe the enemy and win without fighting a single battle. Concerned that Bai Yanhu and his supporters were still looting around Dunhuang, he carefully sketched out plans for supply stations, noting that the troops taking the northern route would be mostly cavalry and the southern ones, infantry. Way stations were set up about every one hundred *li*. Twenty-four were established out to Hami and another twenty-six between Hami and Barkol. Hami would be the staging point. The northern route would extend from Hami to Yili; the southern route to Kashgar.[142] The northern route would embark first, and a special official had oversight of supply matters. Strategic reserves were arranged, and Zuo considered arrangements for purchasing additional livestock from locals as needed.[143] Through the summer and autumn of 1875 Zuo demonstrated his usual vigor in planning and pressuring friends and associates around the empire for additional supplies.[144]

THE RULE OF YAKUB BEG AND HIS FOREIGN RELATIONS

We have a fair sense of Yakub's state and aspirations from a number of surviving Western accounts. Though his rule proved ephemeral, it was impressive in its scope. At the height of his power Yakub claimed overlordship over more than 1 million subjects.[145] This made him a major player in Central Asian affairs. It certainly attracted the attention of the Qing. As early as 1870 Prince Gong told Thomas Wade that the Qing were going to crush Yakub Beg and reclaim control over Xinjiang.[146]

Yakub established himself in Kashgar, occupying the new city built by the Qing in the wake of Jahangir's invasions. He received the honorific *Athalik ghazi*, or "Defender of the Faith," from the emir of Bukhara and proclaimed that he was ready to embark on a jihad against the infidel Qing.[147] He subsequently took the title of emir of Kashgaria, pledging fealty to the Ottoman sultan, and began minting coins to solidify his legitimacy and encourage trade.[148] Yakub sent his nephew as his emissary to Istanbul, interceding through sheikhs in Uzbek lodges who served as contacts for Central Asian

Muslims. To his credit, Yakub cultivated ties with all his neighbors, seeking both legitimation and protection, but his most substantial ties were with the Ottoman Empire.

Yakub's decision to hitch his wagon to the declining Ottoman Empire is interesting in light of the religious and commercial environment of Central Asia in the nineteenth century.[149] Sufi influence remained strong, and most Muslims were oriented toward the west. Although in decline, the Ottoman state was still a major player in Central Asian affairs, and Yakub saw value in their patronage. Kemal Karpat views Yakub as "a new type of Muslim ruler, who sensed that the Sultan-Caliph in Istanbul, as the head of the Muslim community, was potentially a more potent and reliable source of strength than the whimsical local ruling khojas with their own dynastic interests."[150] He credits Yakub with envisioning a pan-Islamic union and considers Yakub's efforts "one facet of the new global Islamic movement and a natural consequence of the institutional ties of Central Asia to the Ottoman state."[151] Karpat adds that Yakub was "the only Muslim ruler to attempt to use the Caliphate to create Muslim unity within his state and secure his survival as an independent entity," though this assertion seems dubious given Yakub's conflicts with the Dungans almost from the start.[152]

Whatever the case, Yakub was certainly savvy enough to keep all his options open by treating with the Russians and British as well, not to mention the Qing.[153] Robert Shaw, a British tea trader, tried to encourage his government to open talks with Yakub. The British dispatched a mission under T. D. Forsyth in 1870, but it failed because Yakub was off campaigning in the east.[154] A second Forsyth mission in 1873 gained Britain many of the same privileges enjoyed by Russia.[155]

Throughout these negotiations Yakub proved himself a canny politician, making vague promises and nebulous assurances to every side while angling to secure the best possible outcome for himself, though the *Qing shigao* portrays him as somewhat of a stooge, claiming that the English secretly aided him to use him as a buffer against the Russians while the Russians used him to curry Muslim support for their occupation of Yili.[156] For a while this balancing act worked. The Russians and the British were suspicious of each other and found themselves forced to respond to allegations of aiding Yakub against the interests of the other party. In one instance the government in London denied they were selling weapons to Yakub.[157] In fact, both sides tended to exaggerate the importance of the other to Yakub in order to gain more traction for their respective governments. As the Russians and British fought over who would give him aid, Yakub happily supplied his troops with weapons purchased from his Ottoman overlords.[158] The Qing were well aware of Yakub's activities in these areas, and his possession of advanced artillery and other firearms figured heavily in Zuo's strategic calculus.[159]

From relatively early in his rule, however, Yakub met resistance from many of those he had incorporated into his "empire," most notably Uighurs, who were unhappy with his strict laws, burdensome impositions, and wide array of new taxes, which contradicted his promises to reorganize tax assessment in favor of the masses. Thousands of Muslims were enslaved in Kashgar and other cities. Yakub also set up secret police to keep tabs on possible political enemies.[160] Some sources contend that Yakub's forces raped, pillaged, and looted, and that his outright favoritism toward his countrymen, especially in the military, exacerbated preexisting tensions. His contemporary British biographer, D. C. Boulger, recognized Yakub's faults along with his good qualities, observing, "Yakoob Beg was a very able and courageous man and the task he did accomplish in Kashgaria was in the highest degree creditable; but he was no Timur or Babur. His internal policy was marred by its severity, and the system of terrorism that he principally adopted; and his external policy, bold and audacious as it often was, was enfeebled by periods of vacillation and doubt."[161] It wasn't long before locals looked wistfully back at the "golden age" of Qing rule as a time of comparative freedom and prosperity, admitting that the Chinese had facilitated commerce better than Yakub did.[162]

Yakub Beg squandered his best opportunities through his own mismanagement. He took to claiming lands and reselling them at high prices. Many of his military followers sublet their holdings and lived the good life in the cities, losing their edge and discipline. Additionally, Yakub neglected public works and other governmental responsibilities in favor of building his army.

But rather than strengthening his own position vis-à-vis the Russians, he had effectively ceded control over the khanates of Khokand, Bukhara, and Kiva by 1873 due to his preoccupation with lands farther east and his ill-conceived jihad against the Qing.

Nevertheless, on the eve of the Qing counterattack, Westerners remained impressed with Yakub and his operation. In the spring of 1876, the *North China Herald* falsely reported that the Chinese had suffered a major defeat and Yakub was "completely in control of the situation," hailing him as "probably the best soldier in Asia." The *Herald* opined that if he did indeed join with his co-religionists in Gansu, the Qing were in serious trouble. Subsequent stories reported mutinies among Zuo's troops at Jiayuguan and the false information that Yakub's forces were already on Chinese soil and that Zuo's army was on the verge of destruction. Unverified reports (again) suggested Zuo had been killed in action. Likewise, the writers cautioned the British government against loaning money to China to fight the rebels because the Qing government was a money pit.[163] As it turned out, these reports could not have been more wrong in their assessments and overall predictions. Zuo's careful planning and training were about to pay major dividends.

SWEEPING AWAY A PAPER TIGER

The success of Zuo's campaign in Xinjiang was truly remarkable. The Qing forces swept across the region almost as if they were on a mere training exercise. Hodong Kim argues that this was primarily because Yakub Beg ordered his troops not to fight, hoping that the aforementioned negotiations would bear fruit.[164] This is possible, though it is also plausible that the Muslim sources Kim cites included this information to justify the poor performance of Yakub's forces. A modern Chinese source credits Zuo's planning, the bravery and patriotism of his soldiers, and the good generalship of his commanders.[165] While the patriotic angle might be anachronistic, the other two points are valid. Zuo calculated costs carefully and proved astute in setting up supply depots and procuring grain from the Russians, even in the midst of unrest there that saw the Russian peasantry on the verge of revolt. Zuo's troops were instructed to maintain discipline and were strictly prohibited from rape and pillage. Zuo wanted the imperial troops to be regarded "like a spring rain" by the local populace.[166] And while it was true that Yakub's forces carried guns acquired from multiple foreign sources, they were no match for Zuo's Krupp guns, repeating rifles, steel cannons with 12- and 15-pound shells, long-range cannons, and mortars.[167] Boulger likewise credits Qing training and experience, likening the Qing force to a Roman legion whose veterans inspired and set examples for the younger troops.[168]

Yakub's realm was also tottering economically. His emphasis on bolstering his military forces and desire for total control resulted in dried-up canals, lousy trade, barren fields, and ruined roads. And though the economy in the heart of Kashgaria to the west was better off, there was still a lot of barter, despite Yakub's efforts to mint coins.[169] He did bring in artisans and miners, but they were not systematically employed and Yakub was suspicious of external trade. His strict implementation of Islamic law and customs alienated many who were used to a more relaxed approach to religion.[170] Finally, his taxes and corrupt tax collectors quickly became even more despised than their Qing predecessors. They demanded more than 75 percent of the yield and added further impositions.[171]

The old Xiang Army arrived in Suzhou in the first month of 1876 with Liu Jintang at its head. Liu Dian reached Lanzhou the next month. About this time Zuo learned that his (now expanded) 10-million-tael loan had come through, via the intercession of his old compatriot Shen Baozhen.[172] As the troops marched forth, Zuo exhorted them onward, explicitly linking Yakub Beg to their old foe Bai Yanhu, noting that the two were in league, with Bai controlling the north (not true) and Yakub the south. He added that Yakub Beg had deluded the masses and purchased Western guns and cannons from India that made the Shaan-Gan traitors even more deadly.[173] Therefore, many local leaders had accepted tokens of his rule and served him instead of their rightful Qing overlords.

Zuo dispatched Xu Zhanbiao to Barkol and Zhang Yao to Hami to guard against rebel incursions. Significantly, the Qing were building and deploying gunboats on the Yellow River in Gansu to bring supplies to the armies in the west, using lessons learned from the West to support their own imperialist designs.[174] Other troops were sent to Dunhuang and other locations to guard against probing attacks from either the north or south.[175] The government forces' early advances, though fairly rapid, were also marked by caution as they wanted to ensure their supply lines and other preparations were adequate. There was heavy skirmishing with Bai Yanhu's forces around Tarbagatai in the late spring.[176] Fighting broke out elsewhere as well, and reports that carts of supplies sent from Russia were being looted by bandits in Yili lent a greater sense of urgency to Qing operations. In retrospect, however, these small-scale actions seem akin to a disturbed anthill. The defenders rush about pell-mell, but if the attacker is purposeful and goes for the queen, the defenders quickly lose all sense of direction and crumble before the invader.[177]

The Qing quickly recovered several of the storehouses seized by the rebels and cleared many of the roads east of Manas, prompting the court to push for a full-out assault on Manas.[178] Meanwhile Liu Jintang raced for Gucheng, roughly eighty miles north of Turfan and ninety miles northeast of Urumqi, which had fallen to the rebels in 1875. His force covered almost 2,000 *li* in just eighty days and captured the city easily.[179] Once he had control of the city, Liu turned it into another supply depot. In many places the defenders simply abandoned stores of weapons and gunpowder, much to the delight of the Qing.[180]

Less than two weeks later, as Liu's army neared Fukang, Bai Yanhu withdrew to Gumudi, another walled city just northeast of Urumqi. At this juncture Zuo's planning and Liu's battlefield experience came to the fore. There were multiple roads leading to Gumudi, but the main water source was at Huangtian, located off the main road and well protected by the rebels. Liu sent a detachment commanded by Jinshun along the larger route to trick the defenders into sending out units to engage them. Meanwhile, he sent units to dig wells along the smaller, more difficult route in advance of the main army, also striking for Huangtian. The Qing force descended on Gumudi in multiple columns.[181] Liu attacked the east and southeast walls while Jinshun assailed the north and west walls. Bai Yanhu dispatched allies from his old base at Hongmiaozi to engage the Qing but lost a thousand men.[182] The Qing force erected platforms for the artillery to fire down into the town. Another five to six thousand rebels were reportedly killed in the capture of Gumudi itself.[183] The walls were breached after five days of fighting. The Qing lost just 158 dead and 400 wounded, attesting to both the level of surprise achieved and the superiority of their weapons and tactics.[184] The dismayed rebels started fleeing south in large numbers.

Liu Jintang led a light cavalry detachment to Jimusa to explore the defenses around Urumqi and also dispatched strike forces around the area. He then linked up with Jinshun to take Fukang, defeating Bai Yanhu's partisans and killing 500–600 of them while losing 130 of their own men.[185] Fukang had been devastated by more than a decade of fighting, so the Qing had to repair the roads to move their artillery.[186] Liu captured secret letters indicating that Urumqi was practically undefended, and indeed, the city was nearly empty when it fell on August 18, 1876, and Tuo Ming submitted to the Qing.[187] Liu sent emissaries into the Tianshan Range to cut deals while he pursued the rebels who had fled south.[188] Late that summer the Qing clashed with Yakub's forces at Taksim. When Liu's forces were poised to take the city, the defenders set their supplies on fire and fled.[189]

Around the same time Zuo dispatched other commanders to secure the areas around Turfan, which was reportedly menaced by seven thousand troops affiliated with Bai Yanhu. Bai thought to sap the superior strength of the Qing forces by luring them into the barren wastes of Central Asia, but Liu Jintang's intelligence network provided him with the location of water sources. Liu's troops also dug their own wells and traveled by night to cut down on water consumption.[190] As they advanced, the Qing seized the false seals granted by Yakub Beg's regime and appointed their own officials to reestablish their legitimacy.[191] Zuo also recognized the rift between Bai and Yakub Beg and realized that the two were unlikely to coordinate their operations going forward.[192]

By the ninth lunar month the Qing were poised to travel more than four thousand *li* south to take the forty-nine cities and fortresses guarding the route to Yakub's base at Kashgar. Zuo was once again cautious, carefully amassing troops and supplies with the intention of fully securing the northern cities before assailing the south.[193] Some of these mop-up operations were hotly contested. The rebels possessed heavy artillery, and taking even smaller locations involved the application of siegecraft. Still, by the autumn of 1876 the Qing had recovered more than 4,000 *li* of territory stretching from east to west, and 1,300 *li* stretching from north to south. Their armies were not particularly large, but the combination of good supply lines and superior firepower proved impossible for the rebels to resist. Zuo credited his military intelligence and superior firepower with facilitating the Qing victories thus far. But speed was of the essence, because his army of 5,000 consumed around 30,000 taels of supplies per month.[194]

Even as the Qing forces steamrolled across Central Asia, many Western observers continued to predict their defeat. An erroneous report in the Chinese newspaper *Shenbao* that the Qing forces had already withdrawn within the Great Wall prompted an angry retort from Zuo. This was not the only time Zuo criticized the paper's shoddy reporting.[195] In response to reports that his forces were beaten and he had been killed in battle, Zuo sent a letter to the Zongli Yamen with an update that highlighted the talent and training of his officers and armies.[196]

Yakub Beg sent a force of five thousand cavalry to defend Dapan,[197] but rifts were emerging in his already fragile coalition. More and more of his subjects were becoming disenchanted with his rule as their misery increased day by day. Russian sources reported many desertions and predicted Yakub Beg was doomed.[198] For his part, Zuo stressed keeping his supply lines open and keeping his plans secret while also keeping tabs on the Russians and the English. He wrote to Liu Jintang that Thomas Wade had floated the idea of investing Yakub as a Qing vassal with control of all of southern Xinjiang, a proposal Zuo roundly rejected.[199]

The Qing forces cautiously advanced on Manas with their artillery in the fore and cavalry units protecting the rear. They initially advanced within three *li* of the city walls, digging ditches the first night and erecting fences by felling trees. Their first barrage, lasting nine hours, killed many, including the rebel commander Ma Xing, but even though the walls were breached at one point the Qing could not take the city. After three days of fighting, they were forced to pull back and wait for reinforcements.[200] Meanwhile they alternated barrages and sapping efforts as the rebels tried to break through the siege.

The assault on Manas was directed by Jinshun, assisted by Xu Xuegong and Liu Jintang. Both sides deployed foreign guns, and the Qing mounted five major assaults before they finally captured the city in November after a two-month siege.[201] The rebels feigned surrender at one point, and some managed to escape, but the Qing killed their leader, Ma Youcai. Some accounts indicate that one of those who came out to surrender started shouting at the Qing, provoking additional violence.[202] The south gate collapsed on September 28, 1876. A bloody street fight ensued as the rebels tried to fill the breach and rained gunfire on their attackers. The final Muslim sally of two thousand to three thousand men was thrust back, and the Qing finally breached the southern walls. The women, children, and elderly were reportedly spared. The Qing recovered and desecrated the corpse of the "false Muslim King," Tuo Delin.[203] Kong Cai occupied the city and posted notices ordering commoners to return to their old occupations. Officials were dispatched to the surrounding towns to restore order. Xu Xuegong mopped up pockets of resistance in the following months.[204]

When the victory was reported in the *North China Herald* in February 1877, Westerners expressed horror at the supposed sack of Manas, likening it to Li Hongzhang's massacre of surrendered rebels during the Taiping Rebellion.[205] A self-righteous diatribe about the civilized treatment of rebels concluded that "such acts exhibit a sufficiently low standard of honor and civilization."[206] Such criticisms drip with irony, particularly coming from the British, who not only strapped rebellious Sepoys to cannons and blew them to pieces in the rebellion of 1857 but later published photos of decapitated Chinese Boxers as a way of "teaching the savages" lessons about proper behavior.[207] The issue would crop up again later when the Russians were said to oppose the appointment of Jinshun as governor of Yili because of his supposed role in perpetrating the massacre at Manas.[208]

Illness struck many of the Qing troops, including Liu Jintang, soon after Manas fell. In addition to worrying about Liu, Zuo was concerned about supplies and troop numbers, telling Jinshun that he might consider paring some men from his ranks to ensure the remainder had adequate food.[209] Zuo decided to rest his troops and regroup, making new appointments, stocking up on supplies, and sending a force under Jinshun north to deter probing actions by the Russians in Yili. Troops were repositioned throughout eastern Xinjiang to keep supply lines open and preserve the Qing reconquests. Tarbagatai was secured, and the Qing fought a number of other minor battles, winning all through their superior firepower. The victories allowed them to get more supplies west in anticipation of the final campaign the following spring.[210]

The Qing rested for most of the winter of 1876–1877, but still Yakub Beg failed to do much to counter them, even though he had more than 28,000 troops in the field garrisoning various cities.[211] Owing to supply concerns, Zuo decided that no more than forty battalions would participate in the southern campaign in 1877, trusting that superior weaponry and training would carry the day. He saw Turfan and Dapancheng as the linchpins to moving south, believing that if they were captured, "the other cities would fall like chopping bamboo."[212] The court pressed the other provinces to rush funds to the northwest so Zuo could finish the job.[213]

When the weather improved, Liu Jintang led nineteen battalions forth from Urumqi early in the third month. Zhang Kui and Xu Zhanbiao led Sichuanese units toward Turfan. Within four days they had defeated rebel defenses in several places, taking Pizhan and slaying hundreds, capturing and executing one leader and recovering many weapons and livestock.[214] Xu Zhanbiao continued to push west, blowing through old and new defenses at Qiketongmu and elsewhere, and soon reached the outskirts of Turfan.[215] The city had been recently reinforced, and the rebels initially showed spunk, coming forth to engage the attackers. The Qing detached their cavalry to attack from the flank, and the defenders quickly broke and scattered. Yakub Beg's designated commander in the area surrendered and was executed before the troops at Turfan.[216] Some ten thousand Muslims surrendered and were allowed to return to their former occupations.

Liu Jintang's army advanced on Dapancheng in several columns on April 14. They encircled the city and hit it two days later, carefully coordinating their infantry and cavalry on the muddy ground. The fighting commenced at dawn, with Liu Jintang directing the Qing forces from horseback. Ditches were dug to deter sallies, and cavalry were dispatched some fifty *li* around the city to beat off the approaching relief forces led by Yakub Beg's second son. While the defenders awaited their arrival, Liu erected siege towers and started lobbing explosive shells into the city. The fighting was fierce, and the muddy fields around the city hampered cavalry operations. At one point Liu Jintang's horse was shot out from under him. The Qing sent pike-wielding infantry at the walls, supported by cavalry. When the Qing assault was delayed, the defenders tried to punch holes in Qing lines with their artillery. The Qing returned fire and hit the rebels' ammunition stores, setting the city ablaze. A great wind arose, and the smoke choked out the defenders. Relief troops coming to aid the defenders were thrown into chaos by people fleeing the burning city.[217] Liu Jintang entered the city himself to receive its surrender.[218] All told, some 2,000 rebels were killed and 1,200 captured, along with significant numbers of livestock and guns.[219] The Qing claimed losses of just 168 men.[220] With these cities taken, Liu and Zhang Yao advanced together toward Tashkent. Xu Zhanbiao stayed in Turfan, where the Qing were already opening relief bureaus.[221]

Still on the run, Bai Yanhu begged for assistance from Yakub. But seeing how rapidly things were unraveling, Yakub supposedly sent an envoy to Liu Jintang to negotiate. As Zuo put it, "from the capture of Gumudi onward the awesomeness of the army increased daily." Even with the winter respite and their new defenses Bai Yanhu and Yakub Beg could not resist the Qing.[222] Zuo bragged that his forces had prevailed easily over vast distances "without a single soldier retreating." He also indicated that Yakub might be looking to turn over Bai Yanhu in exchange for recognizing his control of the south, not fully appreciating the strength of the Qing. Yakub had deceived and misled the Hui, Zuo said, but now a reckoning was coming. Even European observers said that Zuo's army "was that of a strong country" and "the battle skills of the Chinese have advanced considerably." The tables had now turned. Compared to Zuo, Yakub Beg "was like a schoolboy when it came to battle acumen."[223]

Qing sources indicate that Liu offered to listen to Yakub's pleas if he immediately handed over eight cities in the south. He also offered amnesty if Yakub turned over Bai Yanhu.[224] The court authorized the release of another 2 million taels for Zuo's military expenses and expressed delight at reports of Zuo's great victories, apparently conveyed east by newly laid telegraph lines.[225] Zuo's reports from the latter stages of this campaign reference receiving orders and communications by cable, which greatly abetted his ability to act and report, yet another example of the Qing adopting new technologies to facilitate their imperial projects.

As the Qing forces plowed on, Yakub Beg continued to search for allies, hoping that British intervention might help him retain his polity without having to actually fight for it. In 1877 the British ambassador to Russia suggested joint mediation, with Russia and Britain advising China and Yakub Beg, but Thomas Wade rejected the idea owing to Russia's continued occupation of Yili. Nevertheless, he thought China might still lose in Kashgaria. Guo Songtao, Zuo's old Hunan compatriot, then the resident Qing diplomat in London, shared that sentiment.[226] It was in this context that Wade and Guo tried to concoct an agreement whereby Yakub would be invested as a Qing tributary.[227] In exchange, Yakub would help the Qing restore order throughout Central Asia. Both Li Hongzhang and Prince Gong seemed to favor the arrangement, and Guo Songtao even sketched out a basic deal. Wade, a supporter of Li Hongzhang, pushed the deal to the Grand Council.[228] Zuo, however, was enraged by the plan and called Guo a traitor and a fool.[229]

On the verge of his triumph, with his forces ready to sweep across Central Asia, Zuo roundly rejected any such compromises.[230] His preparations and intelligence from the field had convinced him that victory was likely, and he had no wish to alter his course now. Moreover, Zuo perceived that Britain was more concerned with India than China and wanted Yakub to serve as a buffer. Yakub would be a poor buffer, Zuo insisted, and it was far better for the Qing themselves to resume control over southern Xinjiang. As he phrased it, "The awesomeness of the Qing was already manifested in the recapture of Hongmiao and Wuyuan; if they could the same in the south, the Qing would be in good shape."[231] In a letter to the Zongli Yamen, Zuo couched his argument in strategic terms, laying out what he had already achieved and how he was poised to meet all the Qing government's goals without recourse to foreign intercession. Zuo saw Russia as a declining power, and he was confident Yili could be retaken soon after Yakub was swept away. Investing him would thus serve no purpose.[232] Zuo did hold out the possibility that Yakub might be allowed to live if he cooperated in turning in Bai Yanhu and the other rebel leaders.

Through the winter Zuo discussed the situation with Liu Jintang, noting that spies informed him that Russian strength in Yili was low, on the order of just eight hundred to a thousand troops. Once the rebels were defeated, Zuo could capitalize on his momentum to retake Yili. The holdouts in the east should capitulate then as well, contributing even more to stability across the region.[233] To the latter end, the Qing were already appointing officials and expanding *tuntian* operations. Zuo ordered land surveys and discussed different possibilities for growing new crops such as tea with Zhang Yao. In a letter to Zeng Guoquan, Zuo discussed trading tea for horses to revive the economy of the northwest as a whole.[234]

Zuo also sent more letters to the Zongli Yamen discussing the trade situation with Russia and explaining how he thought the Qing could exploit their rivalry over influence in India and Central Asia. Noting Britain's many global commitments, Zuo pushed for fast action to recover Xinjiang and keep the Turks and the Russians on their toes. He explained that Russia was most interested in trade due to its fragile economic situation, so the Qing should use that leverage to get Yili back. Zuo himself was no longer buying grain from Russia for his troops because the Qing supply lines and new cultivation were covering their needs.[235]

Once he received news of Zuo's successes, Guo Songtao changed his position on offering Yakub Beg a deal. As these discussions were unfolding, news came that Yakub was dead. When word of Yakub's demise reached London, talks between the British and Guo were terminated.[236] As Boulger aptly puts it, "England and Kashgar were friends because they had no reason to be foes, but they were indifferent friends."[237] For his part, Zuo politicked to have Wade removed from his post.[238] He also expressed concerns that the British might try to roll back his victories, arguing that they had no right to do so; these were Qing lands of old, not to mention Chinese territory since the Han.[239] He wryly added that if Britain wanted a buffer so badly, they could create one out of India.[240]

Concerning Yakub's death, Qing sources, including Zuo's original report to the throne, generally maintain that he took poison and committed suicide in despair.[241] Muslim scholars attributed Yakub's defeat to his tyranny and pride.[242] Zuo also maintained that Yakub never responded to Liu Jintang's offer and was clearly dismayed by the completeness and rapidity of the Qing victories. In classic Confucian fashion Zuo also criticized Yakub's policies, saying he plundered the people and arrogated resources to himself, thereby incurring the punishment of Heaven.[243] Some sources suggest he was assassinated by those in his organization.[244] The most plausible explanation, derived from reports about his condition just prior to his demise, is that he suffered a massive stroke.[245]

Yakub's second son, Hakim Quli (called Haigula in Chinese sources), performed the Muslim ablutions and took off for Kashgar with his father's corpse. Some of his followers flocked to Bai Yanhu's banner; others decided to go off on their own or align themselves with one of Yakub's heirs. While Zuo crowed about his spectacular success, the court was still concerned about what Bai Yanhu and Yakub's sons might do. Zuo knew this, of course, and had sent his commanders forth in pursuit of Bai and the others.[246] Additionally, Zuo noted that Yili had still not been recovered and start lobbying for making Xinjiang a province and more closely integrating it with the rest of the empire.[247]

DEFEATING THE REMNANTS

After Yakub died, his sons Beg Quli, Hakim Quli, and others vied for control of his floundering state. His eldest son, Beg Quli, was named Yakub's successor at Aksu and moved to Kashgar. Hakim Quli appointed one Hakim Khan to command the defenses of Korla while he went to meet with his brother, but Hakim Khan, having been proclaimed ruler by officials in Korla, turned on his former lord and moved toward Kashgar, hoping to wipe out Yakub's heirs. Meanwhile, Bai Yanhu had been left in charge of Korla. Hakim Quli was killed by his brother before he even reached Kashgar.[248] Beg Quli killed Hakim Khan two months later.[249] Wary of exhausting his forces in the hot summer months, Zuo decided to hold back and let the rebels pick each other off and wait until fall to renew his full pursuit of Bai.[250] In Zuo's assessment, Yakub's surviving sons were on the defensive and Bai was in flight mode, so the Qing held the upper hand.

Liu Jintang finally set forth from Taksim in pursuit of Bai Yanhu on August 25, 1877. Bai was now the last man standing from the great Muslim revolts, and Liu was eager to capture him. The area through which Liu traveled was already swampy, and Bai made it more so by cutting the dikes on the Kaidu River, flooding the area around Korla in October 1877. This barely slowed the Qing advance, though it did force Liu Jintang to travel sixty or seventy *li* in search of a suitable crossing point. The Qing used rafts and constructed makeshift dikes to effect their crossing.[251] Bai seized the autumn harvest and fled to Kuche but was denied entry by the locals and went on toward Ush Turfan. He sent his treasure ahead to Russia and proceeded to Kashgar, where one of Yakub Beg's sons was ensconced. When the Qing approached the city, the rebels split their forces and fled in multiple directions. One unit fled to Aksu, pursued by Zhang Yao. While there was scattered resistance in some places, in others the locals returned their allegiance to the Qing. By the middle of December Kashgar, Yarkand, and Yengisar were all firmly in Qing hands.[252] Upon their arrival at Kashgar, the Qing desecrated Yakub's corpse and built a temple near his tomb.[253]

The Qing nearly caught Bai on October 17, fighting and killing a thousand of his rear guard, but the wily Bai escaped again, heading toward Yili.[254] Liu finally pulled his men back and devoted his efforts to securing the region and stamping out remnant rebel groups. Sensing the changing direction of the political winds, locals shut their gates to Bai and his followers and welcomed the Qing in Aksu and other places.[255] Down to perhaps two thousand followers now, Bai split his forces and fled across the border to take refuge in Russia.[256] Liu Jintang killed more than one thousand rebels around Kashgaria in mop-up operations.[257] Liu's general instructions were to kill those bearing arms and spare the rest. He specifically forbade harming ordinary Muslims. The main part of Liu's army set up camp at Kashgar in December 1877.

Liu Jintang now had all of Yakub's living sons in his hands as well as the seals of authority. He sliced up the sons in the marketplace in Kashgar in the eleventh lunar month of 1877.[258] The women and children were sold into slavery. Some of the young boys were castrated and sold as slaves. These measures were met with outrage in the hypocritical Western press. An editorial published in 1879 in the *North China Herald*, for example, said that China's actions "indicate a contempt for the opinions of the civilized world."[259] "No devils in Hell have ever been credited by medieval priests with more infernal ingenuity in torture than that ascribed to the victorious general in Kashgar," wrote another author.[260] In fact, the Qing's treatment of Yakub Beg's family was in accordance with tradition. The way rebel leaders were handled reinforced "imperially preferred understandings of rebel organization, culpability, Qing legitimacy, and martial success."[261] Their views and actions just happened to differ from those of their Western critics.

The Qing took Khotan in January 1878. When Kuche was recovered, the locals were encouraged to return to their homes and resume their former occupations. More skirmishes followed, but once Liu Jintang killed the Muslim rebel leader Ma Youbu, the enemy forces broke. The Qing also went to Barkol, traversing nine hundred *li* in just six days and receiving a warm welcome from those remaining in the city. Administrators were sent to Aksu and other places along the southern route to distribute relief, seeds, and tools. Post stations were built or repaired, and more boats were constructed to facilitate river transport. Though there was still scattered fighting throughout the region, the central authorities were notified that Xinjiang had been recovered.[262] And as more and more isolated towns were recovered, the populace reverted to Qing allegiance. The British allegedly praised Liu as "the flying general" for the speed at which he took these distant cities.[263]

Liu Jintang's forces captured Bai Yanhu's confederate Ma Youcai and sixteen others at the frozen Humanake River and executed them.[264] The rebels suffered further losses as they alternately skirmished and fled.[265] The survivors finally crossed into Russia around the beginning of 1878. They were disarmed at the border and sent along.[266] Liu Jintang was furious, and the Qing opened negotiations for deportation of Bai but were stymied by the Russians.[267] Later sources suggested that Russia's reluctance to extradite Bai was grounded in Western diplomatic protocols wherein countries would not extradite people simply to be executed.[268] The Russians, in classic diplomatic fashion, claimed that Bai was a political refugee. Although they stressed that returning Bai would "further friendship between Russia and China," the Qing chose to not pursue the point too aggressively, being sensitive to the bigger picture regarding Yili. The Ottomans also got involved in the talks.[269]

Zuo and Liu contemplated sending a strike team into Russia to bring Bai back. Offering veiled threats concerning the Qing military potential in the area, Zuo also sent a letter to his Russian counterpart telling him that he had instructed the Qing troops not to cross the border so as to preserve friendly relations between the two nations and was therefore requesting Bai's extradition, noting that the Qing throne had also submitted a request via the Russian envoy in Beijing.[270]

As the diplomats were arguing, Bai and his partisans were reportedly raiding across the border and stirring up local bandits against the Qing. Liu Jintang organized 2,500 crack cavalry into border patrol units to stop them.[271] Some of the raiders' family members and other followers were apprehended and executed—a total of 1,166 people according to Qing sources. The Qing also recovered more than 100 artillery pieces of various sizes and 11,000 war horses in these battles.[272] In a letter addressed to two of his sons, Zuo exulted in his accomplishments, putting them on a par with anything done in the region in the entire history of China and saying that the outer barbarians now feared China because of him.[273]

At this point even the biased Western press could not deny Zuo's successes. Editorialists now criticized those who formerly sneered at Zuo's prospects, admitting that no Western power could have done better.[274] Zuo's commanders "have well-earned the distinctions conferred on them," one writer noted. "It is painful, however, to read the continued tales of massacre which have disgraced their progress, from the sack of Suzhou to the pacification of Yarkand and Kashgar."[275] Westerners begrudgingly commended Jinshun and other commanders, saying that the Russians now feared China and predicting a larger role in Central Asian affairs for China, though one story walked this praise back a bit, noting that the death of Yakub Beg was presumably by assassination.[276]

In the aftermath of the campaign Zuo moved to consolidate Qing control, stressing rehabilitation efforts. As always, his goal was not only to recover the lost territory but also to regain the hearts of the people. He carefully investigated local conditions, distributing relief and bestowing honors and rewards on those who had aided the Qing cause against Yakub Beg. He tried to get local Muslim officials to participate in the reconstruction process, seeing the creation of a class of culturally and linguistically bi-fluent intermediaries as integral to the recovery that was his long-term goal.[277]

The armies were repositioned and gradually demobilized, and Zuo sought to ensure that they still had supplies, or at least the funds to buy them, so as to not disturb the locals.[278] Troops were strictly forbidden from raping, stealing, looting, or otherwise harming the people. Zuo believed that the strict implementation of martial law was essential to long-term security. He also emphasized rebuilding the infrastructure by repairing roads and irrigation works and stimulating new cultivation via both *tuntian* and incentives for civilian farmers.[279] Demonstrating his open-mindedness in practical matters, Zuo consulted Europeans concerning the latest techniques in water management. New roads were built and existing ones repaired. Walls were built to shield traders from the area's raging winds and sandstorms. Zuo was also keen to restore the old postal routes. Qing officials noted that barely one in ten Hui were able to support themselves in the aftermath of the war, so they prioritized distribution of food, seeds, and winter clothing, noting that the strong might otherwise return to banditry.[280]

It was typical for cities in Xinjiang to have Han, Manchu, and Muslim sections divided by walls. These were restored, but greater emphasis was placed on restoring the outer walls for defense purposes. Smaller, more isolated communities were walled to protect them from wandering bandits. Sections of the Great Wall were repaired, as were the city walls of Kuche, Kashgar, and

Lanzhou.[281] Martyrs' shrines were erected for loyal officials who had died in earlier stages of the rebellion, as they had also been in Shaan-Gan.[282] Rewards were offered for those who contributed funds toward the reconstruction of official buildings. In all these ways the Qing crafted a narrative to situate Xinjiang more properly within the regular domestic sphere of the empire. Newly appointed officials were given peacock feathers symbolizing their reintegration into the Qing imperium.[283] Some places began sending tribute again, and funds recovered from the rebels were distributed for relief and reconstruction efforts.[284]

Finally, Zuo stressed the overall improvement of local administration, which he noted had been in steady decline since the Jiaqing era. "If the government is rotten," he said, "the rest of society follows."[285] Zuo's plan for cleaning up officialdom involved investigating officials, training officials, and compensating officials. In doing so he followed five basic principles: (1) officials must love the people, (2) officials must protect what is upright and not gossip, take bribes, crave profit, or seek petty advantages, (3) officials should be diligent in the pursuit of their duties and not cause trouble, (4) officials must always employ good people, and (5) officials must apply the laws of the realm properly.[286] If the quality of officials was improved, then the overall efficiency of the government would improve as well. To this end he published guidebooks for officials urging them to follow statecraft practices such as those of the famous Cheng Hongmou (1696–1761).[287] He raised their compensation to cut down on the potential for graft. Zuo made sure his own friends and family maintained these principles, even removing his adopted son from a post for impropriety.[288] The court was understandably pleased with Zuo's accomplishments, and he was given the hereditary honorific title of Earl of Jin.[289] Rewards and promotions were showered on the other victorious officials as well. Perhaps more surprising is the praise from the Englishman D. C. Boulger, often a critic, who said that the Qing victory showed that "those independent rulers who establish themselves for a space on the confines of China are mere ephemeral excrescences; birds of passage who must betake themselves away if they can when their little hour has struck."[290]

THE YILI CRISIS

Russia's greater involvement in Central Asian affairs preceded its occupation of the Yili Valley by some five decades and was intimately connected to its larger imperial aims and rivalry with the British Empire.[291] Because of its long territorial border with China, Russia had always been the one European power with "special" trade status vis-à-vis the Qing. The Qing had legalized Russian trade in Yili and Targabatai in the 1840s and formalized it in the Treaty of Kulja in 1851.[292] Russia quickly built warehouses and expanded its trade activities in Central Asia. The Sino-Russian Treaty of 1860 opened Kashgar to Russian trade even as other agreements consolidated the Sino-Russian frontier in the northeast. In the process of these agreements Russia gained nearly 250,000 square miles of territory, something that still riles Chinese nationalists today.[293] Indeed, Sally Paine notes, "For the Chinese people their present northern border is an incarnation and potent symbol of China's failure and humiliation at the hands of foreigners in general and of the Russians in particular."[294]

Modern Chinese sources tend to oversimplify these pragmatic agreements and put them into the category of unequal treaties while also enumerating the various machinations of the Russians and the British in Central Asia, conveniently overlooking the imperialist dimensions of Qing rule in the region.[295] But the agreements were realpolitik in its most pure form. By the late nineteenth century, the Qing and others, including independent agents such as Yakub Beg, were learning how to play the imperialist game by Western rules even as they grounded their assumptions and claims along more traditional lines. This also manifested in Qing relations with Korea, as masterfully traced by Kirk Larsen, though some have criticized late Qing "assimilatory colonialism" as a reaction to the crisis of declining political control.[296] There is no reason it could not be both, of course, as crisis often spurs innovation. Moreover, as Paine notes, because both China and Russia were declining as great powers in the late nineteenth century, this situation had the potential to be especially volatile.[297]

Having defeated Yakub Beg and reestablished their hold over the whole of Central Asia, the Qing were now ready to reoccupy the strategically vital Yili Valley, which Russia had occupied as a "favor" to the Qing back in 1871.

But unsurprisingly, the Russians were loath to relinquish this important foothold in Central Asia. Russia's presence in the Yili Valley strengthened its position vis-à-vis Great Britain in the ongoing Great Game, especially in light of its recent difficulties with the Ottomans. Back in 1872 the Russians had stated they were waiting for the Qing to bring sufficient troops to properly administer the region and refrained from discussing military expenses (for their occupation) or demarcation lines, knowing that the Qing were not in a position militarily to do much. But they had pledged to return Yili once the Qing restored order.[298] The Qing had clearly done that now, but Russia was still there.

The Russian commander Konstantin von Kaufman was especially belligerent and critical of Zuo, even attacking him in letters published in Western papers such as the *North China Herald*.[299] For his part, Zuo felt secure in pressing for a resolution to the Yili Crisis, by force if necessary. He stressed the commercial and military significance of Yili while also linking it to China's overall geostrategic picture. If China abandoned Yili to the Russians, he argued, then the whole area south of the Tianshan Range would be imperiled. Further, once China had recovered the area it should be reinforced with moats, artillery towers, and more garrisons in strategic locales. Improving the infrastructure and establishing *tuntian* would support the additional forces as well as stimulate further growth. Making these improvements would embody the principle of "taking people as the root" of the nation and be a step toward making Xinjiang a regular province. He offered detailed figures on population and land under cultivation in Yili while also sketching out his broad administrative vision for Xinjiang.[300] He also favored banning Russian traders in Yili until the land was returned.[301] More concerning to the court, however, was Zuo's report from the summer of 1878 that Russia had sent an additional two thousand troops to the region.[302]

Once again Li Hongzhang was on the opposite side of the debate, and some contemporary Western observers portrayed their disagreement as just another power struggle between Zuo and Li. As in their original debate over fighting for Xinjiang versus protecting the coast, the realities were more nuanced, but the same basic premises held true. The main difference was that

China was now coming out of a successful war, and Russia was reeling from a series of draining conflicts with the Ottomans and facing rising domestic unrest. Zuo invoked historical precedents for a stable northwestern border to support his argument, but he also accused Li of pursuing selfish interests while his own were grounded solely in love for his country.[303] Zuo also argued that Taiwan should be treated the same as Xinjiang and be converted into a regular province, which did indeed happen a few years later.[304] Zuo was consistent in his statecraft views, believing that best way to integrate these frontier regions into the empire and preserve them from rivals was to formalize their administration and acculturate them.

The Qing decided to send the veteran Manchu diplomat Chonghou (1826–1893) to St. Petersburg to resolve the situation.[305] Chonghou had served as envoy in France and England and was presumed to have the experience necessary for the job. It did not hurt that he was fairly well connected at court. In addition to regaining the lost territory, the court hoped that Chonghou could negotiate new trade deals and hammer out a plan for dealing with fugitives such as Bai Yanhu.[306] It is worth noting that despite his later condemnation of Chonghou, Zuo approved of his appointment at the time, including giving him wide discretionary powers to negotiate.[307]

At the end of 1878 Zuo sent a report on the Yili situation to the court. He noted that Russia occupied much of the western part of the valley, and even though the land was underpopulated on the whole, many Russian merchants and troops remained. He wanted to stimulate Qing settlement in the region and build up agriculture and animal husbandry. The sooner people returned and local prosperity was restored, the faster Yili could be integrated into the regular Qing polity. Greater Han immigration to Yili would help accomplish the former. Tools, seed, and other incentives were to be used to encourage resettlement. To these ends Zhang Yao and Liu Jintang were already diverting rivers and reopening irrigation works. Forts and postal stations were being rebuilt. Zuo also wanted to stamp out the pockets of resistance to the Qing so as not to appear weak before Russia in the ongoing talks. This included dealing with traitorous Hui plotters that Zuo claimed were in league with Bai Yanhu and aiding his followers' raids.[308]

In terms of his initial administrative reforms, Zuo recommended the creation of the post of Grand Minister Consultant at Yili. A similar position had previously been used to govern Outer Mongolia. Thus, even as the Qing were moving to integrate Xinjiang into the administrative hierarchy, they were retaining the flexibility that had always been a hallmark of Qing administration. Other coordinating officials, modeled after those then being used in Qinghai, would be stationed in Hami, Yengisar, Kashgar, and similar places.[309] Zuo recognized that sending administrators who spoke a different language and practiced different customs was problematic, so he supported keeping Muslim intermediaries for the time being; but he also hoped to establish schools to facilitate Sinicization.[310]

Before going to St. Petersburg Chonghou first went to Paris and met with Guo Songtao. Guo found Chonghou to be ignorant of both Yili and the issues at hand and predicted the failure of his mission.[311] Chonghou arrived in St. Petersburg on the last day of 1878 and had his first audience with Tsar Alexander II on January 20, 1879. The subsequent negotiations would drag on for seven months. According to most reports, Chonghou was gaslighted by the Russians, who treated him with the utmost deference as they manipulated him into accepting all their demands. But in fact, the Russians themselves were not in agreement, with some in favor of returning Yili but at a high price and others willing to fight to retain it. The argument in favor of return was that the funds could be used to build the Trans-Siberian Railway and exact further trade concessions. Contrary to later claims, at least some of the Russian demands were relayed back to the Qing court. Many of these involved clemency for Muslims in the region and articulated the Russians' rationale for refusing to return Bai Yanhu, which centered on the potential trouble his return would cause.[312]

Meanwhile Liu Jintang, Dong Fuxiang, and Zhang Yao continued battling rebel elements through 1878–1879. Some of their skirmishes involved hundreds of rebel forces who tried to take advantage of the terrain to harass the Qing and raid their grain stores. But the Qing field commanders were experienced and creative and countered the rebels with better weapons and superior tactics. Thousands were slain in these operations, gaining commendation from the throne and bolstering the Qing negotiating position.[313]

The negotiators in Russia initially asked China to pay a staggering 60 million rubles for the return of Yili, but after extensive discussion—and the realization that the Qing could not pay such a sum—reduced the sum to 5 million. But they also wanted borders redrawn, new trade privileges, and amnesty for Muslims who had fled to Russia. Having been dusted at the recent Congress of Berlin that ended the war with Turkey in 1878, Russia wanted to gain face here and pressed for cession of large swaths of Yili. The new borders they proposed were such that the parts "returned" to the Qing would be nigh indefensible. When informed of the Russians' proposition, Zuo argued that Yili must be returned in its entirety before the Qing could talk about trade concessions, border demarcation, and reparations.[314] He also accused the Russians of fomenting unrest by sending Bai Yanhu's partisans across the border to stir up trouble.[315] As more details of the talks were revealed through cables, Zuo's opposition increased.[316]

Anticipating the need for future military action, Zuo told Zhang Yao to set up weapons factories in Xinjiang. The Qing built a weapons bureau in Aksu and a gunpowder factory in Kuche.[317] In the meantime, the court authorized Liu Jintang to eradicate traitors and proceed with the formal integration of the territory into the regular administrative structure, a process called *junxian*, which literally translates as "prefecturing and districting."[318] This appears to have been calculated to further improve the Qing negotiating position.

But while the Zongli Yamen pressed Chonghou to resist some of the Russians' demands, they also authorized him to make the deal. The resulting Treaty of Livadia included pardons for residents of Yili; the payment of a 5-million-ruble indemnity to cover the Russians' occupation costs; duty-free trading privileges and travel throughout much of Xinjiang for Russians; and the establishment of consulates in a number of cities, including Hami, Gucheng, Turfan, and Urumqi. China also ceded nearly 70 percent of Yili to Russia. The treaty even included navigation rights along the Sungari River in Manchuria.[319] Chonghou ratified the treaty on his own authority on October 2, 1879, but observers in Russia and elsewhere immediately wondered if the Chinese court would ratify it.[320]

The Zongli Yamen's initial response was measured due to concern about the international optics of outright rejection. Paine argues that the Zongli Yamen was also rent by factionalism stemming from earlier political disagreements.[321] So they solicited opinions from high officials, including Zuo, Li Hongzhang, Jinshun, and Xilun.[322] Zuo was outraged at Chonghou's gullibility and lack of resolve. His concessions made China look weak and gave away territory Zuo had just won.[323] Zuo made his views clear:

Our emissary Chonghou has absurdly and ridiculously concluded the negotiations and talks about a quick return home. Although he may sign a treaty with their government, it is in effect only after our Imperial Highness' approval. Much can still be done during the interval and this is completely different from agreeing first and rejecting later. Speaking practically, the whole thing hinges upon how strong or weak we are. If we are strong, we can make justice from injustice. If we are not strong, our justice will be taken as injustice. It has been so in ancient and modern times. The life and death, ebb and flow of a state depend wholly on force and not totally on justice. Now that our emissary has signed a treaty in violation of his instructions; the imperial edicts have already disputed [this] and disowned [his act] so [the treaty] will not be ratified. This is not a case of bad faith.[324]

Zuo offered to move his headquarters to Hami and suggested that the Qing offer to pay the indemnity but reject the border and commercial aspects of the treaty, arguing that the Mingyi Treaty of 1864 was sufficient to govern trade relations with Russia.[325] He also stressed that his assessments were grounded in his practical knowledge of the situation on the ground.

Zuo's ire increased when he saw the full text of the treaty listing all the territorial concessions. He wrote to Beijing again in December 1879 saying that recovering Yili in this fashion "was like getting an empty city without suburbs—Russia could move in anytime." He added, "When a state is devoid of military strength, cession of territory and begging for peace may be in order. But without firing a shot [Chonghou] has abruptly given away territory to satisfy their greed. It is like throwing a bone to a dog. When the bone is finished [the dog] will bark again."[326] In another letter to the Zongli Yamen, Zuo claimed that the Russians were afraid of him, and even though Russia was a big country, its troops were few. He predicted that he could penetrate deep into Russia to retrieve Bai Yanhu and inflict further payback on the Russians. He was "finished with empty words. It's time to unleash the awesomeness of the army."[327]

Zuo recommended disavowing all the treaty's border arrangements and employing a combination of diplomacy and force to resolve the issue.[328] "First we will rely upon negotiations, adopting an amiable stance in the hopes that it will work. But [if not] then we'll take to the battlefields, adopt a resolute stance and pursue victory. Although I may be old and declining, I won't shirk my duty!"[329] Another account asserts that Zuo said, "We have nothing at all to fear from a country like this. Victory will certainly be China's [if we fight]. If the talks between Zeng Jize and Russia are cut off, certainly I won't be able to withdraw."[330] Echoing Wenxiang's words of a few years before, Zuo continued, "If we retreat an inch, they advance a foot, and the end result is that it just gets worse and worse."[331] He feared the court's timorous position was casting away a golden opportunity. The majority at court supported Zuo, at least at first, and authorized the mobilization of troops and urgent delivery of supplies around the Tianshan, though they stressed that they needed time to fully consider the terms of the agreement.

As might be expected, Li Hongzhang was not overly concerned about ceding Yili to the Russians and advocated conciliation to keep the peace. He suggested that China first appoint better-qualified negotiators to seek revision of the border and commercial provisions, arguing that Zuo's aggressive posturing was risky and likely to fail. True to his character, however, he covered his own derriere with a few gentle criticisms of Chonghou before repeating his mantra about the greater importance of coastal defense.[332] In the event of war with Russia, he added, China could seek aid from Britain, France, and Japan. Zuo countered by comparing Li's conciliation policy to a quack doctor's prescription. The doctor would rather let the patient die than prescribe a powerful drug that might save him. So once again it came down to interior versus coastal priorities.[333] Others took up intermediate positions. Shen Baozhen also opposed the treaty but thought China might have to sacrifice Yili for gains elsewhere. Guo Songtao said China should reject the treaty but delay responding to prevent the Russians from upping their demands. Jinshun said talks should be opened to buy time for military preparations.

After much debate and investigation, the Zongli Yamen and Li Hongzhang repudiated Chonghou's actions and the treaty itself. Cixi even contemplated executing Chonghou, but Western diplomats strenuously objected that such acts were beyond the pale.[334] In his own defense Chonghou protested that the Russians drove a hard bargain and had used a variety of threats. He was also apparently under the impression that he possessed the kind of sweeping authority enjoyed by imperial commissioners in domestic appointments. Under the circumstances, he did the best that he could. This was an instance of modern diplomatic conventions and protocols clashing with traditional practices and expectations. The high ministers decided to appoint a new official to renegotiate on the grounds that Chonghou had overstepped his bounds.[335] Chonghou was cashiered immediately, and though calls for his head continued, he was spared due to pressure from Westerners and to Guo Songtao's argument that executing him would give the Russians a pretext for action later.[336] He was formally pardoned in June 1880.

REOPENING NEGOTIATIONS WITH RUSSIA

In February 1880, in the wake of the debacle created by the Treaty of Livadia, Zeng Guofan's son, Zeng Jize (1839–1890), then minister to France and England, was appointed minister to Russia.[337] In fact, Zeng had been initially considered for the post, but Chonghou had many supporters at court and had good ties with Westerners, so the job went to him. When Zeng was appointed, Zhang Zhidong suggested that Chonghou accompany him and pay 1 million taels from his apparently considerable personal funds to assist with the defense of Xinjiang. Prosper Giquel, the Frenchman who had helped Zuo Zongtang set up the Fuzhou Navy Yard, was among the party that accompanied Zeng to Russia.

Believing that military force was needed to reinforce the Qing's diplomatic position, Zuo sent the army into Yili along four routes in 1880. The northern route was commanded by Jinshun, Zhang Yao led the central route armies, Liu Jintang led the eastern route forces, and Xilun's forces were the rear guard. Zuo also moved his own headquarters to Hami, allegedly bringing a coffin with him lest he die on the campaign. He offered assessments to the court concerning Russia's capabilities and possible routes of attack. "Even though Russia's population is large," he reiterated, "they are not skilled in warfare." He predicted that a show of force would get them to back down.[338] Zuo's essential point was that displaying China's willingness to go on the offensive was key to its defense. Zuo turned the tables on Li Hongzhang in a letter to the Zongli Yamen that criticized Li for wasting money on purchasing "useless outdated ironclads" from the British rather than promoting the more important defense of the northwest.[339]

As he continued to promote his case for incorporating Xinjiang into the empire as a regular province, he offered plans for setting up modern factories and posting modern armies across the region to ensure its long-term security.[340] Liu Kunyi was tasked with coastal defense upgrades, and Bao Chao was to raise ten thousand troops to defend Tianjin in the event of an attack by sea on the capital, as there were rumors of a Russian fleet at Nagasaki.[341] Zuo tried to allay the court's concerns in that regard, implying the rumors were fabrications concocted by the British and their allies. With the court focused on Xinjiang, Li Hongzhang and his Huai clique were temporarily shunted aside.[342]

Contemporary newspaper reports indicate that many believed war was nigh. China was buying up guns from foreign sources, including 175 cannons and more than 50,000 hand weapons, including Remingtons, breechloaders, and more Krupp guns. Zuo sent mines and torpedoes to Fujian, where the navy had more than fifty gunboats and forty-one steamers, including the *Wannian Qing*. Russia was building up its frontier defenses, bringing in

Cossacks and regular units, though the British attaché, George Villers, was unimpressed. In August 1880 a story in the *North China Herald* predicted that Russia would move into Kashgar while Zuo was still in Manas.[343] At the same time, the cities in the northeast were riled by rumors of a Russian naval attack from that quarter.[344]

Li Hongzhang continued to voice his concerns that China was not ready to take on a Western power, especially at sea, and called Zuo "senile and boastful."[345] He further called Zuo's achievements in the west mediocre and predicted that the dispute with Russia had the potential to engulf the whole country. He also believed that Zuo had secretly recruited Zhang Zhidong and others to stir up trouble. This brought Li more criticism from Liu Mingchuan, who said Li should be more like Zuo. Li cattily replied, "Generalissimo Zuo commands a big army and huge funds in a place nobody will contest for. Therefore, he gives the appearance of wanting war, but he does not care about the general situation of the state. Those who are at all familiar with the affairs of ancient and modern times can see readily through his falsehood."[346]

Westerners' assessments of China's prospects were mixed. Some thought China could win, but the war would be disastrous even so. Others held that China could win only if Western officers led its troops, claiming that Zuo's triumph was due primarily to Yakub's death. Others pointed to Zuo's acumen in amassing supplies and resources, even as they commended the Russian General Kaufman's leadership abilities. In June 1880, a report circulating in Guangzhou stated that Zuo had already defeated the Russians in battle.[347]

In fact, despite his rhetoric to the contrary, Zuo was not completely confident of victory. Having learned from a cable that Russia might be inclined to fight, he asked Zhang Yao for an update on the state of Russia's preparations and resolve. Zuo then told the Zongli Yamen that war appeared inevitable.[348] He reported that he was ready to take military action in the spring of 1880 and laid out his battle plans.[349] But Zuo's increasingly belligerent stance alarmed some at court who did not wish to be perceived as instigating a conflict, and in May 1880 he was recalled to Beijing, allegedly for a court audience to discuss defense matters, and Liu Jintang was placed in overall command of the Qing forces in Xinjiang.[350] Zuo left his successor detailed instructions indicating where troops were positioned and which officials were entrusted with certain responsibilities. He also suggested entrusting Zhang Yao with greater military authority because he had been shifted to a primarily civilian post.

Worried about the appointment of Zeng as minister to Russia, Zuo wrote a letter to the Zongli Yamen warning them of the craftiness of Westerners and expressing doubt that Zeng would succeed in his mission.[351] Bales argues that Zuo was not really pro-war; he was just convinced that a well-substantiated bluff coupled with the potentially high costs of a war would be enough to deter the Russians and improve the Qing negotiating position.[352] Zuo was certainly better informed than most people in Beijing about conditions in Russia, not to mention the state of affairs in Central Asia, so Bales's argument should not be rejected out of hand. However, Bales's conclusion that the resulting Treaty of St. Petersburg "was almost wholly the handiwork of Zuo Zongtang" is perhaps stretching it.[353] Nevertheless, Zuo was certainly savvy to the nuances of how the Great Game was played and more than willing to take risks to advance China's aims when he felt his hand was strong. He may have been a gambler, but only when the odds favored him. He was definitely not a warmonger.

Li, for his part, was much more the canny and manipulative politician. He tended to have a negative assessment of China's capabilities. As the de facto prime minister Li was afraid that much more might fall on his shoulders (as it would a decade later) should China lose a war. But it seems that Zuo's posturing impacted Russia's considerations more than Li thought, and Li's vocal criticisms of his rival may have weakened the Qing negotiating position. In fact, Russia's internal affairs were a mess owing to the combination of the war with Turkey and Alexander II's failed reforms in the wake of his abolition of serfdom. The Russians falsely believed Zuo had some 180,000 troops (against their 5,000) near Yili and that 40,000 of them were equipped with the latest guns. They also believed that a land war in Manchuria and Siberia would be "prolonged and ruinous" for them.[354] American assessments also noted Russia's poor economic and military situation.

Zuo reached Lanzhou on December 2, 1880. He spent two days there before departing for Xi'an, arriving there just over two weeks later. He reached Beijing on February 24, 1881. Zuo's return came in the midst of the treaty talks and stoked fears that the Qing were readying for war, when in fact he had been recalled to prevent that very outcome.[355]

Disagreements broke out between the various British advisers and diplomats, and criticisms dogged Zeng Jize, including some from Li Hongzhang, who was apparently not close to his former mentor's son. Nonetheless, Zeng soldiered on, studying the history and geography of Yili and reporting back to the throne. He identified three key categories for negotiation: boundaries, trade concessions, and the issue of monetary compensation for the occupation. Though the court was less than pleased, Zeng was allowed to continue. The Russians told Zeng that the pardon of Chonghou was essential and that they were more interested in trade privileges than acquiring territory. He kept up regular communications with Beijing concerning the talks, and the overall response was far more positive than had been the case with the rejected Treaty of Livadia.[356]

The Russians tried to move the treaty talks to Beijing to add legitimacy to the proceedings but to no avail. Russia's plenipotentiary was finally recalled from Beijing amid concerns that another war with Turkey loomed. As Russia now seemed to be facing a war with Turkey, Zeng dragged his feet, feeling he could get a better deal if he waited. Extensions on ratification were negotiated as both sides jockeyed for the upper hand. Zeng Jize proved shrewd in countering the Russians' requests for further indemnities that would have been used to build a Russian fleet in the east. In the end, China ceded some territory for Dungan refugees, agreed to pay 9 million rubles (6 million taels) in "occupation fees," and granted Russia the right to establish consulates in Suzhou and Turfan, with temporary duty-free trade throughout Xinjiang.[357] This Treaty of St. Petersburg would be ratified in August 1881.[358] Jinshun was dispatched to Xinjiang to oversee the transfer of power back to China, and Xilun was recalled to explain the details to the ranking ministers in Beijing.

The Treaty of St. Petersburg was largely viewed as a victory for China at the time. Zeng Jize was lauded abroad and promoted when he came home.

Coming off their unexpectedly rapid military conquest of Xinjiang, the Qing had used a combination of adroit diplomacy and the plausible threat of military force to achieve an outcome that was more favorable than the preceding Treaty of Livadia. Nevertheless, some nationalistic modern scholars criticize the Qing court for selling out or being deceived by the Russians, thereby denying Zuo "his beautiful dream of defeating the Russians."[359] Such interpretations aside, the ability to effect a new treaty agreement without recourse to hostilities from a position of strength was territory the Qing had not charted in some time, though they admittedly failed in their efforts to extradite Bai Yanhu.

In the wake of the treaty agreement, border markers were formally erected, and officials were steadily rotated in. The Qing adopted a much more regularized approach to the frontier that characterized their maturation in the fields of international diplomacy and foreign relations.[360] This experience would inform their subsequent approaches to conflicts with France and Japan, even though the outcomes were less favorable. And there were still logistical difficulties. In 1884 Jinshun reported that there were 17,397 Qing troops stationed in Yili at a cost of 678,900 taels per year, with 3,000 more serving in mobile capacities, but these were insufficient to patrol the extensive border. The 8,000 or so Green Standard troops in Chahar cost 183,000 taels annually to maintain. A requested increase of 15,000 troops from the interior was projected to cost 2.28 million taels, so they were requesting additional subsidies and contributions. Xinjiang as a whole had some 67,800 troops at the time, but if expensive mercenaries were converted into regulars and training plans implemented, costs would drop.[361]

MAKING XINJIANG A PROVINCE

Even before he had defeated Yakub Beg, Zuo, inspired by the statecraft writers of the early nineteenth century, had peppered the court with missives calling for making Xinjiang a regular province. Indeed, many of Zuo's propositions were lifted verbatim from those works. Cognizant of the court's concerns about costs, Zuo painted an overly rosy picture. While initial outlays would in fact be considerable, he admitted, the eventual revenues from developing the untapped resources of the region—expanding agriculture, planting cotton, mining for jade and precious metals, and trading in pelts—would soon balance the scales. He even went so far as to say that three years of subsidies might be all that were needed.[362] An article in the *North China Herald* was critical of Zuo's suggestions and requests, calling his campaigns "wasteful [and] undertaken for arrogant pride," adding that China should have plenty of money, given that nothing serious had happened in the empire since 1864![363] Zuo also tried to sell the court on the inevitable and beneficial process of Sinicization that would follow, thereby binding the region more closely to the rest of the empire, saying that Han culture would "help the Muslims who have just come through fire and water."[364]

Zuo discussed extensively revamping the irrigation and waterway systems, repairing forts, digging more wells, and making other infrastructural improvements. He called for rationalizing the tax system to distribute burdens more evenly and improve revenue collection. He submitted detailed plans for these measures, taking into account census figures and projected population increases. Taxes would be commuted for the first several years. Directives would be issued in Arabic in addition to Chinese, as would documents pertaining to property ownership and other essential matters.[365] As a means of speeding acculturation Zuo recommended translating Chinese classics into Arabic. As of 1880, he said, he had already set up thirty-seven schools to acculturate the Hui.[366] Xiao Xiong, one of Zuo's secretaries, composed a poem praising the success of these efforts:

There are some of ability and distinction
Who rise above the mob's foul reek;
Their intelligence is no less than that of Li Bo—
They finish their outlandish books and study Chinese writing.[367]

Zuo's early proposals called for a governor-general in the north with overarching authority and a governor based at Aksu in the south. The huge area would be split into four circuits (*dao*) with subordinate prefectures and counties. Administrative centers would be established close to the oases.[368] Zuo's ideas saw spirited debates over the next several years concerning the precise form the new administration in Xinjiang would take. Most of them centered on costs and administrative feasibility. Interestingly, Liu Jintang, who became Xinjiang's first governor, had opposed creating a separate province, believing Xinjiang could simply be attached to Gansu with a governor appointed specifically to oversee all land west of Hami.[369] In the end, a compromise was achieved that combined aspects of several proposals. Liu Jintang was appointed the temporary minister in charge in 1881, with Zhang Yao in charge of military affairs.[370] The final plan to make Xinjiang a province was submitted to the throne by the ministries of Revenue, War, and Personnel on November 15, 1884.

The Ministry of Revenue set aside 4.8 million taels per year for the next three years for Xinjiang and Gansu, afterward to be reduced to 3 million taels annually. Local revenues would be used to pay low-level officials at post stations. Land surveys would be conducted and *tuntian* expanded to achieve self-sufficiency as quickly as possible.[371] Ambitious construction plans were laid out including building new barracks, walls, and yamen offices, in addition to repairing existing roads and structures. In his earlier reports Zuo stressed that the benefits reaped in stability, order, and resource extraction would multiply upon themselves, helping the Qing achieve lasting peace. In other words, the key to survival and future progress and prosperity was grounded in the realization of Confucian ideals. Zuo viewed officials as shepherds, and the people, especially the Hui, as sheep in need of guidance. He stressed that officials "should not concern themselves with high and low, but just love the people."[372] If the livelihood of the masses was restored, the state would profit as well. In this sense Zuo's thinking was in line with what some Qing statecraft thinkers had been saying for decades, but it also jibes with the changing views of the central authorities concerning the need to better tap "the profits of nature," as discussed by Peter Lavelle.[373]

The governor of Xinjiang would be based in Urumqi but was subordinate to the governor-general of Shaan-Gan, posted in Lanzhou. As for the lower levels, though Sinicization was the ultimate goal, at least in the eyes of the

Han officials, the Qing realized that they needed locals with expertise in the languages and culture of the area to assist in administration. As we have seen, Zuo himself was a strong advocate of this measure. Some 3,300 Turkic functionaries were retained with new titles as (low-ranking) government officials to help manage Uighur affairs in particular. The Qing made it clear that their status was lower than it had been before, even though many were performing the same functions.

Recognizing that a smaller, better-trained military presence was preferable, the Qing reduced the troop strength of Xinjiang to a mere 30,000. Many soldiers were demobilized and given land grants to become farmers. But demobilization was a tricky process. The soldiers had been fighting for more than a decade. Their pay rates were generally higher than the standards around the empire, but their pay was often in arrears. They would need to receive all their back pay before being discharged lest they mutiny or join secret societies like the Gelaohui. Liu Jintang estimated that this would cost around 40,000 taels per battalion. He suggested gradual demobilization and paying the troops in installments as they returned home, many to distant places like Hunan.[374] For his part, Zuo was opposed to rapid demobilization, feeling that the Qing needed to retain a deterrent against Russia. He convinced Liu to convert some of the mercenaries into a revived Green Standard force for the defense of Xinjiang.[375]

Modern Chinese scholars have given Zuo's establishment of Confucian schools a great deal of attention.[376] From 1866 to 1879 Zuo had established twenty new schools in Gansu and repaired fifteen others. These included free basic elementary schools and other schools for more advanced reading of characters. The total rose above three hundred in Shaan-Gan.[377] By 1883 there were seventy-seven schools in Xinjiang, each with a teacher and fifteen to twenty male students ages eight and up. In addition to the Chinese classics, the reconstruction agencies printed copies of texts that included Arabic translations and parallel versions of texts.[378] Zuo emphasized that the difference between Chinese and Muslims "was not a difference in nature, but a difference in teaching."[379] Thus, he was even open to allowing some Muslims who had been relocated from Suzhou to return to their ancestral lands so long they could prove they had no rebel ties. His rationale was that they might be better integrated into the exam system and social structure in Suzhou than they were in isolated Muslim areas.[380]

The schools did open up more appointments for local scholars, and thousands took the first two rounds of examinations. Some came from as far away as Beijing. Stipends were provided for students and candidates, and it was hoped they could bring more Hui into administration.[381] But though these efforts were noteworthy, the results were mixed at best, and by 1907 schools were following the new curriculums in any case. Traditional Islamic education also continued. The new schools did better in primarily Han areas in the north but seem to have been resented by the Muslims.

Zuo looked to advance acculturation through religion as well. Each imperially sponsored temple was provided with ten thousand taels for construction or repair work. Altars of the state and grain (*shejitan*), enduring symbols of imperial authority, were established for the first time in some places. Confucian temples received priority funding.[382] Zuo established the Chongwen Publishing Company as a vehicle to transmit the culture of the Central Plain to the northwest.

In terms of the administrators themselves, the impact of Zuo Zongtang is undeniable. Liu Jintang served as the first provincial governor from 1884 to 1887, when he was allowed to retire to take care of his elderly grandmother. Sensitive of his background, Liu was modest and always demonstrated concern about his soldiers and the subjects under his rule. It was said that he was warmly greeted and showered with gifts wherever he went on his departure trip. He was made Junior Guardian of the Heir Apparent in 1889 and promoted to Senior the next year before being made a first-grade baron in 1894. The court tried to recall him to service against Japan, but he was ill and died soon thereafter.[383] Wei Guangtao, the first finance commissioner, was a grandnephew of the famous Wei Yuan and the author of an account of Zuo's campaign in Xinjiang used herein. Most of the officials at all levels were connected to Zuo, and they often clashed with Tao Mu, who governed the province after Liu. Appointing officials he knew and trusted allowed Zuo at least temporarily to realize his lofty aims, but as in so many other areas, tying reforms to individuals rather than stable institutions undermined their lasting effectiveness.[384]

While many of the early reports sent back from Xinjiang were positive, most notably those concerning harvests, tax surveys show how small the crop base was.[385] In 1887 there was just 11,480.19 *mu* in Xinjiang under cultivation that provided 203,029.2383 *shi* of grain, 13,958,216.128 catties of hay, and 57,952.162 taels of silver.[386] *Lijin* taxes had been so abused that they were canceled. Petty grievances and abuses accumulated. Muslim revolts would arise in both Gansu and Xinjiang through the end of the Qing era. Larger crises pertaining to the Great Game would also break out, though these are beyond the scope of the present study.

EVALUATING THE XINJIANG CAMPAIGN AND ITS AFTERMATH

There is no arguing that the campaign in Xinjiang was expensive. In total Zuo spent some 26.5 million taels from 1875 to 1877 and another 18 million on reconstruction from 1878 to 1881.[387] This amounted to about one-sixth of the annual expenditures of the Qing.[388] Was it worth it? That depends on one's perspective. Funding for Xinjiang was an issue from the start, and after 1901 its already meager subsidies were slashed due to the need to pay the Boxer Indemnity. Zuo's rosy claims aside, reclaimed lands were often marginally productive or abandoned. Even though the campaign in Xinjiang was successful, some sources claim that it drained Qing coffers to the extent that it weakened naval defenses, opining that the Qing might have won the ensuing Sino-Japanese War had funds not been misallocated to Xinjiang.[389]

One perhaps unanticipated effect of the campaign was that more Uighurs moved north and east, contributing to their collective sense that this was "their land" because their numbers far exceeded those of the Han and Dungans in the region.[390] Additionally, since many documents were destroyed during the conflicts of 1862–1877, the local Uighurs played a major role in gazetteer compilation, affecting both official Qing histories and contemporary perceptions.[391] Campaign diaries, poems, and novels about the events of the conquest were written by participants as well, reinforcing Confucian tropes such as loyalty and filial piety as they incorporated these episodes more broadly into the chaotic history of the late Qing.[392]

The recovery of Xinjiang has been called "the last imperial campaign of a dying empire." Many Western scholars characterize it as a prime example of the "backward continental thinking of the Qing court" rather than correctly seeing it as a strategically sensible response to the dilemma facing China at the time.[393] In fact, more than forty years ago, Nailene Chou argued that the creation of the province of Xinjiang marked a convergence of the aims of proponents of Qing evidential scholarship with strategic concerns, especially with regard to Russia, noting, as I do, the many connections between Zuo Zongtang and early nineteenth-century statecraft scholars such as Wei Yuan.[394] She also correctly notes that the process of creating the province of Xinjiang was a testament to the continued viability of Qing central authority.[395]

Some at the time even saw it as a harbinger of a full-blown Qing revival. Boulger, writing a contemporary account, stated, "The Chinese reconquest of East Turkestan is beyond doubt the most remarkable event that has occurred in Asia in the last fifty years and is quite the most brilliant achievement of a Chinese army led by Chinamen that has taken place since Qianlong subdued the country more than a century ago."[396] He praised China's adaptive faculty in drawing on European weapons, science, and tactics, noting that "even in such minor matters as the use of telescopes and field glasses we find this Chinese army well-supplied," further asserting that "in all essentials [it] closely resembled that of a European power."[397] Boulger was not alone, as even after China's uneven showing against the French, many Western observers predicted a Qing victory in the war with Japan in 1895 on the basis of China's showing in the 1870s.[398]

Modern nationalist scholars in the PRC have praised Zuo's Xinjiang campaign as his greatest accomplishment, one that solidified his position as a "true patriotic hero."[399] They point to Zuo's vision as worthy of emulation even as "outsiders" today try to stir up dissent in Xinjiang between different peoples.[400] The willow trees that still line roads in Gansu and Xinjiang are said to be lasting reminders of Zuo's patriotic vision and are called a "greening movement" by one enthusiastic modern biographer.[401] Indeed, Zuo planted more than 400,000 trees extending more than 1,000 *li* through Gansu and

Shaanxi. Zuo claimed that when he returned through the region in 1880 the many new-growth trees had already changed it.[402]

Modern Chinese sources likewise praise Zuo's efforts to prohibit opium use and eradicate opium production and replace it with more beneficial products, even though these efforts failed in the long run.[403] When Zuo arrived in Xinjiang, an estimated 70 percent of the population used opium and upward of 30 percent of the arable land was used for opium cultivation. Zuo prohibited opium production in 1869 and tried to replace it, most notably with sericulture, bringing in mulberry seeds from the southeast.[404] More than a decade later, as Zuo was pushing for Xinjiang to become a regular province, he claimed that 886,000 mulberry trees had been planted and suggested that Russia could become a major customer for silk produced there. In fact, part of his rationale was strategic, as he believed that if silk was available in Xinjiang, Russian traders would not need to go farther inland to acquire it.[405] At this time he also rejuvenated his push to prohibit opium. He proposed sending new officials out to investigate local conditions and offer farmers seeds for beneficial crops instead of the drug.[406] An 1878 article in *Shenbao* praised Zuo's efforts, noting that if other officials followed Zuo's lead, a real transformation could be achieved.[407] But opium was simply too profitable for too many people, and even some of Zuo's inspectors were suborned, so the antiopium campaign was mostly symbolic. The *North China Herald* recognized that, though the writer expressed mild optimism that the establishment of woolen mills might help curtail poppy cultivation.[408]

With respect to Zuo's Xinjiang campaign being the result of "backward thinking" that took funds and attention away from coastal defense, no one was more acutely aware of the need to defend China's southeast coast than Zuo Zongtang. He simply believed that the recovery and defense of Xinjiang should assume priority. Indeed, as one modern biographer notes, Zuo's policy regarding the northwest in general was in fact more nuanced and encompassing than Li's and was grounded in greater practical experience.[409] The subsequent debacle of the Chinese fleet in the Sino-French War should not be blamed on Zuo or this policy. If anything, primary responsibility for that defeat belongs at the feet of Li Hongzhang, who jealously guarded "his" fleet and resources in the north and refused to render full aid to the southern forces battling the French around Taiwan. Li received his just desserts a decade later in the war against Japan when the southern fleets returned the favor.

More important, the recovery of Xinjiang and its integration into the empire marked the final stage in a process of Sinicization and administrative integration that had been ongoing since the beginning of the Qing, starting with the southwest and extending through Tibet and into Central Asia.[410] The increasing power of Han Chinese officials dovetailed with a rising sense of Han nationalism in the late Qing to create an environment in which the supposedly transformative power of Han civilization supplanted the multiethnic hands-off approach that had previously undergirded Qing imperial practices. It also helped create the basis for the modern PRC discourse concerning the multiethnic nature of the Chinese state and its grounding in Chinese history. Interestingly, this discourse itself has evolved over the course of the PRC. In the early days of the People's Republic, Zuo and the Qing defeat of the rebellion were cast as antiprogressive. Nowadays, his efforts, even if sometimes bloody, are perceived as having been necessary to preserve the unity of the Chinese nation.[411]

Even though they were still in control, the Qing leaders were increasingly forced to accede to these Han initiatives as they desperately tried to prop up their empire by all means available, rightly realizing that the more concessions they made to the Han, the more tenuous their legitimacy became. Formally integrating Xinjiang and Taiwan into the empire as provinces potentially offered both legal and financial benefits to the beleaguered Qing, though in fact, these proved to be phantoms as Taiwan was detached anyhow and Xinjiang's development was retarded by the factors outlined above. Nevertheless, this should not obscure the fact that these decisions made a good deal of sense at the time. The Qing government had just defeated the last of a series of massive rebellions and was still standing. The victory in Xinjiang was as unlikely as any and was achieved without much foreign aid and against considerable odds. Boulger hailed Yakub Beg as the "the most remarkable man Central Asia in its fullest extent, has produced since Nadir Shah," and most Western commentators at the time predicted he would defeat the Qing handily.[412] After the Qing had prevailed against Yakub, some observers warned that this was a "new China," and their victory would have a serious ripple effect vis-à-vis other powers in Central Asia.[413]

This prediction proved to be partly correct. The Qing did retain control over Xinjiang, and the Russian threat receded in the following decades with the combination of domestic unrest and Russia's defeat at the hands of the Japanese. But the threat along China's coast rose, starting with an unexpected war with France over influence in Vietnam. Zuo's limited involvement in this conflict marked the last phase of his storied career. By this point he was a grizzled elder statesman, either respected or considered a played-out relic, depending on one's political leanings. But even in Zuo's final days, his warnings and recommendations remained prescient and true to his character.

Map 6. The Sino-French War

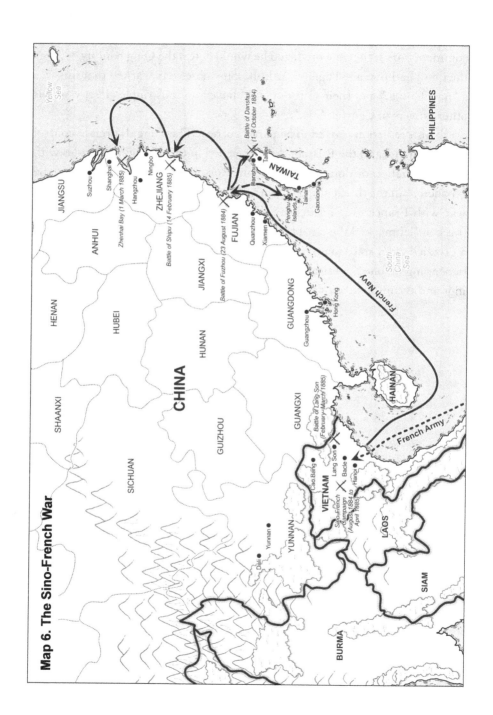

PHILIPPINES

Yellow Sea

Battle of Danshui (1–8 October 1884)

TAIWAN

Danshui

Taibei

Penghu Islands

Tainan

Gaoxiong

JIANGSU

Suzhou

Shanghai

Zhenhai Bay (1 March 1885)

Hangzhou

Ningbo

ZHEJIANG

Battle of Shipu (14 February 1885)

ANHUI

Battle of Fuzhou (23 August 1884)

FUJIAN

Quanzhou

Xiamen

JIANGXI

HENAN

HUBEI

HUNAN

CHINA

GUANGDONG

Guangzhou

Hong Kong

South China Sea

SHAANXI

GUIZHOU

French Navy

HAINAN

SICHUAN

GUANGXI

Battle of Lang Son (February–March 1885)

French Army

Cao Bằng

Lang Son

Bắc Lệ

Hanoi

VIETNAM

Sino-French Campaign (August 1884 to April 1885)

YUNNAN

Dali

Yunnan

LAOS

BURMA

SIAM

7

THE GROGNARD

*Let railways and mines and the construction of ships and guns
be undertaken at once as a means of ensuring our national
prosperity and strength.*
—Zuo Zongtang

Zuo's recall to the capital was publicly portrayed as an honor. He was the undisputed conqueror of Xinjiang, queller of the massive Muslim rebellions that had plagued the northwest for nearly two decades. It was said that when Zuo left Lanzhou, the grateful population came out in droves to cheer him and see him off.[1] The court claimed it wanted to hear Zuo's advice personally as a counterpoint to those favoring a less belligerent stance.[2] But many also knew that some regarded Zuo as a warmonger and that his rivalry with Li Hongzhang had animated most of the key foreign policy debates of the past decade. Thus the "honor" of a desk job in Beijing was a mixed one, to be sure. And it would soon become clear that despite his age and infirmity (his eyes had been deteriorating for some time), Zuo remained a man of action. He had little stomach for court intrigue and was uncomfortable in court settings. He increasingly found himself a grognard, an old soldier admired by many but forced to cede authority and initiative to younger men in a rapidly changing world that he had done much to shape.

THE UNWILLING COURTIER

By the time he returned to Beijing, Zuo had been serving as a military official for three decades. For the vast majority of that time he had been in the field, often in distant and desolate regions of the empire. Never particularly comfortable in social situations, Zuo preferred interacting with commoners in the fields, puttering in his garden, and eating common food, especially dog, with soldiers in camp.[3] While he was certainly capable of conducting erudite discussions on history and the classics with other scholars, he preferred such discussions to be in informal settings and for practical ends. The life of the dilettante and courtier was simply not for him, as became obvious as soon as he reached the capital. Furthermore, the revised treaty with Russia caused Zuo great consternation and exacerbated his ill health.[4]

In any event, he found life in Beijing overly politicized. He was allegedly initially denied entry to the Forbidden City because he refused to bribe the court eunuchs the required 40,000-tael "fee" to gain an audience.[5] Prince Gong interceded, and Zuo got his audience, though Cixi was reportedly ill, so he only met with Dowager Empress Ci'an.[6] He was appointed Minister of the Realm in charge of all military affairs and given oversight of central policy for the Ministry of War.[7] He also received a pair of eyeglasses that had belonged to the deceased Emperor Xianfeng (Zuo had broken his own), though a eunuch allegedly told Zuo he should offer an astounding 100,000 taels as thanks for the gift.[8] He was also given a spot on the Grand Council and accorded the privilege of riding his horse in the Forbidden City.[9]

As he took up his duties Zuo requested reports on provincial military strength across the empire, wanting actual figures so he could devise a coordinated national defense strategy.[10] He also took steps to allocate more modern Western firearms to troops and to spread their manufacture and distribution across the empire, recognizing the vulnerability of having just a couple of major production centers. Zuo was especially concerned about the vital Jiangnan region. Although there already were arsenals at Tianjin and Baoding, he wanted more of them, with the arms they produced supplemented by purchases from Germany. He pushed for each province to set up an armory and munitions factory and to purchase weapons, fuses, and the like from abroad, providing cost estimates of doing so.[11]

Not being one to rest on his laurels, Zuo's first order of business was to restore the waterworks around the capital for agricultural, commercial, and military purposes, something for which he was eminently qualified owing to his experiences in such endeavors across the empire.[12] He worked with Li Hongzhang over a four-month period to dredge canals and open routes to the sea. His ailments worsened during this time, and in the summer of 1881 he was forced to take a two-month sabbatical.[13] Even so, one modern biographer asserts that Zuo accomplished more in less than a year than Li Hongzhang had achieved in a decade.[14] He also investigated ways to expand *lijin* revenues and tap other sources of income.[15] This included finally supporting the legalization and taxation of opium, with higher levies for imported drugs.[16] Opium would become an important governmental revenue stream through the Republican period. Zuo hoped to get even more done, but he vastly underestimated the depths of the Beijing political swamp.

From the start Zuo had trouble with his colleagues in Beijing, where intrigue and bribery were the norm, because of his straightforward, no-nonsense manner. Zuo simply could not stand the endless sniping and gossipy (*simian Chuge*) atmosphere of court, where everyone competed for access to and attention from the powerful dowagers, most notably Cixi.[17] "These people have nothing in the world to say to me," Zuo complained, "and I can't waste my time in formalities."[18] Zuo apparently stepped on the toes of a Manchu prince by wanting to use his own men from the Xiang Army to complete repairs to waterworks when the prince in question already had an "arrangement" with local officials to contract out the work.[19]

Within six months Zuo was named governor-general of Liang-Jiang (Jiangsu and Jiangxi) and sent back to the field.[20] The *North China Herald* praised this as a "good appointment for despite his age and weight, [Zuo's] mind is active and his nerve as strong as ever."[21] He was now lauded not as antiforeign but rather as a "fervent nationalist." The paper also commented on Zuo's disagreements with Li Hongzhang and his general distaste for the poisonous atmosphere of Beijing, observing that Zuo was a man of action who desired to return to the southeast where he could actually get something accomplished.[22] Zuo would have the necessary resources in Nanjing, the paper suggested, and could work better with Li from a distance, crediting the two officials with representing a "utilitarian as opposed to the old futilitarian party in China."[23]

Publicly Cixi said that the appointment was made because of Zuo's skills and knowledge of the area, but it was well known in court circles that it was simply to get him out of Beijing, where he had made more enemies than friends.[24] He left the capital on January 24, 1882, supposedly being inundated by well-wishers as he left. He went to Hunan on the way to his new assignment, his first visit to his old home in more than twenty years. He traveled to Xiangyin, his ancestral home, and then to Changsha, where he supervised the building of his tomb in the hills outside the city.[25]

BACK IN THE FIELD: PUSHING CHANGES IN LIANG-JIANG

As he traveled south by boat Zuo had the opportunity to observe the state of the government's modernization efforts, including military defenses in this most vital region of the empire. He was concerned that matters had not progressed enough since the Taiping Rebellion, suggesting that official corruption and peculation had hindered reform and retarded the economic recovery.[26] He called for better oversight of subordinate officers, noting that there was continued misappropriation of funds and false reporting concerning troop numbers, among other things. He found some Hubei battalions to be at less than half strength, leaving them ill-prepared should a real challenge emerge.

The same was true in Jiangsu.[27] Specifically, Zuo called out Li Hanzhang, Hongzhang's younger brother, who had previously supported Zuo in the frontier policy defense debate, for nepotism and corruption. An imperial investigation resulted in the replacement of some officials and promises to conduct further inquiries, some of which bore fruit and led to more dismissals. The foreign press speculated that Zuo was seeking to purge the administration of Li Hongzhang's protégés, though some writers also suspected that Li was in fact laying traps for Zuo in order to consolidate his own control over foreign affairs. In the end Zuo was allowed to put more of his own men into posts at all levels, lending credence to the idea that the court was interested in cleaning up the administration as well as maintaining a balance of sorts between the two high officials.[28]

Zuo's recommendations at his new post were grounded in the desire to improve the local economy by improving the transportation infrastructure,

removing bad officials, and tapping new sources of revenue by expanding trade and increasing arable land.[29] He forwarded detailed reports on
local revenues and commerce as well as military accounting, comparing
his own records from Xinjiang and Gansu with those in the southeast.[30]
Again drawing on his experiences in the northwest, Zuo set up military
rehabilitation offices around Nanjing.[31] He oversaw the construction of
the steel-plated ship *baomin*, outfitted with eight Krupp guns, though
the project suffered from serious cost overruns.[32] A new jetty was built
there as well. In discussing his achievements as the empire's chief military
official, the *North China Herald* praised Zuo as "a man of progress" and
a "true hero."[33]

Once settled in his new post Zuo set himself three main tasks: (1) repair
waterworks with an emphasis on improving commercial transit, (2) revise
salt revenue collection to improve regional finances, and (3) improve naval
defenses in the region.[34] This entailed repairing the Grand Canal and managing the Huai River. Like the Yellow River to the north, the course of the
Huai had shifted in the 1850s, and Zuo wanted to return it to its former
course in order to spare the people of Yangzhou from flooding. Though he
invested significant resources in this project, he retired before it was finished.
He repaired waterworks elsewhere, however, alleviating a number of problems by building new dikes, embankments, and channels, both decreasing
flooding and expanding cultivated land to feed the growing population.[35]
Local forts, city walls, bridges, and roads were restored as part of his infrastructure improvements. A visit to Shanghai helped raise funds for expanding railways in north China.[36]

The high costs of operating a modern machine industry in a comparatively underdeveloped economy sapped the financial strength of Jiangnan
and gave rise to other social problems as certain aspects of rehabilitation were
glossed over or neglected. Moreover, the ongoing need for foreign technical aid
to update the equipment kept China dependent, a problem Zuo recognized
and hoped to ameliorate through the expansion of schools emphasizing science and technology.[37] Yet another problem was the propensity for Chinese
officials to see modernization projects as opportunities for nepotism, graft,

and corruption.[38] Some also lacked the necessary technical knowledge to run these enterprises. Li Hongzhang, ironically one of the foremost beneficiaries of these practices, called them out, prompting Zuo to revise bidding practices and procedures in projects he oversaw.[39]

Zuo also raised revenues via selling salt certificates.[40] He conducted detailed investigations of the salt trade in south-central China with the aims of lowering duties and curtailing smuggling, though he was dubious about his chances of complete reform because entrenched interests blocked his efforts. But he believed that issuing more licenses (for sale) and lowering customs fees were steps in the right direction. More people would be employed if they could afford licenses, and lower fees would cut down on smuggling.[41]

Zuo embarked on wholesale plans of military reconstruction and training. Boats, shipyards, shore batteries, and emplacements on city walls were upgraded. More weapons and patrol boats were purchased from the Germans, and trainers were hired to instruct the troops in their use.[42] Zuo sketched out ideas for a comprehensive plan of coastal defense, specifying what kinds of ships were needed for which operations and identifying places that needed shore batteries and gun emplacements. He considered different organizational hierarchies, presenting the cases for both provincial and more overarching authority. Belying his reputation, he also stressed that coastal defenses should have priority over riverine defenses at this juncture. Calling gunboats "the heart of Self-Strengthening," Zuo stressed that the process of naval modernization and training in Western methods would still take several years.[43] Surprisingly, Zuo noted that he and Li Hongzhang concurred on these general principles.[44]

In another report on the progress of his naval measures, including the construction of steamers, Zuo stressed the need for appointing an admiral in charge of training the sailors and coordinating all coastal defenses. Echoing points first made when he advocated the creation of the Fuzhou Navy Yard, Zuo emphasized the links between warfare and commerce and explained how having a strong navy would advance China's commercial interests. Coastal defenses should be integrated with riverine defenses, and China, like Britain, needed ships capable of operating in both environments. Zuo recommended a number of officials, including Peng Yulin, for key posts in his new organizational scheme.[45]

In laying out his revised plans for coastal defense, Zuo described a strong defense as another means of "spreading the awe" (*fan tianwei*) of the empire.[46] To this end, Zuo even experimented with creating a coast guard (*yutuan*), which he believed would be an economical way to keep order in the short term as the full-scale upgrades were implemented. Fisherman could be recruited to help fill its ranks. Zuo later conducted an inspection tour of these units in the autumn of 1883, noting their training methods and recording the number of ships and weapons they possessed.[47] He offered a positive assessment of their progress, believing they could serve as a useful adjunct to regular naval forces.[48]

Zuo expanded his idea of using fishermen in the coast guard into other areas as well. Noting how the recent strife had severely depleted the available pool of high officials, Zuo argued that talent should be drawn from other sources. Drawing on his own experiences, Zuo made the case for employing talented *juren*, noting that "in times of chaos, one must take up the martial." Many such individuals had been forced by necessity to take on greater responsibilities, and many now had more practical experience than their book-educated "superiors" in the administrative hierarchy.[49]

Recognizing Zuo's efforts to raise revenues, including via opium taxes, foreigners praised him as "a man of great integrity and mind and purpose" who "honestly holds extreme views on the opium trade." Li Hongzang, in contrast, was held to be sneaky and duplicitous.[50] One story criticized Li for failing to help Zuo restore waterways in north China, though Li maintained that such efforts were both expensive and impractical.[51]

Zuo remained interested in the development of Xinjiang as well and reported on the progress made in appointing officials and expanding the administration. He emphasized skills over numbers and reiterated the importance of appointing capable local officials. He also warned the court of the continued intrigues of the Russians, who were always eager to stir up trouble, particularly among the Muslims. Noting that Liu Jintang's forces were spread dangerously thin, Zuo stressed speeding up infrastructural improvements to ensure the flow of weapons and other supplies to the Qing armies as they prepared the region for provincial status.[52]

As he had in the northwest, Zuo pushed the expansion of modern industry in Liang Jiang, expanding the use of steamboats, telegraph lines, and railroads.[53] He wanted to build a railroad extending west from Hankou, perhaps eventually linking up with the expanding transportation networks in Xinjiang. Dismissing earlier criticism of him as an antiforeign reactionary, the *North China Herald* now highlighted Zuo's progressivism, quoting his statement that "the road to the development of wealth lies in opening of the sources of wealth and regulating the channels of expenditure."[54]

The tireless Zuo even devised a comprehensive plan for the expansion of the national telegraph system, including the projected costs.[55] The Sino-French War, which broke out a couple years later, would galvanize official support for that idea. The telegraph aided communication with the troops in Vietnam during that war, and some sources credit it with facilitating the land victories of the Qing and their Vietnamese allies. Even Li Hongzhang came to view the telegraph as a valuable tool to "enhance communications and extend our sovereignty."[56] The telegraph eventually supplanted the *Capital Gazette*, as newspapers such as *Shenbao* rapidly received and reprinted imperial edicts and reports, including from the fronts of the Sino-French War. This widespread and rapid communication had the added effect of enhancing the importance of public opinion and contributed to the rise of popular nationalism in the waning days of the empire. Indeed, Sun Yatsen indicated that media coverage of the Sino-French War helped radicalize him.[57]

In addition to the telegraph, Zuo advocated for opening more coal and iron mines, rightly seeing these as essential for expanding modern industry, and pushed for businessmen to assume control of them rather than officials, too many of whom saw the lucrative enterprises as new sources of graft. He established one mine at Xuzhou in Jiangsu in October 1882. And though Zuo recognized the talents of Westerners in the business sphere, he remained true to his ideals of Self-Strengthening and pushed for native Chinese to take the lead in both business and industrial developments.[58] The best way to defend against further encroachments by foreign interests was to get China's internal affairs in order, he insisted, with the Chinese themselves spearheading this process. At least some in the foreign community applauded this stance, with one article in the *North China Herald* arguing that foreigners had nothing to fear from Zuo; he could be expected to "strictly respect treaties and act in a fair and high minded spirit."[59]

Zuo recognized that continued reliance on foreigners would simply perpetuate the cycle of dependence the Qing had been mired in for some forty years. Thomas Kennedy summarizes China's need for self-sufficiency when he notes that "the environment of foreign dependency in which the industry developed forced the arsenals to rely on China's potential enemies for the elements necessary to maintain modernized production."[60] To speed the process of self-sufficiency Zuo pushed to expand the Interpreter's College (Tongwenguan) so that the Chinese could more quickly acquire technical skills, though he continued to employ European experts in his arsenals and ordnance factories to stay abreast of the latest developments.[61] On the whole, Kennedy judges the efforts of Zuo and other modernizers a success: "though some products were imperfect or substandard, in a scant thirty-five years production in China's arsenals had progressed from gingals and cannon balls to the most modern types of arms and ammunition."[62]

But Zuo's health continued to decline, and he requested permission to retire yet again after suffering a "stroke of paralysis" in late 1882.[63] Zuo wrote to the emperor that he "was paralyzed; his sight was dim; his mind dark; his memory failing; his pulse fluctuating; he forgets things after he reads them, and he had accumulated huge amounts of unread correspondence."[64] The Western press speculated that Zuo would officially retire when his three-month leave ended, but instead Zuo was recalled to service in 1883 to deal with the rise of sectarians in Shandong, which he handled quickly. After defeating these heterodox elements Zuo recommended the creation of local militia. That advice would have negative repercussions some two decades later in the Boxer Rebellion.[65]

As Zuo was once more shouldering the burdens of command in March 1883, plans going forward to make Xinjiang an official province were attracting much attention in Western circles.[66] Foreigners' assessments of Zuo's policies were mixed, though they agreed that he seemed to have recovered his mental faculties. One writer noted that "despite his advanced age and enormous bulk, his mental vigor still seems unimpaired and he's still highly prized as an adviser, so he'll probably die in harness."[67] Zuo was dealt a political defeat of sorts when his proposals for revamping the salt gabelle were rejected, in part because existing traders donated large amounts of salt to the market, making it less feasible to issue more licenses, though Zuo did apprehend one notorious bandit and salt smuggler known as Little Monkey Xi.[68] On a more positive note, during a visit to Shanghai, Zuo purchased two gunboats from foreign manufacturers. But his attention was forced elsewhere when tensions with the French erupted into war.[69]

THE BACKDROP TO THE SINO-FRENCH WAR

The Qing clash with France over Vietnam (Annam) was inevitable in the context of late-nineteenth-century geopolitics. France had been jockeying with the other European powers for influence around the globe for decades. The French were still stung by their defeat in the Franco-Prussian War and wary of Britain's growing power in South and Southeast Asia after the suppression of the Sepoy Mutiny. Vietnam had ceded Saigon and three provinces in the south of Vietnam, also known as Cochin China, to France in 1862. Twelve years later the king of Vietnam, Nguyen van Trung, was forced to sign the Treaty of Saigon, which, in addition to providing for "peace and alliance" between Vietnam and France, granted the French navigation rights up the Red River all the way to the Chinese border in Yunnan. At this time the French also declared Vietnam a French protectorate.[70] But the Qing refused to relinquish their tributary sovereignty over Vietnam and would not grant the French the right to trade in Yunnan.[71]

Moreover, in the aftermath of the Taiping Rebellion both Taiping remnants and Qing units had moved into the borderlands between China and Vietnam and become embroiled in regional political squabbles that expanded over time. The most infamous of these "imperial bandits" was the Black Flags, though there were numerous other organizations that were intimately tied to both the opium trade and regional politics.[72] Annam continued to send tribute to the Qing, thereby keeping the old relationship with the Qing intact, but by 1880 the French were ready to push their interests in Annam. They likely knew of China's current preoccupation with Russia, since Zeng Jize had been the Qing envoy to France. In April 1882 the French commander Henri-Laurent Rivière (1827–1883) seized Hanoi.[73] The Zongli Yamen responded with a statement of China's position on the matter:

> If the French intend to occupy the whole of Vietnam that state has no means to preserve itself. Regarding China's righteous concern for its dependencies, we should send troops to aid Vietnam, and use peaceful or warlike tactics as suits the situation. But, viewing the situation, the difficulty of settling on a satisfactory policy lies in the fact that the strength of China is not yet adequate and Vietnam is weak and cannot sustain itself. The southern part has already been lost and provinces of the northern part border on Yunnan, Guangdong, and Guangxi. If we wait until the French have entirely occupied the north before we inaugurate a plan of closing the passes for self-defense, then China's defenses will be drawn back and there will be no end to ensuing troubles. Nor will it only be France that rises up on all sides, nor only Vietnam which is imperiled. This is not only a trouble which affects the borders, but one that affects the whole [strategic] situation [of China].[74]

Efforts at reconciliation with France over the next couple of years failed, and a very avoidable war erupted. After Hanoi was occupied, Beijing sent a small naval detachment from Guangdong to patrol the coast and "manifest the awe" of the Qing empire. Some troops were dispatched into the border region to augment the Black Flags and Vietnamese units then engaged with the French. Zeng Jize, once again serving as China's representative in Paris, vociferously restated the previous agreements between France and Vietnam, most notably the 1874 treaty. According to some Chinese sources, Zeng also worked behind the scenes to gain British support for China's position.[75] Talks between Li Hongzhang and the French minister to China, Frédéric Bourée, in late 1882 produced three major agreements: (1) China would withdraw its troops and France would declare it had no intention of conquering Vietnam or diminishing that kingdom's sovereignty; (2) France could establish a market at Lao-Kay on the Red River, south of Yunnan; and (3) a buffer zone would be established in northern Vietnam. These terms required revisions from the Zongli Yamen, and the Qing requested that the Vietnamese participate in the talks as well. Subsequent criticism from various Chinese provincial leaders and a change in the French government scuttled the whole deal, though clearly it influenced the Li-Fournier Agreement discussed below.[76]

Bourée continued to advise Li, telling him that a group of French mine investors in Tonkin were pushing for war although France itself preferred a peaceful settlement. But while Li continued to push for peace, the hawks in Beijing got the ear of the throne, prompting another warning that doubled down on the Qing's determination to defend its traditional tributary rights: "We hear that the French in Vietnam are now even more on the rampage. Vietnam is in an enfeebled condition, encroachments upon it are without end, and it can hardly preserve itself. That state is one of our dependencies and we cannot but protect it. Also, the territories of Yunnan, Guangxi, and Guangdong border on it, and if the screens of defense are drawn back, how can we bear to speak of future troubles?"[77] Li Hongzhang was ordered to proceed to Tonkin (northern Vietnam) to negotiate directly, but he protested, loath to abandon his power base in the north. The court finally relented and authorized Li to hold talks with the French representative Arthur Tricou in Shanghai. But these talks went nowhere as well. Li was not overly concerned. Reports from Zeng Jize in Paris suggested that most of the French people were opposed to war and only a few special interest groups were pushing it. For their part, the Qing continued to deny that Chinese troops were even in Vietnam, claiming the notorious Black Flags were entirely independent actors.[78]

As might be expected, when push finally came to shove, Zuo, buoyed by his apparent success in cowing the Russians during the recent Yili Crisis, favored a more aggressive stance vis-à-vis the French while Li Hongzhang pushed for conciliation. Zuo referenced the Opium War, saying China needed to put up a strong defense and not simply capitulate. He quickly moved to dispatch spies, guard the ports, and establish *baojia* while also sending patrol boats along the coasts, prioritizing defense of the mouth of the Yangzi. Shore batteries were erected up and down the coasts.[79] Artillery students from Nanjing were dispatched to Yunnan and Guangxi to aid in weapons making. Foreigners lamented China's "unwinnable predicament," contending that Zuo was "too old and too fat to command" and placing their hopes in Zeng Jize's negotiating skills.[80]

Zuo informed the court of his willingness to martyr himself in defense of the empire should Western steamers penetrate the coastal defenses. Eighteen cannons were erected on platforms at Wusong, and the defenses around Shanghai were also reinforced. Zuo and Peng Yulin addressed the sailors there in a rousing speech said to have driven the chill from the morning air.[81] In the autumn of 1883 Zuo traveled along the Yangzi on his own steamer reviewing the troops. He proclaimed himself quite impressed by their appearance, declaring the sailors "superior to other people" and with the ability to "fight on water as if it were dry land."[82] Zuo urged the increased production of ships in Fujian, expressing concerns about both the quality of the ships being produced and the training of their crews. Zuo's fears on those scores would be realized sooner than he expected.[83]

As the French agitations mounted, Zuo warned the court that the Black Flag commander Liu Yongfu (1837–1917) was not necessarily reliable as either an ally or a source of information. He recommended sending the Xiang Army south, but they would need secure supply lines. Now that the irrigation work in Zhili was completed, Zuo thought he could shift funds toward military needs in the south. Mercenaries were recruited in Yunnan and Guangxi and supplies were amassed in Guangdong as Wang Depang was contacted to make preparations for a possible Qing intervention.[84] Through the summer of 1883 more troops were dispatched to Guangdong.[85] Military supplies, notably guns and ammunition, followed.[86] Zuo sent letters to Li Hongzhang and the Zongli Yamen with his assessments of the French threat and the state of China's coastal defenses.[87] Zuo noted that he was not impressed with the performance of Liu Yongfu's forces and had dispatched Wang Depang to gather intelligence and coordinate efforts along the border.[88] In the second month of 1884 Wang's army took up defensive positions around Nanning as Kang Guoqi arrived to oversee supplies.[89] More Western-trained gunnery units were also dispatched to the southeast.

Back in the heartland, Zuo made plans to protect the Grand Canal from potential French attacks. Training was stepped up across central and eastern China, and more officials were posted to key areas to oversee local defenses. A long article on Zuo's career in the *North China Herald* captures Zuo's continued dedication: "His short, stout, but powerful figure, with the bull neck and big heavy face might be seen trudging constantly about the camp, his eye upon everybody."[90] Anticipating a naval clash with the French, Zuo experimented with torpedoes in Nanjing, even meeting with a British torpedo instructor there in November 1883 prior to taking another two-month leave.[91] Peng Yulin submitted a long missive to the court in December 1883 detailing preparations and the state of China's coastal defenses.[92]

British observers decried the warmongers Cen Yuying in Yunnan, Zhang Zhidong, and, to a lesser extent, Zuo, who was now criticized as a "bitter conservative."[93] Stories suddenly emerged claiming that Zuo's troops had behaved boorishly during the visit to Shanghai the previous year, supposedly pointing bayonets at unarmed men, firing at ships, and spitting on women.[94]

In the meantime, the Qing continued to prepare for war. Refugee centers were set up along the southern borders. Torpedoes and cruisers were purchased for the defense of Taiwan and the coast. Though his leave had been extended, in the fourth month of 1884 Zuo was recalled to Beijing for an imperial audience concerning the situation in Vietnam.[95] During the meeting Zuo was reportedly questioned about his troops' poor behavior in Shanghai and charges that the gunboats under his purview were of inferior quality.[96] At the same time more troops were dispatched to the southwest, and Huang Shaochun was ordered to hasten to the border.[97]

Zuo again requested permission to retire, citing his declining eyesight in particular.[98] Though he was initially put in charge of the Firearms Division in Beijing and granted oversight over the entire empire's military affairs (again), he protested that age and infirmity prevented him from performing those tasks and was granted another four-month leave. Zeng Guoquan replaced him as governor of Liang Jiang.[99] The court considered Zuo's retirement request but instead made him governor-general of Guangdong and Fujian with concurrent responsibilities for the defense of Taiwan in the summer of 1884.[100] Zuo realized this would require a coordinated national defense, but from the start Li Hongzhang balked at sending "his" fleet from Tianjin to help in the south, arguing that doing so would leave Beijing exposed to attack.[101] Guo Songtao also feared the possibility of expanding hostilities with the Western powers at sea. Zuo countered with his usual logic, pointing out that if France swallowed Vietnam, it would be poised to strike at Guangdong and Yunnan and might dominate the southern seas.[102]

Keeping tabs on the situation in the southwest along the border, Zuo recommended the impeachment of Tang Jiong (1829–1909), the governor of Yunnan, for taking bribes and fumbling relations with the French.[103] As the undeclared war dragged on and tensions rose, the court dispatched Zuo to Fujian.[104] He picked up five thousand of his old soldiers en route to the south and reached Fuzhou in the tenth month of 1884, easing the hearts of the locals by virtue of his arrival, according to one of his biographers.[105] Zuo immediately set about bolstering defenses, sending out more patrol boats, and establishing anti-looting and -raiding procedures to protect local commerce. He sent more ships to aid in the defense of Taiwan and asked the court to dispatch a high-level official to the island to coordinate its defenses, a request echoed by Zeng Guoquan.[106] Zuo's shore batteries reportedly helped prevent French ships from menacing the coast.[107]

The undeclared war between China and Vietnam against the French picked up steam, with semi-independent elements carrying on much of the fighting for the allies. Foremost among these were the Black Flag armies comprised of former Taiping and miscellaneous bandit elements that had taken refuge in the mountainous border region between China and Vietnam in the preceding years. Liu Yongfu, their most prominent leader, largely controlled trade along the upper Red River in the 1870s and had gained fame by killing a French naval lieutenant in a battle near Tonkin in 1873. The Black Flags aided the Vietnamese against the French at the instigation of regional officials from both the Qing and Vietnamese sides, while also clashing with other semi-independent military forces in the region, including groups known respectively as the White Flags and the Yellow Flags.[108]

In 1883 Liu's Black Flags defeated the French, killing their commander, Henri Rivière at the Battle of Paper Bridge just outside Hanoi on May 19.[109] This had the effect of expanding the war and drawing Chinese land forces deeper into the conflict.[110] In the meantime the Vietnamese leadership was in transition, with three emperors dying in the space of six months and factions jockeying for influence.[111] Though their results were mixed, the Black Flags attracted the attention of prominent firebrands such as Zhang Zhidong, who pushed for more overt Qing support of them and an expansion of the war in Vietnam, partly as a means of drawing French power away from Taiwan.[112] More aid was funneled to Liu Yongfu, but the French defeated his forces at Son Tay in the autumn of 1883.[113]

As Chinese victory reports from the land battles in Vietnam rolled in, Zuo pushed the court to step up construction of warships. Zuo and some of the other Qing hawks believed that victory was possible, even though local officials in Vietnam were dragging their feet, citing poor weather conditions. When the court suggested a halt to the actions, Zuo sent a secret letter saying that China should keep fighting to strengthen its negotiating position.[114] He was also furious that despite his nominal command position, his hands were tied because Li Hongzhang appeared to have the ear of the policymakers in Beijing. Meanwhile, talks between China and France were reopened in Shanghai.[115]

Zuo nevertheless continued to amass mines, artillery, and other supplies as some younger scholars and officials, best represented by Zhang Zhidong and calling themselves the "purists" (*qingliu*), clamored for war, condemning appeasement and calling France a "spent arrow." For his part, Zeng Jize argued for a strong stance, echoing many of the concerns expressed by Zuo that if China compromised now, further depredations would likely follow, possibly including serious French encroachments on Chinese territory and resources in the southwest. This in turn might inspire Russia and Britain to press for more concessions. Zeng also argued that France, not unlike Russia a couple of years earlier, was diplomatically isolated in Europe and unable to prosecute a lengthy war.[116] Cixi listened to all sides, alternately favoring one and then the other as she sought to maintain her own superior position at court.[117]

After his defeat in the Battle of Son Tay in December 1883, Liu Yongfu and his diminished army retreated toward the Chinese border.[118] He continued retreating up the Red River in early 1884, falling back toward the border town of Lao Cai. His Black Flags had been nearly wiped out, and many surrendered to the French. The French also skirmished with and defeated elements of the Guangxi Army in the spring of 1884. These defeats lent strength to Li Hongzhang's arguments for conciliation, as did reports that a French fleet was steaming north. France had rejected a proposal to make Vietnam a joint Sino-French protectorate, but Li reopened talks with the French naval captain F. E. Fournier, and a preliminary accord was worked out at Tianjin in May 1884.[119]

The purists lambasted the Li-Fournier Agreement, which called for recognition of all French treaties with Vietnam and the withdrawal of Chinese troops from northern Vietnam. In return the French promised no indemnity and no invasion of China, and no pejorative references to China in future talks. Nearly fifty memorandums poured into the court criticizing Li and the agreement, with the result that it was not confirmed.[120] Li was accused of squandering funds, failing to modernize the military, and misrepresenting the demands of the French.[121]

The agreement having fallen through, the Chinese troops remained in northern Vietnam. The French ratcheted up tensions by concluding the

Treaty of Hue with the Vietnamese on June 6, effectively declaring a French protectorate over the entire kingdom encompassing Tonkin and Annam. British reports floated the notion of a conspiracy created by Zuo and the war cabal that was leading China into war.[122] Decrying Zuo as "a pig-headed old obstructive," they argued that China's rejection of the Li-Fournier Agreement made the Qing government unworthy of recognition.[123] After the war, Western reporters would charge Zuo with filling young Prince Chun with bellicose ideas, thereby swaying Cixi to authorize military action.[124] But there were also allegations that sections of the agreement had been forged or otherwise altered, so it remains unclear exactly what finally swayed Cixi to favor war.[125]

As they neared the Chinese border, the French again clashed with the Guangxi Army. The Chinese ambush of French forces at Bac Le near Lang Son on June 23, 1884 was the tipping point for what was still an undeclared war between China and France.[126] Jules Patrenotre replaced Fournier as the chief French negotiator. On July 12, 1884, the French sent an ultimatum to the Qing demanding both an indemnity of 250 million francs and recognition of the (now apparently altered) Li-Fournier Agreement.[127] Zeng Guoquan was appointed as the new Chinese negotiator. After getting the ultimatum deadline extended, he finally offered to pay a paltry 3.5-million-franc indemnity. Shifting course, the court now appointed Zhang Zhidong governor of Guangdong, stationed at Guangzhou, and appointed Zhang Peilun commander of the Fujian fleet.[128] China also refused to apologize or pay an indemnity. Zuo supposedly solicited half a million U.S. dollars in war funds from Chinese living in San Francisco.[129]

After China refused France's demands, the French instructed Admiral Amédée Courbet to sail his fleet toward Fuzhou and prepare to attack the naval yard there, even though neither side had declared war. The French destroyed Chinese shore batteries at Jilong in northern Taiwan on August 5 but were driven back out to sea by Liu Mingchuan the next day.[130] Zuo was pleased by the news, opining that the French might be overawed or at least forced to divide their strength in Taiwan.[131] While Zuo continued to make preparations to build a string of supply depots to the southwest, the French were about to strike the first and most significant blow of an all-out war. Courbet received his official orders to attack on August 22.

FRANCE GOES ON THE OFFENSIVE

The surprise French strike at the Fuzhou Navy Yard, which ironically France had helped to build, was a devastating blow with enormous implications for the subsequent history and demise of the Qing. The attack took place on August 23, 1884, and within an hour the French force destroyed the entire naval yard and damaged or sank eleven Chinese ships. Zhang Peilun had been among the first to flee. He would be exiled to the frontier for his failure to defend the yard and for lying about the extent of the Qing defeat in his initial report.[132] Though the Qing held their own in the other theaters of the war, this single event came to characterize the "failure" of the Self-Strengthening movement for many, including elements of the Qing court, because it attracted widespread press coverage in China and abroad.[133]

The debacle was largely caused by poor communication and the vagaries of international law. Local officials recognized signs of war in the weeks preceding the attack, but there was no proper chain of command between He Ruzhang (1838–1891), the superintendent of the Fuzhou Navy Yard, and the throne. Because war had not been officially declared, French ships were allowed to sail right past the forts protecting the dockyard despite prior warnings from Li Hongzhang that the French might try to seize it.[134] When the number of French ships increased, the local Manchu commander, Mutushan, protested but could not get the authority to attack from his superior commander He Jing. Zhang Peilun supposedly wanted to block the channel but was denied permission by the Zongli Yamen due to concerns over international law. Repeated requests for aid from Mutushan, He, and Zhang were rebuffed by the court, and the other fleet commanders jealously protected their own interests, as they would throughout the conflict. Zhang Zhidong finally sent two ships, but Li Hongzhang continued to keep his fleet out of the action. On August 12, 1884, Mutushan, He Ruzhang, and Zhang Peilun requested instructions from the throne and asked for forceful action by China.[135] Two days later the court ordered Zeng Guoquan to send a ship south, but he procrastinated.[136]

The court issued an edict on August 18 warning that war should be expected, and all commanders were to attack at will in the event of hostilities, though no specific directives were given. Two days later Zhang Peilun was told that talks were ongoing, but he should make "secret preparations" to deal with any eventualities.[137] The next day Zeng Guoquan was placed in command of the defenses of Jiangnan, and Li Hongzhang was ordered to purchase German guns and send them to Fuzhou. As of August 22, He Ruzhang feared that war was imminent because the American and British ships had left Fuzhou. The court ordered Zeng and Li to send help south, but it was too late.

Thus on August 23 the French destroyed the Chinese fleet at Mawei anchorage. There were eleven ships there, all wooden, the largest displacing 1,400 tons. There were also twelve war junks on hand. The French brought only eight ships, but they were far superior to the Chinese ships, the smallest being 470 tons and the largest more than 4,700 tons. All were armor-clad, some composite, and their guns were "triumphs of mechanical skill."[138] Nevertheless, the Chinese might have held their own had they taken the initiative. But they vacillated and refused to use the tide to their advantage. When the French attacked, the Chinese ships were still at their moorings.

Accounts vary as to what the Chinese knew and when. Some suggest they had credible intelligence that an attack would happen on August 24. Others say that He Jing received a declaration of war from a Catholic priest but kept it secret. Various other versions of the story have the Chinese learning at noon that the attack would commence at 2 p.m. He Ruzhang claimed the French cut the telegraph wire so he could not warn Mutushan.[139] Certainly, lack of communication, organization, and cooperation by the officials on the scene undermined any chances the Chinese might have had. Only two Chinese ships survived the attack. The French seized the outlying forts from the rear on their way back out to sea. In the end, the Qing were undermined by the presence of too many nominal commanders but no actual leader or legitimate chain of command.[140] Rather than proving a stunning tactical or strategic victory for the French, however, the destruction of the Fuzhou Navy

Yard, not unlike Japan's attack on Pearl Harbor decades later, galvanized the populace and firmly turned the masses in favor of war. Modern nationalistic Chinese accounts likely overstate these sentiments, but the Chinese certainly acquitted themselves better against the French than they had in previous anti-imperialist clashes.[141]

ZUO'S FINAL CAMPAIGN

Zuo Zongtang was again recalled to service on September 7, 1884, when he was appointed viceroy of the southeast. Zuo was later said to have "flung his crutch aside" when his desire to go to Fuzhou was approved.[142] After overseeing the completion of a steam launch in Nanjing, Zuo headed south, arriving in Fuzhou on December 13 to a warm welcome.[143] En route Zuo supposedly had a dream in which his wife's ghost visited him and warned that the war would last three years but peace would be restored.[144] Zuo set up coastal batteries and firing stations, laid mines, and restored city defenses, walls, and battlements. He conducted inspection tours along the coast at the end of 1884, checking defenses and ascertaining the range and capabilities of Qing cannons.[145] Iron chains were strung across harbors as barriers and more naval auxiliaries were recruited.[146]

As it turned out, Zuo's defenses were never tested, though one modern scholar suggests that this was because they were "so formidable that the French dared not approach them."[147] Whether or not this was the case, the experience would inform his final recommendations to the Qing government.

The French next turned their attention to Taiwan, which they tried to blockade while also seeking to disrupt grain shipments from south to north China, with mixed results.[148] In general the Chinese troops acquitted themselves well in the clashes on land and prevented the French from making inroads into Taiwan. Though the French managed to seize Jilong on October 1, 1884, they could not advance, and vital nearby coal mines remained in Qing hands.[149] The Qing general Sun Kaihua defeated a French attack on Danshui, the gateway to Taibei, and further French efforts to control Taiwan on land were likewise stymied. Assessing the situation in Taiwan as of late autumn 1884, Zuo said that the Qing should be able to prevail on land because they outnumbered the French two to one. But he was concerned about the lack of ships to break the French blockade and Li Hongzhang's failure to send help. Li even went so far as to send ships to Korea instead, claiming to fear a Japanese attack there.[150] Zuo also criticized Liu Mingchuan, an old ally of Li's, for failing to seize the initiative to recover Jilong. The court agreed with Zuo's overall assessment and dispatched Zuo's former colleague Yang Yuebin to Taiwan.[151] Yang was delayed by illness and allegedly undermined by spies within his organization, and he failed to fully liberate Taiwan, though Taibei and the southern parts of the island remained free of French control.[152]

Zuo expressed hope that an attack from sea, aided by gentry-led partisans on land, could break the blockade, but he admitted that coordinating the attempt would be difficult because the French boats enforcing the blockade did not have fixed schedules. He suggested using the naval militia as spies, possibly in conjunction with an attack from Xiamen.[153] The result was a stalemate, with the French being unable to take Taiwan or mount a serious attack against Fujian, though there were skirmishes through the winter of 1884–1885.[154] Zeng Guoquan finally sent a small force to rescue Taiwan in February 1885 but broke off the attack swiftly. A modern account criticizes the Qing naval commanders for their lack of knowledge and experience, saying that only one of them had even graduated from the Fuzhou Academy.[155]

The naval battles were less successful from the Qing perspective, but this was partly due to Li Hongzhang's continued refusal to commit significant resources. He continued to argue that to send his Beiyang fleet to aid Taiwan would open up north China to a concerted French attack or perhaps machinations by other powers. The French were thus able to carry out a partial blockade that, while not determining the course of the war, put pressure on pacifist elements at court.[156] The British eventually came to China's aid by closing Hong Kong and other Far Eastern ports under their purview to French warships. Strikes by Chinese workers in Hong Kong affected food supplies to the French armies.[157] The French retaliated by attempting a rice blockade, but this was not fully implemented before the war ended. Zuo suggested sinking all French supply ships, but this policy was never enacted. Zuo also apparently tried to buy more supplies and weapons from the British, but they refused to sell.[158] The French briefly occupied the Penghu Islands off the coast of Taiwan, but within weeks an agreement was ironed out to lift the French blockade.

Though it has been argued that China's defeats in the naval sphere were more the result of poor leadership and organization than technical shortcomings, the rather poor performance of the Qing navy caused Zuo to reiterate his calls for faster gunboat construction and higher-quality artillery.[159] Still angry over Li Hongzhang's refusal to come to his aid in the south, Zuo called for the creation of a unified naval construction bureau with a single overseer. He emphasized that study and training were as important as equipment. This started with adding more schools to the training facilities, because too few of China's naval officers were literate.[160]

Though the Guangxi Army had suffered a series of defeats to the French in the early autumn of 1884, their prospects improved when they were joined by the Yunnan Army and Liu Yongfu's Black Flags in November. With assistance from Chinese guerrilla forces that had crossed over from Guangdong, the Qing stabilized the front, prompting extensive debates among the French high command. The Black Flags and the Yunnan Army together besieged the town of Tuyen Quang. The French went back on the offensive in January 1885, winning a victory near the village of Nui Bop that paved the way for an offensive against Lang Son. They captured Lang Son after nine days of bloody fighting and headed toward Tuyen Quang.[161] The uneven performance of Chinese troops in these engagements has been attributed to deficiencies in training and lack of proper artillery, though given the pedigrees of the Chinese officials involved, this assessment is questionable. And in some cases, the Chinese had the technological advantage. Certainly the rugged terrain played a role, as did the fact that the engagements featured mixes of regular and irregular forces.[162]

After nearly a month of bloody fighting the French forced the Chinese to lift their siege at Tuyen Quang. The French pressed onward, even sending probing missions into Guangxi and destroying a customs station. But they were repulsed by Chinese forces led by Wang Depang and Feng Zicai at the Battle of Zhennanguan in late March and fell back to Lang Son.[163] Although a Qing assault on Lang Son was thrown back, the French commander, fearing encirclement, decided to pull out, allowing the Qing forces under Pan Dingxin to rally and retake Lang Son. Around the same time French forces farther west were defeated by combined regular and Black Flag forces. While military historians have questioned the extent and strategic significance of these Qing victories, they undoubtedly bolstered morale back home and emboldened the purists.[164] They also resulted in the Qing recapturing nearly all the territory lost to the French the previous autumn. And news of the defeat led to the fall of the French cabinet.[165]

But even as these victories occurred, the Chinese and French negotiators were finally coming to an accord. Qing sources suggest that the French made the initial request, but both sides were eager to end the conflict.[166] Sir Robert Hart played a key role in the talks. The initial protocols, grounded in the earlier Li-Fournier Agreement, were signed on April 4, 1885, with the treaty itself signed in Tianjin on June 9—much to the outrage of Zuo Zongtang and his fellow hawks.[167] When he heard that the talks had been reopened, Zuo insisted that the French were just stalling for time and hoping to blunt Qing momentum in order to drag the war on into summer, when disease could take its toll on the Chinese troops. Zuo also suggested that the French were conspiring with the Russians.[168]

A DEFEAT SNATCHED FROM THE JAWS OF VICTORY

Coming when it did on the heels of Qing victories near the border, the treaty between the Qing and the French has been condemned by Chinese nationalists ever since as a "defeat snatched from the jaws of victory."[169] Sun Guangyao calls it "a war that France didn't win, but won, and a war that China didn't lose, but lost."[170] With the death of Ci'an and the arrest of Prince Gong, Cixi had assumed near total control of government affairs. The Qing shifted away from policies of restoration and more active engagement with the West to a generally more passive policy steered by Li Hongzhang in particular, who profited greatly from his position but seems to have done fairly little in terms of bettering China's position with respect to the wolves at the door.[171] Memorandums criticizing the peace settlement and its proponents poured into Beijing for months afterward.[172]

In the immediate aftermath of the hostilities, the French withdrew from Jilong, and Yang Yuebin was placed in command of Taiwan. Cen Yuying demobilized his forces as well, though it would take a couple of years to formally delineate the Sino-Vietnamese border. The border settlement helped create a refugee crisis a few years later, though French authorities did help the Qing curtail banditry in the region.[173] The court rewarded Feng Zicai and Cen Yuying, and Wang Depang saw his former rank and privileges restored. Tang Jingsong eventually became the first governor of Taiwan and subsequently served as the president of the Republic of Formosa under Japanese rule. Liu Yongfu remained a prominent figure into the Republican era, succeeding Tang in Taiwan and fleeing Japanese rule to aid in bandit suppression in Guangdong.[174]

Zuo himself was openly disgusted at the "defeatless defeat" and blamed Li Hongzhang for selling out China. He saw the peace agreement as a virtual invitation to Western powers to invade and take more land.[175] The fact that China was forced to pay an indemnity was especially galling, considering that "the French barbarians were begging for peace."[176] In a secret missive to the court, Zuo warned that the French were untrustworthy and unlikely to honor the agreement. He predicted that the British would seize Tibet and put more pressure on China's southwest. He also continued to argue that a more aggressive stance would have paid dividends against France, just as it had against Russia.[177] Zuo's complaints received no reply from the court, but Zhang Zhidong sent Zuo a telegram lamenting the aimlessness of the court and its sycophantic officials and telling Zuo that he was the only high official he trusted.[178] It has been said that no one dared to tell Zuo when the final treaty was signed because he was already quite sick and the news might kill him.

Zuo was indeed distraught when he finally heard the treaty had been confirmed. But he also contended that all hope was not lost if China could quickly resume its naval buildup. To that end, Zuo presented his comprehensive plan for a unified coastal defense to the throne on July 29, 1885.[179] By this point the court had already authorized the creation of a formal navy, albeit with divided northern and southern commands.[180] Zuo was ordered to oversee the construction of a steamship fleet.[181]

On the same day he presented his plan Zuo recommended stationing the governor of Fujian in Taiwan to better oversee the island's defenses.[182] This would be one of the first steps in converting Taiwan into a regular province, reflecting the new Qing strategy of extending and legally reinforcing their sovereignty claims. While some might view these acts as desperate measures adopted by a flailing imperial power, they are better viewed as savvy attempts to adapt to changing international circumstances. While the Sino-French War was certainly no triumph for the Qing, neither was it a ringing defeat. Despite the embarrassment of being hit with an indemnity, no Qing territory was lost and Taiwan was retained, albeit only for another decade. The effort to more closely integrate Taiwan into the empire by raising its status and according it more resources made sense in the context of the times. The Qing simply lacked the means to fully realize their aims.

The Qing court finally responded to Zuo's recommendations regarding coastal defenses with a stinging rejoinder: "After twenty years of naval defense operations, we've had no successes. Of all the ships built in Fujian, they were all useless. So where is this so-called 'Self-Strengthening'? And now you want to build three [more] ironclads but we'd have to authorize the loans for it. The costs of construction alone will be vast and then we'll need a high-level official and others to oversee it and doubtless there will be [cost] increases and we still don't know if this will produce empty names without reality."[183] While the court did not completely reject the idea of military and naval modernization, this response was certainly indicative of the changing political climate in Beijing. Li Hongzhang did nothing to implement Zuo's recommendations. Though Li was generally considered a pro-Western reformer, his desire to retain his personal fortune and influence outstripped everything else. He was by no means interested in sharing or relinquishing authority over the navy. The performance of his Beiyang Navy in the subsequent war against Japan also indicates that he, or more likely sycophantic underlings who used their positions primarily for graft, paid little attention to Zuo's call for much more extensive education and training of naval officers. And indeed it was not technology that doomed the Qing in the conflict with Japan. In fact, some of the Chinese ships were technically superior to their Japanese counterparts, but the officers commanding them lacked the necessary training and discipline. Li's refusal to create a unified naval command came back to haunt him when war came with Japan. His forces were humiliated while the Nanyang Navy stayed in the south and did nothing to help. Indeed, Li's vaunted Beiyang Navy proved to be a paper shark, while the southern fleet had at least rallied after the initial shock at Fuzhou. The Qing, unlike Zuo, proved unable to apply lessons they should have learned.[184]

ZUO'S FINAL DAYS

Once the peace treaty with France was signed, Zuo again requested leave on account of illness. His request was granted in July 1885.[185] Zuo spent his last days writing and reflecting on the recent war. Many of his late writings concerned the creation of a proper coastal defense as the key to China's survival and modernization. In a memorandum from the summer of 1885 Zuo praised China's achievements thus far but admitted that the Chinese were still inferior to Western troops in drill and practice, especially in the naval arena. He recommended bigger dockyards with deeper anchorages and better arsenals and suggested building larger breechloading guns at Jiangnan and Guangdong for practice.

With Japan and Europe growing more powerful and looking to expand into China, Zuo urged a unified response. Lacking that, he said, China would become weaker and weaker: "Let railways and mines and the construction of ships and guns be undertaken at once as a means of ensuring our national prosperity and strength." Ever conscious and respectful of China's traditions, he also urged the emperor to read the sacred books of China and "daily associate with men of principle, and listen to their counsels."[186]

Still smarting from China's recent failures against the French at sea, Zuo urged centralization of the navy under the direction of a minister of coastal defense who would have full power and report directly to the throne. The person appointed to the post should be of excellent character, well versed in foreign studies and affairs, and be respected by Chinese and foreigners alike.[187] Those criteria implicitly disqualified Li Hongzhang for the post. Zuo offered seven major propositions concerning coastal defense:

1. China must construct many warships of different types and functions and needed a minimum of ten squadrons. Zuo proposed putting squadrons at Dagu, Yunchun, Zhefu, Chengming, Jinhai, Fuzhou, Hainan, and Guangdong. Other cities would be guarded by warships detached from those squadrons. Two more squadrons would patrol the oceans, protecting shipping and collecting intelligence, which included observing foreign ships.

2. China must create and implement standard naval regulations. These should include guidelines on appointing commanders, establishing rank, selecting officers, and the like, independent of land forces.

3. Rules were needed to regulate patrolling, guarding, drilling, and naval exercises.

4. Businesses should cooperate with the Navy. The Navy needed chemists, metallurgists, and other experts. There should be a centralized procurement system for the military, with all arsenals under the minister of coastal defense.

5. As for funding, Zuo suggested reducing the regular army size by 60 percent; raising taxes on foreign goods, including opium imports; abolishing existing gun junk patrols and assessing all provinces for subventions, coordinated by the Navy Board.

6. Railroads should be built across the country for communication and economic and military purposes. Zuo noted that there was "every advantage and no detriment" to railroads. Wealthy mandarins and businesspeople should be encouraged to invest in railroads.

7. China needed more new schools teaching science and other necessary subjects. Foreign books must be translated as fast as possible and made available. This should likewise fall under the purview of the minister of coastal defense.[188]

Zuo's interest in coastal defense and his recognition of the strategic significance of Taiwan were recurrent themes in his final recommendations to the Qing court. He sketched out plans for the economic and political development of Taiwan grounded in acculturation. As with Xinjiang, Taiwan could quickly become prosperous and more closely integrated into the regular administrative apparatus if steps were taken to Sinicize the native population. Many of Zuo's suggestions would be implemented by Liu Mingchuan during his brief tenure as governor of Taiwan.[189] Zuo also remained interested in administrative streamlining. In one of his last writings on September 4, 1885, he discussed the demobilization of his fledgling coast guard forces while also calling for rectification of the civil and military official registers in Fujian.[190]

Zuo died in Fuzhou on September 5, 1885. It was said that the public mourned at his passing. His sons collected his body on September 25 and brought it back to Changsha for burial. It arrived there in November and was interred the following year. His family received imperial condolences, and Zuo was accorded a variety of posthumous honors including being canonized as Wenxiang gong (Duke of Promoting Literary Accomplishments).[191] Emperor Guangxu composed a poem chronicling Zuo's many exploits on behalf of the empire.[192] Shrines were erected across the empire to commemorate his achievements, most notably in Hunan, Beijing, and Lanzhou.[193] A stele erected to Zuo in Xi'an praised him for "standing up for what is right in Heaven and Earth."[194] Upon hearing of Zuo's death, Cixi allegedly repeated the famous line about the empire surviving the Taiping Rebellion only because of Hunan, and Hunan surviving only because of Zuo's efforts.[195]

Comments on Zuo's retirement and death in the *North China Herald* were mixed. Zuo was described as "not brilliant, but obstinate, determined with sublime confidence in himself and [having] the moral courage to push through and speak his mind."[196] But he was also said to be far more conservative than Li Hongzhang and less inclined to trust foreigners and foreign ideas, charges that are misplaced, in this writer's opinion. Zuo's Chinese contemporaries were much more laudatory on the whole, with even his political rivals acknowledging his erudition and contributions to the empire and its subjects.[197] Certainly Zuo was one of the luminaries of the nineteenth century. And as our understanding of that era has grown, Zuo's significance as an exemplar of the age has become increasingly evident.

CONCLUSION

MORE THAN JUST A CHICKEN DISH

You should surround yourself with men of principle and heed their counsel.

—Zuo Zongtang

The nineteenth century was undoubtedly one of the bloodiest and most tumultuous periods in the long and storied history of imperial China. The Chinese remember it as the embarrassing "century of humiliation" during which, according to the accepted narrative, China devolved from one of the world's greatest civilizations to semicolonial status, exploited by not only the Western powers but Japan as well. The demise of the Qing ushered in four decades of warlordism, civil war, and foreign invasion until the visionary leaders of the communist revolution—led by a famous son of Hunan, no less—helped China finally stand on its own two feet again. In the West, China's nineteenth-century experience has been viewed as another sordid chapter in the global history of imperialism, yet another case study of the superiority of Western-derived institutions and technologies. Yet the reemergence of China in the late twentieth century has caused scholars to finally start questioning these tenacious narratives. For the China that has emerged, while certainly owing much to Western models and institutions, is also grounded in its own traditions, institutions, and cultural practices, including those of imperialism, albeit an "imperialism with Chinese characteristics," regardless of what Deng Xiaoping or the current leaders of the PRC might have one believe.

It is at this intersection where figures such as Zuo Zongtang become so important. No one embodies the apparent contradictions of these developments more than Zuo. He was a conservative reformer born into poverty but highly conscious of his intellectual heritage and the responsibilities incumbent on his class, no matter their financial circumstances. While he mastered and valued the classical corpus, he also realized that pragmatic solutions were needed to grapple with China's many problems. This meant learning not only from books but also from experience. Reading geographies was edifying, but one could also learn from talking with farmers and interviewing officials who had served on the frontier. One must also not rush to hasty judgments, even when confronted with something that might seem new or repugnant. Zuo's youthful understanding of the Opium War instilled in him a lifelong animosity toward the British in general. But he was more than willing to work with Westerners, including the British, to achieve his aims and help China modernize.

His failures at the highest level of the traditional examination system likewise galvanized him and inspired him to think outside the box. Talent could be found everywhere. It just needed to be properly cultivated. New methods and new subjects of study were needed to overcome new challenges. Moreover, lessons learned needed to be applied and refined to suit new conditions. Time and again, Zuo demonstrated an ability to apply the lessons he learned, freely abandoning plans that proved unworkable, such as his initial ideas concerning the use of military carts against the Nian. Unfortunately for the Qing, most court officials did not share Zuo's outlook or approach, though he did his best to put similar thinkers in important positions to continue his reforms. But unlike Meiji Japan, the Qing was not a modern postrevolutionary government. The kinds of wholesale changes initiated just across the sea simply were not possible under existing conditions.

Furthermore, as recent studies have highlighted, much of the supposed Qing "opposition to technology" had little to do with technology per se but was rooted in personal interests and issues related to maintaining dynastic sovereignty.[1] Viewed in this light, the actions of the Qing are both rational and understandable. Qing leaders and high officials correctly realized that going too far with sweeping changes would bring about their own demise. They constantly experimented with new approaches to old problems in addition to adapting the tools and tactics of the West to prolong their rule. In this, the Qing were more successful than has been generally acknowledged. In the seventy-year period between the outbreak of the First Opium War and the fall of the dynasty, borders were consolidated; government revenues were greatly increased; industrialization and modern communication lines were extended to the far reaches of the empire, albeit unevenly; and a nearly two-thousand-year-old educational system was dismantled in favor of an emphasis on science, technology, and other "practical" subjects needed to help China compete in the modern world.[2] All this was accomplished amid profound internal and external military and social challenges. By contrast, the Tokugawa shogunate in Japan collapsed in just fifteen years under the weight of far fewer pressures in a much more homogeneous society.

It is long past time to dismiss the late Qing reform efforts as "failures" based on the results of conflicts such as the Sino-French and Sino-Japanese Wars, or even the fall of the Qing.[3] Writing several decades ago, Thomas Kennedy noted that the Qing record of achievement and progress "suggests a degree of resilience and a viability which not all writers have found in nineteenth century China."[4] China should be evaluated on the basis of its overall progress from 1840 to 1911 and how that laid the groundwork for later developments, not simply by the results of two limited wars. More recent studies by the likes of Peter Lavelle, Anne Reinhardt, and Stephen Halsey have confirmed Kennedy's findings while also adding new layers of understanding to the complex processes at work in Qing modernization efforts.[5] In short, the Qing, like Zuo, were both conservative and open to change, and each episode served as a wake-up call to new challenges and opportunities. For example, the Sino-Japanese War provoked new ideas about colonialism and national imperialism, whereas the desire to incorporate Xinjiang and Taiwan as provinces was rooted in creating stronger claims of sovereignty and exploiting natural resources as a means of extending imperial power, reflecting an updated understanding of empire in the nineteenth-century context.[6]

The career of Zuo Zongtang serves as a perfect lens through which to view these momentous changes and to assess their relative success or failure, for he personified the idea of conservative change within tradition. As his biographer W. L. Bales notes, Zuo "was the most dominating constructive influence in the Chinese empire during the nineteenth century."[7] This is an important observation, because despite his conservatism on many levels and his frequent frustration at the nature and pace of late Qing reforms, Zuo remained an optimist to the end of his life. His Confucian belief in the possibilities offered by a sound moral education never wavered even though he also embraced the study of practical works on agriculture, sericulture, science, and technology.[8] Zuo's convictions helped sway Zeng Jize increasingly to his side, as Zeng saw the value in Zuo's stances compared with the continued defeatism expressed by Li Hongzhang. By the 1880s Li had essentially degenerated into a pessimist far more concerned with maintaining his personal status and fortune than with charting a positive course for China's future. Li became convinced that China's reform efforts had been for naught and saw little hope that the nation could withstand the depredations of the West and Japan. After Zuo died, Li increasingly assumed a pacifist stance. With the death of Zeng Jize, Li had the political arena largely to himself, at least with respect to the elder Han statesmen of the empire.[9]

Though we have discussed changing perspectives on Zuo's life and works throughout the present book, it is useful to revisit them here. Although Zuo's accomplishments were duly lauded and appreciated by his contemporaries, by the early Republic he was denounced as a Han traitor, only to be rehabilitated somewhat under the Nationalists as a progressive reformer.[10] During World War II, Zuo's example was even used in a song to inspire freedom fighters to resist the Japanese invaders.[11] Qin Hancai, writing in 1943, listed Zuo's accomplishments as including opening roads, expanding trade, establishing new forts and outposts, capturing deserters and restoring military discipline, building new military farms, opening up transit routes to the west, and thwarting bandits' attempts to undermine the Qing.[12] Zuo was also a patriot who combined the best elements of traditional paternalistic Confucianism with modern nationalist sensibilities, both recognizing the threat of the West and realizing the need to learn from it.[13]

In the early years of the People's Republic, Zuo once again became an enemy of the masses, criticized for suppressing the Taiping, Nian, and Muslim rebellions, which were part of the revolutionary heritage of the Chinese

Communists.[14] With the demise of the Gang of Four in the late 1970s there was another revision of attitudes toward Zuo. In the December 19, 1978 issue of *Guangming ribao* Zuo was praised for his great patriotism in resisting foreign invaders, recovering the northwest, and aiding the common folk, albeit as a "shining light of the feudal order."[15] More than a dozen biographies of Zuo were published in subsequent years, most of them focusing on his recovery of Xinjiang and opposition to Russian imperialism.

More complex interpretations of Zuo's contributions began to appear in 1982. Acknowledging the "inherent social contradictions engendered by feudal society and imperialism," Chinese sources pointed to Zuo's positive traits in pushing for education for the masses and in advocating the adoption of science and technology.[16] As an essay in *Red Flag* put it, Zuo could be blamed for suppressing the people and buttressing the feudal order, but he deserved credit for his patriotism in resisting foreign invaders. Subsequent publications in the 1980s took a similar line, culminating in the publication of more balanced biographies grounded in newly collated primary sources.[17] The municipal government of Changsha renovated Zuo's tomb in 1983 and held a celebration to mark the centennial of his death in 1985. In 2012 the provincial government of Hunan held a celebration marking the bicentennial of Zuo's birth, and a new statue of Zuo was recently built near his birthplace in Xiangyin.[18]

This pattern continued over the next thirty years as new editions of Zuo's collected works and other primary sources from the late Qing were published in China. In the last decade a spate of biographies of Zuo appeared in China, most of which, while still colored by nationalistic biases and contemporary political concerns, attempt to better situate Zuo within the context of his time.[19] Unfortunately such studies have generally not engaged new interpretations of imperialism—perpetrated by both the West and the Qing—emerging in Western-language secondary scholarship. It is my hope that the present volume contributes to that engagement.

Along these lines and with reference to current events, we must also consider the broader racial implications of Zuo's campaigns in the northwest and Central Asia. Hannah Theaker contends that in the aftermath of the rebellions a binary emerged that "confirmed a process of minoritization" culminating in the ethnic categories and assimilationist narratives created by the People's Republic that still exist today.[20] Similarly, Eric Setzekorn suggests that "the techniques used by Han officials and military leaders radically shifted the ethnic balance in favor of Han colonists."[21] Setzekorn further notes that while it would be simplistic to assume that none of the Hui bought into the late Qing civilizing project, it is likely that it produced more estrangement than assimilation.[22] There is also the fact of the reduction of the Muslim population, though it seems that the drop in Xinjiang was far less stark than in Shaanxi and Gansu. Still the numbers have been used to cast Zuo as an inveterate foe of the Muslims who consistently used a heavy hand to further his own assimilation policies.[23]

Some records have also been used to support the current government's stance by highlighting the actions of "good and loyal" Muslims in supporting the Qing.[24] These accounts appear in modern textbooks and follow on Qing efforts to honor such individuals with martyrs' shrines and official positions. That does not mean that such individuals were not sincerely loyal; and in any case personal interests may coincide with those of the state. Indeed Schluessel argues that many of the Muslims learned how to "manipulate the ideology and institutions of the civilizing project to advance their own interests as imperial subjects."[25]

The Uighurs have also created their own narrative, of course, selectively identifying key actors and events from the past to support their separatist/independence position. While support for the Uighurs' positions may wax and wane in accordance with global political winds in the coming decades, it seems highly unlikely that the PRC will relinquish control of any part of Xinjiang in the absence of a complete collapse of the communist regime. Still, as Wen-djang Chu observed decades ago, the Muslim problem in Xinjiang is not unsolvable, and "peaceful co-existence and harmonious cooperation can be worked out under any strong central government."[26]

We must also acknowledge the connection between the various Hunan statecraft scholars, Zuo, and his protégés in shaping the direction of late Qing Xinjiang and fashioning the blueprint for assimilation, successful or not. In addition to Liu Jintang, who became the province's first governor, others connected to Zuo included Wei Guangtao, nephew of Wei Yuan; Tao Mu, who had served with Zuo in Gansu; Rao Yingqi, who had been Zuo's secretary; Pan Xiaosu, who had served in the Xiang Army since 1861; and, of course, Zhang Yao. In addition to disseminating Han culture more broadly, these men along with less distinguished settlers imported specific elements of Hunanese culture to the northwest, including the worship of certain city gods.[27] It has been estimated that 71 percent of the officials in Xinjiang from 1877 to 1911 were from the broad homeland of the Xiang Army, with some 45 percent of those whose birthplace is known hailing from the greater Changsha region.[28] And their native province responded in kind, with locals publishing works chronicling the achievements of its native sons in Xinjiang. Thus was manifested the "provincial patriotism" analyzed by Stephen Platt with respect to Hunan, though it could also be said that the Hunanese who settled in Xinjiang became forces for conservatism at the very end of the Qing as they sought to retain their positions.[29]

In the shorter term, in addition to Zuo's many Hunanese compatriots, it is noteworthy that several of Zuo's Muslim allies played key roles in military campaigns in the region over the remainder of the Qing. Many of the other administrators were Xiang Army veterans, often Muslims who had joined the ranks during the campaigns in Shaanxi and Gansu. Ma Zhan'ao helped the Qing fight in Tibet. One of his sons, Ma Anliang, fought under Dong Fuxiang in the He-Huang Rebellion of the 1890s.[30] In the wake of these movements many of the old Sufi tombs were destroyed, severing links with the past and paving the way for the emergence of the new modernizing Muslim warlords who dominated the region until the rise of the PRC.

As this is, at its heart, a biography, I would be remiss if I did not revisit Zuo's achievements and discuss his character and personality here. On the most basic level Zuo was one of the great "Restoration (*zhongxing*) Ministers" of the late Qing alongside Zeng Guofan, Li Hongzhang, Feng Guifen, Hu Linyi, Zeng Guoquan, Guo Songtao, and Ding Richang. As we have seen, a surprising number of these men hailed from Hunan province. They were informed and animated by the statecraft scholarship of the late Ming and early Qing as revived by men such as Wei Yuan in the early nineteenth century. They believed in bringing historical knowledge and scholarship into the practice of government grounded in Confucian principles such as benevolence, loyalty, and respect for education. Many of these officials had friendship or marriage ties. Guo Songtao's daughter, for example, was married to Zuo Zongtang's nephew. Because of their close ties and national status, the Hunanese model of statecraft was transmitted across the empire, with profound implications for the direction of modern China.[31]

In terms of Zuo's concrete accomplishments, there were many. Though the long-term results were mixed, Zuo greatly expanded industry and seri-culture, particularly in the northwest and Central Asia. He had thousands of cases of machinery and hundreds of spindles and looms delivered to the northwest, along with German technicians to aid in setting up the enter-prises.[32] Western methods of digging irrigation canals and mining were also introduced to the northwest, again with mixed results.[33] Zuo even considered mechanizing China's sugar-refining industry. While it is easy to dismiss these less successful enterprises, the importance of floating the ideas and considering the possibilities of such developments, which we see today in the "Belt and Road Initiative," are worthy of praise in themselves.[34] As Gideon Ch'en noted in 1938, albeit with a bit of hyperbole, Zuo was "the first Chinese statesman in the nineteenth century to have the foresight and courage to initiate what might have led to a considerable industrial change in this ancient country."[35] Of course, with the benefit of a longer perspective we can better evaluate the long-term implications of Zuo's actions.

Acting in the capacity of the classic Chinese official, Zuo contributed significantly to famine relief in Central Asia and the northwest.[36] When famine struck in 1877–1878, resulting in widespread reports of cannibalism, Zuo immediately released 100,000 taels of army supply funds for distribu-tion to the masses along with 13,000 taels of superior silver.[37] Grain reserves were set up across the region, and grain was imported from Hubei and else-where. Liu Dian was dispatched to inspect the fields and see if anything else could be harvested for reallocation. The wealthy residents of Shaanxi and other provinces were pressured for donations, with Zuo again relying on his extensive government contacts to procure grain, clothing, and medicine.[38] Liu Jintang reported that funds confiscated from the rebels were redistributed for local relief.[39] But Zuo also contended that 80–90 percent of those who died in the famine were already weakened by their opium addiction, and he worried that funds distributed for famine relief might be used to buy more drugs.[40]

Zuo realized that donations and redistribution efforts alone were no more than a Band-Aid. He drew on his extensive readings in statecraft to promote the lasting expansion of agriculture in the region through the introduction of new crops and seed strains as well as the application of new techniques gleaned from agricultural manuals and his own experiments. New tools were brought in, some modeled on Western prototypes and some manufactured in the factories Zuo established. These also aided in his expansion of irrigation works, a project he stressed later when he returned to China proper. Zuo was credited with restoring the prewar productivity of Pingliao and Ningxia, reportedly donating 13,000 taels of his own money for the latter project.[41] The finished works extended over thirty *li*. The Qing armies also rebuilt irrigation works in Hami and virtually every other major settlement affected by the war. Qing reports suggest significant infrastructural improvements throughout Xinjiang that benefited everyone.[42] Modern accounts claim tens of thousands of acres of land were brought under cultivation due to these new irrigation efforts.[43] The Qing also restored subterranean channels called *karez* in nearly two hundred places.[44] There is also no question that more lands were brought under cultivation, both privately and in the form of *tuntian*, as noted in reports from Liu Jintang.[45]

Zuo's efforts to replace opium with mulberry cultivation were laudable, even if they fell short of his expectations. He at least experimented with new measures and later proved flexible enough to compromise on the opium issue, again because he recognized that in this case the needs of the people trumped his personal moral convictions, at least in the short run. The infrastructure of this region was greatly expanded as well, with positive effects for commerce and other aspects of daily life. Even if one discounts some of the overly laudatory reports concerning the expansion of fields in Xinjiang, there is no doubt that Zuo's irrigation projects were extensive and impactful. Some of the new canals stretched over sixty *li*. Old canals were repaired and more than two hundred new wells were dug.[46] His troops even engaged in beautification projects. Some of the more than half a million trees his troops planted are still alive today and help prevent erosion in this arid landscape.[47]

Under Zuo's watch dozens of new stone bridges were built. Earthen and stone forts were repaired, and new ones constructed. More post stations and rest houses, complete with horses and supplies, were established to aid in the transition to provincial status. Trees were planted in muddy areas to soak up water and facilitate mounted travel. Lands were investigated and new tax quotas assigned, normalizing assessments for everyone, including Muslims.[48] Carpenters were brought in from Guangdong, transforming the architectural landscape of the northwest and integrating it, for better or worse, with that of the interior.[49]

We discussed Zuo's efforts to acculturate the Muslim populace through the establishment of schools above. Even contemporaries noted that the results were mixed, though modern Chinese scholars tend to praise them for helping to unify the country.[50] But they did increase government opportunities for a few good students, and the benefits of literacy that made the scientific and technical manuals Zuo and his successors circulated available to the populace should not be discounted. While some might debate the rationale behind the expansion of the school system that Zuo initiated in northwest China, it was certainly in line with his statecraft principles and intersected with the state-building ambitions of the late Qing, as Zuo said he wished to "cultivate talent and integrate the region culturally" with the rest of China.[51] Academies destroyed by warfare were reconstructed and new ones built. Free schools were established too, especially for Muslim students. Every county was expected to have at least one free school.[52]

Unsurprisingly, modern Chinese accounts tend to stress the unifying aspects of these efforts while also praising how they assisted local officials in bringing order, removing local bullies, ridding the frontier of covetous officials, and reversing existing practices of "making public private."[53] Upon Zuo's arrival in Pingliang and elsewhere he distributed guides to good government by the likes of Chen Hongmou and published teaching manuals and textbooks using printing houses he also established. Effects were more positive in Gansu than Xinjiang, with the former becoming one of the fastest-growing provinces for exam candidates in the last decades of the Qing.[54]

In terms of industrialization, Zuo established spinning factories in Xi'an, Dunhuang, Hami, and Turfan, among other places, to meet the troops' need for winter clothing. Producing cloth locally was cheaper than bringing it from elsewhere, and it stimulated the local economy. In a letter to Liu Jintang, Zuo expressed his hope that Xinjiang would become a major silk- and cotton-producing region.[55] Zuo envisioned factories radiating westward from Lanzhou attracting both domestic and foreign investments. British sources reported that Zuo purchased looms and other machinery from the Germans.[56] He also pushed for the rapid expansion of railway and telegraph lines to better integrate the region with the rest of the empire, not to mention to aid in its defense. He even recommended bringing in French advisers to help with these projects and others.

Although the weaving factory established with German aid lasted just a few years, it was important in introducing the concept of modern industry to China's northwest.[57] It also helped the animal husbandry sector, as it was reported that the productivity of Gansu was restored in six years by virtue of Zuo's efforts. The Russians had previously been quite interested in developing Central Asia as a cotton-producing area during the American Civil War, so Zuo's thinking along these lines did not come out of left field. The Russians also desired silk but had few places to buy it cheaply.[58] Some enthusiastic modern supporters praise Zuo's efforts in this regard as being forerunners of the Four Modernizations and other contemporary projects designed to more closely integrate the state and infrastructure, proclaiming that "China is finally realizing Zuo's dream of more than a century ago."[59] Had the Qing not been burdened with so many other pressing issues in its final decades, progress along these fronts likely would have been greater. But as in so many aspects of Qing modernization, these efforts were tied to specific individuals and networks and were never institutionalized.

With respect to personality, there is no doubt that Zuo was not an easy person to get along with. At the same time, both his friends and his rivals appreciated his clear and open speech and manner. His sometimes calling himself Zhuge Liang, and even signing letters using that nickname, offers ample evidence of his cockiness and arrogance, though contemporaries waited until after Zuo's death to make the comparison.[60] He was proud of his accomplishments, as his private letters reveal. He often clashed with other officials and frequently bore grudges, even against former friends, that could be both personal and professional, though he was generally able to put aside feelings for the sake of the realm.[61] Though he was never particularly close to Zeng Guofan, the latter repeatedly defended Zuo against charges of insubordination and malfeasance. And Zuo bailed Zeng out of military trouble spots repeatedly, even convincing Zeng to abandon thoughts of suicide at one juncture. Such facts prompted one modern writer to raise the possibility that Zeng and Zuo only pretended to be rivals to confound the Manchus and retain their respective posts.[62] Whether or not such speculation is true, Zuo was close to Zeng Guoquan, Guofan's younger brother, even writing a tribute to his wife after her death.[63] He was similarly close to Zeng Jize, Guofan's son.

Zuo's stubbornness was legendary, but it served him well at times. He was relentless when it came to raising funds for his military expeditions and willing to pull every available string to get what he needed. The primary sources are full of Zuo's requests for funds and letters written to colleagues begging, cajoling, warning, and reminding them of their responsibilities to support the empire. This extended to softening his personal stances on things like the sale of offices and the legalization and taxation of opium. Zuo's many connections and long service are signs that he was more successful than many in acquiring the resources needed. But his success in these areas is another indication of the underlying weakness of the Qing system. While measures were in place for interprovincial cooperation and resource coordination, it was personal networks that got things done.[64]

On the other hand, Zuo, unlike many of his contemporaries, appears to have had a legitimate concern for the plight of ordinary people and excelled in interacting with commoners and succoring their needs. As his official biography notes, "He had the talents of a hegemon, yet he followed the Way of Kings in aiding people."[65] He was neither covetous nor greedy, and even when his personal fortunes were at a low ebb, he distributed relief to the poor and donated the produce of his own fields. He seldom accepted gifts or bribes and was noted for donating portions of his own salary to help his soldiers. In Zuo's later years he remained active in soliciting famine relief for the northwest in addition to contributing to the grain reserves he had established there.[66] When he died, Zuo had but 25,000 taels in accumulated savings; the rest had been donated or given away. For example, Zuo gave Liu Dian's family six thousand taels when Liu fell ill.[67] Li Hongzhang, by contrast, bequeathed a fortune in excess of 40 million taels to his descendants when he died.[68]

Zuo's practice of living a thrifty life was in perfect accordance with his Confucian belief that the people were the root of the state. A strong, well-functioning state required a happy, productive populace.[69] This can also be seen in his overriding concern for properly supplying the troops. Zuo was sensitive to the causes of desertion and mutiny and appreciated the value of high morale in facilitating victory, especially in the barren wastes of the northwest. Further, keeping the soldiers happy and well fed was vital to keeping his own position. This is again in contrast with Li Hongzhang, who valued concrete symbols of power, such as the Beiyang Navy, over social stability, a philosophical difference apparently grounded in Li's shortsighted prioritization of foreign over domestic affairs, not to mention his preference for form over function and his penchant for nepotism. For example, in refurbishing canals, Zuo took a scientific approach, planting trees alongside waterways to cut down on erosion and improve their effectiveness, whereas Li's approach was to just keep digging and linking waterworks together to demonstrate concrete evidence of expansion to his superiors.[70]

Zuo was also a master at recognizing men of talent. In professional relations he was guided by two simple rules. First, talent and ability were foremost; one need not be personally close to colleagues. Second, good conduct and model behavior were paramount because they set the example for others to follow. A strong case in point is Zuo's long relationship with

Liu Jintang. Zuo strongly recommended Jintang to replace his uncle Songshan after the latter was slain in the attack on Fort Jinji, despite Jintang's youth. The two worked together over the next decade, frequently clashing over matters related to strategy or supplies and differing on the best way to organize the administration of Xinjiang, but there was always mutual respect between them. Zuo cultivated similar relationships with the likes of Liu Dian, Zhang Yao, Xu Zhanbiao, and Gao Liansheng, who were from varying backgrounds.[71]

With respect to foreigners, as we have seen, Zuo's reputation varied quite a bit. He was often stigmatized as conservative and virulently antiforeign, yet he had long-standing relationships with a number of foreigners, most notably Prosper Giquel. He had no problem with bringing in foreign experts, particularly Germans and Frenchmen, to help train his arsenal and factory workers and sailors. He staunchly supported the expansion of translation schools and tapping into modern Western knowledge as a means of strengthening China. As his first Western biographer, W. L. Bales, notes, "His character was rooted in the Old China, but his outlook on life was fresh and new."[72]

The best summary of Zuo's life and career is perhaps the one offered by Bales: "He was born in obscurity and poverty, schooled himself under great difficulties, suffered many adversities, entered an official career when well past middle age and by his energy and genius rose to the highest posts open to a Chinese during the Manchu period. He was not prepared either by education or by early training for the profession of arms, yet he became the foremost soldier of his generation in China."[73] Nowadays with the shifting of the political winds in China, Zuo is once again receiving proper recognition as one of the great reformers and patriots of the late Qing, not to mention one of the architects of the modern Chinese state by virtue of his recovery of Xinjiang. Whatever one feels about the current policies of the PRC in Xinjiang, Zuo's legacy in helping to preserve the territorial integrity of the Qing is undeniable.[74] Indeed, it has been argued that the Han concept of "China" as articulated by Qing officials laid the foundation for the multiethnic nationalist discourse that animates the PRC today.[75]

This biography offers an interesting counterpoint to Zuo's "fame" in the United States, where the omnipresent chicken dish beloved by so many is unknown to the average Chinese outside the American Chinese restaurant industry. But as I hope the present study has demonstrated, Zuo deserves to be remembered as a great hero, patriot, educator, and military commander. He was far from perfect, but he sincerely tried to put his principles into practice and create a better world for Qing subjects from all walks of life across the empire. To quote Bales once more, Zuo was indeed a "man of the greatness of soul" and a "glory to his land and to his people."[76]

NOTES

CHC	*Cambridge History of China*
ECQP	*Eminent Chinese of the Qing Period*
HMQY	*Shaanxi huimin qiyi ziliao*
HMYD	*Qingmo xibei huimin zhi fan Qing yundong*
KXJ	*Kanding Xinjiang ji*
NCH	*North China Herald*
NJWX	*Nianjun wenxian huibian*
PHZ	*Ping Hui zhi*
PZJL	*Ping Zhe jilue*
QSG	*Qing shigao*
SGXF	*Shaan-Gan Xinjiang huifei fanglue*
SXHMQY	*Tongzhi nianjian Shaanxi huimin qiyi lishi diaocha jilu*
ZNP	*Zuo wenxiang gong nianpu*
ZQHZ	*Zeiqing huizuan*
ZWZX	*Zuo wenxiang gong zai xibei*
ZZQJ	*Zuo Zongtang quanji*

PREFACE

1. There are various romanization systems used to convert Chinese words into the Western alphabet. Tso is an older form, called Wade-Giles after the missionary scholars who invented it in the nineteenth century. Zuo is the current pinyin form that is the official system used by the People's Republic of China (PRC). The Chinese character in question is written 左. Tsao/Cao are romanizations for entirely different Chinese characters, but since most non-Chinese don't know the difference, they creep into restaurant menus.
2. See the IMDB database entry: https://www.imdb.com/title/tt3576038/.
3. See Jennifer 8. Lee, *The Fortune Cookie Chronicles: Adventures in the World of Chinese Food* (New York: Twelve Books, 2009).

4.　Lee, *Fortune Cookie Chronicles,* 68.

5.　Lee, 78–82.

6.　For short biographies of Zeng Guofan and Li Hongzhang, see *ECQP*, 842–47 and 317–24, respectively. For Zuo's biography in the same volume, see 947–54.

7.　See the overview of Zuo's career in Yang Dongliang, *Zuo Zongtang* (Beijing: Renmin wenxue chubanshe, 2004), 1–3.

8　See Yang Dongliang, *Zuo Zongtang,* 3.

9.　The complete biography is W. L. Bales, *Tso Tsung-t'ang: Soldier and Statesman of Old China* (Shanghai: Kelly & Walsh, 1937). Also see Lanny B. Fields, *Tso Tsung-t'ang and the Muslims: Statecraft in Northwest China, 1868–1880* (Kingston, ON: Limestone Press, 1978); and Peter Lavelle, *The Profits of Nature: Colonial Development and the Quest for Resources in Nineteenth-Century China* (New York: Columbia University Press, 2020).

CHAPTER 1. THE NEXUS OF THE CRISES

1.　See *ZWZX*, 5.

2.　Chinese literati often took "styles," or courtesy names, and referred to each other by these monikers. Zuo's "official" biography can be found in *QSG*, 3084–87. In this modern reprint edition there are two paginations because four traditional pages are reproduced on each modern page. So in the original version, Zuo's biography is found on pages 12023–35. For convenience I follow the romanized page numbering on the bottom of the pages.

3.　Bales, *Tso Tsung-t'ang*, 58.

4.　Sun Guangyao, *Zuo Zongtang zhuan* (Beijing: Zhongguo shuji chubanshe, 2015), 3.

5.　Sun Guangyao, *Zuo Zongtang zhuan*, 2; *ZNP*, 539–40.

6.　Yang Dongliang, *Zuo Zongtang*, 4. Also see Fields, *Tso and the Muslims*, 2.

7.　Lanny B. Fields, "Tso Tsung-t'ang and His Campaigns in Northwestern China,1868–1880" (PhD diss., Indiana University, 1972), 20; *ZWZX*, 13–16.

8.　Bales, *Tso Tsung-t'ang*, 59.

9.　Daniel McMahon, "The Yuelu Academy and Hunan's 19th Century Turn towards Statecraft," *Late Imperial China* 26.1 (June 2005), 74. On the significance of this academy in the statecraft tradition, also see Eric Schluessel, *Land of Strangers: The Civilizing Project in Qing Central Asia* (New York: Columbia University Press, 2020), 37–40.

10.　Yang Dongliang, *Zuo Zongtang*, 5. Some sources maintain that Zuo initially was ranked first but was downgraded for political reasons. See Sun Guangyao,

Zuo Zongtang zhuan, 4. For an exhaustive study of the civil service examination system in late imperial China, see Benjamin A. Elman, *A Cultural History of Civil Examinations in Late Imperial China* (Berkeley: University of California Press, 2000).

11. Sun Guangyao, *Zuo Zongtang*, 3.

12. Fields, *Tso and the Muslims*, 3.

13. *ZWZX*, 6.

14. On these interests, see Fields, "Tso Tsung-t'ang (1812–1885) and His Campaigns in Northwestern China," 5; also see Yang Dongliang, *Zuo Zongtang*, 5. On the influence of statecraft scholarship in the late Qing and its connections to military campaigns in the northwest, see Nailene Joseph Chou, "Frontier Studies and Changing Frontier Administration in the Late Ch'ing: The Case of Sinkiang, 1759–1911" (PhD diss., University of Washington, 1976), 27–54.

15. Fields, *Tso and the Muslims*, 38.

16. On Wei Yuan, see *ECQP*, 659–61. On his statecraft impact, see Thomas L. Kennedy, *The Arms of Kiangnan: Modernization in the Chinese Ordnance Industry, 1860–1895* (Boulder: Westview Press, 1978), 20–22. Also see Jane Kate Leonard, *Wei Yuan and China's Rediscovery of the Maritime World* (Cambridge, MA: Harvard University Asia Center, 1984); and Chou, "Frontier Studies and Changing Frontier Administration," chap. 4.

17. *ZWZX*, 7.

18. See the editorial in *NCH*, 1 (August 3, 1850). Accessed via the *North China Herald* online database, http://www.brill.com/products/online-resources/north-china-herald-online.

19. *CHC*, 10.1:1.

20. See Paul A. Cohen, *Discovering History in China: Recent American Writing on the Chinese Past* (New York: Columbia University Press, 2010), especially chapter 1.

21. *CHC*, 10.1:3.

22. Maochun Yu, "The Taiping Rebellion: A Military Assessment of Revolution and Counterrevolution," in *A Military History of China*, ed. David A. Graff and Robin Higham, 135 (Boulder: Westview Press, 2002).

23. *CHC*, 10.1:10.

24. John L. Rawlinson, *China's Struggle for Naval Development, 1839–1895* (Cambridge, MA: Harvard University Press, 1967), 1.

25. James Bonk, "Chinese Military Men and Cultural Practice in the Early Nineteenth Century Qing Empire (1800–1850)" (PhD diss., Princeton University, 2014), 1.

26. See David B. Ralston, *Importing the European Army: The Introduction of European Military Techniques and Institutions into the Extra-European World, 1600–1914* (Chicago: University of Chicago Press, 1990), 108.

27. Emily Mokros, *The* Peking Gazette *in Late Imperial China: State News and Political Authority* (Seattle: University of Washington Press, 2021), 169.

28. Yingcong Dai, *The White Lotus War: Rebellion and Suppression in Late Imperial China* (Seattle: University of Washington Press, 2019).

29. For the classic explanation of late Qing militarization, see Philip A. Kuhn, *Rebellion and Its Enemies: Militarization and Social Structure, 1796–1864* (Cambridge, MA: Harvard University Press, 1980), iv–32. On the social stresses and militarization of late Ming society, see Kenneth M. Swope, *The Military Collapse of China's Ming Dynasty, 1618–44* (London: Routledge, 2014); and Kenneth M. Swope, *On the Trail of the Yellow Tiger: War, Trauma and Social Dislocation in Southwest China during the Ming-Qing Transition* (Lincoln: University of Nebraska Press, 2018).

30. See David Ownby, *Brotherhoods and Secret Societies in Early–Mid Qing China: The Formation of a Tradition* (Stanford: Stanford University Press, 1996).

31. See Dai, *White Lotus War*, 433; and Bonk, "Chinese Military Men."

32. Bonk, 2.

33. Bonk, 15.

34. On military culture in the High Qing, particularly with respect to the Manchus, see Joanna Waley-Cohen, *The Culture of War in China: Empire and the Military under the Qing Dynasty* (London: I. B. Tauris, 2006). On the expansion of military cultural practices such as establishing shrines and honors for war dead for Han Chinese, see Bonk, "Chinese Military Men," 36–81.

35. See Bonk, 237–40. On the *Shengwu ji*, see *CHC*, 10.1:148–52.

36. For a biography of He Changling, see *ECQP*, 209–10.

37. Lavelle, *Profits of Nature*, 22–23. It was He Changling who compiled a new edition of the *Huangchao jingshi wenbian* in 1827.

38. Fields, "Tso and His Campaigns," 61–62.

39. On the significance of this Hunan connection in Zuo's career, see Li Lianli, *Zuo Zongtang pingzhuan: wan Qing di yishi* (Wuchang: Huazhong keji daxue chubanshe, 2013), 15–16; and Lanny B. Fields, "The Importance of Friendships and Quasi-Kin Relationships in Tso Tsung-t'ang's Career," *Journal of Asian History* 10.2 (1976), 72–86.

40. Kuhn, *Rebellion and Its Enemies*, 186. On the significance of the Hunanese in the late Qing, also see Stephen R. Platt, *Provincial Patriots: The Hunanese and Modern China* (Cambridge, MA: Harvard University Press, 2007).

41. See Liao Zhenghua, *Xiangjun zhengzhan shi* (Beijing: Xiandai chubanshe, 2017), 1.
42. *ZWZX*, 14.
43. Sun Guangyao, *Zuo Zongtang*, 5.
44. Bales, "Tso Tsung-t'ang," 63; Sun Guangyao, *Zuo Zongtang*, 6.
45. Yang Dongliang, *Zuo Zongtang*, 7. For Zuo's essays, see *ZZQJ*, 13: 352–64; also see the discussion in Lavelle, *Profits of Nature*, 23–29.
46. *ZZQJ*, 13:362–63.
47. *ZNP*, 544.
48. Yang Dongliang, *Zuo Zongtang*, 8–9. Some of his later essays also discuss military preparations and training. See *ZZQJ*, 13:364–97.
49. Sun Guangyao, *Zuo Zongtang*, 6–7.
50. See Li Lianli, *Zuo Zongtang pingzhuan*, 10–11.
51. See Sun Guangyao, *Zuo Zongtang*, 7.
52. *ZZQJ*, 13:406. Translated in Chou, "Frontier Studies and Changing Frontier Administration," 125.
53. On Tao Zhu, see *ECQP*, 590–91.
54. Yang Dongliang, *Zuo Zongtang*, 10.
55. Kennedy, *The Arms of Kiangnan*, 20.
56. Lavelle, *Profits of Nature*, 27.
57. Useful surveys of the war include Hsin-pao Chang, *Commissioner Lin and the Opium War* (Cambridge, MA: Harvard University Press, 1966); Peter Ward Fay, *The Opium War, 1840–1842: Barbarians in the Celestial Empire in the Early Part of the Nineteenth Century and the War by Which They Forced Her Gates* (Chapel Hill: University of North Carolina Press, 1997); and Arthur Waley, *The Opium War through Chinese Eyes* (Stanford: Stanford University Press, 1958). The inner workings of the Qing bureaucracy leading up to and during the conflict are treated in James Polachek, *The Inner Opium War* (Cambridge, MA: Harvard University Press, 1992). The British context is explored in Stephen R. Platt, *Imperial Twilight: The Opium War and the End of China's Last Golden Age* (New York: Vintage Books, 2019); and Bickers, *Scramble for China*.
58. See Platt, *Imperial Twilight*, 441. Lin's biography can be found in *ECQP*, 364–68.
59. Platt, *Imperial Twilight*, 443–45. On Wei's and other recommendations for naval reform after the war, see Bruce A. Elleman, *A History of the Modern Chinese Navy, 1840–2020* (London: Routledge, 2021), 41–42.
60. *ZZQJ*, 10:28–29.
61. Yang Dongliang, *Zuo Zongtang*, 15–16.

62. See Yang Dongliang, 14–16; and *ZZQJ*, 10: 15–16.
63. *ZNP*, 539; also see Fields, *Tso and the Muslims*, 9.
64. For a biography of Gu, see *ECQP*, 187–92. For translations of Gu's writings, see Gu Yanwu, *Record of Daily Knowledge and Collected Poems and Essays* (New York: Columbia University Press, 2016).
65. Li Lianli, *Zuo Zongtang pingzhuan*, 2.
66. *ZZQJ*, 10:5–6.
67. Fields, *Tso and the Muslims*, 10.
68. *ZNP*, 546.
69. *ZNP*, 547.
70. See Zuo's 1837 letter to He Xiling in *ZZQJ*, 10:3–4.
71. Bales, *Tso Tsung-t'ang*, 68.
72. See *ZZQJ*, 10:11–19.
73. *ZZQJ*, 10:15.
74. *ZZQJ*, 10:16–17.
75. See *ZZQJ*, 10:23–26.
76. Yang Dongliang, *Zuo Zongtang*, 17–18; also see *ZNP*, 549. On the significance of the concept of awesomeness in late imperial Chinese grand strategy, see Kenneth M. Swope, "Being Awesome: Grand Strategy in Late Imperial China, 1368–1911," forthcoming in *The Cambridge History of Grand Strategy*, 4 vols., ed. Beatrice Heuser and Isabelle Duyyesteyn (Cambridge: Cambridge University Press, 2024).
77. For biographies of Hu Linyi, see *ECQP*, 237–39; and *QSG*, 3060–62.
78. *ZNP*, 550–51.
79. *ZZQJ*, 10:45–47.
80. Yang Dongliang, *Zuo Zongtang*, 17. For an overview of social disorder in southeast China during this period, see Frederic Wakeman Jr., *Strangers at the Gate: Social Disorder in South China, 1839–1861* (Berkeley: University of California Press, 1966).
81. *ZZQJ*, 10:42–43 and 53–56.
82. *CHC*, 10.1:266.
83. See *QSG*, 230–32.
84. *QSG*, 233–34.
85. Bales, *Tso Tsung-t'ang*, 71; *ZNP*, 551; and Lavelle, *Profits of Nature*, 35.
86. On Zuo's supposed Elder Brother Society affiliations, see William T. Rowe, *China's Last Empire: The Great Qing* (Cambridge, MA: Harvard University Press, 2009), 182.

87. Cited in Yang Dongliang, *Zuo Zongtang*, 18.
88. Lavelle, *Profits of Nature*, 30.
89. *ZNP*, 552.
90. *ZZQJ*, 10:68–69.
91. Yang Dongliang, *Zuo Zongtang*, 18.
92. For Shen Baozhen's biography, see *ECQP*, 527–29.
93. For a biography of Guo Songtao, see *ECQP*, 197–99. Also see Jenny Huangfu Day, "Searching for the Roots of Western Power: Guo Songtao and Education in Victorian England," *Late Imperial China* 35.1 (June 2014), 1–37.
94. For a biography of Li Xingyuan, see *ECQP*, 339–40. On the Tiandihui, see Dian Murray, *The Origins of the Tiandihui: The Chinese Triads in Legend and History* (Stanford: Stanford University Press, 1994); and Barend ter Haar, *Ritual and Mythology of the Chinese Triads: Creating an Identity* (Leiden: Brill, 2000). On Triad membership among the Taipings, see Jean Chesneaux, *Popular Movements and Secret Societies in China, 1840–1950* (Stanford: Stanford University Press, 1972), 68–70; and Jen Yu-wen, *The Taiping Revolutionary Movement* (New Haven: Yale University Press, 1973), 68–70, which downplays these connections.
95. Yang Dongliang, *Zuo Zongtang*, 19. On the *qingye jianbi* strategy in Chinese history, see Kenneth M. Swope, "Clearing the Fields and Strengthening the Walls: Defending Small Cities in Late Ming China," in *Secondary Cities and Urban Networking in the Indian Ocean Realm*, ed. Kenneth R. Hall, 123–54 (Boulder: Lexington Books, 2008).
96. *ZNP*, 553.
97. For a short biography of Hong Xiuquan, see *ECQP*, 226–32. For a very readable biography of Hong in English, see Jonathan D. Spence, *God's Chinese Son: The Heavenly Kingdom of Hong Xiuquan* (New York: W. W. Norton, 1996). Excellent overviews of the Taiping Rebellion include Franz Michael, *The Taiping Rebellion: A History with Documents*, 3 vols. (Seattle: University of Washington Press, 1966); *CHC*, 10.1:264–317; and Sheng Sunchang, *Shishuo Taiping tianguo* (Shanghai: Shanghai shudian chubanshe, 2017). Hong's official biography in the *Draft History of the Qing Dynasty* is the last and lengthiest biography in the work. See *QSG*, 3296–321.
98. For a critical overview of Qing military institutions at the outset of the Taiping Rebellion, see Richard Smith, "Chinese Military Institutions in the Mid-Nineteenth Century, 1850–1860," *Journal of Asian History* 8.2 (1974), 122–61. Some of Smith's findings have been corrected or revised by more recent scholars, James Bonk in particular.

99. Smith, "Chinese Military Institutions," 148–50.

100. See Yizhu's biography in *ECQP*, 797–99.

101. S. Y. Teng, *The Taiping Rebellion and the Western Powers* (Taibei: Yiwen yin-shuguan, 1977), 22.

102. *QSG*, 237.

103. *NCH*, 1 (August 3, 1850).

104. *QSG*, 237.

105. Cited in J. C. Cheng, *Chinese Sources for the Taiping Rebellion* (Hong Kong: Hong Kong University Press, 1963), 15.

106. *QSG*, 237. For a discussion of the symbolic importance of the queue for Manchu identity and Qing authority, see Philip A. Kuhn, *Soulstealers: The Chinese Sorcery Scare of 1768* (Cambridge, MA: Harvard University Press, 1990).

107. See the story in *NCH*, 43 (May 24, 1851).

108. *QSG*, 238.

109. *QSG*, 238.

110. See *NCH*, 46 (June 14, 1851).

111. *NCH*, 48 (June 28, 1851).

112. *QSG*, 237. For a biography of Xiang Rong, see *ECQP*, 693–95.

113. See Franz Michael, "Military Organization and Power Structure of China during the Taiping Rebellion," *Pacific Historical Review* 18.4 (1949), 782.

114. For an exhaustive examination of the Banner system and its place in Qing society, see Mark C. Elliott, *The Manchu Way: The Eight Banners and Ethnic Identity in Late Imperial China* (Stanford: Stanford University Press, 2001).

115. For Duolonga's biography, see *QSG*, 3072–74.

116. Michael, *Taiping Rebellion* 1:55–57.

117. See Bales, *Tso Tsung-tang*, 83–85; and *ECQP*, 228.

118. *NCH*, 38 (April 19, 1851).

119. See Chesneaux, *Secret Societies and Popular Rebellions*, 70–74, on Hong Daquan and the Triads. Also see Michael, *Taiping Rebellion* 1:65–66; William James Hail, *Tseng Kuo-fan and the Taiping Rebellion with a Short Sketch of His Later Career* (New York: Paragon Books, 1964), 52–62; and Thomas Taylor Meadows, *The Chinese and Their Rebellions* (Stanford: Stanford University Press, 1953), 12–22.

120. See Jen, *Taiping Revolutionary Movement*, 77–84, for details on the activities around Yongan.

121. On the campaign around Guilin, see J. C. Cheng, *Chinese Sources*, 18; and Teng, *The Taiping Rebellion and the Western Powers*, 80–83.

122. Yang Dongliang, *Zuo Zongtang*, 20.

CHAPTER 2. A KINGDOM NEITHER HEAVENLY NOR PEACEFUL

1. Liao, *Xiangjun zhengzhan shi*, 19.
2. *QSG*, 3084; *ZNP*, 553.
3. For an overview of the *mufu* institution in Qing China, see Jonathan Porter, *Tseng Kuo-fan's Private Bureaucracy* (Berkeley: University of California Press, 1972), 14–29.
4. Sheng, *Taiping tianguo*, 139.
5. J. C. Cheng, *Chinese Sources on the Taiping Rebellion*, 21; *QSG*, 239.
6. *ZZQJ*, 9:3–4; Cui Ji'en, "Zuo Zongtang shuping," *Shixue yukan* 1957 (July 1957), 9.
7. Yang Dongliang, *Zuo Zongtang*, 20–21.
8. See *ZZQJ*, 9:3–8, for Luo Bingzhang's overall assessment of the situation at Changsha.
9. Liao, *Xiangjun zhengzan shi*, 14–16.
10. See Shang, *Taiping tianguo*, 146–47.
11. Yang Dongliang, *Zuo Zongtang*, 22; Porter, *Tseng Kuo-fan's Private Bureaucracy*, 81–82.
12. Cui, "Zuo Zongtang shuping," 9. For another assessment of Zeng as a counter-revolutionary, see Jen, *Taiping Revolutionary Movement*, 4. The author of this work was an anti-Manchu Chinese nationalist from Guangdong who sympathized with Hong Xiuquan. He compiled his original work in Chinese over several decades, supposedly burning the first draft because it was grounded in "distorted" Qing sources. He then traveled the countryside interviewing survivors, including descendants of the Hong clan. He also conducted archival work in China and in Hong Kong after 1949. The present work is a translation and abridgement of the Chinese original.
13. *ZZQJ*, 9:15–18.
14. Liao, *Xiangjun zhengzan shi*, 21–22.
15. *ZNP*, 555.
16. See the discussion in Kenneth M. Swope, "Of Bureaucrats and Bandits: Confucianism and Antirebel Strategy at the End of the Ming Dynasty," in *Warfare and Culture in World History*, 2nd ed., ed. Wayne E. Lee, 123–53 (New York: New York University Press, 2020).
17. Sun, *Zuo Zongtang zhuan*, 17.
18. *ZZQJ*, 10:78–80.
19. *ZZQJ*, 10:104.

20. *ZZQJ*, 10:80–82.

21. *ZZQJ*, 9:19–20.

22. See the reports in *ZZQJ*, 9:28–37; and a letter Zuo wrote to Tao Guang in *ZZQJ*, 10:92–93.

23. For a discussion of the Qing military rewards system, see Ulrich Theobald, "Monetary and Non-monetary Rewards in the Early and High Qing Period (1673–1795)," in *Money in Asia (1200–1900): Small Currencies in Social and Political Contexts*, ed. Jane Kate Leonard and Ulrich Theobald, 398–419 (Leiden: Brill, 2015).

24. Sun, *Zuo Zongtang zhuan*, 24. The municipality of Wuhan technically consists of three cities: Hanyang, Hankou, and Wuchang. The sources sometimes refer to Wuhan and sometimes reference one of the smaller units, sometimes called the "Three Towns of Wuhan" (*Wuhan san zhen*).

25. Jen, *Taiping Revolutionary Movement*, 100–105.

26. J. C. Cheng, *Chinese Sources on the Taiping Rebellion*, 25.

27. *ZZQJ*, 9:42–45.

28. J. C. Cheng, *Chinese Sources on the Taiping Rebellion*, 27. On the *Capital Gazette*, see Mokros, *The* Peking Gazette *in Late Imperial China*.

29. *ZZQJ*, 9:51–54.

30. *QSG*, 239.

31. Lai Yi-faai, "River Strategy: A Phase of the Taipings' Development," *Oriens* 5.2 (December 1952), 302.

32. See J. C. Cheng, *Chinese Sources on the Taiping Rebellion*, 31; and Sheng, *Taiping tianguo*, 139. Xiao Chaogui was Hong Xiuquan's brother-in-law. Some sources state Xiao was killed in a later attack on Changsha, in 1853, but he was slain in the initial siege in the fall of 1852. See *ZZQJ*, 10:81.

33. *NCH*, 138 (March 19, 1853).

34. Jen, *Taiping Revolutionary Movement*, 118.

35. On the strategic debate between the Taiping leaders, see Michael, *Taiping Rebellion*, 1:72–74.

36. Teng, *Taiping Rebellion and the Western Powers*, 125–27.

37. See Bales, *Tso Tsung-t'ang*, 94–96.

38. Michael, *Taiping Rebellion*, 1:93–96. Details on the Northern Expedition can also be found in Jen, *Taiping Revolutionary Movement*, 172–215. For a discussion of the Northern Expedition's influence on Jinan in Shandong province, see Daniel Knorr, "Fragile Bulwark: The Qing State in Jinan during the Taiping and Nian Wars," *Late Imperial China* 43.1 (June 2022), 46–60.

39. Jen, *Taiping Revolutionary Movement*, 166.

40. *NCH*, 152 (June 25, 1853).

41. *QSG*, 3050.

42. See *NCH*, 173 (November 19, 1853); *QSG*, 240–41. For Senggelinqin's biography, see *ECQP*, 520–22. On the exaggeration of Shengbao's victory at Linqing, see *NCH*, 200 (May 27, 1854).

43. *QSG*, 3051.

44. For a biography of Jiang, see *ECQP*, 277–78. On the Battle of Suoyi Ferry, see Jen, *Taiping Revolutionary Movement*, 88–90.

45. *ZZQJ*, 10:77. This is a common expression in classical Chinese.

46. For detailed discussions of the Hunan Army and its operations, see Guanhe Wushizhou, *Xiangjun jueqi* (Beijing: Xiandai chubanshe, 2018); and Liao, *Xiangjun zhengzhan shi*.

47. On Zeng's adoption of Qi's practices, see Teddy Sim and Sandy J. C. Liu, "Zeng Guofan's Applications of Qi Jiguang's Doctrines in Crushing the Taiping Uprising," in *The Maritime Defence of China: Ming General Qi Jiguang and Beyond*, ed. Y. H. Teddy Sim, 93–104 (Singapore: Springer, 2017); and Kuhn, *Rebellion and Its Enemies*, 146–47. For biographies of Qi, see Goodrich and Fang, eds., *Dictionary of Ming Biography*, 220–24; and Fan Zhongyi, *Qi Jiguang zhuan* (Beijing: Zhonghua shuju, 2003).

48. For details on Xiang Army training methods, see Liao, *Xiangjun zhengzhan shi*, 32–42.

49. Michael, *Taiping Rebellion*, 1:102. On the role of Jiangxi in financing the war, see David Pong, "The Income and Military Expenditure of Kiangsi Province in the Last Years (1860–1864) of the Taiping Rebellion," *Journal of Asian Studies* 26.1 (1966), 49–65.

50. Jen, *Taiping Revolutionary Movement*, 221–25.

51. Sheng, *Taiping tianguo*, 212.

52. Yu, "Taiping Rebellion," 148; also see Chu Wen-djang, *The Moslem Rebellion in Northwest China, 1862–1878: A Study of Government Minority Policy* (The Hague and Paris: Mouton, 1966), 16–17; and Sim and Liu, "Zeng Guofan's Application," 95–96.

53. Sheng, *Taiping tianguo*, 214–15.

54. See Tobie Meyer-Fong, "To Know the Enemy: The *zei qing huizuan*, Military Intelligence, and the Taiping Civil War," *T'oung Pao* 104.3–4 (2018), 407.

55. See Bales, *Tso Tsung-t'ang*, 48–50.

56. Jen, *Taiping Revolutionary Movement*, 225–30.

57. Meyer-Fong, "To Know the Enemy," 416.
58. Meyer-Fong, 418–20.
59. Meyer-Fong, 422.
60. *ZZQJ*, 9:68–73.
61. *ZZQJ*, 9:73–75.
62. See Liao, *Xiangjun zhengzhan shi*, 34–36.
63. *ZZQJ*, 9:98–101.
64. *ZZQJ*, 9:111–13.
65. Sun, *Zuo Zongtang zhuan*, 18.
66. Bales, *Tso Tsung-t'ang*, 106.
67. For a biography of Luo, see *ECQP*, 404–5; also see *QSG*, 3058–60.
68. *ZNP*, 553.
69. Bales, *Tso Tsung'-t'ang*, 106–7.
70. Bales, 108–11.
71. Bales, 108; Jen, *Taiping Revolutionary Movement*, 247–48; and Sun, *Zuo Zongtang zhuan*, 28.
72. *ZNP*, 557–58.
73. Kennedy, *Arms of Kiangnan*, 15.
74. Jen, *Taiping Revolutionary Movement*, 254–56.
75. See Kennedy, *The Arms of Kiangnan*, 15. Like many authors of his era, Kennedy blames Confucianism for China's "slow development" of arms. See Kennedy, *Arms of Kiangnan*,16.
76. *ZNP*, 558; also see Ch'en, *Tso Tsung-t'ang, Pioneer Promoter of the Dockyard and Woolen Mill in China* (New York: Paragon, 1968), 6–7; and Fields, "Tso-tsung-t'ang (1812–1885) and His Campaigns in Northwestern China," 73.
77. See Ch'en, *Tso Tsung-t'ang: Pioneer Promoter*, 8–12. On Qing experiments with boat design, see Liao, *Xiangjun zhengzhan shi*, 38–42. Emperor Xianfeng ordered the construction of steamships to defend the rivers in 1856. See *QSG*, 243.
78. Laai, "River Strategy," 320.
79. Laai, 320–21.
80. Meyer-Fong, "To Know the Enemy," 386.
81. *ZHQZ*, 791.
82. *ZHQZ*, 791.
83. *ZHQZ*, 28.
84. *ZZQJ*, 9:140–45.
85. Jen, *Taiping Revolutionary Movement*, 217–21.

86. *QSG*, 241.

87. *ZZQJ*, 9:165.

88. Liao, *Xiangjun zhengzhan shi*, 49–52.

89. See *CHC*, 10.1:413; and *QSG*, 3071–72. For more details on the Battle of Xiangtan, see *ZNP*, 558; *ZZQJ*, 9:162–71; and Yang Dongliang, *Zuo Zongtang*, 24–25.

90. *ZZQJ*, 9:168–74; *ZZQJ*, 10:98–110. For biographies of Taqibu, see *ECQP*, 591; and *QSG*, 3071–72. Taqibu was a member of the Bordered Yellow Banner who had served in the imperial bodyguards and specialized in firearms training. His defense of Changsha brought him to the attention of Zeng Guofan. On Peng Yulin, see *ECQP*, 465–67; and *QSG*, 3077–79. Unsurprisingly, Peng was a native of Hunan. He had risen to prominence through military exploits at the local level after rapacious neighbors stole his family lands after his father's death. This brought him to the attention of Zeng Guofan, who brought him on while he was creating his initial river patrols in support of the Hunan Army. See Liao, *Xiangjun zhengzhan shi*, 7–9.

91. *ZZQJ*, 9:175–77.

92. *ZZQJ*, 9:210.

93. Yang Dongliang, *Zuo Zongtang*, 25.

94. *ZZQJ*, 9:228–29.

95. *ZNP*, 555.

96. See Fields, "Tso Tsung-t'ang and His Campaigns in Northwest China," 77.

97. Laai, "River Strategy," 321, citing the *Yuefei fanglue*.

98. Laai, 322.

99. *ZNP*, 558.

100. For Luo's biography, see *ECQP*, 407–8. On the fall of Wuchang, see *ZZQJ*, 9:239–42; and Liao, *Xiangjun zhengzhan shi*, 69–73.

101. *ZNP*, 560; *ZZQJ*, 9:254–55.

102. *ZZQJ*, 9:268–75.

103. *ZZQJ*, 9:285–94.

104. *QSG*, 242.

105. *ZZQJ*, 9:304–13; *ZZQJ*, 10:113.

106. *ZZQJ*, 10:114.

107. *ZZQJ*, 10:122.

108. *ZZQJ*, 10:25.

109. *ZZQJ*, 10:133.

110. *ZNP*, 564.

111. *ZZQJ*, 10:139.

112. *ZZQJ*, 10:139.

113. *ZZQJ*, 10:147. For other letters, see *ZZQJ*, 10:140–46.

114. Yang Dongliang, *Zuo Zongtang*, 26.

115. On the Miao connection, see *ZZQJ*, 9:329–35; and *ZZQJ*, 10:160. Miao also fought on the Qing side.

116. See Robert Jenks, *Insurgency and Social Disorder in Guizhou: The "Miao" Rebellion, 1854–1873* (Honolulu: University of Hawaii Press, 1994).

117. *ZZQJ*, 10:187.

118. See the strategic overview in *ZZQJ*, 9:442–46; also see *QSG*, 3060.

119. See *ZZQJ*, 10:188–89.

120. *ZZQJ*, 10:207.

121. *ZNP*, 567; *ZZQJ*, 10:189.

122. Shi had returned to Nanjing the previous year and tried to mediate the dispute between the other leaders. Fearing for his own life he fled, and his family was subsequently murdered. Shi returned to Nanjing and removed Wei Changhui but fell afoul of members of Hong's clan, so he returned to the field, operating almost independently from this point onward. See Jen, *Taiping Revolutionary Movement*, 294–309.

123. See *ZZQJ*, 9:497–527, for accounts of these victories.

124. See *ZZQJ*, 10:191–93.

125. *ZNP*, 568.

126. The reader may recall the probably apocryphal story that Shi Dakai had met Zuo several years earlier and offered him a position in the Taiping ranks. See Li Lianli, *Zuo Zongtang pingzhuan*, 25–27.

127. *QSG*, 3072–73. For Bao Chao's biography, see *ECQP*, 16–17. Bao had also been involved the battle to retake Yuezhou, Wuchang, Hanyang, and Tianjiazhen earlier in the war. See *QSG*, 3074. On the campaigns leading up to the recapture of Jiujiang, see Liao, *Xiangjun zhengzhan shi*, 81–83.

128. *ZZQJ*, 10:291.

129. For Liu's biography, see *ECQP*, 371–72; and *QSG*, 3110–11. On his communications with Zuo at this time, see *ZZQJ*, 10:311–18.

130. *QSG*, 3060. On Jiang's death at Luzhou, see Liao, *Xiangjun zhengzhan shi*, 44–47.

131. *QSG*, 3110.

132. Jen, *Taiping Revolutionary Movement*, 309; *QSG*, 3061–62; and *ZZQJ*, 9, 661–70; also see Liao, *Xiangjun zhengzhan shi*, 105–11.

133. *QSG*, 248.

134. *QSG*, 3110.
135. *ECQP*, 540; and Michael, *Taiping Rebellion*, 3:1097–99. For his final confession, see Michael, *Taiping Rebellion*, 3:1200–1204.
136. Jen, *Taiping Revolutionary Movement*, 333.
137. See Jen, 338–41; and Liao, *Xiangjun zhengzhan shi*, 98–104.
138. Liao, 112–20.
139. *ZZQJ*, 9:695–700.
140. See *ZZQJ*, 10:319; Yang Dongliang, *Zuo Zongtang*, 34–35; and *ECQP*, 950.
141. Sun, *Zuo Zongtang zhuan*, 32.
142. See *ZNP*, 575; Yang Dongliang, *Zuo Zongtang*, 35–36; and Li Lianli, *Zuo Zongtang pingzhuan*, 37–39. Chu is another name for the area around northern Hunan province.
143. See the table in Yang Dongliang, *Zuo Zongtang*, 36.
144. *ZZQJ*, 9:711–13. On Liu Songshan, see *QSG*, 3076–77. His career started when he answered a call for mercenaries and was attached to the army of Wang Xin, where he rose to the post of chiliarch. He was subsequently promoted for his exploits in battle and rose steadily through the ranks as he fought the Taipings in Jiangxi.
145. Liao, *Xiangjun zhengzhan shi*, 107.
146. Yang Dongliang, *Zuo Zongtang*, 37.
147. *ZNP*, 576.
148. See *ZNP*, 572–74; and *ZZQJ*, 10:333–35; also see Sun, *Zuo Zongtang zhuan*, 28–30.
149. There is a discrepancy in the sources concerning Zuo's promotions at this time. See Yang Dongliang, *Zuo Zongtang*, 28.
150. *ZNP*, 574; also see Li Lianli, *Zuo Zongtang pingzhuan*, 31–34.
151. *ZZQJ*, 10:339. Officials were normally exempt from corporal punishment.
152. *ZZQJ*, 10:351.
153. See the letters in *ZZQJ*, 10:363–70.
154. For a detailed discussion of the origins of this tax, see Edwin G. Beal, *The Origin of Likin, 1854–1873* (Cambridge, MA: Harvard University Press, 1958); also see *ZNP*, 562.
155. Beal, *Origins of Likin*, 3. For a discussion of the impact of the Taiping Rebellion on the Qing fiscal system in general, see James T. K. Wu, "The Impact of the Taiping Rebellion upon the Manchu Fiscal System," *Pacific Historical Review* 19.3 (1950), 265–75.
156. Beal, *Origins of Likin*, 18.

157. For discussion of proposed methods to raise revenues, including by adjusting the salt monopoly, see *ZZQJ*, 9:397–406.

158 See Beal, *Origins of Likin*, 25–27; and *ECQP*, 198. Lei's original memorandum is translated in Beal, 83–87.

159. Beal, *Origins of Likin*, 78–82. For a more recent discussion of *lijin* and its implications for military operations, see Stephen R. Halsey, *Quest for Power: European Imperialism in the Making of Chinese Statecraft* (Cambridge, MA: Harvard University Press, 2015), 87–99.

160. See Yang Dongliang, *Zuo Zongtang*, 29–30; and *CHC*, 10.1:454.

161. *CHC*, 10.1:445.

162. See Yang Dongliang, *Zuo Zongtang*, 28–29.

163. See *QSG*, 3058–59.

164. *ZZQJ*, 9:569–71.

165. Halsey, *Quest for Power*, 131.

166. *ZZQJ*, 10:149.

167. Elizabeth Kaske, "Fund-Raising Wars: Office Selling and Interprovincial Finance in Nineteenth-Century China," *Harvard Journal of Asiatic Studies* 71.1 (June 2011), 69–141, 84.

168. Kaske, "Fund-Raising Wars," 125. On the decline in revenue percentage, see Wu, "Manchu Fiscal System," 273.

169. Kaske, "Fund-Raising Wars," 102–4.

170. Kaske, 110–13.

171. See Kaske, 129; and *ZZQJ*, 5:375–76.

172. Kaske, 135.

173. Meadows, *Chinese and Their Rebellions*, 208–12.

174. Meadows, 252–53; Jen, *Taiping Revolutionary Movement*, 270–71.

175. Yuan Chung Teng, "American-China Trade, American-Chinese Relations and the Taiping Rebellion," *Journal of Asian History* 3.2 (1969), 102.

176. *NCH*, 157 (July 30, 1853).

177. *NCH*, 159 (August 13, 1853).

178. Zuo, for example, suggested getting Westerners' help to defend Hangzhou and Ningbo by sea but was more interested in buying foreign ships and guns for his own use. See *PZJL*, 36.

179. *NCH*, 116 (October 16, 1852).

180. For an overview of the impact of treaty revisions on Western approaches to the Taipings, see Teng, *The Taiping Rebellion and the Western Powers*, 231–50.

181. *QSG*, 241.

182. See *QSG*, 242–44.
183. Teng, *Taiping Rebellion and Western Powers*, 247.
184. Yang Dongliang, *Zuo Zongtang*, 31.
185. Yang Dongliang, 32–33.
186. On Zuo's distrust of Westerners, see *ZZQJ*, 1:125.
187. Teng, *Taiping Rebellion and Western Powers*, 296. On F. T. Ward, see Caleb Carr, *The Devil Soldier: The Story of Frederick Townsend Ward* (New York: Random House, 1992).
188. Meadows, *Chinese and Their Rebellions*, 292–93.
189. See *NCH*, 52 (July 26, 1851).
190. The British press in China had been making that argument since at least 1850. See the editorial in *NCH*, 10 (October 5, 1850); also see Meadows, *Chinese and Their Rebellions*, 487–88.
191. *NCH*, 12 (October 19, 1850).
192. *ZZQJ*, 10:191.
193. *ZZQJ*, 10:271.
194. *QSG*, 245.
195. See *CHC*, 10.1:249–52; and Bruce Elleman, *Modern Chinese Warfare, 1795–1989* (London: Routledge, 2001), 50–52.
196. *QSG*, 245–46.
197. Details on the sacking of the Summer Palace and its cultural and diplomatic significance can be found in James Hevia, *English Lessons: The Pedagogy of Imperialism in Nineteenth-Century China* (Durham: Duke University Press, 2003), 74–118.
198. For a biography of Prince Gong, see *ECQP*, 793–96.
199. *QSG*, 249.
200. *QSG*, 249.
201. For a complete narrative account of the *Arrow* War, see J. Y. Wong, *Deadly Dreams: Opium and the Arrow War (1856–1860) in China* (Cambridge: Cambridge University Press, 1998). Also see Hevia, *English Lessons*, 31–48. A short account connecting it to the broader military situation of the late Qing can be found in Elleman, *Modern Chinese Warfare*, 45–48.
202. Hong Ren'gan's activities and contributions to the Taiping movement are fully treated in Stephen R. Platt, *Autumn in the Heavenly Kingdom: China, the West and the Epic Story of the Taiping Civil War* (New York: Vintage Books, 2012). The so-called Taiping Restoration is also treated in Teng, *Taiping Rebellion and the Western Powers*, chapter 6.

203. Jen, *Taiping Revolutionary Movement*, 380–82; and *ECQP*, 341.

204. Jen, 382–83.

205. Jen, 399–420.

206. For a detailed account of the battle for Anqing, see Liao, *Xiangjun zhengzhan shi*, 121–46.

207. Yang Dongliang, *Zuo Zongtang*, 38.

208. *QSG*, 3079–80. Yang was subsequently named governor of Jiangxi with Peng as his naval commander in chief. They created a flotilla for protecting the Yangzi in 1869. See *QSG*, 3078, for details.

209. *QSG*, 3047.

210. The name Shengbao literally translates as "secure/protect victory." See Liao, *Xiangjun zhengzhan shi*, 100. Shengbao was described as a specialist in fabricating victories and overselling his accomplishments.

211. *QSG*, 3047.

212. *QSG*, 244.

213. Sun, *Zuo Zongtang zhuan*, 25.

214. See Hail, *Tseng Kuo-fan*, 210–19.

215. *QSG*, 244.

216. Liao, *Xiangjun zhengzhan shi*, 130–31.

217. Sun, *Zuo Zongtang zhuan*, 36.

218. *QSG*, 3084; Yang Dongliang, *Zuo Zongtang*, 38–39; and Liao, *Xiangjun zhengzhan shi*, 134–35.

219. Sun, *Zuo Zongtang zhuan*, 38–39.

220. *ZZQJ*, 13:23–24.

221. See *ZZQJ*, 13:36–37.

222. Sun, *Zuo Zongtang zhuan*, 27.

223. *QSG*, 3233.

224. *QSG*, 3233.

225. *ZZQJ*, 13:33.

226. *ZNP*, 576. On Zeng Guoquan, see *ECQP*, 847–48.

227. *ZNP*, 578.

228. *ZZQJ*, 13:45.

229. *QSG*, 250.

230. *QSG*, 252; and Sheng, *Taiping tianguo*, 390–91.

231. Li had been placed in charge of riverine defenses around Zhenjiang at the end of 1861. See *QSG*, 252.

232. Sheng, *Taiping tianguo*, 350–60, covers the battles for Shanghai.

233. For Li Xiucheng's biography, see *ECQP*, 340–44.

234. See Sheng, *Taiping tianguo*, 374–75.

235. *QSG*, 253–55.

236. For Zaichun's biography, see *ECQP*, 836–38.

237. *QSG*, 251. On the intrigue at court, see the discussion in Daniel Barish, *Learning to Rule: Court Education and the Remaking of the Qing State, 1861–1912* (New York: Columbia University Press, 2022), 29–31.

238. For a short biography of Cixi, see *ECQP*, 698–704. For a modern revisionist but rather flawed biography, see Jung Chang, *Empress Dowager Cixi: The Concubine Who Launched Modern China* (New York: Anchor Books, 2013).

239. See Li Lianli, *Zuo Zongtang pingzhuan*, 39–40.

240. *ZZQJ*, 10:430.

241. *QSG*, 3062.

242. See Mary C. Wright, *The Last Stand of Chinese Conservatism: The T'ung-chih Restoration, 1862–1874* (Stanford: Stanford University Press, 1957).

243. Halsey, *Quest for Power*. For an overview of the "Restoration" era and the historiography pertaining to it, see Rowe, *China's Last Empire*, 202–23.

244. *QSG*, 3085.

245. Sun, *Zuo Zongtang zhuan*, 43.

246. Sun, 44–46.

247. Teng, *Taiping Rebellion and Western Powers*, 306.

248. *PZJL*, 21; *ZZQJ*, 1:8–10.

249. *QSG*, 3084–85.

250. *ZNP*, 579–80.

251. *ZZQJ*, 1:14–15.

CHAPTER 3. EMBRACING SELF-STRENGTHENING

1. *CHC*, 10.1:491. Also see the Richard J. Smith, "Reflections on the Comparative Study of Modernization in China and Japan: Military Aspects," *Journal of the Royal Asiatic Society Hong Kong Branch* 16 (1976), 12–24.

2. Bales, *Tso Tsung-t'ang*, 127.

3. See *ZNP*, 581–82.

4. Yang Dongliang, *Zuo Zongtang*, 40.

5. Yang Dongliang, 40.

6. *QSG*, 3085.

7. For an outline of Zuo's plan of attack, see *PZJL*, 8–11. On the importance of securing supplies first, see *PZJL*, 19. This work, compiled by two low-ranking

officials in Zuo's service, offers great insight into Zuo's strategic thinking as well as a view of the campaign in Zhejiang from the ground. It includes both official correspondence and private writings.

8. *ZZQJ*, 14:42.
9. *PZJL*, 23.
10. *PZJL*, 25.
11. Jen, *Taiping Revolutionary Movement*, 479.
12. *PZJL*, 30.
13. *PZJL*, 31.
14. See *ZZQJ*, 1:1–5.
15. *PZJL*, 42–43.
16. *ZZQJ*, 1:18.
17. Yang Dongliang, *Zuo Zongtang*, 41.
18. See the account in *PZJL*, 43–53.
19. See *ZZQJ*, 1:29–31.
20. *ZNP*, 583; *ZZQJ*, 1:36–38; and *PZJL*, 55. On the throne's acknowledgment of these victories, see *ZZQJ*, 1:42.
21. *ZZQJ*, 1:175. On the battles in Anhui as they pertained to Zhejiang, see *PZJL*, 383–418.
22. Li Lianli, *Zuo Zongtang pingzhuan*, 43.
23. For an appraisal of the overall strategic situation from Zuo, see *ZZQJ*, 1:55–58; also see Yang Dongliang, *Zuo Zongtang*, 41–42.
24. *QSG*, 253.
25. *PZJL*, 60–63.
26. *ZZQJ*, 1:74–77; and Xiaowei Zheng, "Loyalty, Anxiety, and Opportunism: Local Elite Activism during the Taiping Rebellion in Eastern Zhejiang, 1851–1864," *Late Imperial China* 30.2 (December 2009), 74.
27. *PZJL*, 65–69.
28. *PZJL*, 71–75.
29. See *ZZQJ*, 1:102–7, for Zuo's account of the battle for Longyou. His final report can be found in *ZZQJ*, 1:134–38.
30. *PZJL*, 78.
31. *PZJL*, 80.
32. *PZJL*, 82.
33. See the account in *PZJL*, 84–90.
34. *PZJL*, 91–110.
35. *PZJL*, 112–19.

36. *ZNP*, 584.
37. On the recovery of Jinhua, see *ZZQJ*, 1:219–22; and Liao, *Xiangjun zhengzhan shi*, 162.
38. Sun, *Zuo Zongtang zhuan*, 49. Sources vary on whether Jinhua or Yanzhou was taken first.
39. *ZZQJ*, 1:112–15; Sun, *Zuo Zongtang zhuan*, 48.
40. Sheng, *Taiping tianguo*, 504.
41. *QSG*, 3085; *PZJL*, 128–29. For Zuo's pitch to the court concerning the importance of attacking Fuyang, see *ZZQJ*, 1:159–61.
42. Sun, *Zuo Zongtang zhuan*, 50.
43. Mokros, *The* Peking Gazette *in Late Imperial China*, 144.
44. Sun, *Zuo Zongtang zhuan*, 51–52.
45. *PZJL*, 128 and 319–20.
46. See *PZJL*, 133–46, 283–84, and 353–54.
47. Zheng, "Local Elite Activism," 58.
48. See Ulrich Theobald, "Craftsmen and Specialist Troops in Early Modern Chinese Armies," in *Civil-Military Relations in Chinese History: From Ancient Times to the Communist Takeover*, ed. Kai Filipiak, 191–209 (London: Routledge, 2015).
49. On pay rates, see Theobald, "Craftsmen and Specialist Troops," 205–9.
50. *ZZQJ*, 14:12.
51. *ZZQJ*, 1:178.
52. *ZZQJ*, 13:62 and 13:64.
53. Giquel's diary has been translated into English. See Steven Leibo, trans. and ed., *A Journal of the Chinese Civil War, 1864 by Prosper Giquel* (Honolulu: University of Hawaii Press, 1985). On the creation of the Ever Triumphant Army, see Leibo, *Giquel*, 16.
54. Leibo, *Giquel*, 68.
55. Jen, *Taiping Revolutionary Movement*, 488; Yang Dongliang, *Zuo Zongtang*, 43.
56. *ZZQJ*, 10:455–56.
57. On the recovery of Fuyang, see *ZZQJ*, 1:244–46; and *ZZQJ*, 14:25.
58. *ZZQJ*, 1:147–55. On rewards for the European troops, see *ZZQJ*, 1:236–37.
59. *ZZQJ*, 1:163–65; *ZZQJ*, 10:475.
60. *PZJL*, 36.
61. *ZZQJ*, 1:156–59; Li Lianli, *Zuo Zongtang pingzhuan*, 45.
62. See Li Lianli, *Zuo Zongtang pingzhuan*, 45–46.
63. *ZZQJ*, 14:27–28.

64. *ZNP*, 587. For details on operations in the summer of 1863, see *PZJL*, 324–37.

65. *ZZQJ*, 13:79–80.

66. Sun, *Zuo Zongtang zhuan*, 53.

67. *PZJL*, 146–48.

68. See *ZNP*, 587–88; and *ZZQJ*, 10:471.

69. *ZZQJ*, 1:205–9.

70. See Lavelle, *Profits of Nature*, 65.

71. Lavelle, 73.

72. *ZNP*, 586.

73. See *ZZQJ*, 1:54, 74–75, and 178; and Lavelle, *Profits of Nature*, 67.

74. On the rhetoric of catastrophe in imperial China, see Swope, *On the Trail of the Yellow Tiger*, especially chapter 9.

75. *ZZQJ*, 1:245.

76. See *ZZQJ*, 1:251–60.

77. *PZJL*, 155–56.

78. *PZJL*, 291.

79. See *ZZQJ*, 1:266–67.

80. *ZZQJ*, 1:271–74.

81. Sheng, *Taiping Tianguo*, 507–8.

82. These battles are covered in *PZJL*, 157–67.

83. *PZJL*, 169.

84. *PZJL*, 172.

85. *PZJL*, 175.

86. See *ZZQJ*, 1:276–81, on the battles for Hangzhou.

87. *PZJL*, 175–77; *ZZQJ*, 1:288–94.

88. *PZJL*, 178–80.

89. *PZJL*, 182; *ZZQJ*, 1:332–43.

90. *ZNP*, 591.

91. Leibo, *Giquel*, 71.

92. See Yang Dongliang, *Zuo Zongtang*, 45; and Bales, *Tso Tsung-t'ang*, 177–78. On the propensity of the troops under Gordon's command to loot, see Smith, *Mercenaries and Mandarins*, 138.

93. *ZZQJ*, 1:346–55.

94. See *PZJL*, 187–89.

95. *PZJL*, 194–96.

96. *ZZQJ*, 1:360–66.

97. *ZZQJ*, 1:369–71.

98. *ZZQJ*, 13:48.
99. See Leibo, *Giquel*, 63.
100. *ZZQJ*, 1:391–96.
101. *PZJL*, 362–66.
102. *PZJL*, 214; Bales, *Tso Tsung-t'ang*, 153.
103. *PZJL*, 217.
104. *PZJL*, 231–35.
105. *PZJL*, 238–54.
106. *ZZQJ*, 1:405–9.
107. *PZJL*, 226–27 and 375–76.
108. See *PZJL*, 101–8. On expanded use of exploding shells, see *PZJL*, 356.
109. Yang Dongliang, *Zuo Zongtang*, 46.
110. The full official name of the Zongli Yamen was Zongli geguo shiwu yamen, which translates as "Office of the Administration of the Affairs of the Various Countries." See *CHC*, 10.1:416–18, on its origins.
111. Richard J. Smith, "The Employment of Foreign Military Talent: Chinese Tradition and Late Ch'ing Practice," *Journal of the Royal Asiatic Society Hong Kong Branch* 15 (1975), 114. Nonetheless, Smith condemns late Qing antiforeignism grounded in a supposed "Neo-Confucian ideological straightjacket" (124).
112. *PZJL*, 309.
113. *ZZQJ*, 10:451.
114. See Smith, *Mercenaries and Mandarins*, 43–46; and Zheng, "Local Elite Activism," 62–65, on these discussions and the process of creating these forces.
115. *ZNP*, 584.
116. There are many biographies of Ward available. For a colorful but deeply flawed popular account that relies on many outdated generalizations, see Carr, *Devil Soldier*.
117. Carr, *Devil Soldier*, 49; Teng, *Taiping Rebellion and Western Powers*, 296.
118. Carr, *Devil Soldier*, 3. The error-laden entry on the Ever Victorious Army in Wikipedia (https://en.wikipedia.org/wiki/Ever_Victorious_Army) attributes many of the characteristics already present in the Xiang Army to "innovations" proposed by Ward.
119. Carr, *Devil Soldier*, 33.
120. See, for example, the dated account in Smith, *Mercenaries and Mandarins*, 98.
121. Cited in Teng and Fairbank, *China's Response*, 69.
122. *ZNP*, 586.
123. Yang Dongliang, *Zuo Zongtang*, 49.

124. See the letter to Zuo from Li Hongzhang complaining about Lay's intrigues in Cheng, *Chinese Sources*, 116–17.
125. On the Lay-Osborn Flotilla debacle, see *CHC*, 10.1:429–31; and Cheng, *Chinese Sources*, 113–18.
126. Yang Dongliang, *Zuo Zongtang*, 48.
127. *ZNP*, 582; *ZZQJ*, 1:60.
128. *PZJL*, 307–12. Incidentally, native troops brought from India served in some of the British contingents.
129. *PZJL*, 261. On Zuo's changing position regarding the Ever Triumphant Army, see Leibo, *Giquel*, 40–42.
130. *PZJL*, 338.
131. On Li's efforts to take Shanghai, see Sheng, *Taiping tianguo*, 418–29.
132. Carr, *Devil Soldier*, 254–61; Zheng, "Local Elite Activism," 69; and Jen, *Taiping Revolutionary Movement*, 485.
133. *QSG*, 254; Carr, *Devil Soldier*, 293–94. On these battles, also see Michael, *Taiping Rebellion*, 1:170–73.
134. On the Burgevine debacle, see Smith, *Mercenaries and Mandarins*, 111–14; Danny Orbach, "Foreign Military Adventurers in the Taiping Rebellion, 1860–1864," *Journal of Chinese Military History* 10.2 (2021), 65; Carr, *Devil Soldier*, 297–312; and Cheng, *Chinese Sources*, 104–9.
135. See Bales, *Tso Tsung-t'ang*, 161–62.
136. Cheng, *Chinese Sources*, 122–23.
137. On the Qing advance to Nanjing, see Sheng, *Taiping tianguo*, 455–66.
138. See Sheng, 503.
139. Teng, *Taiping Rebellion and the Western Powers*, 318.
140. See Cheng, *Chinese Sources*, 124–30, for accounts of these events.
141. Jen, *Taiping Revolutionary Movement*, 503–4.
142. See *ZNP*, 591; *ECQP*, 71; and Carr, *Devil Soldier*, 313–14.
143. *ZZQJ*, 1:423–27; *ZZQJ*, 14:39–40. Also see Sun, *Zuo Zongtang zhuan*, 62–63.
144. *ZZQJ*, 1:428–37.
145. *ZZQJ*, 1:444–454. Huang Wenjin's corpse was publicly dismembered, as were those of many rebel leaders.
146. See Teng, *Taiping Rebellion and Western Powers*, 392; and Jen, *Taiping Revolutionary Movement*, 530.
147. See *QSG*, 258; and Sheng, *Taiping tianguo*, 524.
148. See Sun, *Zuo Zongtang zhuan*, 61–62; Bales, *Tso Tsung-t'ang*, 171–73; and *ECQP*, 230.

149. *ECQP*, 344. For a translation of Li's confession, see Michael, *Taiping Rebellion*, 3:1387–496.
150. *ZNP*, 594.
151. Sun, *Zuo Zongtang zhuan*, 64.
152. *ZNP*, 594.
153. *ZZQJ*, 1:464–67.
154. See *ZZQJ*, 1:457–64, on the plight of Zuo's troops, his requests for relief, and measures he implemented.
155. *ZNP*, 596; also see *PZJL*, 425–30.
156. Sheng, *Taiping tianguo*, 572.
157. Yang Dongliang, *Zuo Zongtang*, 50.
158. See the details in Yang Dongliang, 51.
159. On this siege, see *ZZQJ*, 1:524–28; and *ZZQJ*, 2:1–4. Also see *PZJL*, 435–39.
160. *ZZQJ*, 1:469–70; *PZJL*, 431.
161. *ZZQJ*, 1:478–85; *ZZQJ*, 2:53–54.
162. *ZZQJ*, 1:511–14.
163. See the reports in *ZZQJ*, 2:5–19.
164. *ZZQJ*, 2:22–27.
165. *ZZQJ*, 2:29–30.
166. *PZJL*, 438.
167. Yang Dongliang, *Zuo Zongtang*, 52.
168. *ZZQJ*, 13:90–91.
169. *ZNP*, 598.
170. *ZZQJ*, 10:589–91.
171. *ZZQJ*, 2:72–75
172. *ZZQJ*, 2:273–76.
173. *ZZQJ*, 1:521–24; Sun, *Zuo Zongtang zhuan*, 68–69.
174. *PZJL*, 442–44.
175. *PZJL*, 444–46.
176. *PZJL*, 453.
177. *PZJL*, 451–52.
178. *ZNP*, 597; *ZZQJ*, 2:32–35.
179. On Wang's battles with the Qing, see *PZJL*, 458–60.
180. See, for example, *ZZQJ*, 2:40.
181. Yang Dongliang, *Zuo Zongtang*, 52.
182. *PZJL*, 461.
183. On the battles, see *ZZQJ*, 2:54–58.

184. *PZJL*, 465–66.
185. Bales, *Tso Tsung-t'ang*, 180.
186. *ZZQJ*, 10:562–63.
187. *ZZQJ*, 2:62–63.
188. *ZZQJ*, 10:572–74; also see *ZZQJ*, 13:87–89.
189. *ZZQJ*, 2:235–36.
190. Yang Dongliang, *Zuo Zongtang*, 53; *ZZQJ*, 2:173–74; Liao, *Xiangjun zhengzhan shi*, 191–92; and *ZZQJ*, 10:607.
191. Sheng, *Taiping tianguo*, 576.
192. On the battle for Zhenping, see *ZZQJ*, 2:150–70 and 238–41.
193. Yang Dongliang, *Zuo Zongtang*, 53.
194. *ZZQJ*, 10:611–12; *ZZQJ*, 2:239–40; and Sun, *Zuo Zongtang zhuan*, 70.
195. Sheng, *Taiping tianguo*, 578.
196. *ZNP*, 599–600.
197. *ZNP*, 601.
198. *ZZQJ*, 10:638.
199. *ZZQJ*, 10:648. Also see Zuo's criticisms of local officials in *ZZQJ*, 2:48–51.
200. *ZZQJ*, 2:81–82.
201. See Cai, "On the Origins of the Gelaohui," 481–508; Teng, *Taiping Rebellion and Western Powers*, 361.
202. *ZZQJ*, 2:107–10.
203. *ZZQJ*, 2:110–120.
204. *ZZQJ*, 2:132–33. It is not clear if these units included foreign soldiers in addition to the foreign weapons.
205. *ZZQJ*, 10:631–34; *ZZQJ*, 2:100–102.
206. *ZZQJ*, 2:277–78.
207. *ZZQJ*, 2:282–84.
208. *ZZQJ*, 2:283.
209. See *ZZQJ*, 2:284–302.
210. Sheng, *Taiping tianguo*, 576–80.
211. *ZZQJ*, 2:302–7.
212. See Zuo's battle report in *ZZQJ*, 2:313–15.
213. *ZZQJ*, 2:315. Some sources claim the Qing killed Wang on the battlefield, but it makes sense to follow Zuo's official report here.
214. Michael, *Taiping Rebellion*, 1:181.
215. *ZZQJ*, 2:322.
216. See *PZJL*, 472–79, for casualty figures and summaries of the mop-up operations.

217. Sheng, *Taiping tianguo*, 583.
218. *ZZQJ*, 13:96–100; *ZZQJ*, 2:323–25. On Bao Chao's exploits, see *QSG*, 3074–75.
219. *ZZQJ*, 2:326. A summary of these battles and a list of rewards and promotions can be found in *ZZQJ*, 2:326–34.
220. On Tang's execution and career, see *ZZQJ*, 3:15–16. Also see Yang Dongliang, *Zuo Zongtang*, 54; and Sheng, *Taiping tianguo*, 581–82.
221. See *ZZQJ*, 2:334–35.
222. For very detailed reports on the successes, promotions, and rewards for the military units and soldiers present at Zhenping and Jiaying, see *ZZQJ*, 3:178–222.
223. See Zuo's victory report to the Zongli Yamen in *ZZQJ*, 10:650–52.
224. *NCH*, 765 (March 25, 1865).
225. Anne Reinhardt, *Navigating Semi-Colonialism: Shipping, Sovereignty, and Nation-Building in China, 1860–1937* (Cambridge, MA: Harvard University Press, 2018), 44–45.
226. See *ZZQJ*, 3:5–8.
227. *ZZQJ*, 3:8.
228. *ZZQJ*, 3:13–14.
229. *PZJL*, 483–84.
230. *PZJL*, 487–92.
231. *PZJL*, 495.
232. See the reports in *ZZQJ*, 3:22–43.
233. *ZZQJ*, 3:38.
234. *ZZQJ*, 3:43; *QSG*, 262.
235. See *PZJL*, 592–93.
236. Cheng, *Chinese Sources*, 115.
237. For a recent analysis of the importance of steamships and navigation as a means of interrogating China's experience of imperialism, see Reinhardt, *Navigating Semi-Colonialism*.
238. Halsey, *Quest for Power*, 211.
239. Stephen Halsey, "Sovereignty, Self-Strengthening and Steamships in Late Imperial China," *Journal of Asian History* 48.1 (2014), 88.
240. *ZZQJ*, 10:553.
241. *ZZQJ*, 3:52.
242. See Yang Dongliang, *Zuo Zongtang*, 56–58; and *ZZQJ*, 10:553–57.
243. *ZZQJ*, 3:53.
244. *QSG*, 255–56.

245. *ZNP*, 602; *ZZQJ*, 10:652. Li Hongzhang made the same point about needing machines to make machines in a memorandum to the throne concerning revision of the examination system. See *CHC*, 10.1:499.
246. On why Fuzhou was selected with French input, see Ch'en, *Tso Tsung-t'ang: Pioneer Promoter*, 22–23.
247. Yang Dongliang, *Zuo Zongtang*, 59.
248. *ZNP*, 602.
249. See *ZNP*, 602–3; and *ZZQJ*, 3:52–57. Zuo's letter to the Zongli Yamen outlining his plans can be found in *ZZQJ*, 10:658–60. Also see Ch'en, *Tso Tsung-t'ang: Pioneer Promoter*, 26.
250. *ZZQJ*, 3:55–56.
251. *ZNP*, 603; *ZZQJ*, 3:56.
252. For a biography of Zhang, see *ECQP*, 893–97. On Zhang's positions regarding China's modernization, see Adam Chang, "Reappraising Zhang Zhidong: Forgotten Continuities during China's Self-Strengthening, 1881–1901," *Journal of Chinese Military History* 6.2 (2017), 157–92. On the *"ti-yong* paradigm," see Kennedy, *Arms of Kiangnan*, 29–33.
253. Sun, *Zuo Zongtang zhuan*, 85.
254. See Day, "Searching for the Roots of Western Wealth and Power," 30.
255. *ZZQJ*, 10:666–68.
256. Yang Dongliang, *Zuo Zongtang*, 59–60.
257. *ZZQJ*, 3:59–60.
258. *ZZQJ*, 3:56.
259. See the discussion in *CHC*, 10.1:525–29. On networks, also see Halsey, *Quest for Power*, 72.
260. See *ZZQJ*, 3:61–62.
261. On Shen's appointment, see *ZZQJ*, 3:138–40. Also see Yang Dongliang, *Zuo Zongtang*, 60–61.
262. *ZZQJ*, 3:113. For his reports and directives, see *ZZQJ*, 3:109–20.
263. See the cost estimates in *ZZQJ*, 3:298–300.
264. *ZZQJ*, 3:175–77.
265. *ZZQJ*, 10:655.
266. *ZZQJ*, 10:481.
267. Yang Dongliang, *Zuo Zongtang*, 70.
268. Rawlinson, *China's Struggle for Naval Development*, 57–59.
269. Chen, *Tso Tsung-t'ang*, 33; Rawlinson, *China's Struggle for Naval Development*, 46.
270. Rawlinson, *China's Struggle for Naval Development*, 48.

271. *ZZQJ*, 10:660–61.
272. *NCH*, 129 (December 29, 1869).
273. *NCH*, 129 (December 29, 1869).
274. See the table in Yang Dongliang, *Zuo Zongtang*, 63–66.
275. Yang Dongliang, 68–69.
276. *ZZQJ*, 11:386.
277. See *ZZQJ*, 11:404–5.
278. See *ZZQJ*, 11:372–75 and 406–10.
279. *ZZQJ*, 11:430–38.
280. Rawlinson, *China's Struggle for Naval Development*, 56.
281. Rawlinson, 98–99.
282. David Pong, "Keeping the Foochow Navy Yard Afloat: Government Finance and China's Early Modern Defense Industry," *Modern Asian Studies* 21.1 (1987), 128.
283. Rawlinson, *China's Struggle for Naval Development*, 103.
284. For a biography of Wang, see *ECQP*, 638–41.
285. Lin Qiyan, "Wang Tao de haifang sixiang," *Jindaishi yanjiu* 2 (1999), 137.
286. See Halsey, *Quest for Power*, 156–57. Ding was a native of Guangdong who also served as *daotai* in Shanghai. For his biography, see *ECQP*, 104–5.
287. Elleman, *Modern Chinese Navy*, 58.
288. On Li's stance toward the navy, see Kennedy, *Arms of Kiangnan*, 77–86.
289. Halsey, *Quest for Power*, 174.
290. *NCH*, 794 (October 14, 1865).
291. For example, see Smith, "Reflections," 14–15.
292. See the overview in Ricard S. Horowitz, "Beyond the Marble Boat: The Transformation of the Chinese Military, 1850–1911," in Graff and Higham, eds., *Military History of China*, 153–74.
293. Halsey, "Warfare, Imperialism and the Making of Modern China,"62.
294. These arguments are summarized in Benjamin Elman, "Naval Warfare and the Refraction of China's Self-Strengthening Reforms into Scientific and Technological Failure, 1865–1895," *Modern Asian Studies* 38.2 (1996), 283–326; and Halsey, "Warfare Imperialism and the Making of Modern China," 47–72.
295. Chen, *Tso Tsung-t'ang*, iii.
296. Halsey, *Quest for Power*, 5.
297. Yang Dongliang, *Zuo Zongtang*, 66–67.
298. See Chang, "Reappraising Zhang Zhidong," 163–64. For an older, much more negative appraisal of Qing efforts in this arena, see Richard Smith, "The Reform

of Military Education in Late Ch'ing China," *Journal of the Royal Asiatic Society Hong Kong Branch* 18 (1978), 15–40.

299. On the Tianjin Academy, see Smith, "Reform of Military Education," 24–25.

300. Elleman, *Modern Chinese Navy*, 56.

301. Chang, "Reappraising Zhang Zhidong," 180–81.

302. On the criticism, see Smith, "Reform of Military Education," 21.

303. Halsey, *Quest for Power*, 82.

304. Halsey, "Sovereignty, Self-Strengthening, and Steamships," 111.

305. Elleman, *Modern Chinese Warfare*, 58.

CHAPTER 4. CORALLING THE NIAN

1. For recent studies of the late Ming wandering bandits in English, see Swope, *Military Collapse*; and Swope, *On the Trail of the Yellow Tiger*.

2. See *NJWX*, 1:1.

3. See Elizabeth J. Perry, *Rebels and Revolutionaries in North China, 1845–1945* (Stanford: Stanford University Press, 1980), 3–5, for her definitions of these survival strategies.

4. Perry, *Rebels and Revolutionaries*, 96.

5. Perry, 51.

6. Perry, 18–27.

7. Perry, 96. On the environmental backdrop to the Nian Rebellion, also see *CHC*, 10.1:312–13; and Elizabeth J. Perry, *Chinese Perspectives on the Nien Rebellion* (London: Routledge, 1981), 25–32.

8. Chiang Siang-tseh, *The Nien Rebellion* (Seattle: University of Washington Press, 1954), v–vi; also see *CHC*, 10.1:459.

9. Perry, *Rebels and Revolutionaries*, 96.

10. *NJWX*, 1:13.

11. Perry, *Chinese Perspectives on the Nien*, 34.

12. Knorr, "Fragile Bulwark," 52.

13. Perry, *Chinese Perspectives on the Nien*, 40–42.

14. Chiang, *Nien Rebellion*, 7. On the different theories concerning the proper meaning of *"nian,"* see Perry, *Chinese Perspectives on the Nien*, 76–77; and S. Y. Teng, *The Nien Army and Their Guerrilla Warfare, 1851–1868* (Paris and London: Mouton, 1961), 17–20.

15. Perry, *Chinese Perspectives on the Nien*, 77 and 88–93.

16. On these activities, see Perry, *Rebels and Revolutionaries*, 100–113; Perry, *Chinese Perspectives on the Nien*, 23–54; and Teng, *Nien Army*, 47–55.

17. Perry, *Rebels and Revolutionaries*, 111–12. On the heavy Muslim presence in the region, which is unchanged today, see Teng, *Nien Army*, 42–44.

18. Perry, *Chinese Perspectives on the Nien*, 37; and Perry, *Rebels and Revolutionaries*, 106.

19. See Teng, *Nien Army*, 90–98.

20. *QSG*, 249.

21. *CHC*, 10.1:457; and Teng, *Nien Army*, 69–70. For the classic study of the "social bandit," see Eric Hobsbawm, *Bandits* (New York: New Press, 2000). On the social bandit tradition in this region of China, see Perry, *Rebels and Revolutionaries*, 64.

22. Chiang, *Nien Rebellion*, 18–19.

23. Chiang, 5.

24. Chiang, 32; *CHC*, 10.1:459.

25. Teng, *Nien Army*, 172.

26. Chiang, *Nien Rebellion*, 33.

27. Teng, *Nien Army*, 76–79.

28. See Chiang, *Nien Rebellion*, 25–28, for details on the banners and their leaders.

29. On the significance of the banners for Nian identity and organization, see Teng, *Nien Army*, 80–82.

30. *NJWX*, 1:13.

31. Perry, *Rebels and Revolutionaries*, 127.

32. *QSG*, 254.

33. See Chiang, *Nien Rebellion*, 38–42.

34. Chiang, 45–54.

35. *CHC*, 10.1:463.

36. Chiang, *Nien Rebellion*, 62–65; *NJWX*, 1:13.

37. *QSG*, 260; *ECQP*, 522–23.

38. See *CHC*, 10.1:461–62, where K. C. Liu calls Miao Peilin "Modern China's first warlord." Also see Teng, *Nien Army*, 102–6. On his execution by Senggelinqin, see *QSG*, 257 and 3052.

39. For Yuan Jiasan's biography, see *ECQP*, 823–24. He was the grandfather of the late Qing general and future president of the Republic Yuan Shikai (1859–1916). Yuan Jiasan's son, Yuan Baoheng, served under Zuo Zongtang for six years in the northwest as a logistics officer.

40. See *NJWX*, 1:2. Shengbao was among those who impeached Yuan Jiasan.

41. On Miao Peilin's reversion to banditry, see *QSG*, 251. On Nian leaders submitting to the Qing, see *QSG*, 246–47.

42. *QSG*, 3048.

43. On criticism of Shengbao, see *QSG*, 247; and Teng, *Nien Army*, 204.
44. *QSG*, 3048.
45. *QSG*, 256; 3052; Teng, *Nien Army*, 141.
46. *NJWX*, 1:3.
47. *NJWX*, 1:14; *QSG*, 3052–53.
48. See Chiang, *Nien Rebellion*, 81–84.
49. *QSG*, 3232; Bales, *Tso Tsung-t'ang*, 332–34.
50. *NJWX*, 1:4.
51. *NJWX*, 1:5 and 14; *QSG*, 3053.
52. *QSG*, 3053. On the significance of this last honor in the Qing period, see Waley-Cohen, *Culture of War*, 42–44.
53. Chiang, *Nien Rebellion*, 86–88.
54. On Zeng's appointment, see *NJWX*, 1:13; and *QSG*, 263.
55. Teng, *Nien Army*, 176.
56. *ZZQJ*, 11:98–99.
57. See *NJWX*, 1:17–18.
58. Chiang, *Nien Rebellion*, 100–102; *CHC*, 10.1:470–71.
59. *NJWX*, 1:19.
60. *NJWX*, 1:20.
61. Chiang, *Nien Rebellion*, 136.
62. See Teng, *Nien Army*, 143–48.
63. Chiang, *Nien Rebellion*, 107; Teng, *Nien Army*, 147–50.
64. *NJWX*, 1:6 and 24.
65. *NJWX*, 1:25. Nanyang was repeatedly attacked by both the Nian and the Taipings due to its strategic location on the Bai River in southern Henan. On some of these campaigns, see Xun Liu, "In Defense of the City and the Polity: The Xuanmiao Monastery and the Late Qing Anti-Taiping Campaigns in Late Nineteenth-Century Nanyang," *T'oung Pao* 94.4–5 (2009), 287–333.
66. See *NJWX*, 1:27–30.
67. Hail, *Tseng Kuo-fan*, 300–301; Teng, *Nien Army*, 157.
68. Chiang, *Nien Rebellion*, 122.
69. See *CHC*, 10.1: 470.
70. *ZZQJ*, 11:126–27.
71. *ZZQJ*, 3:120–21.
72. *QSG*, 3110.
73. *ZZQJ*, 3:310–11; Yang Dongliang, *Zuo Zongtang*, 78.
74. *QSG*, 3085; and *SGXF*, 13:7381–84. Also see *ZWZX*, 89.

75. *ZWZX*, 48–49.
76. Yang Dongliang, *Zuo Zongtang*, 77; *ZNP*, 612. For an overview of the classic Confucian pacification strategies that were employed by Yang as utilized in the Ming, see Swope, "Of Bureaucrats and Bandits," 123–54
77. Yang Dongliang, *Zuo Zongtang*, 79–80. Xi'an had also been besieged in 1862, and Shengbao had gone to the rescue. See *QSG*, 254–55.
78. *NJWX*, 1:8.
79. *ZZQJ*, 11:101.
80. *ZZQJ*, 11:101–4.
81. Yang Dongliang, *Zuo Zongtang*, 78–79.
82. See *ZNP*, 605; and Chu, *Moslem Rebellion*, 91–92.
83. *ZNP*, 610. For the full battle array, see Yang Dongliang, *Zuo Zongtang*, 80.
84. *ZZQJ*, 11:25.
85. *ZZQJ*, 11:30.
86. See *ZZQJ*, 3:57–58, 13, 105; and *ZNP*, 605.
87. *QSG*, 3085; *ZZQJ*, 11:13; and *ZZQJ*, 14:52–53.
88. See Fan, *Qi Jiguang zhuan*, 212–98. On Qi's actual formulation of these plans, see Qi Jiguang, *Jixiao xinshu*.
89. *ZZQJ*, 3:58; *ZZQJ*, 13:106–8.
90. *ZWZX*, 50.
91. *ZZQJ*, 11:37–38.
92. *ZZQJ*, 11:23–24.
93. *ZZQJ*, 13:117.
94. *ZZQJ*, 14:81–82.
95. *SGXF*, 13:7389–92.
96. *SGXF*, 13:7387–88.
97. Yang Dongliang, *Zuo Zongtang*, 79.
98. *ZZQJ*, 11:7–8.
99. *ZNP*, 611.
100. *ZZQJ*, 11:1.
101. Bales, *Tso Tsung-t'ang*, 199–200.
102. Yang Dongliang, *Zuo Zongtang*, 79.
103. *ZZQJ*, 3:329–30; and *ZZQJ*, 11:16–17.
104. *ZWZX*, 53–54.
105. *ZNP*, 611.
106. *ZZQJ*, 3:271–72.
107. *ZWZX*, 55–56.

108. *ZZQJ*, 3:266–71.
109. *ZWZX*, 32–33.
110. *ZNP*, 611. On the Sun Chuanting debacle, see Swope, *Military Collapse*, 184–87.
111. See *ZWZX*, 35; and Bales, *Tso Tsung-t'ang*, 200–202.
112. Chu, *Moslem Rebellion*, 94; *ZWZX*, 49.
113. *ZZQJ*, 11:17–21.
114. *ZWZX*, 62.
115. See *ZNP*, 612–14.
116. *ZNP*, 616; *ZZQJ*, 13:108.
117. *ZNP*, 617; *ZWZX*, 53.
118. *ZZQJ*, 3:326.
119. *ZZQJ*, 14:54–56. Also see *ZZQJ*, 3:315–25, which includes discussions of the rebels' attack on Xi'an.
120. See Chu, *Moslem Rebellion*, 103–5; and *ZWZX*, 51–52, for estimates of troop numbers.
121. *ZZQJ*, 14:50.
122. *ZZQJ*, 14:51–52.
123. *ZZQJ*, 14:59–63.
124. *ZZQJ*, 3:341–42.
125. *NJWX*, 1:34.
126. *ZZQJ*, 14:76–77.
127. *ZZQJ*, 14:92–94.
128. *ZZQJ*, 3:344–49.
129. See *NJWX*, 1:37–43.
130. *NJWX*, 1:35.
131. *NJWX*, 1:44–45.
132. *NJWX*, 1:32.
133. *NJWX*, 1:52.
134. *NJWX*, 1:54.
135. *NJWX*, 1:8–9 and 52–53.
136. *NJWX*, 1:56–57.
137. See *NJWX*, 1:57–59.
138. *QSG*, 261.
139. *NJWX*, 1:59–65.
140. *QSG*, 263.
141. *ZZQJ*, 11:43–44; Yang Dongliang, *Zuo Zongtang*, 81.
142. *ZZQJ*, 3:367–69.

143. See *ZZQJ*, 3:374–77.
144. *ZZQJ*, 3:371.
145. *ZZQJ*, 3:371–72.
146. Cited in *ZZQJ*, 13:109.
147. See *ZZQJ*, 3:498–505.
148. *ZZQJ*, 11:51–54.
149. *ZZQJ*, 3:379.
150. *ZWZX*, 66.
151. *QSG*, 3085.
152. On Zuo's deployments and court approval, see *ZZQJ*, 3:379–82; and Yang Dongliang, *Zuo Zongtang*, 82.
153. *NJWX*, 1:69. Suide had previously been captured by Zhang Zongyu. See *QSG*, 264.
154. *ZNP*, 618–19.
155. *ZNP*, 619.
156. *ZZQJ*, 3:411–31.
157. *ZZQJ*, 3:506–19.
158. *ZZQJ*, 3:520.
159. See *ZZQJ*, 3:387–95.
160. *ZZQJ*, 3:401–6.
161. *ZZQJ*, 3:446–47.
162. On these engagements at the end of 1867, see *ZZQJ*, 3:463–75.
163. *ZZQJ*, 3:484–91.
164. See Sun, *Zuo Zongtang zhuan*, 91–93, on these battles.
165. *QSG*, 3085.
166. *NJWX*, 1:10; *ZZQJ*, 14:98–99.
167. *QSG*, 3085.
168. *ZZQJ*, 14:99.
169. *ZZQJ*, 3:523–26.
170. *ZNP*, 620.
171. *ZZQJ*, 3:524.
172. *ZZQJ*, 14:100–106.
173. *QSG*, 3085–86; *NJWX*, 1:69.
174. *ZZQJ*, 3:527–28.
175. See *ZZQJ*, 14:111–18.
176. See *NJWX*, 1:8–10; 67; *QSG*, 264; and Yang Dongliang, *Zuo Zongtang*, 83.
177. *ZZQJ*, 14:126–30.

178. *QSG*, 264.

179. See *ZZQJ*, 3:533–39; *ZNP*, 620; and *NJWX*, 1:69–70.

180. Yang Dongliang, *Zuo Zongtang*, 85.

181. *ZNP*, 621.

182. *ZZQJ*, 3:574–76; Sun, *Zuo Zongtang zhuan*, 94.

183. For Zuo's reports on these battles, see *ZZQJ*, 3:540–57.

184. *ZZQJ*, 3:561–64.

185. *ZNP*, 622. On the reconstruction of the batteries, see *QSG*, 246.

186. Yang Dongliang, *Zuo Zongtang*, 85–86.

187. *ZZQJ*, 3:557–58.

188. *NJWX*, 1:11; 74–75; also see *QSG*, 265. On the rejection of an earlier recommendation to appoint Prince Huitong to such a post, see *NJWX*, 1:70–71.

189. Yang Dongliang, *Zuo Zongtang*, 85–86.

190. Yang Dongliang, 86; Teng, *Nien Army*, 152.

191. *ZZQJ*, 3:566–69.

192. Sun, *Zuo Zongtang zhuan*, 95.

193. *QSG*, 265.

194. Teng, *Nien Army*, 200.

195. *NJWX*, 1:71.

196. *ZZQJ*, 3:581–84 and 595–96. For a biography of Chen, see *ECQP*, 45–46.

197. *NJWX*, 1:72.

198. On Guo's earlier defeat, see Liao, *Xiangjun zhengzhan shi*, 197.

199. *NJWX*, 1:72–73.

200. *ZZQJ*, 3:587–90.

201. Zuo had reassigned Zhang Yao from the northwest to Shandong because he was deemed ill-suited for combat leadership, but after this experience Zuo came to trust him more, and he proved a valuable asset in subsequent operations against the Muslim rebels. See *ZWZX*, 53.

202. *NJWX*, 1:74.

203. *QSG*, 265.

204. *ZZQJ*, 3:605–10.

205. See *ZZQJ*, 3:619–41.

206. *NJWX*, 1:76.

207. *NJWX*, 1:76–77.

208. *NJWX*, 1:77–78.

209. *NJWX*, 1:78; Yang Dongliang, *Zuo Zongtang*, 87.

210. For more details on the defeat of Zhang Zongyu, see *ZZQJ*, 3:650–56.

211. *NJWX*, 1:78.
212. *ZZQJ*, 3:656–57.
213. *ZZQJ*, 3:659–61.
214. *ZNP*, 624.
215. See *ZZQJ*, 3:661–65, for routes of advance and details on troop organization.

CHAPTER 5. "THERE ARE ONLY GOOD AND BAD PEOPLE"

1. *ZNP*, 4:48–49; Bales, *Tso Tsung-t'ang*, 209.
2. *ZWZX*, 28.
3. *ZWZX*, 28.
4. *ZWZX*, 35. On the backdrop to subsidizing the northwestern provinces, see *HMYD*, 107–15.
5. *HMYD*, 110.
6. *HMYD*, 145.
7. *ZNP*, 4:49–50; Bales, *Tso Tsung-t'ang*, 211.
8. For details, see *HMYD*, 115–18.
9. For an overview of Islam in China prior to the Qing, see *HMYD*, 1–59.
10. *ZWZX*, 22.
11. On the Old versus New Teachings differences and rivalry, see Jonathan Lipman, *Familiar Strangers: A History of Muslims in Northwest China* (Seattle: University of Washington Press, 1997), 103–5; David Atwill, *The Chinese Sultanate: Islam, Ethnicity and the Panthay Rebellion in Southwest China, 1856–1873* (Stanford: Stanford University Press, 2005), 131–33; and Theaker, "Moving Muslims," 10–11. On various Sufi lineages in Central Asia, see Theaker, 31–53.
12. On Ma Mingxin's background and travels, see *HMYD*, 229–33.
13. On the interrelationship between Muslim religious and commercial networks, see *ZWZX*, 21–22.
14. Fields, *Tso and the Muslims*, 65. Also see Hodong Kim, *Holy War in China: The Muslim Rebellion and State in Chinese Central Asia, 1864–1877* (Stanford: Stanford University Press, 2004), 159–60, on the various Sufi sects operating in the region.
15. Fields, "Campaigns in the Northwest," 103–4.
16. Fields, *Tso and the Muslims*, 70. On the ties to Du Wenxiu and the Yunnan rebellion, see *HMYD*, 189.
17. On corrupt Qing governance in Central Asia, see *ZWZX*, 24–25.
18. *ZWZX*, 5; *HMYD*, 155–56.
19. *ZWZX*, 6.
20. See *SXHMQY*, 1–2.

21. See Atwill, *Chinese Sultanate*, 6. For various definitions and designations of Hui, see Theaker, "Moving Muslims," 8–12. On the background in northwest China, also see *ZWZX*, 21–24.
22. *SXHMQY*, 3.
23. Atwill, *Chinese Sultanate*, 7. On the portrayal of Muslims in general as being violent in Chinese historiography, see Lipman, *Familiar Strangers*, xxx.
24. Yang Dongliang, *Zuo Zongtang*, 89.
25. Yang Dongliang, 89.
26. Atwill, *Chinese Sultanate*, 10.
27. See *SGXF*, 2:727–31; *SXHMQY*, 77–84; 91–99; and Bales, *Tso Tsung-t'ang*, 221–22. Other accounts maintain the Muslims were angry over price gouging by the Han. See Teng, *Taiping Rebellion and Western Powers*, 377. For additional references to Han provocations of the Hui, see Eric Setzekorn, "Qing Dynasty Warfare and Military Authority: Discipline and the Ethnic Cleansing of 1860s Shaanxi," *Journal of Chinese Military History* 7.2 (2018), 189. Also see *SXHMQY*, 17–31 and 68, which takes a Maoist approach to analyzing the "contradictions" that arose between the Han and Hui.
28. See *SGXF*, 2:655; *CHC*, 11:216–17.
29. *SGXF*, 2:667; Chu, *Moslem Rebellion*, 25. On the early clashes between the Han and Hui, see *SXHMQY*, 91–94; and *HMYD*, 168–74.
30. *HMYD*, 175.
31. *SXHMQY*, 85–86; also see Lipman, *Familiar Strangers*, 118–20.
32. *HMYD*, 175. Zuo tended to place the blame more on the Hui than on the Han. On Zuo's desire to improve local administration, see *ZZQJ*, 14:151–52.
33. *SXHMQY*, 36–57.
34. *SXHMQY*, 321.
35. *SXHMQY*, 322.
36. *SGXF*, 2:657–60; *HMYD*, 205–8.
37. *SGXF*, 2:682–83; *SXHMQY*, 82–85. On the scale of militarization in Shaanxi, see *SXHMQY*, 329–31; and *HMYD*, 167–68.
38. Lei Duan, "Between Social Control and Popular Power: The Circulation of Private Guns and Control Policies during the Mid to Late Qing, 1781–1911," *American Journal of Chinese Studies* 24.2 (October 2017), 122.
39. Duan, "Between Social Control and Popular Power," 123. On the role of firearms contributing to violence in Shaanxi as aided and abetted by Qing officials, see *SXHMQY*, 333–45.
40. *SGXF*, 2:708–10.

41. *SGXF*, 2:752–55.
42. On the rationale for the suasion policy, see *ZWZX*, 27–28.
43. *SGXF*, 2:764–65.
44. *SGXF*, 2:775.
45. *SGXF*, 2:795–97.
46. Military details of these campaigns are amply covered in *SGXF*, volumes 2–4.
47. *SGXF*, 2:1110–14.
48. *SGXF*, 2:1134.
49. *SGXF*, 4:1792–809.
50. *SGXF*, 5:2663–65.
51. *CHC*, 11.1:219.
52. *SGXF*, 5:2691.
53. *SGXF*, 5:2700–12.
54. *SGXF*, 5:2740–50.
55. *SGXF*, 6:2851–66.
56. *SGXF*, 6:2887–91.
57. See the discussion in *SGXF*, 6:3290–96.
58. On these issues, see *SGXF*, 6:2927–46.
59. *QSG*, 260; *SGXF*, 9:4651–78.
60. *HMYD*, 215.
61. Chu, *Moslem Rebellion*, 76–77.
62. *SGXF*, 9:5111–12.
63. See the reports in *SGXF*, 9:5118–48. The Qing claimed two thousand rebels killed in a series of summer battles around Ningxia.
64. *SGXF*, 9:5200–14.
65. *SGXF*, 9:5250–54.
66. *SGXF*, 9:5219–25.
67. *SGXF*, 9:5227–32.
68. *SGXF*, 10:5514–16.
69. *SGXF*, 10:5590–95.
70. *HMYD*, 106.
71. *SGXF*, 10:5781.
72. On fundraising efforts, see *SGXF*, 10:5664–88; also see *SGXF*, 10:5696–722. On the process of setting up collection bureaus in other provinces, which included raising funds by the sale of offices, see Elizabeth Kaske, "Total War: Military Supplies and Civilian Resources during China's Era of Rebellions," in *Chinese and Indian Warfare—From the Classical Age to 1870*, ed. Peter Lorge and

Kaushik Roy, 257–88 (London: Routledge, 2015). Sales of offices are also discussed in *SGXF*, 11:5893–94.

73. *SGXF*, 11:5986–95.
74. *SGXF*, 10:5802–11.
75. Chu, *Moslem Rebellion*, 62–63.
76. *SGXF*, 11:6217–20.
77. *SGXF*, 11:6404–6; *HMYD*, 237.
78. *SGXF*, 11:6224–39.
79. *SGXF*, 11:6424.
80. Yang Dongliang, *Zuo Zongtang*, 91.
81. *CHC*, 11.1:219; Elleman, *Modern Chinese Warfare*, 66.
82. *PHZ*, 4:1b–2a.
83. See assorted reports in *SGXF*, 12:6522–605.
84. *HMYD*, 217. On the mutiny, see *PHZ*, 3:25b–26a.
85. Chu, *Moslem Rebellion*, 82.
86. *SGXF*, 13:7207.
87. *SGXF*, 13:7118–31.
88. *SGXF*, 13:7230–33.
89. *SGXF*, 13:7585–96.
90. *SGXF*, 13:7262.
91. *SGXF*, 13:7262.
92. *ZNP*, 626.
93. *ZNP*, 626.
94. *SGXF*, 13:7262–63.
95. *SGXF*, 13:7271–76. On the reaction at court to Zuo's plan, see *SGXF*, 13:7279–87 and 13:7379–81.
96. *SGXF*, 13:7283–84.
97. *SGXF*, 13:7307.
98. *SGXF*, 14:7679–82.
99. *SGXF*, 14:7713.
100. *SGXF*, 14:7714–17.
101. *SGXF*, 14:7699–701.
102. *SGXF*, 14:7724–38.
103. *SGXF*, 14:7749–52.
104. *SGXF*, 14:7743–48.
105. *SGXF*, 15:8266–68.
106. See *SGXF*, 15:8378–428.

107. *SGXF*, 15:8472–80 and 8540–42.

108. *SGXF*, 15:8578.

109. *SGXF*, 15:8615–20 and 8629–32.

110. *SGXF*, 15:8649–62.

111. For one of Zuo's requests, see *ZZQJ*, 4:26–28. Also see *ZZQJ*, 3:676–79; and *SGXF*, 16:9020–21, on supply costs and projections.

112. *ZZQJ*, 3:689–90. On the debates, see *NCH*, 204 (March 29, 1871).

113. *ZNP*, 627–29; *CHC*, 11:230. On the mutiny at Suide, see *SGXF*, 16:9377–79 and 16:9387–91.

114. *ZZQJ*, 3:671.

115. *ZZQJ*, 3:686–87; *SGXF*, 16:8958–60.

116. *ZWZX*, 36.

117. Fields, *Tso and the Muslims*, 80–81.

118. *ZZQJ*, 14:134.

119. Cited in Raphael Israeli, "The Muslims under the Manchu Reign in China," *Studia Islamica* 49 (1979), 163–64.

120. *ZZQJ*, 13:124–25.

121. On the articulation and implementation of "benevolent assimilation" in the Philippines, see Brain McCallister Linn, *The Philippine War, 1899–1902* (Lawrence: University Press of Kansas, 2000), 30–32 and 200–206.

122. *ZWZX*, 38.

123. *HMYD*, 93.

124. *HMYD*, 95.

125. *HMYD*, 94.

126. See Yang Dongliang, *Zuo Zongtang*, 90, for details of postings and duty assignments.

127. *ZWZX*, 41–42. On pay rates, also see *SGXF*, 16:9346–47.

128. See Cai Shaoqing, "On the Origins of the Gelaohui," *Modern China* 10.4 (October 1984), 495–96, on Zuo's prohibition against joining this organization.

129. *ZWZX*, 43.

130. See *ZZQJ*, 5:207; Yang Dongliang, *Zuo Zongtang*, 103; and *PHZ*, preface, 2a–3a.

131. *ZWZX*, 46.

132. *ZWZX*, 45.

133. See *ZZQJ*, 3:691–98; *ZZQJ*, 11:139–43; *SGXF*, 16:9113; and *ZWZX*, 67.

134. Bales, *Tso Tsung-t'ang*, 234; Sun, *Zuo Zongtang zhuan*, 98.

135. *SGXF*, 16:9135–40.

136. *ZZQJ*, 3:712–21.

137. *ZZQJ*, 4:1–7; *ZZQJ*, 14:146–47. On these battles, also see *SGXF*, 16:9266–84.

138. *ZZQJ*, 4:6–13.
139. *SGXF*, 16:9171.
140. *NCH*, 94 (February 6, 1869).
141. *PHZ*, 2:25b–27a; *SGXF*, 16:9164–71.
142. See *QSG*, 266; Sun, *Zuo Zongtang zhuan*, 99–100; and *ZZQJ*, 4:52–54. Some sources place the death toll at 127.
143. *ZZQJ*, 4:54–60. Also see Liu Songshan's report, in *ZZQJ*, 4:68–71. On Gao's death, see *SGXF*, 16:9415–18.
144. *QSG*, 12,029; *HMYD*, 258–63.
145. On efforts to eliminate Gelaohui influence in the ranks, see *SGXF*, 16:9418–24.
146. *ZZQJ*, 14:160.
147. See *ZWZX*, 75–76; *ZZQJ*, 14:161; and *CHC*, 11:230. Zuo apparently believed that the Gelaohui evolved from older groups, most notably the Guludang, or Guluhui. See Cai Shaoqing, "On the Origin of the Gelaohui," 485. Di Wang, "Mysterious Communication: The Secret Language of the Gowned Brotherhood in Nineteenth-Century Sichuan," *Late Imperial China* 29.1 (June 2008), 80, contends that as many as 70 percent of the men in Sichuan were still affiliated with the organization in the 1940s. It is unclear if these are the same Gelaohui uprisings reported by the *North China Herald* noted above, but it seems likely. On Zuo's general concerns regarding Gelaohui infiltration, see *ZZQJ*, 13:124; and *ZZQJ*, 11:133–35.
148. *ZZQJ*, 4:38–43 and 87–90.
149. *ZZQJ*, 4:13–28.
150. Chu, *Moslem Rebellion*, 133–34; Sun, *Zuo Zongtang zhuan*, 101. See Zuo's detailed reports and the court's issuance of rewards from the battle in *SGXF*, 16:9479–96.
151. *ZNP*, 631; *SGXF*, 16:9487–88. The expression that there was "no smoke from cooking fires" is part of the rhetoric of catastrophe in China and refers to the absence of homes and families. On these tropes, see Swope, *On the Trail of the Yellow Tiger*, 291–312.
152. *ZNP*, 632.
153. *QSG*, 3234; *PHZ*, 2:29a.
154. *SGXF*, 16:9364–65.
155. Sun, *Zuo Zongtang zhuan*, 102. For Zuo's detailed plan, see *SGXF*, 17:9700–705.
156. On the strategic importance of Jinjibao for the Qing, see *HMYD*, 255–62.
157. *SGXF*, 16:9533.
158. *ZZQJ*, 4:357–58; *SGXF*, 17:9603–15.

159. *ZWZX*, 77.

160. *ZZQJ*, 4:358–59.

161. *ZWZX*, 78.

162. *ZZQJ*, 11:175–77. On Zuo's concerns about Ma Hualong/Chaoqing, see *SGXF*, 16:9403–7.

163. Cited in Schluessel, *Land of Strangers*, 45.

164. *ZZQJ*, 4:359–60.

165. *ZWZX*, 78.

166. See *NCH*, 109 (May 29, 1869). For one of Zuo's victory reports, see *ZZQJ*, 4:11–14.

167. *NCH*, 112 (June 17, 1869).

168. *ZZQJ*, 4:127–29.

169. *ZZQJ*, 4:131–41.

170. Chu, *Moslem Rebellion*, 137–40.

171. *ZNP*, 634.

172. See *ZNP*, 634; *ZZQJ*, 4:142–47; and Yang Dongliang, *Zuo Zongtang*, 93. On Mutushan's defense of Ma Hualong, see Bales, *Tso Tsung-t'ang*, 241; and Sun, *Zuo Zongtang zhuan*, 104. Some modern scholars also credit Ma Hualong with keeping the peace and inducing others to submit. See *HMYD*, 263.

173. *ZNP*, 634; Yang Dongliang, *Zuo Zongtang*, 92.

174. For Zuo's discussions with Liu and Mutushan, see *ZZQJ*, 11:149–54.

175. *ZZQJ*, 14:576.

176. *ZZQJ*, 14:579.

177. *CHC*, 11:226; *HMYD*, 243–55.

178. *ZNP*, 634.

179. *HMYD*, 222–23; Li Lianli, *Zuo Zongtang pingzhuan*, 62–63; and Fields, *Tso Tsung-t'ang and the Muslims*, 81.

180. *SGXF*, 18:9933–39.

181. *ZNP*, 637; Yang Dongliang, *Zuo Zongtang*, 92–93.

182. *ZNP*, 638; and *ZZQJ*, 14:173–74.

183. *SGXF*, 18:9997–10004.

184. *QSG*, 266. On the accusations that Liu's troops killed all Muslims indiscriminately, thereby causing some previously loyal Muslims to join the rebels, see *HMYD*, 264; and *SGXF*, 18:9840–46. See the official inquiry in *SGXF*, 18:9851–52. Some sources claim this rumor was circulated by Ma Hualong. See *PHZ*, 4:25a.

185. *SGXF*, 18:10127–36; *PHZ*, 4:23b–24b.

186. *ZZQJ*, 11:168.

187. *ZNP*, 640–41.
188. *ZZQJ*, 4:160–66.
189. For a description of the defenses around Jinjibao, see Sun, *Zuo Zongtang zhuan*, 103.
190. See *CHC*, 11:229–30; *HMYD*, 267–68; and Yang Dongliang, *Zuo Zongtang*, 93.
191. *ZZQJ*, 14:191.
192. On these battles, see *ZNP*, 641–42; *SGXF*, 18:10063–72; and Sun, *Zuo Zongtang zhuan*, 103.
193. *ZZQJ*, 4:172.
194. *ZZQJ*, 4:172–73.
195. *ZZQJ*, 4:194.
196. Sun, *Zuo Zongtang zhuan*, 106.
197. *ZNP*, 643.
198. Sun, *Zuo Zongtang zhuan*, 106–7.
199. *ZZQJ*, 4:195; see 195–99 for more battle details.
200. Zuo's report on the progress of Liu Songshan can be found in *SGXF*, 18:10211–22.
201. *SGXF*, 18:10233–46.
202. See the reports in *ZZQJ*, 4:200–38; and *SGXF*, 18:10259–65.
203. *PHZ*, 4:26b–32a.
204. *ZZQJ*, 4:258–59; and *SGXF*, 19:10344–56, cover riverine operations.
205. *SGXF*, 19:10303–11.
206. *SGXF*, 19:10388–95.
207. *ZZQJ*, 4:259–62.
208. See *QSG*, 3076; Sun, *Zuo Zongtang zhuan*, 107.
209. *ZZQJ*, 11:175.
210. *SGXF*, 19:10395; *QSG*, 3077. Liu's death was reported to the foreign press in Shanghai via Shaanxi bankers. See *NCH*, 154 (April 12, 1870).
211. *PHZ*, 5:4a.
212. For a list of Qing commanders slain, see *HMYD*, 271.
213. Sun, *Zuo Zongtang zhuan*, 108. Zuo's eldest son personally traveled to the front to deliver the news despite a serious illness that eventually claimed his own life.
214. *NCH*, 154 (April 12, 1870).
215. *NCH*, 161 (June 2, 1870).
216. *ZZQJ*, 4:262–63; *ZZQJ*, 15:280–81; *SGXF*, 19:10399–400; and *QSG*, 3231.
217. See Yang Dongliang, *Zuo Zongtang*, 94.
218. *SGXF*, 19:10403–4.
219. *SGXF*, 20:10945–54.

220. *SGXF*, 19:10415–18.
221. See *ZZQJ*, 14:22–27; Sun, *Zuo Zongtang zhuan*, 109.
222. *ZNP*, 644.
223. *SGXF*, 19:10512–23.
224. *ZZQJ*, 14:231–43; Sun, *Zuo Zongtang zhuan*, 109–10.
225. *ZZQJ*, 4:277–81.
226. See *SGXF*, 19:10572–620, on the spring battles.
227. *SGXF*, 19:10692–99.
228. *SGXF*, 19:10745–48
229. *ZZQJ*, 14:243–49; *QSG*, 3231; and *ZZQJ*, 4:307–16 and 321–25.
230. *ZZQJ*, 4:345–52; *ZZQJ*, 11:183–84. On the summer battles, also see *ZZQJ*, 4:366–86.
231. *ZWZX*, 68.
232. *ZNP*, 645–46. For Liu Songshan's reports on the widespread devastation in the countryside, see *ZZQJ*, 14:157–59.
233. *SGXF*, 20:10980–95.
234. Sun, *Zuo Zongtang zhuan*, 111.
235. *ZZQJ*, 4:386–96.
236. *ZNP*, 647. Zuo's report on recent activities around Jinjibao can be found in *SGXF*, 20:11034–42.
237. *PHZ*, 5:15a–b.
238. On supply efforts over the summer, see *SGXF*, 20:10809–16.
239. *SGXF*, 20:10,790–98.
240. *ZNP*, 648–49; *SGXF*, 20:10841–42 and 10910–15.
241. *ZZQJ*, 11:210–12.
242. *ZZQJ*, 4:406–7.
243. *ZZQJ*, 4:415.
244. *ZZQJ*, 4:431–36; *PHZ*, 5:6a. On later efforts to root out endemic local corruption, see *ZZQJ*, 15:10–12.
245. *SGXF*, 20:11120–29.
246. *HMYD*, 275.
247. *SGXF*, 21:11540–43.
248. *ZNP*, 649–50; *ZZQJ*, 4:396–97, 442; and Sun, *Zuo Zongtang zhuan*, 111–12.
249. *ZZQJ*, 5:15–16; *SGXF*, 21:11,715–16. In some places all Muslims were forced to bow before copies of Kangxi's Maxims erected in public places. See Schluessel, *Land of Strangers*, 27.
250. *ZNP*, 651

251. *ZZQJ*, 4:442–42.

252. *SGXF*, 21:11555–58.

253. *QSG*, 267; Kim, *Holy War*, 161; and Bales, *Tso Tsung-t'ang*, 268. Some sources fix the date as March 2. See Sun, *Zuo Zongtang zhuan*, 113.

254. *SGXF*, 21:11721.

255. *PHZ*, 5:16a–b. Zuo's report on the final defeat and surrender of Ma Hualong can be found in *SGXF*, 21:11699–704.

256. *SGXF*, 21:11577–86.

257. See *SGXF*, 21:11746–49.

258. *SGXF*, 21:11639–43. For more on the mop-up operations, see *SGXF*, 21:11705–11.

259. Sun, *Zuo Zongtang zhuan*, 112.

260. *ZZQJ*, 11:225.

261. Zuo claimed that 190,000 taels in recovered booty was used to buy seeds and repair irrigation works for the people of Lingzhou. See *SGXF*, 21:11704.

262. *HMYD*, 282–88.

263. *ZZQJ*, 4:443–44. For additional details and figures on resettlement, see *SGXF*, 21:11711–15.

264. *ZZQJ*, 14:252–53.

265. *ZZQJ*, 14:267. Also see *NCH*, 373 (June 27, 1874). On Zuo's initial proclamation prohibiting opium cultivation from 1869, see *ZZQJ*, 14:577.

266. See Lavelle, *Profits of Nature*, 92–95.

267. *NCH*, 300 (January 30, 1873).

268. Lavelle, *Profits of Nature*, 97–107.

269. *NCH*, 319 (June 7, 1873).

270. Lavelle, *Profits of Nature*, 110.

271. *ZZQJ*, 14:272.

272. *ZNP*, 651; *CHC*, 11:232.

273. *SGXF*, 22:11923.

274. *SGXF*, 22:11923–24.

275. *CHC*, 11.2:233. See *ZZQJ*, 14:203–4, for Zuo's argument. Also see *QSG*, 268; *HMYD*, 287–90; and *ZZQJ*, 5:44–47.

276. *SGXF*, 22:11926.

277. *ZNP*, 654; *ZZQJ*, 6:118–20.

278. *ZNP*, 657. On the significance of reviving local trade networks, see *SGXF*, 17:9760–63.

279. *SGXF*, 22:12027.

280. *HMYD*, 296–99.
281. *HMYD*, 299.
282. *ZZQJ*, 5:91–93.
283. *SGXF*, 22:11833.
284. Bales, *Tso Tsung-t'ang*, 268.
285. Zuo's plans for attacking Hezhou are detailed in Yang Dongliang, *Zuo Zong-tang*, 96.
286. *ZZQJ*, 5:105–10.
287. Zuo's letter to the Zongli Yamen regarding Russia's occupation of Yili can be found in *ZZQJ*, 11:217–18.
288. *SGXF*, 23:12487–90.
289. *SGXF*, 23:12727.
290. *SGXF*, 23:12639.
291. *HMYD*, 310.
292. On supply and logistical matters, see *SGXF*, 23:12644–59.
293. *SGXF*, 22:12113–18.
294. Sun, *Zuo Zongtang zhuan*, 115; *HMYD*, 311. On earlier difficulties crossing the Tao River, see *ZZQJ*, 14:273–77; and *ZZQJ*, 5:132–39.
295. Bales, *Tso Tsung-t'ang*, 273–75.
296. *ZZQJ*, 5:189–94; Theaker, "Moving Muslims," 98–99.
297. *ZZQJ*, 14:292–94; *HMYD*, 313.
298. *NCH*, 246 (January 18, 1872). Interestingly the same issue has a piece about the many gifts Zuo received from the emperor on the recent celebration of his sixtieth birthday.
299. *NCH*, 254 (March 14, 1872).
300. *HMYD*, 315.
301. *ZZQJ*, 11: 235.
302. On the context and circumstances of Ma Zhan'ao's surrender, see *HMYD*, 316–25.
303. *HMYD*, 316.
304. *HMYD*, 317.
305. *ZWZX*, 70. Much smaller figures are given by Zuo. See *ZZQJ*, 5:193.
306. For Zuo's version of events, see *SGXF*, 22:12173–79.
307. *HMYD*, 324–30; Sun, *Zuo Zongtang zhuan*, 117.
308. *ZZQJ*, 13:146.
309. Sun, *Zuo Zongtang zhuan*, 116. For Zuo's report on Bai, see *SGXF*, 22:12103–6.
310. *SGXF*, 23:12171–83.

311. *SGXF*, 23:12342–51.

312. *SGXF*, 23:12566.

313. *ZWZX*, 71; *ZZQJ*, 13:153–54.

314. *HMYD*, 344–46.

315. *SGXF*, 25:13378.

316. *ZZQJ*, 14:308–9. Hannah Theaker notes that the main rebel bases corresponded to the old lineage networks. See Theaker, "Moving Muslims," 83.

317. *SGXF*, 25:13281–85.

318. *ZZQJ*, 5:239–45; *ZZQJ*, 13:144; and *ZZQJ*, 14:296–98. On Zuo's relief efforts and the pursuit of rebels around Xining, see *SGXF*, 25:13530–37.

319. *ZZQJ*, 11:206.

320. *ZZQJ*, 5:262.

321. Cited in Theaker, "Moving Muslims," 116.

322. Linn, *The Philippine War*, 323.

323. *ZZQJ*, 5:225–27.

324. *ZNP*, 666.

325. See *ZZQJ*, 14:300–303 and 322.

326. *ZZQJ*, 11:255–58.

327. *ZZQJ*, 11:262.

328. *ZZQJ*, 11:267.

329. Sun, *Zuo Zongtang zhuan*, 118–19.

330. Sun, 119.

331. *ZZQJ*, 15:286–87.

332. See Zuo's reports in *ZZQJ*, 5:279–84, 291–94, 354–58, and 375–77; *QSG*, 269; and *SGXF*, 25:13440–47.

333. *QSG*, 269. Although modern scholars generally conclude that the uprising in Yunnan was not connected to the ones in the northwest, Zuo Zongtang apparently entertained the idea that an *ahong* had come from Yunnan to stir things up in Shaanxi. See *HMYD*, 189.

334. *SGXF*, 25:13540–41.

335. *ZZQJ*, 11:335–37.

336. *ZZQJ*, 11:327–31. On Zuo's praise of the Muslim defectors, see *SGXF*, 25:13542–44.

337. *ZZQJ*, 11:304–7.

338. On Liu's activities, see *SGXF*, 25:13598–605.

339. *SGXF*, 26:13758–59.

340. *HMYD*, 373; *ZNP*, 669; *ZZQJ*, 5:428–31.

341. *SGXF*, 25:13614–21.
342. *ZZQJ*, 11:365.
343. *ZNP*, 667–68.
344. *ZZQJ*, 11:297–98.
345. See *SGXF*, 26:13770–74.
346. *SGXF*, 25:13716.
347. *SGXF*, 26:13746–48.
348. On the significance of Chinese wall construction and its implications for artillery-based siege warfare, see Tonio Andrade, *The Gunpowder Age: China, Military Innovation and the Rise of the West in World History* (Princeton: Princeton University Press, 2016), 96–102.
349. *SGXF*, 26:13801.
350. *HMYD*, 374.
351. *SGXF*, 25:13650–52.
352. *ZNP*, 670. On the Bai Yanhu threat, also see *SGXF*, 26:13834–37.
353. *ZZQJ*, 5:431–35, 446–48, and 460–68.
354. *HMYD*, 375; *SGXF*, 26:13869–74 and 26:13991–95. See Zuo's reports in *ZZQJ*, 5:279–84, 291–94, 354–58, and 375–77. Xu Zhanbiao could not be in the vanguard owing to his wounds.
355. *QSG*, 269.
356. *SGXF*, 26:13996–97.
357. *PHZ*, 6:20b; *ZZQJ*, 5:478; Yang Dongliang, *Zuo Zongtang*, 100; and *HMYD*, 375–78. Specific surrender dates and figures concerning the number of Muslims killed vary by source. Bales states that just four thousand were executed. See Bales, *Tso Tsung-t'ang*, 292. Also see *ZNP*, 671–72, for details on the surrender and executions.
358. *ZZQJ*, 5:462–63; *SGXF*, 26:14005–25. For Western reports on the conclusion of the siege of Suzhou, see *NCH*, 348 (January 1, 1874), and 352 (January 29, 1874).
359. *HMYD*, 377–78.
360. *ZZQJ*, 13:330.
361. *QSG*, 12030.
362. *ZZQJ*, 14:339–40.
363. Ch'en, *Tso Tsung-t'ang, Pioneer Promoter*, 51.
364. Ch'en, *Tso Tsung-t'ang, Pioneer Promoter*, 52–58.
365. *ZZQJ*, 11:348–49.
366. There were widespread reports of arson and weapon stockpiling in Hezhou. See *ZZQJ*, 14:355–61.

367. See *ZZQJ*, 14:382–89, concerning flexibility in implementing new regulations.
368. *ZZQJ*, 14:340–47.
369. *ZZQJ*, 5:481; *ZWZX*, 72.
370. *HMYD*, 377.
371. *QSG*, 270.
372. *ZZQJ*, 11:291. In the same letter Zuo praised the loyalty of Ma Zhan'ao.
373. *SGXF*, 26:13902–14.
374. See *SGXF*, 26:14002–5 and 26:14029–32.
375. *SGXF*, 26:13813.
376. *ZWZX*, 31.
377. *ZZQJ*, 14:369–71.
378. *ZZQJ*, 14:278.
379. See Zhang Duoyan, "Zuo Zongtang dui Lanzhou," 86.
380. *ZZQJ*, 13:171; Zhang Duoyan, 87–89.
381. See Zuo's report on the reconstruction of the Lanzhou city walls in 1877 in *ZZQJ*, 15:59–60.
382. Chu, *Moslem Rebellion*, vii; Setzekorn, "Qing Dynasty Warfare and Military Authority," 199.
383. Setzekorn, 184.
384. Cui, "Zuo Zongtang shuping," 10.
385. Cui, 11–12.
386. *SXHMQY*, 332.
387. Chu, *Moslem Rebellion*, vii; Hou Chunyan, "Tongzhi huimin qiyi hou xibei diqu renkou qianyi ji yingxiang," *Shanxi daxue xuebao* 1997.3 (1997), 68. Theaker provides figures of 19 million in 1842 compared to 6 million in 1879. See Theaker, "Moving Muslims," 75.
388. Cui, "Zuo Zongtang shuping," 11.
389. Setzekorn, "Qing Dynasty Warfare and Military Authority," 185.
390. See Lavelle, *Profits of Nature*, 80. On wild animal attacks in the Ming-Qing transition and their association with the decline of civilization, see Swope, *On the Trail of the Yellow Tiger*, 296–99.
391. Lavelle, *Profits of Nature*, 87.
392. Hou, "Tongzhi huimin qiyi," 69.
393. Chou, "Frontier Studies and Changing Frontier Administration," 136.
394. Yang Dongliang, *Zuo Zongtang*, 104.
395. Yang Dongliang, 105–6.
396. Theaker, "Moving Muslims," chap. 4.

CHAPTER 6. PLAYING THE GREAT GAME

1. See the discussion in Lavelle, *Profits of Nature*, 39–62.

2. James Millward, *Eurasian Crossroads: A History of Xinjiang Revised and Updated* (New York: Columbia University Press, 2022), 135–36.

3. Millward, *Eurasian Crossroads*, 138; Peng Dacheng, "Zuo Zongtang kaifa xibei de zhanlue jucuo yu shenyuan yingxiang," *Hunan shifan daxue shehui kexue xuebao* 2001.1 (January 2001), 13.

4. For an overview of the history of Xinjiang, see Yu Taishan, ed., *Xiyu tongshi* (Zhengzhou: Zhengzhou guji chubanshe, 1996).

5. See Peter Perdue, *China Marches West: The Qing Conquest of Central Eurasia* (Cambridge, MA: Harvard University Press, 2005), for an extensive treatment of these campaigns. On Qing logistical innovations, see Ulrich Theobald, *War Finance and Logistics in Late Imperial China: A Study of the Second Jinchuan Campaign (1771–1776)* (Leiden: Brill, 2013).

6. See James A. Millward, *Beyond the Pass: Economy, Ethnicity and Empire in Qing Central Asia, 1759–1864* (Stanford: Stanford University Press, 1998), 36–43.

7. Nicola Di Cosmo, "Qing Colonial Administration in Central Asia," *International History Review* 20.2 (1998), 288.

8. Millward, *Eurasian Crossroads*, 100.

9. For an overview of begs and their place in Qing administration and local society, see Laura Newby, "The Begs of Xinjiang: Between Two Worlds," *Bulletin of the School of Oriental and African Studies* 61.2 (1998), 278–97.

10. Di Cosmo, "Qing Colonial Administration in Central Asia," 304–5.

11. *CHC*, 10.1:78–79.

12. Nailene Joseph Chou, "Frontier Studies and Changing Frontier Administration in Late Ch'ing China: The Case of Sinkiang, 1759–1911" (PhD diss., University of Washington, 1976), 21–22.

13. See David Brophy, "Kings of Xinjiang: Muslim Elites and the Qing Empire," *Études orientales* 25 (2008), 69–90.

14. Immanuel C. Y. Hsu, *The Ili Crisis: A Study in Sino-Russian Diplomacy, 1871–1881* (Oxford: Oxford University Press, 1965), 20.

15. Hodong Kim, *Holy War in China: The Muslim Rebellion and State in Chinese Central Asia, 1864–1877* (Stanford: Stanford University Press, 2004), 17–18.

16. Millward, *Eurasian Crossroads*, 100. For a more focused examination of Qing governance from 1759 to 1864, see Millward, *Beyond the Pass*.

17. Millward, *Eurasian Crossroads*, 102; Millward, *Beyond the Pass*, 50–56. For a discussion of different types of agricultural colonies in Xinjiang, see Bartosz Kowalski, "Holding an Empire Together: Army, Colonization and State-Building in Qing Xinjiang," *Ming Qing Studies* (2017), 45–70.
18. Scott Levi, *The Rise and Fall of Khoqand, 1709–1876: Central Asia in the Global Age* (Pittsburgh: University of Pittsburgh Press, 2012), 182–83.
19. The standard English-language survey of these events remains Peter Hopkirk, *The Great Game: The Struggle for Empire in Central Asia* (New York: Kodansha, 1992).
20. Kwangmin Kim, *Borderland Capitalism: Turkestan Produce, Qing Silver and the Birth of an Eastern Market* (Stanford: Stanford University Press, 2016). For a discussion of the merchant presence in Xinjiang as a whole, see Millward, *Beyond the Pass*, 113–52.
21. On the origins of the Uighurs and their earliest kingdoms in Central Asia, see Millward, *Eurasian Crossroads*, 41–53.
22. Millward, *Eurasian Crossroads*, 108.
23. Millward, 85–86 and 108. For a detailed treatment of the Afaqi and Ishaqi and their rivalry and affiliations, see David Brophy, "Confusing Black and White: Naqshbandi Sufi Affiliations and the Transition to Qing Rule in the Tarim Basin," *Late Imperial China* 39.1 (June 2018), 30–46.
24. See V. G. Kiernan, "Kashgar and the Politics of Central Asia, 1868–1878," *Cambridge Historical Journal* 11.3 (1955), 317; Demetrious Charles Boulger, *Life of Yakoob Beg: Athalik Ghazi, and Badaulet; Ameer of Kashgar* (1878; reprint, London: Andesite Press, 2015), 52–54; Laura Newby, *The Empire and the Khanate: A Political History of Qing Relations with Khoqand, c. 1760–1860* (Leiden: Brill, 2005), 50–58; and Kim, *Holy War*, 14–15 and 20–23.
25. *CHC*, 10.1:377–78.
26. Millward, *Eurasian Crossroads*, 111–12, citing Joseph Fletcher in *CHC*, 10.1:378–83. Also see the discussion in Newby, *Empire and the Khanate*, 184–209.
27. Newby, 10 and 250.
28. Kim, *Holy War*, 31–33; *SGXF*, 1:121–31, 161–80.
29. *SGXF*, 1:233.
30. *SGXF*, 1:187–92.
31. *SGXF*, 1:43–45.
32. *SGXF*, 1:241–42.
33. Kim, *Borderland Capitalism*, 151–73.
34. *SGXF*, 1:272–97.

35. *SGXF*, 1:358–62.
36. See *PHZ*, 7.2b–3a.
37. *QSG*, 259; *KXJ*, 452–54.
38. See Kim, *Holy War*, 4–7.
39. See Yang Dongliang, *Zuo Zongtang*, 109; *KXJ*, 454.
40. *HYMYD*, 391–92.
41. Kim, *Holy War*, 63–64.
42. *PHZ*, 7:3a.
43. Kim, *Holy War*, 45–47; *PHZ*, 7:3b–4a.
44. Kim, 52–55.
45. *KXJ*, 455.
46. Boulger, *Life of Yakoob Beg*, 101.
47. Kim, *Holy War*, xiv; Chung Chien-peng, "China's War on Terror: September 11 and Uighur Separatism," *Foreign Affairs* 81.4 (July–August 2002), 8–9.
48. On the significance of the telegraph for military communications in late Qing China, see Halsey, *Quest for Power*, 224–28.
49. *PHZ*, 7:5a–5b; Sun, *Zuo Zongtang zhuan*, 126. Xu's biography can be found in *QSG*, 3237.
50. See the accounts of Xu's exploits around Urumqi in *SGXF*, 21:11465–71.
51. Kiernan, "Kashgar and the Politics of Central Asia," 319; Boulger, *Life of Yakoob Beg*, 12; Tsing Yuan, "Yakub Beg (1820–1877) and the Muslim Rebellion in Chinese Turkestan," *Central Asiatic Journal* 6.2 (1961), 139.
52. Boulger, 79.
53. See Kim, *Holy War*, 72–83; Boulger, 79–81, 106.
54. Tsing, "Yakub Beg and the Muslim Rebellion," 139–45.
55. Kim, *Holy War*, 87; Boulger, *Life of Yakoob Beg*, 112.
56. Kim, 91.
57. Schluessel, *Land of Strangers*, 11–12.
58. *PHZ*, 7:4b.
59. Hsu, *Ili Crisis*, 30–31.
60. *SGXF*, 22:11912–15.
61. Kiernan, "Kashgar and the Politics of Central Asia," 318.
62. *SGXF*, 22:11649–75.
63. *SGXF*, 22:11694–96.
64. Kim, *Holy War*, 100–102; Boulger, *Life of Yakoob Beg*, 135–37.
65. Kim, *Holy War*, 103–8.
66. Feng, *Wan Qing mingchen*, 359.

67. On military details, see Boulger, *Life of Yakoob Beg*, 143–45.
68. Kim, *Holy War*, 114–19.
69. On the propensity of entrenched hereditary elites to cling to their old ways, see Kenneth Chase, *Firearms: A Global History to 1700* (Cambridge: Cambridge University Press, 2003), 106–7.
70. Boulger, *Life of Yakoob Beg*, 192.
71. A colorful account of the meeting is in Boulger, 193–95.
72. Kim, *Holy War*, 142–46; for the texts of the deals, see 187–93.
73. On pan-Islamic ideology in the nineteenth century, see Joseph Peterson, *Sacred Rivals: Catholic Missions and the Making of Islam in Nineteenth-Century France and Algeria* (Oxford: Oxford University Press, 2022).
74. Tsing, "Yakub Beg and the Muslim Rebellion," 147–50.
75. *SGXF*, 25:13362.
76. A summary of the clashes between Yakub and his allies and the Qing in 1872–73 can be found in *SGXF*, 25:13555–60.
77. *SGXF*, 25:13660–66.
78. *SGXF*, 26:13921–22.
79. *SGXF*, 26:13931–38.
80. *SGXF*, 26:13943–59.
81. *SGXF*, 26:13963–65.
82. *SGXF*, 26:14050–59. For a list of rewards and promotions concerning the Qing victory at Hami, see *SGXF*, 26:14136–41.
83. *SGXF*, 26:14062–69.
84. *KXJ*, 462–63.
85. *SGXF*, 26:14145–61.
86. On Zuo's reconstruction efforts, see *ZZQJ*, 6:14–55.
87. *SGXF*, 26:14203–7; *SGXF*, 27:14268–77.
88. *SGXF*, 27:14261; *ZZQJ*, 6:96–103.
89. *ZZQJ*, 6:112–15.
90. *SGXF*, 27:14293–305.
91. *SGXF*, 27:14392.
92. *SGXF*, 27:14519–54.
93. *SGXF*, 27:14560.
94. *NCH*, 391 (November 5, 1874).
95. See *NCH*, 409 (March 11, 1875); and *NCH*, 423 (June 19, 1875). The paper also erroneously reported Zuo's death.
96. *NCH*, 430 (August 7, 1875).

97. *NCH*, 435 (September 11, 1875).

98. See *NCH*, 447 (December 9, 1875).

99. See Lavelle, *Profits of Nature*, 113; and Lloyd Eastman, *Throne and Mandarins: China's Search for a Policy during the Sino-French Controversy, 1880–1885* (Cambridge, MA: Harvard University Press, 1967), 14.

100. Immanuel C. Y. Hsu, "The Great Policy Debate in China, 1874: Maritime Defense versus Frontier Defense," *Harvard Journal of Asiatic Studies* 25 (1964–65), 217; Li Lianli, *Zuo Zongtang pingzhuan*, 92–94.

101. Chu, *Moslem Rebellion*, 171.

102. Chou, "Frontier Studies and Changes in Frontier Administration," 221; Li Lianli, *Zuo Zongtang pingzhuan*, 80–90; Sun, *Zuo Zongtang zhuan*, 130–33; Hsu, "Great Policy Debate," 224–26.

103. See Eastman, *Throne and Mandarins*, 18–29.

104. Eastman, 16; Li Lianli, *Zuo Zongtang pingzhuan*, 83–85.

105. Zuo's initial argument, dating from the third month of 1875, is laid out in *ZZQJ*, 6:176–83. Also see Chou, "Frontier Studies and Changes in Frontier Administration," 199; and Hsu, *Ili Crisis*, 38.

106. *ZZQJ*, 11:504–5. From around 1840 the Qing generally referred to the Ottoman Empire as Turkey. See Matthew W. Mosca, "Empire and the Circulation of Frontier Intelligence: Qing Conceptions of the Ottomans," *Late Imperial China* 70.1 (June 2010), 198.

107. Hsu, "Great Policy Debate," 221–23.

108. See *ZNP*, 686–911; and *ZWZX*, 84–85.

109. On Taiwan in Qing calculations regarding Xinjiang, also see Yang Dongliang, *Zuo Zongtang*, 118–21. Taiwanese aboriginals had slain some shipwrecked natives of Ryukyu (Okinawa) in 1871, and Japan had demanded restitution.

110. *CHC*, 11.2:82–84.

111. *ZZQJ*, 11:512–13; also see *QSG*, 12,032.

112. Hsu, "Great Policy Debate," 218–19. Ironically, Zuo would later impeach Li Hanzhang for corruption.

113. Cited in Hsu, *Ili Crisis*, 38.

114. Mosca, "Empire and the Circulation of Frontier Intelligence."

115. *SGXF*, 27:14427–28.

116. *ZZQJ*, 11:519–23.

117. See *QSG*, 12032. A biography of Wenxiang can be found in *ECQP*, 669–71. Liao Zhenghua claims Wenxiang only favored retaking the north, but Zuo's vision was broader. See Liao, *Xiangjun zhengzhan shi*, 220.

118. *ZZQJ*, 6:191–92.
119. *SGXF*, 27:14408–10; Li Lianli, *Zuo Zongtang pingzhuan*, 108–10; Elleman, *Modern Chinese Warfare*, 76–78.
120. On his solicitation of the latest maps of Xinjiang, see *ZZQJ*, 5:509. On Zuo's Russian contacts, see *ZZQJ*, 12:21.
121. *ZZQJ*, 6:183–91.
122. "The Ming Withdrawal from Korea and the Beginning of the Imjin War's Aftermath," online lecture delivered by Masato Hasegawa as part of the Research Seminar Program of the Aftermath Project at Autonomous University of Barcelona, September 28, 2022.
123. *ZNP*, 675; *SGXF*, 27:14589–90.
124. About 40,000 of the troops were designated frontline combat forces with the rest being reserves. For more on Zuo's planning, see Yang Dongliang, *Zuo Zongtang*, 123–29.
125. *ZWZX*, 97–98.
126. On Zuo's request for the loan, see *ZZQJ*, 6:340–45; Millward, *Eurasian Crossroads*, 126–27; and Chou, "Frontier Studies and Changing Frontier Administration," 222–23. For particulars on the loan and other funding sources, see *ZZQJ*, 6:371–76 and 391–99; and Immanuel C. Y. Hsu, "The Late Ch'ing Reconquest of Sinkiang: A Reappraisal of Tso Tsung-t'ang's Role," *Central Asiatic Journal* 12 (1968), 54–57. The HSBC loan was for 5 million taels with an interest rate of 1.25 percent per month. See *ZZQJ*, 6:641–43.
127. *ZNP*, 679.
128. *ZNP*, 699–700; *ZZQJ*, 6:266–68. He received 3 million taels' worth of grain from Russia totaling 5 million catties of grain. See *ZZQJ* 12, 5–8; Hsu, "Late Ch'ing Reconquest of Sinkiang," 59; Bales, *Tso Tsung-t'ang*, 336–38; and Kim, *Holy War*, 163.
129. See *ZZQJ*, 6:300–308.
130. Yang Dongliang, *Zuo Zongtang*, 129–31; Li Lianli, *Zuo Zongtang pingzhuan*, 108–10.
131. *ZZQJ*, 6:320.
132. *ZWZX*, 86–87.
133. See Yang Dongliang, *Zuo Zongtang*, 131; and Meadows, *Chinese and Their Rebellions*, 275. On European assessments of Zuo's manufactured weapons, see *ZWZX*, 138–40.
134. Bales, *Tso Tsung-t'ang*, 340–41. Zuo's own praise of the factories is in *ZZQJ*, 12:23–28.

135. *ZZQJ*, 12:31–32.
136. *ZZQJ*, 6:389–91.
137. Chou, "Frontier Studies and Changing Frontier Administration," 138.
138. Zuo's detailed route plans can be found in *SGXF*, 27:14637–55; and *ZWZX*, 89–92.
139. *PHZ*, 7.8a–b; Yang Dongliang, *Zuo Zongtang*, 133.
140. *ZZQJ*, 12:66–69.
141. Yang Dongliang, *Zuo Zongtang*, 132; *ZZQJ*, 3:17 and 116.
142. *ZNP*, 680–81.
143. *ZNP*, 677–84. For details on routes of advance and the evolving supply situation in 1876, see *ZZQJ* 12, 37–59. For specifics on supplies from different provinces, see *ZWZX*, 93–96.
144. See *SGXF*, 27:14680–708.
145. Immanuel C. Y. Hsu, "British Mediation of China's War with Yakub Beg, 1877," *Central Asiatic Journal* 9.2 (June 1964), 142.
146. Hsu, "British Mediation," 143.
147. Kiernan, "Kashgar and the Politics of Central Asia," 319.
148. Kiernan, 327; Feng, *Wan Qing mingchen*, 356. On Yakub's coinage, see T. D. Yih, "The Typology of Xinjiang Silver Tenga and Copper Fulus of Yakub Beg (1820–1877)," *Numismatic Chronicle* 169 (2009), 287–329.
149. On the topic of Islamic proto-nationalism, see Tsing, "Yakub Beg and the Muslim Rebellion," 163–64.
150. Kemal H. Karpat, "Yakub Bey's Relations with the Ottoman Sultans: A Reinterpretation," *Cahiers du monde russe et soviétique* 32.1 (March 1991), 17.
151. Karpat, "Yakub Bey's Relations with the Ottoman Sultans," 22.
152. Karpat, 30.
153. Bales, *Tso Tsung-t'ang*, 316–17; Yang Dongliang, *Zuo Zongtang*, 112–15.
154. Hopkirk, *The Great Game*, 324–28.
155. Tsing, "Yakub Beg and the Muslim Rebellion," 157.
156. *QSG*, 12031.
157. Kiernan, "Kashgar and the Politics of Central Asia," 327.
158. Karpat, "Yakub Beg's Relations with the Ottoman Sultans," 24.
159. *PHZ*, 7:10a; *ZNP*, 706.
160. Boulger, *Life of Yakoob Beg*, 146–49.
161. Boulger, vii.
162. Yang Dongliang, *Zuo Zongtang*, 110–12; Boulger, 5.
163. See *NCH* (April 29, 1876; May 13, 1876; and June 10, 1876).

164. Kim, *Holy War in China*, 167–71.
165. Liao, *Xiangjun zhengzhan shi*, 220.
166. *QSG*, 12,032.
167. *CHC*, 11:239–40.
168. Boulger, *Life of Yakoob Beg*, 236.
169. See Yih, "Typology of Xinjiang Silver Coins."
170. Kim, *Holy War*, 129–37.
171. Boulger, *Life of Yakoob Beg*, 161–63.
172. *ZNP*, 703–5.
173. *SGXF*, 28:14755.
174. *SGXF*, 28:14764–67.
175. *SGXF*, 28:14771; Yang Dongliang, *Zuo Zongtang*, 134.
176. *SGXF*, 28:14876–93.
177. On these early responses and the Qing reaction, see *SGXF*, 28:14799–809.
178. *SGXF*, 28:14831–33.
179. On the fall of Gucheng to the rebels, see *SGXF*, 27:14672–73. On Liu's recapture of it, see *SGXF*, 28:14833–39; and *ZZQJ*, 6:440–42.
180. *KXJ*, 467–68.
181. See *QSG*, 3232; *ZZQJ*, 6:454–58; *SGXF*, 28:14861–65; Li Lianli, *Zuo Zongtang pingzhuan*, 105–7; and Yang Dongliang, *Zuo Zongtang zhuan*, 136.
182. *ZZQJ*, 6:457.
183. *SGXF*, 28:14867–68; *ZNP*, 708; Bales, *Tso Tsung-t'ang*, 357; and Yang Dongliang, *Zuo Zongtang*, 137. Zuo specifically references the superiority of his artillery in *ZZQJ*, 12:80–81.
184. *PHZ*, 7:13a–14a; *ZZQJ*, 6:468–80.
185. *SGXF*, 28:14910–11.
186. *SGXF*, 28:14857–58.
187. *PHZ*, 7:14a–14b.
188. *PHZ*, 7:15b–16a.
189. *PHZ*, 7:20b; *KXJ*, 471.
190. Yang Dongliang, *Zuo Zongtang*, 136.
191. *KXJ*, 470.
192. *SGXF*, 28:14842.
193. *PHZ*, 7:16b–18a.
194. *ZNP*, 710.
195. *ZZQJ*, 12:71. Zuo also criticized *Shenbao*'s shoddy reporting in a letter to Zeng Guoquan. See *ZZQJ*, 12:101.

196. *ZZQJ*, 12:81–83.
197. *ZZQJ*, 6:472; *ZZQJ*, 12:91–93.
198. Boulger, *Life of Yakoob Beg*, 245.
199. *ZZQJ*, 12:98–100; Feng, *Wan Qing mingchen*, 358.
200. *SGXF*, 28:14849–53; *ZZQJ*, 6:524–33.
201. *PHZ*, 7:17b–18b; *SGXF*, 28:14854–55 and 14890–905.
202. *SGXF*, 28:14993–15003.
203. *SGXF*, 28:14971–72; *ZZQJ*, 6:527.
204. *SGXF*, 28:14874–75. For detailed accounts of the battles leading to the capture of Manas, see *SGXF*, 28:14975–86.
205. See *NCH*, 508–10 (February 1–15, 1877).
206. *NCH*, 513 (March 8, 1877).
207. See Hevia, *English Lessons*, 273–81.
208. *NCH* (November 2, 1877).
209. *SGXF*, 28:14900; *ZZQJ*, 12:122–23; Yang Dongliang, *Zuo Zongtang*, 139. On the ongoing problem of sickness among the troops, see *ZZQJ*, 12:148; and *SGXF*, 28:14990.
210. *SGXF*, 28:15003–19.
211. Kim, *Holy War*, 167.
212. Yang Dongliang, *Zuo Zongtang*, 138.
213. *ZZQJ*, 6:572–78.
214. *SGXF*, 28:15022–23.
215. *ZZQJ*, 6:581–83.
216. *SGXF*, 28:15025; *ZZQJ*, 6:583.
217. Liao, *Xiangjun zhengzhan shi*, 227.
218. See Zuo's reports in *SGXF*, 28:15040–48; and *ZZQJ*, 6:605–16.
219. *PHZ*, 7:19b–20a; *ZNP*, 713.
220. Yang Dongliang, *Zuo Zongtang*, 141. Sun Guangyao claims the losses were even lower. See Sun, *Zuo Zongtang zhuan*, 145.
221. *ZZQJ*, 6:620–25; *QSG*, 3232.
222. *ZZQJ*, 6:609.
223. Sun, *Zuo Zongtang zhuan*, 146.
224. *ZNP*, 713; Kim, *Holy War*, 172.
225. *SGXF*, 28:15054–56.
226. Guo was first sent to London in 1875. See *QSG*, 272.
227. Hsu, "British Mediation," 145–46.
228. Kiernan, "Kashgar and the Politics of Central Asia," 329–30.

229. Bales, *Tso Tsung-t'ang*, 361–62.
230. *ZZQJ*, 6:679–82.
231. *ZZQJ*, 12:100.
232. See *ZZQJ*, 12:105–7.
233. *ZZQJ*, 12:165–71.
234. *ZZQJ*, 12:201–3 and 206–8. On Zuo's efforts to clean up the tea administration, also see *NCH* (August 18, 1877).
235. *ZZQJ*, 12:187–90 and 208–16.
236. Kiernan, "Kashgar and the Politics of Central Asia," 337.
237. Boulger, *Life of Yakoob Beg*, 234.
238. *ZZQJ*, 12:132.
239. *ZZQJ*, 12:216–17.
240. *KXJ*, 474; also see Liao, *Xiangjun zhengzhan shi*, 228–31.
241. See Zuo's report from August 10, 1877, in *SGXF*, 28:15,072–75; and *ZZQJ*, 6:645–48. Also see a letter in *ZZQJ*, 12:255–56; and *QSG*, 273.
242. Schluessel, *Land of Strangers*, 194–96.
243. *ZZQJ*, 6:647.
244. Boulger, *Life of Yakoob Beg*, 250–52.
245. For varying accounts of the cause and circumstances of Yakub's death, see *PHZ*, 7:21a; Kim, *Holy War*, 167–69; *ZNP*, 714; and *ZZQJ*, 12:245–46.
246. *ZZQJ*, 12:261–62.
247. *SGXF*, 28:15077–91.
248. *ZZQJ*, 12:268–69; Kim, *Holy War*, 173.
249. Hsu, "British Mediation," 148.
250. *ZWZX*, 103.
251. *HMYD*, 401–2 and 414–15; *ZZQJ*, 6:698–703; Boulger, *Life of Yakoob Beg*, 267; Kim, *Holy War*, 174. This was also reported in *NCH* (January 17, 1878).
252. See details in *ZWZX*, 104–5.
253. Kiernan, "Kashgar and the Politics of Central Asia," 340.
254. *SGXF*, 28:15139; *ZZQJ*, 6:715–22; Yang Dongliang, *Zuo Zongtang*, 143.
255. *PHZ*, 7:24b–27a; *ZZQJ*, 6:716–17; *ZZQJ*, 14:433–35.
256. A more sympathetic account toward Bai and his "heroics" can be found in *HMYD*, 407–24.
257. *PHZ*, 7:24a–b; Bales, *Tso Tsung-t'ang*, 375.
258. *ZNP*, 720; *KXJ*, 477.
259. *NCH* (July 29 and August 5, 1879). On general British attitudes toward China's actions and their portrayal of them in this era, see Hevia, *English Lessons*.

260. *NCH* (October 24, 1883).

261. Daniel McMahon, "Making Men of Iniquity: Imperial Purpose and Imagined Boundaries in the Qing Processing of Rebel Ringleaders, 1768–1828," *Journal of Chinese Military History* 7.2 (2018), 141.

262. *ZNP*, 718; *ZZQJ*, 8:27–41.

263. *QSG*, 3232.

264. *ZNP*, 719.

265. Liao, *Xiangjun zhengzhan shi*, 241–44.

266. *ZNP*, 720; *ZZQJ*, 8:29; and *SGXF*, 29:15191–95.

267. *SGXF*, 29:15197; *ZZQJ*, 8:89–92.

268. See *HMYD*, 416–20; and *SGXF*, 29:15668–69. On different interpretations of international law and its applicability in Europe and China, see S. C. M. Paine, *Imperial Rivals: China, Russia, and Their Disputed Frontier* (Armonk, NY: M. E. Sharpe, 1996), 80–82.

269. *SGXF*, 29:15280–84.

270. *ZZQJ*, 12:313–18.

271. *ZNP*, 718.

272. *PHZ*, 7:29a–30b; *SGXF*, 29:15198–207.

273. *ZZQJ*, 13:181.

274. *NCH*, 583 (July 13, 1878).

275. *NCH*, 570 (April 20, 1878). Romanization updated.

276. *NCH*, 590 (September 2, 1878).

277. Schluessel, *Land of Strangers*, 52. On Zuo's early efforts, see the Imperial Decree of December 4, 1877, reprinted in *NCH*, 557 (January 17, 1878).

278. Yang Dongliang, *Zuo Zongtang*, 154–61.

279. *ZZQJ*, 8:52–54; *ZZQJ*, 14:464–66; *ZWZX*, 124–33.

280. *SGXF*, 28:15111–17.

281. *ZWZX*, 134–38.

282. *SGXF*, 28:15,156–58; *ZZQJ*, 8:117–18 and 310–11.

283. *SGXF*, 29:15,334–35.

284. On the restoration of tribute, see *NCH* (July 22, 1879)

285. Yang Dongliang, *Zuo Zongtang*, 168. On Zuo's efforts to revamp local administration, also see Peng, "Zuo Zongtang kaifa xibei," 9–10.

286. Yang Dongliang, 168–69; *ZZQJ*, 12:265–68; and *SGXF*, 29:15,214–16.

287. A biography of Chen can be found in *ECQP*, 46–47. Also see William T. Rowe, *Saving the World: Chen Hongmou and Elite Consciousness in Eighteenth-Century China* (Stanford: Stanford University Press, 2001).

288. Yang Dongliang, *Zuo Zongtang*, 171. Cui Ji'en, writing in the early years of the PRC, criticized Zuo's children and grandchildren for buying land but offered no evidence for why this was corrupt beyond the ideological taint of capitalism. See Cui Ji'en, "Zuo Zongtang shuping," *Shixue yukan* 1957 (June 1957), 11

289. *QSG*, 12,033; *SGXF* 29, 15,263; and *ZZQJ* 8, 74.

290. Boulger, *Life of Yakoob Beg*, 257.

291. See Alexander Morrison, "Russian Rule in Turkestan and the Example of British India, c. 1860," *Slavonic and East European Review* 84.4 (October 2006), 666–707, for an overview of Russia's activities in Central Asia in the nineteenth century.

292. *CHC*, 10.1:330.

293. Paine, *Imperial Rivals*, 96; also see *CHC*, 10.1:334–39. On earlier treaties with Russia, see Paine, 66–80.

294. Paine, 94.

295. See, for example, the discussion in Yang Dongliang, *Zuo Zongtang*, 145–50.

296. See Kirk W. Larsen, *Tradition, Treaties, and Trade: Qing Imperialism and Choson Korea, 1850–1910* (Cambridge, MA: Harvard University Press, 2008); and Schluessel, *Land of Strangers*, 6.

297. Paine, *Imperial Rivals*, 13.

298. Hsu, *Ili Crisis*, 33–34.

299. See Fields, *Tso and the Muslims*, 97.

300. *ZNP*, 730–33; *ZZQJ*, 8:170–79; and *SGXF*, 29:15,318–22.

301. *ZZQJ*, 8:204–5.

302. *ZZQJ*, 12:347–48.

303. See Zuo's letter in Liu Dian in *ZZQJ*, 12:296–99.

304. *ZZQJ*, 12:305.

305. *QSG*, 274; *PHZ*, 8:11b–12a; *SGXF*, 29:15315–18. A biography of Chonghou can be found in *ECQP*, 72–73.

306. *ZNP*, 723; *SGXF*, 29:15324–30.

307. Hsu, *Ili Crisis*, 49.

308. See *SGXF*, 29:15349–56; and *ZZQJ*, 8:217–21.

309. *SGXF*, 29:15356–57; *ZZQJ*, 12:355–58.

310. *SGXF*, 29:15358–59. On Zuo's plans for a blended administration in Xinjiang, see *SGXF*, 29:15538–46; and *ZZQJ*, 8:156–60.

311. Hsu, *Ili Crisis*, 50.

312. Hsu, 50.

313. *KXJ*, 478–80; *SGXF*, 29:15416–30; *ZZQJ*, 8:259–65.

314. *ZZQJ*, 8:333–38.
315. *ZZQJ*, 12:371–91.
316. See *SGXF*, 29:15434–45, 15465–83; and *ZZQJ*, 12:363–73.
317. *ZWZX*, 140.
318. *ZZQJ*, 8:352.
319. Full stipulations can be found in Hsu, *Ili Crisis*, 57. Also see *SGXF*, 29:15473–83. Many of the original Chinese records pertaining to the original treaty have been destroyed or lost. See Paine, *Imperial Rivals*, 133–35.
320. Chonghou's report can be found in *SGXF*, 29:15513–15.
321. Paine, *Imperial Rivals*, 134–40.
322. *SGXF*, 29:15483–90.
323. *ZZQJ*, 8:374–82; *ZZQJ*, 12:494–502.
324. *ZZQJ*, 12:494–95.
325. Hsu, *Ili Crisis*, 61–62.
326. Cited in Hsu, 62.
327. *ZZQJ*, 12:507–9.
328. *SGXF*, 29:15494–501.
329. *ZZQJ*, 8:381. Some Western sources indicate that Prince Gong supported Zuo. See *NCH* (March 18, 1880).
330. Cited in Liao, *Xiangjun zhengzhan shi*, 251.
331. Liao, 253.
332. Hsu, *Ili Crisis*, 63–64.
333. See *ZZQJ*, 8:386–87; and Hsu, *Ili Crisis*, 66–67.
334. *SGXF*, 29:15517–21. On the foreign response, see *NCH* (January 29, 1880).
335. *SGXF*, 29:15523–34.
336. *QSG*, 275; and Hsu, *Ili Crisis*, 81–89.
337. *PHZ*, 8:14a–15b; *SGXF*, 29:15561–66. Zeng Jize's biography can be found in *ECQP*, 850–52. For a full examination of his diplomatic career, see Li Enhan, *Zeng Jize de waijiao* (Taibei: Zhongyang yanjiuyuan jindaishi yanjiusuo, 1966).
338. *ZZQJ*, 12:533–40; also see *ZZQJ*, 12:578–82.
339. *ZZQJ*, 12:558.
340. See *ZNP*, 740–46; and Li Lianli, *Zuo Zongtang pingzhuan*, 128–31.
341. Zuo references these rumors in a letter to his son Xiaotong. See *ZZQJ*, 13:206.
342. See *ZZQJ*, 12:595–96; and Hsu, *Ili Crisis*, 93–94.
343. *NCH* (August 24, 1880).
344. *QSG*, 12033.
345. Hsu, *Ili Crisis*, 103.

346. Cited in Hsu, 104.
347. See *NCH* (April 1–June 1, 1880).
348. *ZZQJ*, 12:601–4.
349. *ZZQJ*, 8:441–46.
350. On the circumstances of Zuo's recall, see *PHZ*, 8.15b–17a; and *ZZQJ*, 8:508–12.
351. Yang Dongliang, *Zuo Zongtang*, 186.
352. Bales, *Tso Tsung-t'ang*, 382–83.
353. Bales, 387. Romanization in the original has been modified.
354. Hsu, *Ili Crisis*, 158.
355. Hsu, 184–85.
356. See *SGXF*, 29:15582–97.
357. Hsu, *Ili Crisis*, 186. The seemingly high indemnity was the result of a miscalculation by Zeng, according to Sally Paine. See Paine, *Imperial Rivals*, 161.
358. *SGXF*, 29:15606–14.
359. Liao, *Xiangjun zhengzhan shi*, 253.
360. *SGXF*, 30:15830–40 and 15867–77.
361. *SGXF*, 30:15915–41. In fact, these estimates are in line with Zuo's projections of 3 million taels per year in the early years of provincialization.
362. See *SGXF*, 29:15381–96; and Chou, "Frontier Studies and Changing Frontier Administration," 224.
363. *NCH* (March 1, 1881).
364. *ZWZX*, 119. Also see *ZNP*, 724–28; and Yang Dongliang, *Zuo Zongtang*, 165–66.
365. *SGXF*, 29:15547–56; Peng, "Zuo Zongtang kaifa xibei," 13.
366. On the state of schools as of 1880, see *ZZQJ*, 8:431–40.
367. Cited and translated in Schluessel, *Land of Strangers*, 100. Li Bo or Li Bai (701–762) is generally regarded as China's greatest classical poet.
368. Chou, "Frontier Studies and Changing Frontier Administration," 229–31.
369. For a discussion of various proposals, see Chou, 234–43. For Liu's recommendations, see *PHZ*, 8:9b–10a.
370. *SGXF*, 29:15647.
371. Chou, "Frontier Studies and Changing Frontier Administration," 249–50.
372. *ZWZX*, 165–67.
373. See *ZZQJ*, 8:468–72; Schluessel, *Land of Strangers*, 215; and Lavelle, *Profits of Nature*.
374. Chou, "Frontier Studies and Changing Frontier Administration," 245–46.
375. *SGXF*, 30:15770–73. On demobilization, also see *NCH* (February 2, 1880), which links efforts in Gansu and Xinjiang.

376. See Peng, "Zuo Zongtang kaifa xibei," 14–16.

377. Yang Dongliang, *Zuo Zongtang*, 183.

378. Millward, *Eurasian Crossroads*, 140–41. On the translation efforts, see Schluessel, *Land of Strangers*, 88–93.

379. Cited in Schluessel, 43.

380. *ZZQJ*, 14:483–85.

381. Peng, "Zuo Zongtang kaifa xibei," 16–17.

382. *SGXF*, 30:15808.

383. *QSG*, 3232.

384. Peng, "Zuo Zongtang kaifa xibei," 14.

385. On good harvests, see *ZZQJ*, 8:167–68.

386. Chou, "Frontier Studies and Changing Frontier Administration," 261.

387. Hsu, "Late Ch'ing Reconquest of Sinkiang," 57–59.

388. Millward, *Eurasian Crossroads*, 127.

389. Hsu, "Great Policy Debate," 227–28.

390. Millward, *Eurasian Crossroads*, 149–51.

391. Kevin Kind, "Musulman Knowledge, Local History and the Making of the Qing Nation-State," *Late Imperial China* 42.2 (December 2021), 91.

392. See Schluessel, *Land of Strangers*, 156–60.

393. Millward, *Eurasian Crossroads*, 123; Hsu, "Great Policy Debate," 225–28.

394. Chou, "Frontier Studies and Changing Frontier Administration," 5–6.

395. Chou, 252.

396. Boulger, *Life of Yakoob Beg*, 275.

397. Boulger, 275.

398. See Paine, *The Sino-Japanese War of 1894–95*.

399. Yang Dongliang, *Zuo Zongtang*, 107.

400. Yang Dongliang, 166.

401. Peng, "Zuo Zongtang kaifa xibei," 7.

402. *ZZQJ*, 7:634–35; Yang Dongliang, *Zuo Zongtang*, 179–80. On the scope of tree planting, also see Peng, "Zuo Zongtang kaifa xibei," 12; and Li Lianli, *Zuo Zongtang pingzhuan*, 76–78.

403. Peng, "Zuo Zongtang kaifa xibei," 11; *ZWZX*, 179–82.

404. *ZZQJ*, 14:426–27.

405. *SGXF*, 29:15558; Lavelle, *Profits of Nature*, 138–39. For more on his experiments with mulberry trees in the northwest, see *ZZQJ*, 14:520–32.

406. *ZZQJ*, 8:128–32 and 139–40.

407. Cited in Yang Dongliang, *Zuo Zongtang*, 173.

408. See *NCH*, 596 (October 10, 1878). For Zuo's complaints about continued opium cultivation, see *ZZQJ*, 14:445–48; and *ZZQJ*, 12:427–28.

409. Li Lianli, *Zuo Zongtang pingzhuan*, 98–101 and 118–20; *ZWZX*, 120.

410. The inception of this process will be discussed in Kenneth M. Swope, *The Rebellion of the Three Feudatories: The Consolidation of China's Qing Dynasty*, 2024. On the late Qing efforts in Xinjiang, see Kowalski, "Holding an Empire Together," 60–68.

411. See Cui, "Zuo Zongtang shuping," 10; and Peng, "Zuo Zongtang kaifa xibei," 8–10.

412. Boulger, *Life of Yakoob Beg*, 257.

413. Boulger, 277–301.

CHAPTER 7. THE GROGNARD

1. *ZNP*, 748.

2. *ZNP*, 747; Sun Guangyao, *Zuo Zongtang zhuan*, 162.

3. Sun Guangyao, *Zuo Zongtang zhuan*, 162.

4. See Yang Dongliang, *Zuo Zongtang*, 186–87; and *ZZQJ*, 3:748.

5. Bales, *Tso Tsung-t'ang*, 391.

6. Sun Guangyao, *Zuo Zongtang zhuan*, 163.

7. *QSG*, 275.

8. When another official told Zuo he could get away with paying a mere ten thousand taels, he just laughed it off. When Zuo inquired later about the exchange, he was informed that the prince had settled for eight thousand taels.

9. *ZNP*, 748–49.

10. *ZZQJ*, 8:35–36.

11. See *ZZQJ*, 8:49 and 225–32. For reports on actual costs associated with the arsenal at Shanghai, see *ZZQJ*, 8:291–94 and 302–6.

12 *ZZQJ*, 8:22–28; *ZZQJ*, 12:654–57.

13. In addition to trouble with his eyesight, Zuo complained of sore feet and a bad hand, possibly gout. See *ZZQJ*, 8:35 and 38–41.

14. Li Lianli, *Zuo Zongtang pingzhuan*, 256.

15. *ZZQJ*, 12:680–88.

16. See *ZZQJ*, 12:722–23; and *NCH* (July 1, 1881).

17. See Yang Dongliang, *Zuo Zongtang*, 188–89; and *NCH* (September 2, 1881). The expression *simian Chuge* refers to a famous event from Sima Qian's *Shiji* where the protagonist, Xiang Yu, is surrounded by enemies on all sides.

18. *NCH* (September 2, 1881).

19. Sun, *Zuo Zongtang zhuan*, 168–69.

20. *ZZQJ*, 8:45.
21. *NCH* (November 8, 1881).
22. *NCH* (November 15, 1881).
23. *NCH* (November 15, 1881).
24. *NCH* (December 6, 1881).
25. *ZZQJ*, 8:50–55.
26. On the lag in recovery, see Tobie Meyer-Fong, *What Remains: Coming to Terms with Civil War in Nineteenth-Century China* (Stanford: Stanford University Press, 2013).
27. *ZZQJ*, 8:79–81.
28. *ZZQJ*, 8:54–55 and 150–53. For foreigners' takes on the Li Hanzhang affair, see *NCH* (March 2, 9, and 15, 1882).
29. See *ZZQJ*, 8:63–75; and *NCH* (April 28, 1882).
30. *ZZQJ*, 8:82–86, 95–106, and 175–81.
31. *ZZQJ*, 8:212–13.
32. Kennedy, *Arms of Kiangnan*, 101.
33. *NCH* (April 5, 1881).
34. Yang Dongliang, *Zuo Zongtang*, 189.
35. *ZNP*, 750–51.
36. *NCH* (June 23, 1882).
37. Kennedy, *Arms of Kiangnan*, 150–52.
38. Li Lianli, *Zuo Zongtang pingzhuan*, 158–59.
39. Kennedy, *Arms of Kiangnan*, 103.
40. Yang Dongliang, *Zuo Zongtang*, 190–91; *NCH* (August 4, 1882).
41. See the long article in *NCH* (August 4, 1882).
42. *ZZQJ*, 8:106–9; Sun, *Zuo Zongtang zhuan*, 170–71.
43. *ZZQJ*, 8:245–47.
44. *ZZQJ*, 8:123–26.
45. *ZZQJ*, 8:165–70.
46. *ZZQJ*, 8:239.
47. *ZZQJ*, 8:267–70 and 328–30.
48. *ZZQJ*, 8:361–66.
49. *ZZQJ*, 8:320–22.
50. See *NCH* (July 15 and 22, 1881).
51. *NCH* (August 5 and 12, 1881)
52. *ZZQJ*, 8:134–38.
53. *ZZQJ*, 8:182–83; *ZNP*, 752; Yang Dongliang, *Zuo Zongtang*, 190–93.

54. *NCH* (March 29, 1881).

55. *ZZQJ*, 8:184–85.

56. Halsey, *Quest for Power*, 215.

57. Bickers, *The Scramble for China*, 299.

58. See *ZZQJ*, 8:224–25.

59. *NCH* (November 1, 1881).

60. Kennedy, *Arms of Kiangnan*, 150–51.

61. Kennedy, 108–9.

62. Kennedy, 154.

63. See *NCH* (November 15 and 29, 1882).

64. *NCH* (December 12, 1882).

65. *ZZQJ* 8, 353–55. On the militia and the Boxer Rebellion, see Joseph W. Esherick, *The Origins of the Boxer Uprising* (Berkeley: University of California Press, 1988), chapters 1–4.

66. See articles in the *North China Herald* from January through March 1883.

67. *NCH* (May 18, 1883).

68. *NCH* (May 25 and July 6, 1883).

69. *ZNP*, 753; *ZZQJ*, 8:234–37.

70. See Eastman, *Throne and Mandarins*, 31–39; and Rawlinson, *China's Struggle for Naval Development*, 110.

71. On the differences of opinion between the Qing and French with respect to Vietnam's status, see Eastman, *Throne and Mandarins*, 42–44.

72. This backdrop is described in detail in Bradley Camp Davis, *Imperial Bandits: Outlaws and Rebels in the China-Vietnam Borderlands* (Seattle: University of Washington Press, 2016), chapters 1–3. Davis argues that the Black Flags themselves were not actually remnant Taiping forces but derived from other regional armies in southwest China.

73. *ECQP*, 148. Also see Davis, *Imperial Bandits*, 90–100, concerning the French occupation of Hanoi.

74. Cited and translated in Eastman, *Throne and Mandarins*, 54. Translation slightly modified.

75. See Li Lianli, *Zuo Zongtang pingzhuan*, 165–66.

76. Eastman, *Throne and Mandarins*, 60–65. The French saw Yunnan as a vast reservoir of resources waiting to be tapped. See Davis, *Imperial Bandits*, 62.

77. Translated and cited in Eastman, *Throne and Mandarins*, 72. Translation modified.

78. Eastman, 77–80. On the dynamic Sino-Vietnamese border situation and the role of the Black Flags in it, see Davis, *Imperial Bandits*, 32–49.

79. *ZZQJ*, 8:21–22; Yang Dongliang, *Zuo Zongtang*, 195; and Li Lianli, *Zuo Zongtang pingzhuan*, 143.
80. *NCH* (July 27, 1883).
81. Liao, *Xiangjun zhengzhan shi*, 256–58.
82. Yang Dongliang, *Zuo Zongtang*, 196.
83. *ZZQJ*, 8:364–66.
84. *ZZQJ*, 8:282–86.
85. *ZZQJ*, 8:318–19.
86. *ZZQJ*, 8:369–72.
87. See *ZZQJ*, 12:723–24 and 731–33.
88. *ZZQJ*, 12:732–36 and 740–42.
89. *ZZQJ*, 8:414–15.
90. *NCH* (October 24, 1883).
91. *NCH* (November 28, 1883).
92. *NCH* (December 19, 1883).
93. *NCH* (December 26, 1883).
94. *NCH* (March 5, 1884).
95. *ZZQJ*, 8:435.
96. See *NCH* (May 2 and 9, 1884). It is unclear if the gunboats in question were purchased by Zuo or manufactured under his direction.
97. *ZZQJ*, 8:454–55.
98. *ZZQJ*, 8:319–20 and 379–88.
99. *QSG*, 278. The *North China Herald* states that Cen Yuying and Zhang Zhidong successively replaced Zuo before Zeng. See *NCH* (May 30, 1884).
100. *ZZQJ*, 8:465–67.
101. *ZNP*, 753–54.
102. Yang Dongliang, *Zuo Zongtang*, 198.
103. See *ZZQJ*, 8:469–71; and *ECQP*, 588–89, which includes a biography of Tang Jiong.
104. *ZNP*, 755.
105. *ZNP*, 755.
106. *ZZQJ*, 8:473–75.
107. *ZNP*, 756.
108. Davis, *Imperial Bandits*, 64.
109. *QSG*, 277; Davis, 101–3.
110. Yang Dongliang, *Zuo Zongtang*, 197.
111. See Davis, *Imperial Bandits*, 103–8.

112. See *ECQP*, 148 and 894.

113. Eastman, *Throne and Mandarins*, 97–98; *QSG*, 277.

114. *ZNP*, 756.

115. Yang Dongliang, *Zuo Zongtang*, 199–200.

116. *CHC*, 11.2:99.

117. See Barish, *Learning to Rule*, 70–72.

118. Yang Dongliang, *Zuo Zongtang*, 200; Davis, *Imperial Bandits*, 113.

119. *ECQP*, 321; Eastman, *Throne and Mandarins*, 114–18.

120. *CHC*, 11.2:99–100; Eastman, *Throne and Mandarins*, 117–18.

121. Eastman, *Throne and Mandarins*, 123–24.

122. Li Lianli, *Zuo Zongtang pingzhuan*, 146.

123. *NCH* (July 18, 1884).

124. *NCH* (July 5, 1885).

125. See Eastman, *Throne and Mandarins*, 130–34.

126. *QSG*, 278; Yang Dongliang, *Zuo Zongtang*, 200; Davis, *Imperial Bandits*, 118.

127. Eastman, *Throne and Mandarins*, 139.

128. Sun Guangyao, *Zuo Zongtang zhuan*, 174.

129. *NCH* (August 22, 1884).

130. Eastman, *Throne and Mandarins*, 150–52.

131. *ZZQJ*, 8:475 and 480–81.

132. *CHC*, 11.2:100. See Zuo's criticism of Zhang and others in *ZZQJ*, 8:496–503. Zhang was recalled from exile three years later and assigned as an aide to Li Hongzhang. See Eastman, *Throne and Mandarins*, 159–61.

133. Bickers, *The Scramble for China*, 299.

134. Rawlinson, *China's Struggle for Naval Development*, 112.

135. Eastman, *Throne and Mandarins*, 158.

136. Rawlinson, *China's Struggle for Naval Development*, 113–14.

137. Rawlinson, 115.

138. Rawlinson, 116. For an assessment of the relative capabilities of the French and Chinese naval forces, see Li Lianli, *Zuo Zongtang pingzhuan*, 146–48.

139. Rawlinson, *China's Struggle for Naval Development*, 117–18.

140. Rawlinson, 119.

141. Li Lianli calls the struggle for Taiwan a "People's War," perhaps projecting contemporary PRC aspirations concerning reunification with Taiwan. See Li Lianli, *Zuo Zongtang ingzhuan*, 161–65.

142. Zuo apparently used a crutch topped with a gold-headed dragon that was a personal gift from Cixi. See *NCH* (June 19, 1885).

143. Sun, *Zuo Zongtang zhuan*, 177.
144. *NCH* (November 12, 1884).
145. Yang Dongliang, *Zuo Zongtang*, 210.
146. Liao, *Xiangjun zhengzhan shi*, 260.
147. Liao, 260.
148. On the battles on and around Taiwan, see Yang Dongliang, *Zuo Zongtang*, 207–9; and Liao, *Xiangjun zhengzhan shi*, 263–93, which includes a discussion of battles around Hainan.
149. *QSG*, 279.
150. On Li Hongzhang's reluctance to send aid south, see Rawlinson, *China's Struggle for Naval Development*, 123–26; Eastman, *Throne and Mandarins*, 181–93; and Li Lianli, *Zuo Zongtang pingzhuan*, 152–54.
151. *ZZQJ*, 8:484.
152. Liao, *Xiangjun zhengzhan shi*, 262.
153. *ZZQJ*, 8:488–93.
154. *ZZQJ*, 8:504–7.
155. See Gordon, *Confrontation over Taiwan*, 148; and Eastman, *Throne and Mandarins*, 168.
156. See Zuo's report on the blockade in *ZZQJ*, 8:486–88.
157. Li Lianli, *Zuo Zongtang pingzhuan*, 165.
158. Gordon, *Confrontation over Taiwan*, 149.
159. On Zuo's support of continued modernization as well as a refutation of the notion that China's ships were merely "big toys," see Li Lianli, *Zuo Zongtang pingzhuan*, 155–61.
160. *ZZQJ*, 8:508–12.
161. *QSG,* 279.
162. See Barend Noordam, "Technology, Tactics, and Military Transfer in the Nineteenth Century: Qing Armies in Tonkin, 1884–1885," in *Structures on the Move*, ed. A. Flutcher and S. Richter, 182 (Heidelberg: Springer, 2012).
163. This battle is covered in detail in Liao, *Xiangjun zhengzhan shi*, 293–304. Also see Yang Dongliang, *Zuo Zongtang,* 213; and Li Lianli, *Zuo Zongtang pingzhuan*, 197. For a biography of Feng, see *ECQP*, 147–49.
164. See Zuo's report praising Qing land forces in *ZZQJ*, 8:512–13.
165. *ECQP*, 149.
166. *QSG,* 279; also see Sun, *Zuo Zongtang zhuan*, 178.
167. See the full terms in Yang Dongliang, *Zuo Zongtang*, 215.
168. *ZZQJ*, 8:519–20.

169. Li Lianli, *Zuo Zongtang pingzhuan*, 172.
170. Sun, *Zuo Zongtang zhuan*, 180.
171. See Yang Dongliang, *Zuo Zongtang*, 201–3.
172. Eastman, *Throne and Mandarins*, 200–202.
173. Davis, *Imperial Bandits*, 132–36 and 144–47.
174. Davis, 152–54.
175. Li Lianli, *Zuo Zongtang pingzhuan*, 197–98.
176. *ZZQJ*, 12:755.
177. Yang Dongliang, *Zuo Zongtang*, 204; Liao, *XIangjun zhengzhan shi*, 303.
178. Liao, *Xiangjun zhengzhan shi*, 303.
179. See *ZZQJ*, 8:542–46.
180. *QSG*, 279.
181. *QSG*, 279.
182. *ZZQJ*, 8:546–48.
183. See *ZZQJ*, 8:534.
184. Elleman, *History of the Modern Chinese Navy*, 61.
185. *ZZQJ*, 8:541–42.
186. Cited in *NCH* (October 7, 1885).
187. On the problem of fractured leadership in China's modernization efforts, especially in the military sphere, see Kennedy, *Arms of Kiangnan*, 156–57.
188. Published and translated in *NCH* (October 7, 1885)
189. Lavelle, *Profits of Nature*, 169.
190. *ZZQJ*, 8:551–52.
191. *ZNP*, 756–57; *ZZQJ*, 8:553–55.
192. Sun, *Zuo Zongtang zhuan*, 182–83.
193. *QSG*, 12,035.
194. Yang Dongliang, *Zuo Zongtang*, 217–20.
195. Sun, *Zuo Zongtang zhuan*, 182.
196. *NCH* (September 5, 1885).
197. Assorted epitaphs and letters are gathered in Sun, *Zuo Zongtang zhuan*, 186–224. A memorial park to Zuo featuring a giant statue was opened in his hometown of Xiangyin in 2014.

CONCLUSION. MORE THAN JUST A CHICKEN DISH

1. See, for example, the discussions in Reinhardt, *Navigating Semi-Colonialism*; Halsey, *Quest for Power*; and Lavelle, *Profits of Nature*.
2. See Halsey, *Quest for Power*, 242–50.

3.   Unfortunately, many recent texts still perpetuate such falsehoods. See, for example, Bickers, *Scramble for China*, 324–27.

4.   Kennedy, *Arms of Kiangnan*, 159.

5.   See, for example, the discussion in Halsey, *Quest for Power*, 244–56.

6.   Lavelle, *Profits of Nature*, 174.

7.   Bales, *Tso Tsung-t'ang*, 404.

8.   Yang Dongliang, *Zuo Zongtang*, 184.

9.   Li Lianli, *Zuo Zongtang pingzhuan*, 202–5.

10. See Yang Dongliang, *Zuo Zongtang*, 1. On the appreciation of the late Qing reformers by Nationalist politicians, most notably Chiang Kaishek, see Wright, *Last Stand of Chinese Conservatism*.

11. Yang Dongliang, *Zuo Zongtang*, 218.

12. *ZWZX*, 82. Qin's work has gone through seventeen editions in mainland China and Taiwan.

13. Zhang Duoyuan, "Zuo Zongtang dui Lanzhou jiaoyu de gongxian ji yiyi chutan," *Lanzhou jiaoting daxue xuebao* 2010.2 (February 2010), 87.

14. Yang Dongliang, *Zuo Zongtang*, 2.

15. Yang Dongliang, 2.

16. See *ZZQJ*, 1, preface, 10–13.

17. Yang Dongliang, *Zuo Zongtang*, 3–5.

18. See Yang Dongliang, 219–20, on these recent commemorations.

19. See, for example, *ZWZX*, 220–21, which calls Zuo's achievement in conquering Xinjiang unprecedented in Chinese history for its integration of Xinjiang into the regular administrative apparatus of the empire, while also criticizing bumbling politicians for almost losing it.

20. Theaker, "Moving Muslims," 5–6.

21. Setzekorn, "Chinese Imperialism, Ethnic Cleansing, and Military History," 81.

22. Schluessel, *Land of Strangers*, 1.

23. *HMYD*, 426–30.

24. Kind, "Musulman Knowledge," 101–4.

25. Schluessel, *Land of Strangers*, 3.

26. Chu, *Moslem Rebellion*, 205.

27. Schluessel, *Land of Strangers*, 172–74.

28. Schluessel, 58–61.

29. See Schluessel, 55; and Platt, *Provincial Patriots*.

30. Theaker, "Moving Muslims," 202–10.

31. See Fields, *Tso and the Muslims*, 105–6; and Platt, *Provincial Patriots*.

32. Ch'en, *Tso Tsung-t'ang: Pioneer Promoter*, 68–72.
33. Ch'en, 74–76.
34. On linking Zuo to current development initiatives in Xinjiang, see Peng, "Zuo Zongtang kaifa xibei," 18.
35. Ch'en, *Tso Tsung-t'ang: Pioneer Promoter*, 88.
36. *ZWZX*, 175–79.
37. Yang Dongliang, *Zuo Zongtang*, 173. Also see *SGXF*, 30:16064–68.
38. For an overview of responses to famine in late Qing China, see Kate Edgerton-Tarpley, *Tears from Iron: Cultural Responses to Famine in Nineteenth-Century China* (Berkeley: University of California Press, 2008).
39. *ZZQJ*, 8:154.
40. *ZWZX*, 180.
41. Yang Dongliang, *Zuo Zongtang*, 174–77; Peng, "Zuo Zongtang kaifa xibei," 7–8 and 10–12.
42. *SGXF*, 30:15992–93.
43. Peng, "Zuo Zongtang kaifa xibei," 12.
44. Lavelle, *Profits of Nature*, 122.
45. *SGXF*, 30:16024–30.
46. Peng, "Zuo Zongtang kaifa xibei," 11–13. Some sources suggest several thousand new *mu* of land were brought under cultivation.
47. Hou, "Tongzhi Huimin qiyi," 70.
48. Peng, "Zuo Zongtang kaifa xibei," 12–14.
49. Hou, "Tongzhi Huimin qiyi," 70–71.
50. Peng, "Zuo Zongtang kaifa xibei," 7. See Liu Jintang's report in *SGXF*, 30:16033–35.
51. Peng, 14.
52. Peng, 15. For a full list of places Zuo set up schools, see *ZWZX*, 216–20.
53. Peng, 9 and 15.
54. Peng, 16.
55. *ZZQJ*, 12:428–30.
56. *NCH*, 583 (July 13, 1878), citing an article from the *Pall Mall Budget*.
57. See Ch'en, *Tso Tsung-t'ang: Pioneer Promoter*; and Peng, "Zuo Zongtang kaifa xibei," 14.
58. See Hopkirk, *The Great Game*, 302–3; and *ZWZX*, 197–98.
59. Peng, "Zuo Zongtang kaifa xibei," 18. For an overview of Zuo's infrastructure efforts in Xinjiang, see *ZWZX*, 185–203.
60. *PHZ* 8, 21a–21b.

61. *QSG,* 12,035.

62. S. Y. Teng, *Taiping Rebellion and the Western Powers,* 397.

63. Fields, *Tso Tsung-t'ang and the Muslims,* 23.

64. *ZWZX,* 223.

65. *QSG,* 12,035.

66. *ZWZX,* 225–26.

67. Li Lianli, *Zuo Zongtang pingzhuan,* 250.

68. Li Lianli, 249.

69. Li Lianli, 226–30.

70. Li Lianli, 256.

71. Li Lianli, 230–37.

72. Bales, *Tso Tsung-tang,* xii.

73. Bales, v.

74. The editors of the most recent version of Zuo's collected works call this his most significant achievement and one that elevated him above Zeng Guofan and the other late Qing reformers. See *ZZQJ,* 1, preface, 1.

75. See Gang Zhao, "Reinventing China: Qing Imperial Ideology and the Rise of Chinese National Identity in the Early Twentieth Century," *Modern China* 32.1 (January 2006), 3–30.

76. Bales, *Tso Tsung-t'ang,* 424.

BIBLIOGRAPHY

Afinogenov, Gregory. *Spies and Scholars: Chinese Secrets and Imperial Russia's Quest for World Power.* Cambridge, MA: Harvard University Press, 2020.

Andrade, Tonio. *The Gunpowder Age: China, Military Innovation and the Rise of the West in World History.* Princeton: Princeton University Press, 2016.

Antony, Robert J. *Like Froth Floating on the Sea: The World of Seafarers and Pirates in Late Imperial China.* Berkeley: University of California Press, 2003.

———. *Unruly People: Crime, Community, and the State in Late Imperial South China.* Hong Kong: Hong Kong University Press, 2016.

Atwill, David. "Blinkered Visions: Islamic Identity, Hui Ethnicity, and the Panthay Rebellion in Southwest China, 1856–1873." *Journal of Asian Studies* 62.4 (November 2003): 1079–1108.

———. *The Chinese Sultanate: Islam, Ethnicity and the Panthay Rebellion in Southwest China, 1856–1873.* Stanford: Stanford University Press, 2005.

Bales, W. L. *Tso Tsung-t'ang: Soldier and Statesman of Old China.* Shanghai: Kelly and Walsh, 1937.

Barish, Daniel. *Learning to Rule: Court Education and the Remaking of the Qing State, 1861–1912.* New York: Columbia University Press, 2022.

Beal, Edwin G. *The Origin of Likin, 1853–1864.* Cambridge, MA: Harvard University Press, 1958.

Beijing Zhongguo shudian, comp. *(Qinding) Pingding qi sheng fanglue*, volume 21: [Imperial pacification campaigns of seven provinces, volume 21: The pacification of the Muslim bandits of Shaanxi, Gansu, and Xinjiang]. Beijing: Zhongguo shudian, 1985.

Bello, David A. *Across Forest, Steppe, and Mountain: Environment, Identity and Empire in Qing China's Borderlands.* Cambridge: Cambridge University Press, 2016.

Bickers, Robert. *The Scramble for China: Foreign Devils in the Qing Empire, 1832–1914.* London: Penguin, 2012.

Bohr, P. Richard. "The Taipings in Chinese Sectarian Perspective." In *Heterodoxy in Late Imperial China*, ed. Kwang-ching Liu and Richard Shek, 393–430. Honolulu: University of Hawaii Press, 2004.

Bonk, James. "Chinese Military Men and Cultural Practice in the Early Nineteenth Century Qing Empire (1800–1850)." PhD dissertation, Princeton University, 2014.

———. "Patronage and Personal Bonds in the Early Nineteenth Century Green Standards: Yang Yuchun and His Proteges (1795–1840)." *Journal of Chinese Military History* 4.1 (2015): 5–43.

———. "Rewriting the Ningshan Mutiny: Changing Conceptions of Military Authority in the Early Nineteenth-Century Qing Empire." *Journal of Chinese Military History* 7.2 (2018): 119–40.

Borei, Dorothy V. "Ethnic Conflict and Qing Land Policy in Southern Xinjiang, 1760–1840." In *Dragons, Tigers, and Dogs: Qing Crisis Management and the Boundaries of State Power in Late Imperial China,* ed. Robert J. Antony and Jane Kate Leonard, 273–302. Ithaca: Cornell University Press, 2002.

Boulger, Demetrius Charles. *The Life of Yakoob Beg; Athalik Ghazi, and Badaulet; Ameer of Kashgar.* 1878. Reprint. London: Andesite Press, 2015.

Bregel, Yuri. *A Historical Atlas of Central Asia.* Leiden: Brill, 2003.

Brophy, David. "Confusing Black and White: Naqshbandi Sufi Affiliations and the Transition to Qing Rule in the Tarim Basin." *Late Imperial China* 39.1 (June 2018): 29–65.

———. "Kings of Xinjiang: Muslim Elites and the Qing Empire." *Études orientales* 25 (2008): 69–90.

Brown, Jeremy. "Rebels, Rent, and Tao Xu: Local Elite Identity and Conflict during and after the Taiping Occupation of Jiangnan." *Late Imperial China* 30.2 (December 2009): 9–38.

Cai Shaoqing. "On the Origins of the Gelaohui." *Modern China* 10.4 (October 1984): 481–508.

Carr, Caleb. *The Devil Soldier: The Story of Frederick Townsend Ward.* New York: Random House, 1992.

Chang, Adam. "Reappraising Zhang Zhidong: Forgotten Continuities during China's Self-Strengthening, 1884–1901." *Journal of Chinese Military History* 6.2 (2017): 157–92.

Chang, Hsin-pao. *Commissioner Lin and the Opium War.* Cambridge, MA: Harvard University Press, 1966.

Chang, Jung. *Empress Dowager Cixi: The Concubine Who Launched Modern China.* New York: Anchor Books, 2013.

Chappell, Jonathan. "The Limits of the Shanghai Bridgehead: Understanding British Intervention in the Taiping Rebellion 1860–62." *Journal of Imperial & Commonwealth History* 44.4 (August 2016): 533–50.

Ch'en, Gideon. *Tso Tsung-t'ang, Pioneer Promoter of the Modern Dockyard and the Woolen Mill in China.* New York: Paragon, 1968.

Chen Jiang. "Recent Chinese Historiography on the Western Affairs Movement: Yangwu yundong, ca. 1860–1895." *Late Imperial China* 7.1 (June 1986): 112–27.

Cheng, J. C. *Chinese Sources for the Taiping Rebellion.* Hong Kong: Hong Kong University Press, 1963.

Chesneaux, Jean, ed. *Popular Movements and Secret Societies in China, 1840–1950.* Stanford: Stanford University Press, 1972.

Chiang, Siang-tseh. *The Nien Rebellion.* Seattle: University of Washington Press, 1954.

Chin, Shinshun. *The Taiping Rebellion.* Trans. Joshua Fogel. Armonk, NY: M. E. Sharpe, 2001.

Chou, Nailene Joseph. "Frontier Studies and Changing Frontier Administration in Late Ch'ing China: The Case of Sinkiang, 1759–1911." PhD dissertation, University of Washington, 1976.

Chu, Wen-djang. *The Moslem Rebellion in Northwest China 1862–1878: A Study of Government Minority Policy.* The Hague and Paris: Mouton, 1966.

Chung, Chien-peng. "China's War on Terror: September 11 and Uighur Separatism." *Foreign Affairs* 81.4 (July–August 2002): 8–12.

Cohen, Paul A. *Discovering History in China: American Writing on the Recent Chinese Past.* New York: Columbia University Press, 2010.

Crossley, Pamela Kyle, Helen F. Siu, and Donald S. Sutton, eds. *Empire at the Margins: Culture, Ethnicity, and Frontier in Early Modern China.* Berkeley: University of California Press, 2006.

Cui Ji'en. "Zuo Zongtang shuping" [Evaluation of Zuo Zongtang]. *Shixue Yukan* 1957 (July 1957): 9–12.

Dai, Yingcong. *The White Lotus War: Rebellion and Suppression in Late Imperial China.* Seattle: University of Washington Press, 2019.

Davis, Bradley Camp. *Imperial Bandits: Outlaws and Rebels in the China-Vietnam Borderlands.* Seattle: University of Washington Press, 2016.

Day, Jenny Huangfu. "Searching for the Roots of Western Wealth and Power: Guo Songtao and Education in Victorian England." *Late Imperial China* 35.1 (June 2014): 1–37.

Desnoyers, Charles A. *Patterns of Modern Chinese History.* Oxford: Oxford University Press, 2017.

Di Cosmo, Nicola. "Qing Colonial Administration in Inner Asia." *International History Review* 20.2 (1998): 287–309.

Duan, Lei. "Between Social Control and Popular Power: The Circulation of Private Guns and Control Policies during the Mid to Late Qing, 1781–1911" *American Journal of Chinese Studies* 24.2 (October 2017): 121–39.

Eastman, Lloyd A. *Throne and Mandarins: China's Search for a Policy during the Sino-French Controversy, 1880–1885.* Cambridge, MA: Harvard University Press, 1967.

Edgerton-Tarpley, Kate. *Tears from Iron: Cultural Responses to Famine in Nineteenth-Century China.* Berkeley: University of California Press, 2008.

Elleman, Bruce. *A History of the Modern Chinese Navy, 1840–2020.* London: Routledge, 2021.

———. *Modern Chinese Warfare, 1795–1989.* London: Routledge, 2001.

Elliott, Mark C. *Emperor Qianlong: Son of Heaven, Man of the World.* New York: Pearson, 2009.

———. *The Manchu Way: The Eight Banners and Ethnic Identity in Late Imperial China.* Stanford: Stanford University Press, 2001.

Elman, Benjamin. *A Cultural History of Civil Examinations in Late Imperial China.* Berkeley: University of California Press, 2000.

———. "Naval Warfare and the Refraction of China's Self-Strengthening Reforms into Scientific and Technological Failure, 1865–1895." *Modern Asian Studies* 38.2 (2004): 283–326.

Esherick, Joseph W. *The Origins of the Boxer Uprising.* Berkeley: University of California Press, 1988.

Fairbank, John K., ed. *The Cambridge History of China.* Volume 10: *Late Ch'ing 1800–1911,* part 1. Cambridge: Cambridge University Press, 1978.

Fairbank, John K., and Kwang-ching Liu, eds. *The Cambridge History of China.* Volume 10: *Late Ch'ing 1800–1911,* part 2. Cambridge: Cambridge University Press, 1980.

Fan Wenlan, ed. *Nian jun* [The Nian Army]. 6 vols. Shanghai: Shenzhou guoguang she, 1953.

Fan Zhongyi. *Qi Jiguang zhuan* [Biography of Qi Jiguang]. Beijing: Zhonghua shuju, 2003.

Fay, Peter Ward. *The Opium War, 1840–1842: Barbarians in the Celestial Empire in the Early Part of the Nineteenth Century and the War by Which They Forced Her Gates.* Chapel Hill: University of North Carolina Press, 1997.

Feng Jingzhi. *Wan Qing mingchen: Gaoji zhishi fenzimen ruhe zhina junquan* [Famous officials of the late Qing: How high-ranking intellectuals seized military authority]. Nanchang: Ershiyi shiji chubanshe, 2014.

Fields, Lanny B. "The Importance of Friendships and Quasi-Kinship Relations in Tso Tsung-t'ang's Career." *Journal of Asian History* 10.2 (1976): 172–86.

———. "Tso-Tsung-tang (1812–1885) and His Campaigns in Northwestern China, 1868–1880." PhD dissertation, Indiana University, 1972.

———. *Tso Tsung-t'ang and the Muslims: Statecraft in Northwest China, 1868–1880.* Kingston, ON: Limestone Press, 1978.

Foreign Languages Press. *The Taiping Revolution.* Beijing: Foreign Languages Press, 1976.

Gao Wenyuan. *Qingmo xibei huimin zhi fan Qing yundong* [Anti-Qing Muslim rebel movements in northwest China in the late Qing]. Taibei: Xuehai shuju, 1988.

Goetz, Nicole, ed. *The Age of Gunpowder: An Era of Technological, Tactical, Strategic, and Leadership Innovations.* Atlanta: Emory University Press, 2013.

Goodrich, L. Carrington, and Chaoying Fang, eds. *Dictionary of Ming Biography.* 2 vols. New York: Columbia University Press, 1976.

Gordon, Leonard H. D. *Confrontation over Taiwan: Nineteenth-Century China and the Powers.* Lanham, MD: Lexington Books, 2007.

Graff, David A., and Robin Higham, eds. *A Military History of China.* Boulder: Westview Press, 2002.

Gregory, John S. "British Intervention against the Taiping Rebellion." *Journal of Asian Studies* 19.1 (1959): 11–24.

Gu Yanwu. *Record of Daily Knowledge and Collected Poems and Essays: Selections.* Trans. Ian Johnston. New York: Columbia University Press, 2016.

Guanhe Wushizhou [pseudonym]. *Xiangjun jueqi* [Rise of the Hunan Army]. Beijing: Xiandai chubanshe, 2018.

Guy, R. Kent. *Qing Governors and Their Provinces: The Evolution of Territorial Administration in China, 1644–1796.* Seattle: University of Washington Press, 2010.

Hail, William James. *Tseng Kuo-fan and the Taiping Rebellion with a Short Sketch of His Later Career.* 2nd ed. New York: Paragon Books, 1964.

Halsey, Stephen R. *Quest for Power: European Imperialism in the Making of Chinese Statecraft.* Cambridge, MA: Harvard University Press, 2015.

———. "Sovereignty, Self-Strengthening, and Steamships in Late Imperial China." *Journal of Asian History* 48.1 (2014): 81–111.

———. "Warfare, Imperialism and the Making of Modern Chinese History." *Frontiers of History in China* 13.1 (2018): 47–72.

Han Min. *Shaanxi Huimin qiyi ziliao* [Historical materials on the Muslim revolts in Shaanxi]. Xi'an: Shaanxi sheng defang zhibianzuan weiyuanhui, 1987.

Han Min and Shao Hongmo. *Shaanxi Huimin qiyi shi* [A history of the Muslim revolts in Shaanxi]. Xi'an: Shaanxi renmin chubanshe, 1992.

Hanes, W. Travis III, and Frank Sanello. *The Opium Wars: The Addiction of One Empire and the Corruption of Another.* Naperville, IL: Sourcebooks, 2002.

Hasegawa, Masato. "The Ming Withdrawal from Korea and the Beginning of the Imjin War's Aftermath." Online lecture presented as part of the Research Seminar Program of the Aftermath Project at the Autonomous University of Barcelona, September 28, 2022.

Headrick, Daniel R. *The Tools of Empire: Technology and European Imperialism in the Nineteenth Century.* Oxford: Oxford University Press, 1981.

Hevia, James. *Cherishing Men from Afar: Qing Guest Ritual and the Macartney Embassy of 1793.* Durham: Duke University Press, 1995.

———. *English Lessons: The Pedagogy of Imperialism in Nineteenth-Century China.* Durham: Duke University Press, 2003.

Hillman, Ben, and Gray Tuttle, eds. *Ethnic Conflict and Protest in Tibet and Xinjiang: Unrest in China's West.* New York: Columbia University Press, 2016.

Hobsbawm, Eric. *Bandits.* Rev. ed. New York: New Press, 2000.

Hopkirk, Peter. *The Great Game: The Struggle for Empire in Central Asia.* New York: Kodansha, 1992.

Horowitz, Richard S. "Beyond the Marble Boat: The Transformation of the Chinese Military, 1850–1911." In *A Military History of China*, ed. David A. Graff and Robin Higham, 153–74. Boulder: Westview Press, 2002.

Hou Chunyan. "Tongzhi Huimin qiyi fou xibei diqu renkou qianyi ji yingxiang" [An investigation into the impact on population in the Muslim revolts of the northwest in the Tongzhi reign]. *Shanxi daxue xuebao* 1997.3 (1997): 68–72.

Hsu, Immanuel C. Y. "British Mediation of China's War with Yakub Beg, 1877." *Central Asiatic Journal* 9.2 (June 1964): 142–49.

———. "The Great Policy Debate in China, 1874: Maritime Defense versus Frontier Defense." *Harvard Journal of Asiatic Studies* 25 (1964–65): 212–28.

———. *The Ili Crisis: A Study in Sino-Russian Diplomacy, 1871–1881*. Oxford: Oxford University Press, 1965.

———. "The Late Ch'ing Reconquest of Sinkiang: A Reappraisal of Tso Tsungt'ang's Role." *Central Asiatic Journal* 12 (1968): 50–63.

Hummel, Arthur W., ed. *Eminent Chinese of the Qing Period*. Reprint. Great Barrington, MA: Berkshire, 2018.

Huntington, Rania. "Chaos, Memory, and Genre: Anecdotal Recollections of the Taiping Rebellion." *Chinese Literature: Essays, Articles, Reviews* 27 (2005): 59–91.

Israeli, Raphael. "The Muslims under the Manchu Reign in China." *Studia Islamica* 49 (1979): 159–79.

Jackman, Steven D. "Shoulder to Shoulder: Close Control and 'Old Prussian Drill' in German Offensive Infantry Tactics, 1871–1914." *Journal of Military History* 68.1 (January 2004): 73–104.

Jen Yu-wen. *The Taiping Revolutionary Movement*. New Haven: Yale University Press, 1973.

Jenks, Robert D. *Insurgency and Social Disorder in Guizhou: The "Miao" Rebellion, 1854–1873*. Honolulu: University of Hawaii Press, 1994.

Jin, Huan. "Stitching Words to Suture Wounds: A Manuscript Diary from the Taiping-Qing Civil War (1851–64)." *Late Imperial China* 40.2 (December 2019): 141–82.

Jones, Seth G. *Waging Insurgent Warfare: Lessons from the Vietcong to the Islamic State*. Oxford: Oxford University Press, 2017.

Karpat, Kemal H. "Yakub Bey's Relations with the Ottoman Sultans: A Reinterpretation." *Cahiers du monde russe et soviétique* 32.1 (March 1991): 17–32.

Kaske, Elizabeth. "Fund-Raising Wars: Office Selling and Interprovincial Finance in Nineteenth-Century China." *Harvard Journal of Asiatic Studies* 71.1 (June 2011): 69–141.

———. "Total War: Military Supply and Civilian Resources during China's Era of Rebellions." In *Chinese and Indian Warfare—From the Classical Age to 1870*, ed. Kaushik Roy and Peter Lorge, 257–88. London: Routledge, 2015.

Kennedy, Thomas L. *The Arms of Kiangnan: Modernization in the Chinese Ordnance Industry, 1860–1895*. Boulder: Westview Press, 1978.

Kiernan, V. G. "Kashgar and the Politics of Central Asia, 1868–1878." *Cambridge Historical Journal* 11.3 (1955): 317–42.

Kim, Hodong. *Holy War in China: The Muslim Rebellion and State in Chinese Central Asia, 1864–1877*. Stanford: Stanford University Press, 2004.

Kim, Kwangmin. *Borderland Capitalism: Turkestan Produce, Qing Silver, and the Birth of an Eastern Market*. Stanford: Stanford University Press, 2016.

———. "Profit and Protection: Emin Khwaja and the Qing Conquest of Central Asia, 1759–1777." *Journal of Asian Studies* 71.3 (August 2012): 603–26.

Kim, Woosang. "Power Parity, Alliance, Dissatisfaction, and Wars in East Asia, 1860–1993." *Journal of Conflict Resolution* 46.5 (October 2002): 654–71.

Kind, Kevin. "Musulman Knowledge, Local History, and the Making of the Qing Nation-State." *Late Imperial China* 42.2 (December 2021): 91–135.

Knorr, Daniel. "Fragile Bulwark: The Qing State in Jinan during the Taiping and Nian Wars." *Late Imperial China* 43.1 (June 2022): 43–84.

Kowalski, Bartosz. "Holding an Empire Together: Army, Colonization and State-Building in Qing Xinjiang." *Ming Qing Studies* (2017): 45–70.

Kuhn, Philip A. "Origins of the Taiping Vision: Cross-Cultural Dimensions of a Chinese Rebellion." *Comparative Studies in Society and History* 19.3 (1977): 350–66.

———. *Rebellion and Its Enemies in Late Imperial China: Militarization and Social Structure, 1796–1864*. Cambridge, MA: Harvard University Press, 1980.

———. *Soulstealers: The Chinese Sorcery Scare of 1768*. Cambridge, MA: Harvard University Press, 1990.

Laai Yi-faai. "River Strategy: A Phase of the Taipings' Military Development." *Oriens* 5.2 (December 1952): 302–29.

Larsen, Kirk W. *Tradition, Treaties, and Trade: Qing Imperialism and Choson Korea, 1850–1910*. Cambridge, MA: Harvard University Press, 2008.

Lavelle, Peter B. *The Profits of Nature: Colonial Development and the Quest for Resources in Nineteenth-Century China*. New York: Columbia University Press, 2020.

Lee, Jennifer 8. *The Fortune Cookie Chronicles: Adventures in the World of Chinese Food*. New York: Hachette, 2008.

Leibo, Steven A., ed. *A Journal of the Chinese Civil War, 1864 by Prosper Giquel*. Honolulu: University of Hawaii Press, 1985.

Leonard, Jane Kate. *Controlling from Afar: The Daoguang Emperor's Management of the Grand Canal Crisis, 1824–1826*. Ann Arbor: University of Michigan Press, 1996.

———. *Stretching the Qing Bureaucracy in the 1826 Sea-Transport Experiment*. Leiden: Brill, 2018.

———. *Wei Yuan and China's Rediscovery of the Maritime World*. Cambridge, MA: Harvard University Asian Center, 1984.

Levi, Scott. *The Rise and Fall of Khoqand, 1709–1876: Central Asia in the Global Age*. Pittsburgh: University of Pittsburgh Press, 2012.

Li Enhan. *Zeng Jize de waijiao* [Zeng Jize's foreign exchanges]. Taibei: Zhongyang yanjiuyuan jindaishi yanjiusuo, 1966.

Li Fanwen. *Xibei Huimin qiyi yanjiu ziliao huibian* [Compilation of historical materials on Muslim revolts in northwest China]. Yinxiang: Ningxia renmin chubanshe, 1992.

Li Lianli. *Zuo Zongtang pingzhuan: wan Qing di yi shi* [Biography of Zuo Zongtang: The leading official of the late Qing]. Wuchang: Huazhong keji daxue chubanshe, 2013.

Liao Zhenghua. *Xiangjun zhengzhan shi* [Battle history of the Hunan Army]. Beijing: Xiandai chubanshe, 2017.

Lin Gan. *Qingdai Huimin qiyi* [Qing era Muslim uprisings]. Shanghai: Xin zhishi chubanshe, 1957.

Lin Qiyan. "Wang Tao de haifang sixiang" [Wang Tao's thoughts on maritime defense]. *Jindaishi yanjiu* 2 (1999): 136–50.

Lindey, Augustus. *Ti-Ping Tien-Kwoh: The History of the Ti-Ping Revolution*. London: Day & Son, 1866.

Linn, Brian McAllister. *The Philippine War, 1899–1902*. Lawrence: University Press of Kansas, 2000.

Lipman, Jonathan. *Familiar Strangers: A History of Muslims in Northwest China*. Seattle: University of Washington Press, 1997.

Liu, Kwang-ching. "The Limits of Regional Power in the Late Ch'ing Period: A Reappraisal." *Tsing Hua Journal of Chinese Studies* 10.2 (1974): 207–23.

———. "World View and Peasant Rebellion: Reflections on Post-Mao Historiography." *Journal of Asian Studies* 40.2 (February 1981): 295–326.

Liu, Kwang-ching, and Richard Shek, eds. *Heterodoxy in Late Imperial China*. Honolulu: University of Hawaii Press, 2004.

Liu, Lydia H. *The Clash of Empires: The Invention of China in Modern World Making*. Cambridge, MA: Harvard University Press, 2004.

Liu, Xun. "In Defense of the City and Polity: The Xuanmiao Monastery and the Late Qing Anti-Taiping Campaigns in Mid-Nineteenth-Century Nanyang." *T'oung Pao* 94.4–5 (2009): 287–333.

Luo Zhengjun. *Zuo wenxiang gong nianpu* [Chronological biography of Zuo Zongtang]. In *Xuxiu siku quanshu* [Supplement to the Four Treasuries]. 1,200 vols. Volume 557, 539–757. Shanghai: Shanghai guji chubanshe, 1997.

Ma Changshou, ed. *Tongzhi nianjian Shaanxi Huimin qiyi lishi diaocha jilu* [A historical investigation of the Hui Rebellion in Shaanxi during the Tongzhi reign]. Xi'an: Shaanxi renmin chubanshe, 1993.

Ma Xiao. *Zuo Zongtang zai Gansu* [Zuo Zongtang in Gansu]. Lanzhou: Gansu renmin chubanshe, 2005.

McCarthy, Susan K. *Communist Multiculturalism: Ethnic Revival in Southwest China*. Seattle: University of Washington Press, 2009.

McMahon, Daniel. "Making 'Men of Iniquity': Imperial Purpose and Imagined Boundaries in the Qing Processing of Rebel Ringleaders, 1786–1828." *Journal of Chinese Military History* 7.2 (2018): 141–83.

————. *Rethinking the Decline of China's Qing Dynasty: Imperial Activism and Borderland Management at the Turn of the Nineteenth Century.* London: Routledge, 2014.

————. "The Yuelu Academy and Hunan's Nineteenth-Century Turn towards Statecraft." *Late Imperial China* 26.1 (June 2005): 72–109.

Meadows, Thomas Taylor. *The Chinese and Their Rebellions.* Reprint. Stanford: Stanford University Press, 1953.

Meyer-Fong, Tobie. "To Know the Enemy: The *zei qing huizuan,* Military Intelligence, and the Taiping Civil War." *T'oung Pao* 104.3–4 (2018): 384–423.

————. *What Remains: Coming to Terms with Civil War in Nineteenth-Century China.* Stanford: Stanford University Press, 2013.

Michael, Franz. "Military Organization and Power Structure of China during the Taiping Rebellion." *Pacific Historical Review* 18.4 (1949): 469–83.

Michael, Franz, with Chung-li Chang. *The Taiping Rebellion: A History with Documents.* 3 vols. Seattle: University of Washington Press, 1966.

Miles, Steven B. *Upriver Journeys: Diaspora and Empire in Southern China, 1570–1850.* Cambridge, MA: Harvard University Press, 2017.

Millward, James A. *Beyond the Pass: Economy, Ethnicity and Empire in Qing Central Asia, 1759–1864.* Stanford: Stanford University Press, 1998.

————. *Eurasian Crossroads: A History of Xinjiang Revised and Updated.* New York: Columbia University Press, 2022.

Millward, James A., and Laura Newby. "The Qing and Islam on the Western Frontier." In *Empire at the Margins: Culture, Ethnicity, and Frontier in Early Modern China,* ed. Pamela Kyle Crossley, Helen F. Siu, and Donald S. Sutton, 113–34. Berkeley: University of California Press, 2006.

Mokros, Emily. *The Peking Gazette in Late Imperial China: State News and Political Authority.* Seattle: University of Washington Press, 2021.

Morrison, Alexander. "Russian Rule in Turkestan and the Example of British India, c. 1860–1917." *Slavonic and East European Review* 84.4 (October 2006): 666–707.

Mosca, Matthew W. "Empire and the Circulations of Frontier Intelligence: Qing Conceptions of the Ottomans." *Late Imperial China* 70.1 (June 2010): 147–207.

Murray, Dian H. *The Origins of the Tiandihui: The Chinese Triads in Legend and History.* Stanford: Stanford University Press, 1994.

————. *Pirates of the South China Coast, 1790–1810.* Stanford: Stanford University Press, 1987.

Naquin, Susan. *Millenarian Rebellion in China: The Eight Trigrams Uprising of 1813.* New Haven: Yale University Press, 1976.

———. *Shantung Rebellion: The Wang Lun Uprising of 1774*. New Haven: Yale University Press, 1989.

North China Herald. Koninklijke Brill NV. *North China Herald* Online Database, http://www.brill.com/products/online-resources/north-china-herald-online.

Newby, Laura. "The Begs of Xinjiang: Between Two Worlds." *Bulletin of the School of Oriental and African Studies* 61.2 (1998): 278–97.

———. *The Empire and the Khanate: A Political History of Qing Relations with Khoqand, c. 1760–1860*. Leiden: Brill, 2005.

Nie Chongqi, ed. *Nianjun ziliao bieji* [Historical materials on the Nian Army]. Shanghai: Shanghai guji chubanshe, 1958.

Noordam, Barend. "Technology, Tactics, and Military Transfer in the Nineteenth Century: Qing Armies in Tonkin, 1884–1885." In *Structures on the Move*, ed. A. Flutcher and S. Richter, 169–88. Heidelberg: Springer, 2012.

Ocko, Jonathan K. *Bureaucratic Reform in Provincial China: Ting Jih-ch'ang in Restoration Kiangsu, 1867–1870*. Cambridge, MA: Harvard University Press, 1983.

Oidtmann, Max. "Overlapping Empires: Religion, Ethnicity and Politics in Nineteenth-Century Qinghai." *Late Imperial China* 37.2 (December 2016): 41–91.

Onuma Takahiro. "The Qing Dynasty and Its Central Asian Neighbors." *Saksaha* 12 (2014): 33–48.

Orbach, Danny. "Foreign Military Adventurers in the Taiping Rebellion, 1860–1864." *Journal of Chinese Military History* 10.2 (2021): 41–72.

Ownby, David. *Brotherhoods and Secret Societies in Early–Mid Qing China: The Formation of a Tradition*. Stanford: Stanford University Press, 1996.

Paine, S. C. M. *Imperial Rivals: China, Russia, and Their Disputed Frontier*. Armonk, NY: M. E. Sharpe, 1996.

———. *The Sino-Japanese War of 1894–1895: Perceptions, Power, and Primacy*. Cambridge: Cambridge University Press, 2005.

Parker, Geoffrey. *Global Crisis: War, Climate Change and Catastrophe in the Seventeenth Century*. New Haven: Yale University Press, 2014.

Peng Dacheng. "Zuo Zongtang kaifa xibei de zhanlue jucuo yu shenyuan yingxiang" [Zuo Zongtang's strategic moves to open up northwestern China and their profound significance]. *Hunan shifan daxue shehui kexue xuebao* 2001.1 (January 2001): 7–19.

Perdue, Peter. *China Marches West: The Qing Conquest of Central Eurasia*. Cambridge, MA: Harvard University Press, 2005.

Perry, Elizabeth J. *Chinese Perspectives on the Nien Rebellion*. London: Routledge, 1981.

———. *Rebels and Revolutionaries in North China, 1845–1945*. Stanford: Stanford University Press, 1980.

———. "Worshipers and Warriors: White Lotus Influence on the Nien Rebellion." *Modern China* 2.1 (January 1976): 4–22.

Peterson, Joseph. *Sacred Rivals: Catholic Missions and the Making of Islam in Nineteenth-Century France and Algeria.* Oxford: Oxford University Press, 2022.

Phillips, Gervase. "Military Morality Transformed: Weapons and Soldiers on the Nineteenth Century Battlefield." *Journal of Interdisciplinary History* 41.4 (Spring 2011): 565–90.

Platt, Stephen R. *Autumn in the Heavenly Kingdom: China, the West, and the Epic Story of the Taiping Civil War.* New York: Vintage Books, 2012.

———. *Imperial Twilight: The Opium War and the End of China's Last Golden Age.* New York: Vintage Books, 2019.

———. *Provincial Patriots: The Hunanese and Modern China.* Cambridge, MA: Harvard University Press, 2007.

———. "War and Reconstruction in 1860s Jiangnan." *Late Imperial China* 30.2 (December 2009): 1–8.

Polachek, James M. *The Inner Opium War.* Cambridge, MA: Harvard University Press, 1992.

Pong, David. "The Income and Military Expenditure of Kiangsi Province in the Last Years (1860–1864) of the Taiping Rebellion." *Journal of Asian Studies* 26.1 (1966): 49–65.

———. "Keeping the Foochow Navy Yard Afloat: Government Finance and China's Early Modern Defense Industry." *Modern Asian Studies* 21.1 (1987): 121–52.

Porter, Jonathan. *Tseng-Kuo-fan's Private Bureaucracy.* Berkeley: University of California Press, 1972.

Qi Jiguang. *Jixiao xinshu* [A new training manual]. Taibei: Wuzhou chubanshe, 2000.

Qin Hancai. *Zuogong wenxiang zai xibei* [Zuo Zongtang in the northwest]. Reprinted in *Minguo congshu* [Collectanea of the Republic]. Volume 85. Shanghai: Shanghai shudian, 1989.

Qin Xiangye and Chen Zhongying. *Ping Zhe jilue* [Record of the pacification of Zhejiang]. In Shen Yunlong, comp., *Jindai Zhongguo shiliao congkan* [Compilation of historical materials on modern China]. Volume 24. Taibei: Wenhai chubanshe, 1968.

Ralston, David B. *Importing the European Army: The Introduction of European Military Techniques and Institutions into the Extra-European World, 1600–1914.* Chicago: University of Chicago Press, 1990.

Rawlinson, John L. *China's Struggle for Naval Development, 1839–1895.* Cambridge, MA: Harvard University Press, 1967.

Reilly, Thomas H. *The Taiping Heavenly Kingdom: Rebellion and the Blasphemy of Empire.* Seattle: University of Washington Press, 2004.

Reinhardt, Anne. *Navigating Semi-Colonialism: Shipping, Sovereignty, and Nation-Building in China, 1860–1937.* Cambridge, MA: Harvard University Press, 2018.

Rhoads, Edward J. *Manchus and Han: Ethnic Relations and Political Power in Late Qing China, 1861–1928.* Seattle: University of Washington Press, 2000.

Rowe, William T. *China's Last Empire: The Great Qing.* Cambridge, MA: Harvard University Press, 2009.

———. *Saving the World: Chen Hongmou and Elite Consciousness in Eighteenth-Century China.* Stanford: Stanford University Press, 2001.

———. "Violence in Ming-Qing China: An Overview." *Crime, History, and Societies* 18.2 (2014): 85–98.

Schluessel, Eric. *Land of Strangers: The Civilizing Project in Qing Central Asia.* New York: Columbia University Press, 2020.

Setzekorn, Eric. "Chinese Imperialism, Ethnic Cleansing, and Military History, 1850–1877." *Journal of Chinese Military History* 4.1 (2015): 80–100.

———. "Qing Dynasty Warfare and Military Authority: Discipline and the Ethnic Cleansing of 1860s Shaanxi." *Journal of Chinese Military History* 7.2 (2018): 184–202.

Sheng Sunchang. *Shishuo Taiping tianguo* [A true account of the Taiping Heavenly Kingdom]. Shanghai: Shanghai shudian chubanshe, 2017.

Sim, Y. H. Teddy, and Sandy J. C. Liu. "Zeng Guofan's Applications of Qi Jiguang's Doctrines in Crushing the Taiping Uprising." In *The Maritime Defence of China: Ming General Qi Jiguang and Beyond*, ed. Y. H. Teddy Sim, 93–104. Singapore: Springer, 2017.

Skinner, G. William. "Chinese Peasants and the Closed Community: An Open and Shut Case." *Comparative Studies in Society and History* 13 (1971): 270–81.

Smith, Richard. "Chinese Military Institutions in the Mid-Nineteenth Century, 1850–1860." *Journal of Asian History* 8.2 (1974): 122–61.

———. "The Employment of Foreign Military Talent: Chinese Tradition and Late Ch'ing Practice." *Journal of the Royal Asiatic Society Hong Kong Branch* 15 (1975): 113–36.

———. *Mercenaries and Mandarins: The Ever Victorious Army in Nineteenth-Century China.* Millwood, NY: KTO Press, 1978.

———. "Reflections on the Comparative Study of Modernization in China and Japan: Military Aspects." *Journal of the Royal Asiatic Society Hong Kong Branch* 16 (1976): 14–24.

———. "The Reform of Military Education in Late Ch'ing China." *Journal of the Royal Asiatic Society Hong Kong Branch* 18 (1978): 15–40.

Spector, Stanley. *Li Hung-chang and the Huai Army: A Study in Nineteenth Century Chinese Regionalism.* Seattle: University of Washington Press, 1964.

Spence, Jonathan D. *God's Chinese Son: The Taiping Heavenly Kingdom of Hong Xiuquan.* New York: W. W. Norton, 1996.

Sun Guangyao. *Zuo Zongtang zhuan* [Biography of Zuo Zongtang]. Beijing: Zhongguo shuji chubanshe, 2015.

Swope, Kenneth M. "Being Awesome: Grand Strategy in Late Imperial China, 1368–1911." In *The Cambridge History of Applied Strategy*, 4 vols., ed. Beatrice Heuser and Isabelle Duyvesteyn. Cambridge: Cambridge University Press, 2024.

———. "Bestowing the Double-Edged Sword: Wanli as Supreme Commander." In *Culture, Courtiers and Competition: The Ming Court (1368–1644)*, ed. David M. Robinson, 61–115. Cambridge, MA: Harvard University Press, 2008.

———. "Boats, Barbarians, and Bandits: Riverine Warfare & the Taiping Rebellion." *Journal of Chinese Military History* 12.1 (2023): 1–29.

———. "Clearing the Fields and Strengthening the Walls: Defending Small Cities in Late Ming China." In *Secondary Cities and Urban Networking in the Indian Ocean Realm*, ed. Kenneth R. Hall, 123–54. Boulder: Lexington Books, 2008.

———. "General Zuo's Counter-insurgency Doctrine." *Small Wars and Insurgencies* 30.4–5 (2019): 937–67.

———. *The Military Collapse of China's Ming Dynasty, 1618–1644*. London: Routledge, 2014.

———. "Of Bureaucrats and Bandits: Confucianism and Antirebel Strategy at the End of the Ming Dynasty." In *Warfare and Culture in World History*, 2nd ed., ed. Wayne E. Lee, 123–54. New York: New York University Press, 2020.

———. *On the Trail of the Yellow Tiger: War, Trauma, and Social Dislocation in Southwest China during the Ming-Qing Transition*. Lincoln: University of Nebraska Press, 2018.

———. *The Rebellion of the Three Feudatories, 1673–1681: The Consolidation of China's Qing Dynasty*. London: Routledge, 2024.

Teng, S. Y. *The Nien Army and Their Guerrilla Warfare, 1851–1868*. Paris: Mouton, 1961.

———. *The Taiping Rebellion and the Western Powers*. Taibei: Yiwen yinshuguan, 1977.

Teng, Ssu-yu, and John K. Fairbank. *China's Response to the West: A Documentary Survey, 1839–1923*. Cambridge, MA: Harvard University Press, 1979.

Teng, Yuan Chung. "American China-Trade, American-Chinese Relations and the Taiping Rebellion, 1853–1858." *Journal of Asian History* 3.2 (1969): 93–117.

ter Haar, Barend J. *Ritual and Mythology of the Chinese Triads: Creating an Identity.* Leiden: Brill, 2000.

———. *The White Lotus Teachings in Chinese Religious History*. Honolulu: University of Hawaii Press, 1999.

Theaker, Hannah Rebecca. "Moving Muslims: The Great Northwestern Rebellion and the Transformation of Chinese Islam, 1860–1896." PhD dissertation, University of Oxford, 2018.

Theobald, Ulrich. "Craftsmen and Specialist Troops in Early Modern Chinese Armies." In *Civil-Military Relations in Chinese History: From Ancient China to the Communist Takeover*, ed. Kai Filipiak, 191–209. London: Routledge, 2015.

————. "Monetary and Non-monetary Military Rewards in the Early and High Qing Period (1673–1795)." In *Money in Asia (1200–1900): Small Currencies in Social and Political Contexts*, ed. Jane Kate Leonard and Ulrich Theobald, 398–419. Leiden: Brill, 2015.

————. *War Finance and Logistics in Late Imperial China: A Study of the Second Jinchuan Campaign (1771–1776)*. Leiden: Brill, 2013.

Thilly, Peter. "Opium and the Origins of Treason in Modern China: The View from Fujian." *Late Imperial China* 38.1 (June 2017): 155–97.

Wakeman, Frederic Jr. *Strangers at the Gate: Social Disorder in South China, 1839–1861*. Berkeley: University of California Press, 1966.

Waley, Arthur. *The Opium War through Chinese Eyes*. Stanford: Stanford University Press, 1958.

Waley-Cohen, Joanna. *The Culture of War in China: Empire and the Military under the Qing Dynasty*. London: I. B. Tauris, 2006.

————. *Exile in Mid-Qing China: Banishment to Xinjiang, 1758–1820*. New Haven: Yale University Press, 1991.

Wang, Di. "Mysterious Communication: The Secret Language of the Gowned Brotherhood in Nineteenth-Century Sichuan." *Late Imperial China* 29.1 (June 2008): 77–103.

Wang Ermin. *Huai jun zhi* [History of the Huai Army]. Taibei: Institute of Modern History, Academia Sinica, 1967.

Wang Hongzhi. *Zuo Zongtang ping Xibei huiluan liangxiang zhi chouhua yu zhuanyun yanjiu* [Researches into the financing and transportation of military supplies during Zuo Zongtang's pacification of the rebellions in the northwest]. Taibei: Zhengzhong shuju, 1973.

Wang, Wensheng. *White Lotus Rebels and South China Pirates: Crisis and Reform in the Qing Empire*. Cambridge, MA: Harvard University Press, 2014.

Wang Yanzhen. *Zuo Zongtang faji shi* [History of Zuo Zongtang's rise to fame]. 2 vols. Shanghai: Shanghai jinxiu wenzhang chubanshe, 2010.

Wei Guangtao. *Kanding Xinjiang ji* [A record of the rectification of Xinjiang]. In *Zhongguo yeshi jicheng* [Compilation of unofficial histories of China]. Volume 43, 448–525. Chengdu: Ba Shu shushe, 1993.

Weller, Robert P. "Historians and Consciousness: The Modern Politics of the Taiping Heavenly Kingdom." *Social Research* 54.4 (1987): 731–55.

Wills, John E. Jr. "Functional, Not Fossilized: Qing Tribute Relations with Dai Viet (Vietnam) and Siam (Thailand), 1700–1820." *T'oung Pao* 98.4–5 (2012): 439–78.

Wong, J. Y. *Deadly Dreams: Opium and the Arrow War (1856–1860) in China*. Cambridge: Cambridge University Press, 1998.

————. "Historical Memory and Political Culture: The Ballad about Commissioner Yeh in Modern Chinese History." *War and Society* 21.1 (May 2003): 15–39.

———. "The Limits of Naval Power: British Gunboat Diplomacy in China from the *Nemesis* to the *Amethyst.*" *War and Society* 18.2 (October 2000): 93–120.

Wooldridge, Chuck. "Writing the Taiping War into the History of the Southern Ming: Xu Zi, the Militia of Luhe, and the *Annals of a Fallen State.*" *Frontiers of History in China* 13.2 (2018): 227–58.

Wooldridge, William Charles [Chuck]. "Building and State Building in Nanjing after the Taiping Rebellion." *Late Imperial China* 30.2 (December 2009): 84–126.

Wright, Mary Clabaugh. *The Last Stand of Chinese Conservatism: The T'ung-chih Restoration, 1862–1874.* Stanford: Stanford University Press, 1957.

Wu, James T. K. "The Impact of the Taiping Rebellion upon the Manchu Fiscal System." *Pacific Historical Review* 19.3 (1950): 265–75.

Yang Dongliang. *Zuo Zongtang* [Biography of Zuo Zongtang]. Beijing: Renmin wenxue chubanshe, 2014.

Yang Jialuo, comp. *Nianjun wenxian huibian* [Compilation of materials on the Nian Army]. 6 vols. Taibei: Dingwen shuju, 1973.

Yang Yuxiu. *Ping hui zhi* [Account of the pacification of the Muslims]. 4 vols. Ningxia: Ningxia renmin chubanshe, 1987.

Yeung, King-to. "Suppressing Rebels, Managing Bureaucrats: State-Building during the Taiping Rebellion, 1850–1864." PhD dissertation, Rutgers University, 2007.

Yih, T. D. "The Typology of Xinjiang Silver Tenga and Copper Fulus of Yakub Beg (1820–1877)." *Numismatic Chronicle* 169 (2009): 287–329.

Yixin and Chen Banrui, et al., comps. *Qinding pingding Shan-Gan-Xinjiang hui (fei) fanglue* [Campaign history of the pacification of the Muslim bandits of Shaanxi, Gansu, and Xinjiang]. 30 vols. Taibei: Chengwen chubanshe, 1968.

Youn Dae-young. "The Loss of Vietnam: Korean Views of Vietnam in the Late Nineteenth and Early Twentieth Centuries." *Journal of Vietnamese Studies* 9.2 (Winter 2014): 62–95.

Yu, Maochun. "The Taiping Rebellion: A Military Assessment of Revolution and Counterrevolution." In *A Military History of China,* ed. David A. Graff and Robin Higham, 135–52. Boulder: Westview Press, 2002.

Yu Taishan, ed. *Xiyu Tongshi* [Survey history of the western regions]. Zhengzhou: Zhengzhou guji chubanshe, 1996.

Yuan, Tsing. "Yakub Beg (1820–1877) and the Moslem Rebellion in Chinese Turkestan." *Central Asiatic Journal* 6.2 (June 1961): 134–67.

Zhang Daye. *The World of a Tiny Insect: A Memoir of the Taiping Rebellion and Its Aftermath.* Trans. Xiaofei Tian. Seattle: University of Washington Press, 2013.

Zhang Dejian. *Zeiqing huizuan* [Compendium of rebel intelligence]. Taibei: Wenhai chubanshe, 1968.

Zhang Duoyan. "Zuo Zongtang dui Lanzhou jiaoyu de gongxian ji yiyi chutan" [Zuo Zongtang's contribution to the education of Lanzhou and an investigation of its significance]. *Lanzhou jiaotong daxue xuebao* 2010.2 (February 2010): 86–90.

Zhang Hongfu. *Zuo Zongtang* [Biography of Zuo Zongtang]. 2 vols. Wuhan: Changjiang wenyi chubanshe, 2014.

Zhang Zhenpei. *Zuo Zongtang zhuan* [Biography of Zuo Zongtang]. Changsha: Hainan guoji xinwen chuban zhongxin, 1993.

Zhao Erxun et al., comps. *Qing shigao* [Draft history of the Qing dynasty]. 4 vols. Beijing: Zhonghua shuju, 1998.

Zhao, Gang. "Reinventing China: Imperial Qing Ideology and the Rise of Chinese National Identity in the Early Twentieth Century." *Modern China* 32.1 (January 2006): 3–30.

Zheng Wang. *Never Forget National Humiliation: Historical Memory in Chinese Politics and Foreign Relations.* New York: Columbia University Press, 2014.

Zheng, Xiaowei. "Loyalty, Anxiety, and Opportunism: Local Elite Activism during the Taiping Rebellion in Eastern Zhejiang, 1851–1864." *Late Imperial China* 30.2 (December 2009): 39–83.

Zheng Yangwen. *The Social Life of Opium in China.* Cambridge: Cambridge University Press, 2005.

Zhou Shideng. *Huaijun ping nian ji* [Account of the Huai Army's pacification of the Nian]. In Shen Yunlong, comp., *Jindai Zhongguo shiliao congkan* [Compilation of historical materials on modern China]. Volume 5. Taibei: Wenhai chubanshe, 1966–73.

Zhu Xueqin, comp. *Qin ding jiaoping nian (fei) fanglue* [Campaign history of the pacification of the Nian bandits]. In *Zhongguo fanglue congshu* [Collected campaign histories of China]. 32 vols. Volume 1. Taibei: Chengwen chubanshe, 1968.

Zou Yihong. "Zuo Zongtang xibei jin yapian shulun" [Overview of Zuo Zongtang's opium prohibition in the northwest]. *Xinjiang shifan daxue xuebao* 2 (1992): 29–31.

Zuo Jingyi. *Zuo Zongtang zhuan* [Biography of Zuo Zongtang]. Beijing: Huaxia chubanshe, 1997.

Zuo Zongtang. *Zuo Zongtang quanji* [Collected works of Zuo Zongtang]. 15 vols. Changsha: Yuelu shushe, 2014.

Zuo Zongtang and Ma Daozong. *Zuo Zongtang: Aojing: wo xing wo su* [Zuo Zongtang: Peerless spirit: My actions and dispositions]. Taibei: Fengyun shidai chubanshe gufen youxian gongsi, 2012.

INDEX

agriculture: crop cultivation instead of opium, 179–80, 261, 356n265, 376n408; farm purchase by Zuo, xxii, 14; interest in and experiments by Zuo, xxii, 3, 11, 13, 303–4, 313n14; military farms (*tuntian*), 118, 154, 157, 190, 193, 204, 235, 303, 362n17; programs for, 8, 70, 90–91, 91, 121, 198–99, 255, 259; seeds for Hui, 180, 198–99, 356n261; writings about by Zuo, 9, 12, 62

army: Banner system, 18, 318n114; demobilization of troops, 257, 374n375; funding for, 47–50, 326n159; Green Standard troops, 32, 153, 206, 254, 257; modernization ideas of Zuo for, 11–12; serving the people, importance of army role of, 38. *See also specific armies*

Arrow incident/*Arrow* War, xxiii, 42, 52–54, 62, 75, 79, 327n201

awesomeness (*wei*), 12, 53, 57, 65, 68, 134, 146, 154, 316n76

Bai Yanhu, xvi; alliance with Yakub Beg, xxiv, 194, 217, 222, 227, 229, 233–34; defeat of, 168, 185; escape from Jinjibao, xxiv; extradition from Russia, 248, 254; fleeing to Russia by, xxv, 237–39; force strength of rebels under, 214; leadership role of, 141, 182; pursuit of, 193, 194–95, 236–39, 370n256; repulsed relief attack of, 170; submission offer from, 162; Suzhou operations of, 190, 191; tactics of, 163; Xining operations of, 185–86, 189; Xinjiang operations of, 213, 228–29

Bales, W. L., 252, 297–98, 308, 309, 312n9 (preface)

bamboo, 11, 134, 145, 348n27

Bao Chao, xvi, 43, 56–57, 58, 87, 89, 126, 250, 324n127

Beijing: Anglo-French attacks on, 54, 327n197; British minister in, 53–54; fleet for protection of, 100; recall of Zuo to, xxv, 251–53, 265; Summer Palace at, xxiii, 54, 327n197

benevolent assimilation, 159, 351n121

Britain: Beijing attacks by, 54, 327n197; distrust of British, 9–10, 52, 62, 77–78, 94–95, 327n186, 334n124; empire building in Central Asia by, 204, 362n19; Guo Songtao as minister to, 15; nonintervention policy of, 52; Qing relations with, 52, 53–54; Shanghai defense by, 50, 52, 78–79; Taiping Rebellion involvement of, 50–52, 54, 58–59, 75–79, 334n128; Tianjin attack by, xxiii, 54; Yakub relations and treaty with, xxiv, 212, 217, 222, 224, 224–25, 234–36

brotherhoods. *See* secret societies and brotherhoods

Buzurg Khan, xxiv, 209, 210

cannons: battle carts with, 119, 124, 154; building under Zuo, 94–95; defense ideas of Zuo and use of, 24; foreign-made cannons, 37, 38, 221; mountain-splitting cannons, 34–35, 37, 164; riverine warfare use of, 32, 36, 37, 38, 39; steel cannons, 38; wood shortage for mounting cannons, 32

Cao Kezhong, xvi, 153, 154

career/military career: courtier duties and accomplishments after military officer career, 265–68; defense of empire by Zuo, 59; effects of Opium War on interests of Zuo, 9–15; eye for talent of Zuo, 7, 15, 40–41, 307–8; honorific title given to Zuo, 241; influence on subordinates, 258, 297–98; insubordination/corruption charges, xxiii, 46; jealousy of Zeng toward Zuo, 79; Lin discussion, effects on career of Zuo, 14–15; Lujiang Academy role, 11; national/public figure status in Qing bureaucracy, 60–61, 62; practical experience gained under Luo, 40–41; praise of successes by Western press, 239–40; promotions of, 32, 46, 52,

194, 325n149; recall to Beijing, xxv,
251–53, 265; relationships, *guanxi*,
and advances in, 6–9, 19, 33, 40–41,
314n39; retirement, xxiii, xxv, 32–33,
137, 273, 279; supreme commander
appointment of Zuo to recover
Xinjiang, xxiv; victories against rebels
and honors from the court/throne, 57,
58, 60–61, 73, 81, 89, 134, 137; warfare
style of Zuo, 71
Cen Yuying, xvi, 278, 379n99
Central Asia: empire building in, 204,
362n19; famine in, 302–3; Great
Policy debate over, xxiv, 215, 216–19,
365n117; intelligence operations in, 217;
reconquest of, viii, 299–300; reconquest
of, map of, 200; reconquest of, plans and
preparations for, 214–16, 220–23; trade
network in, 186, 204, 242, 253, 358n316,
362n20; unrest and revolts in, 205–8;
Yakub Beg control of, viii
Changsha: boat construction program at, 37;
defense of, xxiii; memorial to Zuo in,
299; property owned by Zuo family in,
2–3; siege of and battle for, 19, 22–25,
29, 32, 320n32; Zuo family move to,
xxii, 2, 14, 43
Chen Hongmou, 241, 305, 371n287
Chen Yucheng, xvi, 58, 89, 106, 111
Cheney, Ian, vii, viii
Cheng Hongmou, 305
Chenglu, xvi, 157, 159, 185
Chengnan Academy, xxii, 6
Chiang Kaishek, 60, 383n10
chicken dish, vii–viii, x, 309, 311n1
China: ambassador to United States, 219;
criticisms, concerns, and fears about
policies and intentions of, ix; legacy
of Zuo and significance for history of,
viii–x, 1, 260–61, 295–309; modern
nation of, 4, 60; multiethnic nature
of, 262, 308; power disparity between
the West and, 103; relationship with
Russia, Zuo support for, 219; return
of territory occupied by Russia, viii;

rhetoric of catastrophe in, 70, 332n74;
self-perception of place in the world,
x; stereotypes about people from,
7; Taiping Rebellion reforms and
modern China, 15; technical skills as
important as philosophical principles
in, 93–94, 102, 273; territorial integrity
of, x, 63, 94; treaty with Japan, 219;
walls around cities in, 190, 359n348.
See also Sino-French War
Chinggis Khan, viii
Chonghou, xvi, 244–49, 253, 372n305
Chu Army: battling Muslims by, 159–64;
battling Taipings by, xxiii, 46, 64; cost
of and funding for, 47, 69, 159; creation
and organization of, xxiii, 45, 325n142;
discipline of, 159–60; experience and
training of, 46; force strength of, 64;
Jiangxi rescue mission by, 42; pay rates
for, 45, 159; prohibited behaviors, 30,
159–60; relationship between troops
and Zuo, 160; Zhejiang recovery by,
60–61
Ci'an, xvi, 137, 266, 288
Cixi (Yehonala), xvi, xxiii, 59, 137, 249,
266, 267, 268, 281, 282, 288, 293–94,
329n238, 380n142
coast guard, 271, 293
Cochin China, xxiii, 274. *See also* Vietnam
Confucianism: distribution of Confucian
works, 3–4; education of Zuo in
Confucian classics, 3, 298; filiality
virtues, 3; military matters and
principles of, 5; paternalism of, 24, 298;
schools established by Zuo, 257–58
Courbet, A. P., xvi, 282–83

Dagu Fort, xxiii, 54
D'Aiguebelle, Paul, xvi, 69, 70, 71, 72, 75, 98
Daoguang, xiv, xvi, xxii, xxiii, 16, 206
Ding Richang, xvi, 100, 173, 301–2, 339n286
Dongzhiyuan, 160, 161, 163–64, 167,
352nn150–151
Dungan Rebellion: alliance between Nian
and, 90, 107, 108, 114, 123, 155;

Henan province, 28–29, 50, 56, 107, 109, 112, 114–15, 122, 124, 127, 129, 130–33, 134
Hezhou, xxiv, 146, 160–61, 164, 181–85, 357n285, 359n366
Hong Kong, 50, 120, 286
Hong Ren'gan, xvii, 55, 80, 327n202
Hong Xiuquan, xvii, xxii, xxiv, 15, 18–19, 23, 28, 55, 81, 106, 184, 317n97, 319n12, 320n32
Hope, James, 60, 76
horses and horsemanship for fighting Nian, 112–13, 121–22, 123, 124
Hu Linyi, xvii; battling Taipings by, 34, 40, 43, 46; career of, 12, 15; contributions of, 301–2; death of, 63; discussions with and letters from Zuo, 15, 47; diversion of Zuo to *mufu* by, xxiii; education of, 7; intercession in charges against Zuo, xxiii, 46; Qing power restoration role of, 60; relationship with Zuo, xxii, 12; secretariat invitation from, 13; strategy for defeating Taipings, role in, 56; support for Zuo from, 21, 63
Huai Army, xxiii, 183, 184, 193
Huang Ding, 122, 128, 155, 166, 168, 173, 175
Huang Shaochun, xvii, 65, 83, 84, 87
Hubei, 35, 36, 39, 40, 41–42, 43, 45, 55
Hunan: character of and stereotypes about people from, 7; coordination of supplies and armies in, 37–38; government role of natives of (Hunan mafia), 7, 201–2, 293, 300–302, 314nn39–40; governor-generals from, 65; governors of, 12, 33; personal ties with natives of, 7, 19, 33; role of Zuo in local society, 12, 13
Hunan Army. *See* Xiang (Hunan) Army
Huzhou, 55, 74–75

industrialization, 94, 127, 269, 272–73, 302, 305
infrastructure: modernization projects and nepotism and graft, 269–70; post-war rehabilitation of Shaan-Gan,

155, 181, 196, 198–99; projects and improvements under Zuo, xxv, 127, 298, 303–4, 305; public works efforts to improve life of common folk, x, 2–4, 38, 90–92
irrigation, viii, 3, 7–8, 255, 302, 303–4, 313n14, 356n261

Jahangir, xvii, xxii, 206, 210, 223
Japan: fleet for war against, 262, 290–91; Meiji Japan defeat of Qing, 59–60, 62, 101; reform of military by, 12; Taiwan interests of, xxiv, 218, 219, 365n109; treaty with China, 219
Jiang Zhongyuan, xvii, 29, 35, 36, 44
Jiangxi, 35, 39, 41–42, 43, 45, 46, 60, 81, 91, 325n144, 328n208
Jiaqing, xiv, xvii, 1, 1–3, 241
Jinglian, xvii, 179, 214–15, 222
Jinjibao (Fort Jinji), xxiv, 141, 149, 151–52, 153, 160, 162, 164, 166–79
jinshi examinations and degree, xxii, xxiii, 8–9, 11, 45, 194
Jinshun, xvii, 161, 166, 181, 192, 193, 215, 221, 222, 231–32, 240, 250, 254
juren degree and exam, 7–8

Kang Guoqi, xvii, 70, 83, 84, 87, 89
Kangxi, xiv, 12, 178, 222, 355n249
Khokand, viii, 205–6, 209, 212, 213, 226
Krupp guns, 120, 192, 227, 250, 269

Lai Wenguang, xvii, 114, 115, 124, 125, 130, 131
land: allocation for Hui, 164–66, 196; competition for, 5; owned by Zuo's family, 2–3, 372n288
Lanzhou, xxiv, 120, 155, 164, 176, 193, 196, 222, 360n381, 366n134
Lee, Jennifer, vii–viii
Lei Zhengwan, xvii, 153, 156, 162, 166, 168, 169–70, 173, 175
Li Bo, 255, 374n367
Li Hanzhang, xviii, 218, 268, 365n112
Li Hongzhang, xviii; battling Nian by,

Mutushan, xix, 122, 152–53, 154, 156–57, 164, 166–67, 169, 283, 284, 353n172

Nanjing: attack on from multiple directions, 56–59; British response to being fired on by Taipings in, 51; recovery of, 45, 75, 79–82, 84; rehabilitation of areas around, 269; siege of, xxiii, 26–28, 33, 39, 50, 55, 80; Taipings advance to, 25–27; Taipings defeat at, xxiv
Nanjing, Treaty of, xxii, 50, 327n198
nationalism/nationalist politics: changing attitudes toward Zuo, x, 298–99, 308; Han Chinese outlook focus of, 4, 103, 201, 262; Uighurs, 208
navy: benefits of, 94–95; building a modern navy, 91–101, 102; coastal and naval defenses, xxv, 12, 70, 94–95, 98–99, 100–101, 270–71, 289–90, 291–93; coastal defense oversight by Li and support for strengthening defenses, 195, 216–17, 218, 243, 249, 250, 251, 261–62; fleet created by Yang and Peng, 55, 328n208; fleet for Sino-French War, 261–62, 283–85, 286, 380n138, 381n150; modernization ideas of Zuo, 10, 12, 14–15, 270–71, 287, 289–90, 291–93, 381n159, 382n187; riverine navy for the Yangzi, 134; shipyards and ship building for, viii, 3, 15, 79, 92–93, 95–100, 103, 338n246; Xiang Army naval battalions, 30. *See also* riverine warfare
Nian Rebellion: alliance between Muslims and, 90, 107, 108, 114, 123, 155; combating by Qing, 110–15; defeat of, xxiv, 59, 298–99; encirclement strategy against, 127–30; force strength of rebels, 42, 120, 124; funds for fighting, 121, 124, 127; leadership of, 90, 108–10, 120; longevity of, 107–8; map of rebellion, 104; Muslim rebels alliance with, 115, 128–29, 130; organization of, 108–10; origins of, 105–8, 340n14; outbreak of, xxiii, 90; Shengbao and

Senggelinqin battle against, 28–29, 111–13, 341n40; strategy for defeating, 118–20, 122, 133; strengths of, 113; surrender of, 131–32; tactics of, 105, 109, 123, 340n1; Taiping units joining with Nian forces, 89, 115; victories against, 115, 122, 125, 126, 128, 129, 131–33, 134–37; Zuo role in battling and stamping out, viii, xxiv, 114, 115–26
Ningbo, 58, 75, 78, 79, 93, 326n178
Ningxia, 147, 148–49, 151–53, 169, 303, 349n63
North China Herald, xiii

opium, 10, 11, 30, 53, 179–80, 261, 271, 303, 327n190, 356n265, 376n408
Opium War, First, xxii, 6, 9–10, 13, 52, 315n57
Opium War, Second. See *Arrow* incident/ *Arrow* War
Ottoman Empire, xxiv, 204, 212, 213, 217, 223–24, 362n19, 365n106

Panthay Rebellion, xxiii, xxiv, 144
Peng Yulin, xix, 37, 39–40, 55, 117, 271, 277, 278, 323n90, 328n208
People's Republic of China (PRC), 262, 308, 311n1, 380n141
publishing companies and printing presses, 3–4, 181, 196, 258, 304–5

Qi Jiguang, 29, 45, 46, 119, 321n47, 343n88
Qianlong, xiv, 180, 181, 202–3, 205, 222, 223, 260
Qing: achievements and reforms of, 296–98; civil officials roles in victories of, 6; criticism of by Western allies, 89–90; fall of, 102, 297; fiscal system and revenue for, 47–50, 59–60, 325nn154–155; foreign relations practices of, 9, 58–59, 75–79, 127, 205–6, 333nn110–111; local gentry role in saving, 24; map of empire of, xxvi; Meiji Japan defeat of, 59–60, 62, 101; officialdom

ranks in, 2; power restoration under Tongzhi, 59–60; reign titles and dates, xiv; selection of officials, 40–41, 51–52; social disorder and appointments and dismissals of officials, 13; state of dynasty and decline and fall of, 4–5; Taiping Rebellion threat to and reforms after rebellion, 15; virtues of loyalists, 31; Western powers relations with, 52, 53–54. *See also* Self-Strengthening (*ziqiang*)
Qishan, xix, 13

railroads/railways, 127, 245, 269, 272, 291, 292, 305
research and sources, ix–x, xiii
rhetoric of catastrophe, 70, 332n74
rice, 2, 11, 43, 70, 180
riverine warfare: boats for, 32, 35, 36, 37, 38–39, 51, 322n77, 326n178; fleet for, 35, 36–37, 66, 323n90; Fuyang river battle, 68; navy for the Yangzi, 134; Nian, river defenses against, 119, 123, 133–34, 135–36; Qing use and understanding importance of, 26, 34–39, 65; river defense ideas of and strategy development by Zuo, 12, 24, 37; weapons for, 32, 34–35, 36, 37, 38, 39
romanization systems and stylistic conventions for names and words, xiii, 311n1
Russia: Bai Yanhu flight to, xxv, 237–39; Central Asian trade of, 242, 253; empire building in Central Asia by, 204, 362n19; grain purchase from, 221, 226, 366n128; negotiations and treaty with over Yili, 245–49, 373n319; negotiations and treaty with over Yili, reopening with military force reinforcements, 249–54; relationship with China, Zuo support for, 219; return of Chinese territory occupied by, viii; threat from, 14; treaty with to restore border, 189; Urumqi

occupation by, 189; Yakub relations and treaty with, xxiv, 212, 217, 222, 224–25, 234, 364n69; Yili occupation by, 182–83, 189, 209–10, 216, 234, 235, 242–49

Saishanga, xix, 17, 22
salt and salt monopoly, 7, 37, 43, 48, 69, 81, 181, 270, 326n157
schools: building of by Zuo, x, 3–4, 179, 181, 196, 257–58, 304, 384n52; Fuzhou Navy Yard school and curriculum, 96–97; military academies, 102–3
Search for General Tso, The, vii, viii
secret societies and brotherhoods, 5, 13, 13–14, 30, 107
Self-Strengthening (*ziqiang*): concept of, 62; military technology purchases and deployment under, 76, 102; modern navy building as part of, 91–101, 102; progress in and evaluation of efforts, 62–63, 101–3, 339n294; support for by Zuo, 62, 102, 218, 272–73
Senggelinqin, xix, xxiii, xxiv, 28–29, 54, 111–13, 115, 123, 321n42
Shaan-Gan: conditions in and damage from war in, 156–57, 174, 355n232; governor-general appointment of Yang Yuebin, 150–51; governor-general appointment to, xxiv, 139; governor-general relationship to Xinjiang, 256; immigration of Han to, 143–44; Liu oversight of military affairs in, 116, 130; map of Dungan rebellion in, 138; massacres at, 192, 194, 207; Muslim revolt in, 137; restoration and rehabilitation efforts in, 155, 163–64, 179–81, 196, 198–99, 214–15, 356n261
Shaanxi province: battling Nian in, 116–22, 125–26, 127–30, 343n77, 345n153; battling Taipings in, 34; firearm ownership in, 146, 348n39; funding for campaigns in, 50; governor-general appointment to, 118, 139; move to

by Zuo, xxiv; Muslim population in, 179, 196, 300; Qishan oversight of, 13; restoration and rehabilitation efforts in, 163–64, 179–81, 196, 198–99, 356n261. *See also* Dungan Rebellion

Shandong: battling Nian in, 132, 133–35; battling Taipings in, 28–29, 32, 34; Nian raids into, 107, 115; recall of Zuo to combat sectarians in, xxv, 273–74

Shanghai: defense of and Western support in defense of, 50, 52, 78–79; fleet at, 100; Taipings advances to, 27, 28, 52, 55, 58, 79; United Defense Bureau in, 76

Shen Baozhen, xix, 15, 95, 97, 98, 116, 227, 249

Shengbao, xix, 17, 28–29, 55–56, 111–12, 321n42, 328n210, 341n40, 343n77

Shengwu ji (Wei), 6, 12

Shi Dakai, xix, 18, 23, 24, 34, 39, 43–44, 89, 324n122, 324n126

shipyards and ship building, viii, 3, 14–15, 79, 92–93, 95–100, 103, 338n246

Shunzhi, xiv, 166

silk production and mulberry trees, 11, 180, 261, 303, 305, 375n405

Sino-French War: backdrop to and start of, xxv, 274–83, 378n72; Chinese fleet for, 261–62, 283–85, 286, 380n138, 381n150; end of, xxv; Fuzhou Navy Yard strike by France, 282–85; Lang Son battle, 287–88; map of, 264; offensive operations of France, 283–85; role of Zuo in, viii, 263, 277–83, 285–88; treaty to end, 288–90

social bandits, 108, 341n21

society: common people as vital to state, 11; concern for and public works efforts to improve life for common folks, x, 2–4, 12, 38, 70, 73–74, 81, 90–92, 129–30, 306–7; militarization of, 5, 7, 119–20, 314n29; modernization of traditional societies, ix, 89–90; reordering traditional political and social norms, 9; study of the past by officials for

a better society, 8; unrest and social disorder, 13, 316n80

Song Qing, xix, 132, 134, 136, 162, 188, 189, 192, 219

sources and research, ix–x, xiii

statecraft: implementation of principles of by Zuo, 61; interest in and study of, 3, 6, 8, 9, 313n14; interest in practical statecraft, 6; security crises and development of new concepts of, 103; Wei's proposals and influence on Zuo, 3

steamers, steamboats, and steamships, 35, 51, 75, 91–92, 95, 99, 127, 322n77, 326n178

styles (courtesy names), 1, 312n2

stylistic conventions and romanization systems for names and words, xiii, 311n1

Suo Huanzhang, xix, 207–8

supply bases/depots and lines: capture of Taiping supplies, 68; Central Asia operations support, 190, 193; cost of and funding for supplies, 137; food and supplies for battling Muslims, 136, 140–41, 149, 153–55, 156, 157–58, 161; food and supplies for battling Nian, 117–18, 122, 123, 125, 127, 129–30; food and supplies for Central Asia operations, 190; food and supplies for troops under Zuo, 45, 46, 69, 70, 82–83, 87, 88; Liu role in keeping supply lines open, 57–58; shortages of supplies for battling Muslims, 153–54; shortages of supplies for battling Taipings, 32, 42–43; Wuhan base, xxiv; Xinjiang operations support, 156, 157, 193, 195, 214, 215, 220–21, 222, 223, 226, 228, 231–32, 366n128; Yili operations support, 193; Zhejiang food shortages, 69, 70, 73–74; Zhejiang operations support, 63, 64, 65, 329–30n7

Suzhou: arsenal at, 193; battle for and recovery of, xxiv, 70, 80, 161, 183, 187–94, 213, 359n354, 359nn357–358;

Zuo Zongtang, xxi; biographies of,
viii, viii–x, 299, 309, 312n2, 312n9
(preface); birth, family, and early
years of, viii, xxii, 1–3, 299; character
and personality of, 1–2, 7, 9–10, 19,
52, 58–59, 59, 265–66, 301–2, 306–8;
crutch used by, 285, 380n142; death
and burial of and memorials to, xxv,
293–94, 299, 382n197; death of parents
of, xxii, 2, 7; death of wife, xxiv, 172,
354n213; familiarity of and interest
in by Chinese people, viii–ix, 293–94;
hardscrabble early life of, 2–3, 38,
306–7; health of, 267, 273, 291, 376n13;
legacy and significance of, viii–x,
1, 260–61, 295–309; marriage and
family of, xxii, 8, 11, 12, 43, 91, 120;
mountains, fleeing to with family, 14,
15, 21, 34; plowing and reading life of,
10–15; prodigy status and aspirations
of, 6–9; timeline of life of, xxii–xxv;
writings by and collected works of, ix,
3, 8–9, 12, 62, 385n74
Zuo Zongzhi, xxii, xxiv, 7, 21

ABOUT THE AUTHOR

Kenneth M. Swope earned his BA from the College of Wooster (OH) and his MA and PhD degrees from the University of Michigan. He is the author or editor of numerous books and articles on late imperial Chinese and East Asian military history, including *On the Trail of the Yellow Tiger: War, Trauma, and Social Dislocation in Southwest China during the Ming-Qing Transition*. He has taught at a number of institutions, including serving as the Dr. Leo A. Shiffrin Distinguished Chair of Naval and Military History at the U.S. Naval Academy. A board member of the Chinese Military History Society, Dr. Swope is Professor of History and Senior Fellow of the Dale Center for the Study of War and Society at the University of Southern Mississippi. Finally, he is a lifelong (perpetually disappointed) fan of all the Cleveland professional sports teams.